PROFITS AND POLITICS

GREGORY P. MARCHILDON

Profits and Politics: Beaverbrook and the Gilded Age of Canadian Finance

UNIVERSITY OF TORONTO PRESS
Toronto Buffalo London

Printed in Canada

ISBN 0-8020-0740-6

Printed on acid-free paper

Canadian Cataloguing in Publication Data

Marchildon, Gregory P., 1956–
    Profits and politics : Beaverbrook and the gilded
age of Canadian finance

    Includes index.
    ISBN 0-8020-0740-6

    1. Beaverbrook, Lord, 1879–1964.   2. Capital investments –
Canada – History.   3. Canada – Economic conditions –
1867–1918.*   I. Title.

    HC120.P7M3 1996   332'.092   c96-931070-6

This book has been published with the help of a grant from the Humanities
and Social Sciences Federation of Canada, using funds provided by the Social
Sciences and Humanities Research Council of Canada.

University of Toronto Press acknowledges the financial assistance to its publishing program of the Canada Council and the Ontario Arts Council.

Contents

Photos follow page xvi.

Tables

Maps and Figures

Preface

The reader should be warned. This book is not a biography of Max Aitken, later Lord Beaverbrook, during his Canadian years – basically the first decade of the twentieth century if you jump over his childhood in New Brunswick. Rather, it is a study of high finance during the Laurier boom of 1896–1913 as seen through the lens of Aitken and his combination bond house and investment bank, the Royal Securities Corporation. As a consequence, I have sacrificed much of the art of biographical storytelling in favour of the analytics of business organization and management, although I readily admit that I might have found a more comfortable equilibrium between the two if I had possessed greater literary skill.

The choice of methodology was determined in part by my own philosophical proclivities. I have never been able to accept the 'great man' theory of history, in which individual action is posited as the decisive element producing societal change. Personal experience and some a priori prejudice have led me to a more 'environmental' philosophy in which the socio-institutional context assumes greater significance than any one individual, including Max Aitken. This is dangerous stuff given that my personal guide to this epoch of Anglo-Canadian business was, in Lady Diana Cooper's arresting description, 'a strange attractive gnome with an odour of genius about him.' Certainly, 'no other Canadian carved his name so large upon his times,' and one must seem peculiar in daring to use him as a means to a nonbiographical end – a study of modern financial capitalism at the beginning of the twentieth century.[1]

At the same time, I had to have some understanding of Aitken's interaction with fellow business associates, absorbing as they did virtually all of his energies from the turn of the century until his move to England in 1910.

These relationships covered the spectrum from unquestioning loyalty and respect at one extreme to intense hatred and distrust at the other, and few remained the same over time. Close and friendly associates one year could become bitter enemies a few years later. Even the friendships that survived a lifetime were subject to the occasional sharp break.

Without doubt, Aitken was a difficult person. He was also a very dangerous man to get close to. Always tormented, often selfish, sometimes generous, never satisfied, he was unpredictable with both friends and enemies. Incredibly complex and contradictory, his personality has eluded the grasp of his biographers. Even while concentrating only on those aspects of his personality that enabled him to become the most dynamic financier of his generation, I must confess that I, too, have had tremendous difficulty understanding what made the man tick.

Enigmatic personality aside, Aitken's real claim to fame during the Laurier boom, reflected in the innovative approach that would make him a very rich man while he was still in his twenties, was his ability to create organizational structures capable of achieving his ends. His goal was to attain the power necessary to lead a riveting life, one full of adventure and novelty, and the means to this end were profit and, to a lesser extent, politics. Simply put, Aitken's road to fame was paved by the fortune he made as a Canadian financier. His more infamous qualities – his sharp practice in the Canada Cement affair, his joy in crushing business rivals, his need to dominate associates – caused him no end of problems and ultimately cost him dearly in terms of his reputation.

On the other hand, organizations such as Royal Securities and Montreal Engineering were money-making machines because they were innovative and purposeful organizations that harnessed individual and institutional strengths. By funnelling large amounts of capital to existing companies, these organizations added real value to the Canadian economy. They also augmented substantially Aitken's profit-making capacity by allowing him to do progressively bigger deals with more influential people and institutions, thereby constantly expanding his horizons, something at least as important to Aitken as the rather unimaginative and static matter of consuming wealth. In other words, Aitken's organizations were designed to feed a voracious appetite for profit, and almost all of that profit was thrown back into his financial machine to generate even more. Aitken was a capitalist in the classical meaning of the word, at least until he left Canada for England; that is, he emphasized reinvestment far more than consumption, and he found in profit the ultimate yardstick of success. He was unashamedly ambitious, but unlike many of those he worked alongside, he seemed incapable of hiding his greed for profit behind a veneer of personal propriety and societal respectability.

My view of entrepreneurship differs in some important respects from that of Joseph Schumpeter, who characterized entrepreneurs as a distinct caste, separated from the unwashed masses by their superior foresight and abilities. These rare individuals are presumably born – genetically endowed, if you like – with entrepreneurial abilities, and they thus form an aristocracy of sorts in any society. In Schumpeter's view, therefore, innovation is strictly an individual accomplishment, although later in life he saw individual efforts becoming aggregated and routinized by corporations through organized research and development efforts.[2]

What do I find wrong with this picture? First, I would suggest that Max Aitken, like most entrepreneurs, did not inherit his 'special' abilities. They were learned over time from those he associated with, in particular, his early mentor in Halifax, John F. Stairs. Second, Schumpeter's world, while it places emphasis on the importance of curiosity and adventurousness, does not give due weight to greed as an incentive. Aitken was greedy for profit and for the power that invariably accompanies great wealth. As David Landes has said of the sixteenth-century European conquistadors, this type of greed was 'not a commendable quality,' but it was both 'powerful and devilishly effective.'[3] Aitken, like the conquistadors before him, was hardly heroic in his unrestrained pursuit of profit.

Finally and most significantly, Schumpeter's theory of entrepreneurship misses what I think is the essential linkage between organization and innovation. There is much evidence that business organizations are little more than the cooperative processes required to employ 'technological and managerial personnel who are able and willing to combine and coordinate their specialized talents to bring the innovation to fruition,' as William Lazonick has so aptly expressed it.[4] Aitken's innovations in particular could only have been implemented through the cooperation of the talented individuals whom he lured into the tent of his Halifax and Montreal organizations. In the pages that follow, careful attention is paid to the interplay between Aitken's entrepreneurial strategy and the various organizational structures with which he experimented.

I recently read three biographies of junk bond king Michael Milken in an effort to understand what happened to American finance capitalism during the heady decade of the 1980s.[5] Although all three were written by journalists rather than scholars, I did expect to find some revealing detail on the evolution of new forms of securitization and the rise of the junk bond market, and on the connection between these innovations and the savings and loan débâcle on the one hand, and the dismemberment of some of America's corporate giants after hostile takeovers fuelled by junk bonds on the other. In the end, I was amazed at how little the authors knew – or cared to know – about the business of the person they were judging, even though it was something Milken did in the course of his business that presumably led to his rise – and perhaps to his fall.

This tendency among writers in the area of high finance is, in part, understandable, as the subject is complex and tremendously slippery. In my own attempt in this book to capture the basic essence of capital forma- tion before the Great War, I have been very much aware of the limitations of my knowledge. I have depended heavily on the scholarship of others to fill in as much of the general picture as possible. When even this was not sufficient, I pestered many colleagues who knew far more than I about the history of finance, and most were extremely generous in donating their time and knowledge to a young scholar.

To avoid confusion, I should explain at the outset what I mean by the term 'investment banking.' In contrast to deposit (commercial) banks, which receive money on deposit and then lend it as advances on a short- term basis, investment banks facilitate long-term advances to industry through the sale of *new* corporate securities. The word 'new' is critical. Unlike stockbrokers, who simply act as agents in the resale of securities to investors, investment banks promote, issue, and underwrite newly created securities. The name of the financial intermediary is unimpor- tant; if a securities dealer, a trust company, or even a stockbroking firm acts as a principal in the new issue market, it is engaging in the business of investment banking in my opinion. And the fact that a securities dealer such as Aitken's Royal Securities Corporation also retailed securi- ties is unimportant. The litmus test is the core activity of the institution in question. In the case of Royal Securities, this was unquestionably the promotion of new companies, which then created securities floated by Royal Securities.[6]

Finally, I owe an explanation for my use of the name Beaverbrook, rather than Max Aitken, in the title despite the fact that Aitken did not receive a peerage until 1916, well after his Canadian financial career had ended. Unfortunately, he is now recognizable as Aitken by only a few ded- icated students of Canadian history; most people know him as Lord Bea- verbrook. I regret the necessity of using the latter in the title but hope that this book will make the name Max Aitken more familiar in the end.

Acknowledgments

The origins of *Profits and Politics* can be traced to a fateful decision in December 1987, when I suddenly resolved to change the direction of my doctoral research at the London School of Economics (LSE). For months, I had been accumulating research on the origins of Canadian antitrust law and attempting to measure its impact, if any, on the Canadian business structure and industrial organization. I had begun to write the more theoretical chapters but was dissatisfied with the poor quality of the existing empirical research on Canadian mergers and acquisitions. I needed both time and money to tackle the job properly, and in the process of preparing a research grant proposal to construct a new statistical series for Canadian mergers, I was given a tip that permanently changed my dissertation and ultimately my research program for the next seven years.

Ian Drummond, who was then a visiting scholar at the LSE, was kind enough to review my grant application. While I had methodically laid out the statistical information on mergers that I expected to cull from the records of the London Stock Exchange and Canadian financial periodicals, Ian suggested that I could go even further by examining the most interesting promoter of the era, given that his records happened to be situated in London. At the time, I had no idea of the significance of the Beaverbrook Papers at the House of Lords Record Office. While I was aware of Aitken and his infamous Canada Cement merger, it had not occurred to me that his Canadian business correspondence would be gathering dust in Westminster. Moreover, as an economic historian who had been trained more in the methodology of neoclassical economics than in history, I was unconcerned about my ignorance: after all, why would I want to know about the individual operations of certain merger promoters? I was trying to reconstruct an outline of all mergers and acquisitions in order to ascertain their aggregate impact on Canadian industrial structure over a number of years. I felt I had little time for the personal motivations of the stock market types who had specialized in the business of making mergers.

Despite this, I set aside one day in December to check out what I could find at the House of Lords Record Office. At that time, Aitken's Canadian business papers, since they were of little interest to the majority of scholars visiting the Beaverbrook collection, remained the only unorganized portion of his papers. Within a few hours, however, I realized that the papers provided a most spectacular view of a world that I had known only in its crudest outlines from my previous research. Then and there, I decided to embark on a far more exciting journey of inquiry than the one on Canadian antitrust that I had been undertaking for the past two years.

Fortunately, my thesis adviser, Leslie Hannah, trusted my instincts when I told him of my discovery, and he allowed me to jettison my existing work so that I could explore this new world. Soon afterwards, he and his LSE colleagues invited me to take up an appointment as a lecturer in American economic history. The salary was not rich, but I was provided with an office, where I could store my fast-growing pile of research notes and photocopies, and most important of all, I was given a telephone with which I was permitted, as an LSE lecturer, to make the occasional transatlantic call to prepare a Canadian archival research trip funded by my new grant from the Canadian High Commission. Voyages of discovery are hardly possible without some money and patronage, and I shall always appreciate these early votes of confidence.

In 1989 I left the LSE to become an assistant professor at Johns Hopkins University's School of Advanced International Studies (SAIS), in Washington, DC. My dissertation – in large part a macro study of Canada's first merger wave, including an econometric model of merger causation – was completed a year later. Only one chapter was devoted exclusively to Max Aitken and the Royal Securities Corporation. Concerned about publishing the very different methodological approaches encompassed in the thesis, I resolved to complete a less schizophrenic study that would concentrate on Max Aitken and the Royal Securities Corporation, using a business history methodology throughout.

Since my position at SAIS required that much of my time be devoted to more contemporary issues in Canada–U.S. relations, I was continually working on other, quite different, projects during my next five years in Washington. As a consequence, I relied heavily on some of my extremely

Acknowledgments xv

talented students when completing the research for *Profits and Politics*. Vivian Noble and Mark Whitcomb helped me plough through years of *Industrial Canada*, the *Monetary Times*, and the *Canadian Journal of Commerce*, and Mark also assisted me in Montreal with the archival records of the Canada Cement Company. Chris Sands helped organize and type up hundreds of pages of my handwritten notes from the Beaverbrook Papers – a monumental task, without which the book would have taken much longer to write. In the process, Chris patiently allowed me to bounce around my half-baked ideas about Aitken's business methods. John Meehan and Nicolas Crowley combed through months of specialized trade periodicals, including the *Street Railway Journal*, and accompanied me on a hectic research trip to New Brunswick and Nova Scotia; they also critiqued the partial, and painful, drafts of the first few chapters.

Since the research was conducted in various locations in North America and Britain without grant money after 1989, I depended on the goodwill of numerous friends who allowed me to stay with them for many days at a time. In the process, I met many archivists, librarians, and corporate custodians who went far beyond the call of duty to help me out. Katherine Bligh, at the House of Lords Record Office, not only proved to be an excellent guide to Aitken's vast collection of correspondence, she also renumbered all of my endnote references after her staff had completed classification of the Canadian papers, so that anyone desirous of following up on my sources would not be confused. Barry Cahill, of the Public Archives of Nova Scotia, was wonderfully obliging in helping me locate a great deal of information concerning Aitken's Halifax years, and when I was unable to visit Halifax, he took the time to locate and send me research material without any prompting on my part. Dave Kelly helped me and my research assistants find virtually every Canadian business and trade periodical I needed for this study in the labyrinth that calls itself the Library of Congress. Alain Fredette and John Redfern, of Lafarge Canada, permitted me access to the remaining records of the Canada Cement Company, while Alex Percy, of the Steel Company of Canada (Stelco), was instrumental in eventually permitting me access to the records of his company.

I am particularly indebted to Christopher Armstrong, Barry Cahill, and Duncan McDowall, all of whom had the fortitude to read earlier, primitive drafts and gave me constructive criticism when I most needed it. Naturally, none should be implicated in the final product, for I am sure all would have written a very different book than this one. Throughout, Gerald Hallowell, of the University of Toronto Press, has been extremely supportive of this project. His guidance, along with the superb editing of Carlotta Lemieux and the expert production work of Darlene Zeleney, as well as the constructive criticism of two anonymous referees, has helped improve this book immensely.

By the time I was ready to write my final draft, I had already changed my occupation. As deputy minister of intergovernmental affairs for the Government of Saskatchewan, I found myself concentrating all my efforts on current problems within the Canadian federation, and I was forced to write in short bursts during the few vacation days which I managed to steal away from my regular work. This pressure may not have improved the quality of the resulting book, but it certainly gave me a new perspective on Max Aitken's first years in Britain, divided as they were between politics and the business of making profit.

Finally and most importantly, I would like to thank my wife and partner, Giovanna Pirro, for putting up with this seemingly endless project since we first met in 1988. She has been my toughest and, at times, my most insightful critic. While reminding me that the conflicting deadlines of numerous disparate tasks do not provide the optimal environment in which to write a book, she always, in the end, forgave my self-defeating propensity to take on yet another article or project, and even another profession, before this book was finished.

'Maxie' Aitken (centre back) at Harkins Academy, c. 1893

Rev. William Aitken, 1900

R.B. Bennett as a young lawyer in
Chatham, New Brunswick

John F. Stairs

Max Aitken as John F. Stairs's
executive assistant, 1903

Aitken's eventual nemesis in
Halifax, Robert E. Harris

Charles H. Cahan, politician,
journalist, lawyer, and adventurer

W.B. Ross and B.F. Pearson of the Dominion Group

Max Aitken in 1905, roughly a year after John F. Stairs's death

Blake Burrill, Aitken's 'indispensable' manager of the Royal Securities' Halifax office

Aitken's golden boy, Arthur J. Nesbitt, 1907

Walton Killam, Aitken's eventual successor

The spendthrift Gerald Farrell in 1909

Edward Clouston in 1904

Interior of Clouston's office at the Bank of Montreal

The Bank of Montreal's head office on St James Street, Montreal, 1906

Richard Wilson-Smith, the last anglophone mayor of Montreal

Sir Sandford Fleming

Arthur Doble at the beginning of
the Canada Cement affair

Nathaniel Curry in 1910

Rodolphe Forget

Mackenzie King, the 'Minister of Combines,' in ceremonial dress

Prime Minister Wilfrid Laurier on his 1910 Western tour

Soon to be prime minister Robert Borden campaigning

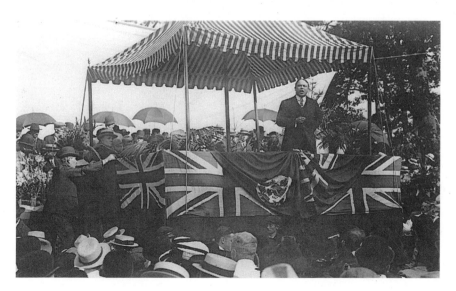

Mackenzie King campaigning on a lost cause, 1911

From left: J.C. Buckley, Conservative agent for Ashton-under-Lyne;
R.B. Bennett; Aitken; and Izaak Walton Killam. England, c. 1913

Ward Pitfield in First World War air-corps uniform

Lord Beaverbrook – newspaper baron, philanderer, and political intriguer

Gladys Aitken shortly after the war

PROFITS AND POLITICS

1

Max Aitken and the Nature of Finance Capitalism during the Laurier Boom

Promoter's profit is neither a swindle, nor some kind of indemnity or wage. It is an economic category *sui generis*.

Rudolf Hilferding, 'Finance Capital,' 1910[1]

Max Aitken came from Newcastle, New Brunswick. Newcastle wasn't big enough for Max so he went to Halifax. But Halifax wasn't big enough either so he went to Montreal. Montreal wasn't big enough so he went to London. Even London isn't big enough. So he'll go to hell.

British cabinet minister J.H. Thomas[2]

Max Aitken, later to become Lord Beaverbrook, captured the English imagination as a social and political phenomenon who rose to prominence despite his obscure colonial origins. His immense wealth, his rapid ascension to the peerage, his scandalous affairs, his political mischief making, and his control over the Express family of newspapers both attracted and repelled some of the most talented writers of his era.[3] As a result, he appeared as Lord Copper in Evelyn Waugh's *Scoop*, Sir Bussy Woodcock in H.G. Wells's *Autocracy of Mr. Parham*, Lord Raingo in Arnold Bennett's novel of the same name, Lord Ottercove in William Gerhardie's *Jazz and Jasper*, and Francis Pitt in Rebecca West's novel *Sunflower*.[4]

The son of a Presbyterian minister, Aitken grew up in the backwoods of New Brunswick at the close of the nineteenth century and never received any formal education past grade ten; he was little more than an insurance salesman until his early twenties. Humble beginnings perhaps, but there was nothing obscure about Aitken's final years in Canada. When he left Canada at the age of thirty-one, he was already recognized as one of the foremost financiers of his generation and the country's most prominent merger promoter. It was precisely this reputation, along with considerable wealth, that allowed him to penetrate London society and politics in the years immediately preceding the First World War. From the day he arrived in England in 1910 until he died in 1964, Aitken carved out an iconoclastic place for himself in modern British history.[5]

Despite this astonishing track record, Aitken remains an uncomfortable enigma in Canadian history. The conventional wisdom is that he created three immense Canadian mergers within less than a year and then fled to Britain with millions of dollars of profit in order to avoid investigation or even prosecution. Aitken is accordingly seen as a scoundrel and a crook who betrayed business associates and robbed the treasuries of the companies he had helped create.[6]

This view was held from the beginning by Aitken's many detractors. Prairie grain farmers, seeking reform of the Canadian political system and refuge from the 'monopolies of the east' through free trade with the United States, pilloried Aitken as the malevolent force behind the Canada Cement Company. Attacking an incentive system that allowed 'get-rich-overnight' financiers to amass millions of dollars in uncarned profit by creating 'trusts,' many populists and progressives argued that it was not the efficiency of these new 'combines' that produced large dividends and rising share prices; it was their tariff-protected ability to gouge the Canadian consumer.

Aitken's business enemies were far more subtle and, ultimately, devastating in their assault on him. His reputation was forever blackened by a clever strategy that exploited the antimonopoly sentiments of the country, which were reaching a feverish pitch during the 1911 reciprocity election campaign. The charge against him was publicly led by an old and arguably venerable doyen of the Canadian establishment, Sir Sandford Fleming, who asserted that Aitken had grabbed $12 million of common stock from the treasury of the Canada Cement Company.[7]

The allegation overshot the mark by a substantial margin, but Aitken and his Royal Securities Corporation had certainly profited handsomely from the merger. Moreover, Aitken was undeniably guilty of what was then called stockwatering – overissuing securities, whose face value exceeded the underlying value of the properties entering the merger. But all the other merger promoters of the day were also guilty of this. The financial practices of the time, combined with an archaic system of listing par (nominal) share values in units of $100 irrespective of their real (market) value, dictated that virtually all corporate financing during this era involved stockwatering. The real issue was one of degree. Canada Cement suffered no more from stockwatering than the average merger of the period (and, it appears, significantly less than many).[8] But in the politically charged atmosphere of 1911, the allegation of stockwatering added ammunition to the populist and progressive attack on Aitken, Canada Cement, and the 'combines' in general, and the general public soon came to share Sir Sandford Fleming's depiction of Aitken.

Years later, Aitken tried to change the image of himself as having been a crook in his youth, but it was too late; the image was too deeply embedded in the public's consciousness.[9] Even some of his closest friends and most powerful defenders thought the worst of Beaverbrook's Canadian years. Lord Northcliffe, for example, was fond of saying that Aitken 'only just got away [from Canada] in time from the arm of the law.'[10] Few since have suggested that Max Aitken's Canadian career was anything other than a (thankfully) brief exercise in unrestrained buccaneering. One exception was A.J.P. Taylor who, in his voluminous biography published eight years after Beaverbrook's death, tried his best to change this conventional wisdom. Most reviewers, however, felt that Taylor was swayed far too much by his close friendship with Aitken to be objective.[11] In his preface to the biography, Taylor admitted as much.[12] More importantly, he knew too little about the Canada Cement business and the world of finance to make a discerning judgment on the issue.

Over time, Aitken did attract a few defenders, who pointed out that his mergers were not permanent monopolies, if they were monopolies at all. They contended that all of his consolidations – Canada Cement, Canadian Car and Foundry and the Steel Company of Canada – performed better than the typical industrial merger created during the Laurier boom. Since they were all sound business enterprises, his profits were deserved, or so the argument runs.[13]

This same line of reasoning has recently been used to defend J.P. Morgan's activities during the gilded age of American finance.[14] However, unlike Aitken's consolidations, not all of Morgan's business enterprises were sound, and he did suffer at least one spectacular failure. Economies of scale based on new high-throughput technologies were central to Aitken's industrial mergers, whereas Morgan made the mistake of attempting a shipping company merger in which such economies were absent.[15] There were other differences too. When Morgan entered the field of industrial merger promoting at the turn of the century, he was head of a famous and long-established private bank. Well past middle age by then, he stood at the very pinnacle of the American financial pyramid. By comparison, when Aitken launched the Canada Cement Company, he was a brash young man who had just broken into the inner sanctum of the Canadian business establishment.

Despite the seventy years separating their careers, Aitken more resembled Michael Milken – the modern junk bond* king – than J.P. Morgan.[16] Both were young and pushy intruders in their respective financial establishments, both concentrated on promoting companies in the leading sector industries of their age, and both used high-risk methods to finance these companies. Mergers and acquisitions were a key part of their respective strategies to raise new capital, and they both raked in millions of dollars in profit, often in the form of the very high-risk securities that their businesses depended on. In the end, both became symbols of the financial excesses of their respective eras and were scorned by the general public.[17]

Unlike Milken, Aitken did not have to spend two years in jail to atone for the sins of his generation, though this was largely because of the widespread acceptance of insider trading and the absence of rules concerning security issues and financial disclosure during the Laurier boom.[18] As difficult as it was, the political environment in Canada was not nearly as punishing as in the United States, either then or seventy years later, when the riptide of mergers seemed to shake the American economy and society to its knees.[19] In Canada, merger waves, from the Laurier boom onwards, never seemed quite so threatening, and Aitken never had to contend with the degree of political backlash that spawned the Money Trust investigation into J.P. Morgan's activities.[20] While the 'cement combine' produced an outcry, it was muted by the political reality that both sides in Parliament found it inconvenient to order an investigation into the affair.

Although Aitken was never investigated, charged, or sentenced, his early reputation suffered no less than Milken's, and perhaps more than J.P. Morgan's. The purpose in unravelling the Canada Cement merger, for example, is not so much to determine who was right and who was wrong, but to tell the story as accurately as possible, given the evidence available, and to see what light this sheds on the investment banking practices of the time. Indeed, the overriding objective of all the chapters that

---

*'Junk bond' refers to a modern high-risk, high-yield security either rated below investment grade (BB or lower) or unrated altogether by commercial rating companies such as Moody's or Standard & Poor's.

follow is to understand the nature of the finance capitalism that evolved during the Laurier boom and to ascertain Max Aitken's place in it. From the turn of the century until the First World War, the industrial world experienced a financial, managerial, and organizational revolution that has many parallels with the tumultuous changes of the 1980s and early 1990s. Understanding this past is an important step in understanding the function of corporate promoters and investment bankers in a modern economy.

The Laurier Boom in Perspective

Canadian industry and finance were fundamentally transformed during the years preceding the First World War. This was the great Laurier boom, so-named by political historians because much of this remarkable period coincided with Prime Minister Wilfrid Laurier's tenure in office. Starting in 1896, the beginning of an inflationary cycle for most of the advanced industrial world, the boom reached its apogee during the first Canadian merger wave that began in 1909, only to die out with the world-wide recession of 1913.

In their novel *The Gilded Age*, Mark Twain and Charles Dudley Warner satirized the 'all-pervading speculativeness,' optimism, materialism, and low ethical standards that seemed to become part of the American character after the hard years of the Civil War.[21] The term 'gilded age' was a metaphor for conspicuous wealth, particularly the wealth that flowed so abundantly to those engaged in what appeared to be nonproductive pursuits. Corporate promoters and their world of high finance became the living embodiment of all the qualities portrayed with contempt by Twain and Warner.

The term 'gilded age,' however, is better applied to the period following the 1870s and 1880s, when a long cycle of inflationary growth set in, spreading the fever of optimism and speculation beyond the United States. The years after 1896, until the depression of 1913 and the horrors of the First World War, were similarly experienced throughout the industrial world. Remembered variously as *la belle époque*, the Edwardian years, and the Laurier boom, it was truly the gilded age of the industrialized world.[22]

These were good times for all, but no country enjoyed a faster rate of economic growth than Canada. Despite the fact that the 1870s and 1880s were sluggish decades, business had so picked up by the turn of the century that Canada's average growth rate for the decades of the second

TABLE 1.1 Canadian growth relative to that of other countries, 1870–1913[a]

Real GDP growth rate		Real GDP per capita growth rate		Real GDP per labour-hour	
%	Countries	%	Countries	%	Countries
4.1	Canada	2.3	Canada	2.3	Canada
3.9	U.S.A.	1.8	U.S.A.	1.9	U.S.A., Germany, Japan
3.5	Australia	1.6	Germany, Denmark	1.8	Austria, Finland
2.8	Germany	1.5	Sweden, Austria	1.7	Italy, Sweden
2.7	Denmark, Finland	1.4	Japan, Finland	1.6	France, Norway
2.4	Austria	1.3	France, Italy, Norway	1.5	Switzerland
2.3	Japan, Netherlands	1.2	Switzerland	1.3	Netherlands
2.2	Sweden	1.0	Britain, Belgium,	1.2	Britain, Belgium
2.1	Switzerland, Norway		Netherlands	1.1	Australia
2.0	Belgium	0.9	Australia		
1.9	Britain, Italy				
1.5	France				

Source: Angus Maddison, *Dynamic Forces in Capitalist Development: A Long-Run Comparative View* (Oxford 1991), 49–51
[a] Average annual compound growth rates based on 1985 U.S. prices at purchasing power parity

industrial revolution towered above that of every other country. As can be seen in table 1.1, output per person and per labour-hour was, on average, between 0.4 and 0.5 per cent per annum higher than in the United States, the fastest-growing country after Canada. This remarkable growth rate reflected both high capital intensity and rapid technological innovation and adaptation. Starting from a relatively undeveloped industrialized position at the time of the birth of the country in 1867, Canada had grown into a vital manufacturing nation by 1914.

A recently reworked series of historical national income statistics, briefly summarized in table 1.2, can be used to pinpoint the source of Canada's rapid growth rate during these years.[23] Real gross national product (GNP) grew more than twice as fast in the period 1896–1913 as in the periods preceding and following it.[24] During the Laurier boom (also known as the 'wheat boom' by economic historians), growth was actually most rapid in infrastructure. Both the transportation and construction sectors experienced an average annual growth rate in excess of 10 per cent. Manufacturing grew at a vigorous average of more than 6 per cent per year, while agriculture (led by wheat production) fell in behind at 5 per cent.[25]

TABLE 1.2 Average annual real growth rates (per cent), Canada (GNP and sectoral) and United States (GNP)

Years	Total GNP	GNP per capita	Mfg. output	Constr. output	Agr. output	Trans. output	Mining output	Forestry output	Fishing output	U.S. GNP
1877–96	2.8	1.5	3.0	1.0	1.7	8.6	8.0	1.9	1.8	3.7
1896–1913[a]	6.6	4.2	6.3	12.0	5.0	12.4	8.7	0.7	0.5	4.4
1913–26	3.6	1.9	2.3	-3.5	0.7	2.2	2.1	4.3	1.0	3.1

Source: GNP growth rates from Morris Altman, 'Revised Real Canadian GNP Estimates and Canadian Economic Growth, 1870–1926,' *Review of Income and Wealth* 38, no. 4 (Dec. 1992), 468. Sectoral growth rates derived from annual data in Morris Altman, 'Revised Estimates of Real Canadian GNP and Growth and Pre and Post World War Two Volatility of the Canadian Business Cycle with Some Comparison to the American Record' (unpublished working paper, Department of Economics, University of Saskatchewan, 1989)

[a] The years of the Laurier boom

TABLE 1.3 Canadian population and rates of growth by decade

Decade	Population[a] (thousands)	Rate of population increase by decade (per cent)	Net immigration
1871–81	3,689	17.2	−1.5
1881–91	4,325	11.7	−3.4
1891–1901	4,833	11.1	−2.7
1901–11[b]	5,371	34.2	15.1
1911–21	7,207	21.9	4.3
1921–31	8,788	18.1	2.6
1931–41	10,377	10.9	−0.9

Source: M.C. Urquhart, 'Canadian Economic Growth, 1870–1980' (discussion paper no. 734, Institute for Economic Research, Queen's University, 1988), 6
[a] Population at beginning of decade
[b] The central years of the Laurier boom

The Laurier boom was therefore a product of the enormous infrastructure investment that accompanied the rapid industrialization of central Canada and the opening of the western prairies for farm settlement. Three characteristics distinguished this period of remarkable economic growth: a positive and high rate of net immigration to western Canada and to the newly industrializing cities of central Canada; a very high rate of gross fixed capital formation; and an enormous net capital inflow from Britain.[26]

The closing off of the American frontier, the opening up of the Canadian prairies for settlement – the 'last best west,' as it was known – and the emergence of new industry in central Canada all combined to encourage record numbers of foreigners to immigrate to Canada , as can be seen in table 1.3. Moreover, rather than using the country as an entry point for the United States as had been common practice before the Laurier boom, most new immigrants remained in Canada. The growing prosperity also meant that fewer nonimmigrant Canadians moved to the United States seeking employment. The result was a high rate of population growth, which helped generate an average rate of real GNP growth that was 2.2 per cent above the American annual average for the same period.[27]

The level of investment in infrastructure, transportation, industry, and agriculture was on such a large scale that even a relatively high level of domestic savings was insufficient to pay for it. The Laurier boom consequently witnessed a deluge of foreign investment. Capital came mainly from Britain in the form of portfolio investment. Indeed, in the decade preceding the First World War, Canada received almost all the capital flowing from Britain to its empire. According to Michael Edelstein's calculations, 'Canada was the largest borrower in the last great surge of British lending that started in 1902–3, absorbing perhaps a third of British lending.'[28] Although American direct investment, particularly in manufacturing and resource extraction, began to flow into Canada at an accelerated pace, the total amount remained small relative to British investment.[29] In 1900, for example, from the total of $1.2 billion in foreign investment received from Canada, 85 per cent came from Britain. By 1910, the total had more than doubled to $2.5 billion, 77 per cent of which was from Britain.[30]

As a result of this dramatic increase in British investment during the Laurier boom, Canadian finance became more closely linked with the mother country than ever before, with the securities of the largest Canadian enterprises trading almost as easily in London as in Montreal and Toronto. Business practices were heavily influenced by this trend. Canadian investment bankers and brokers established agency arrangements with their British counterparts; and a handful, including Aitken's Royal Securities Corporation, set up branch offices in the 'City,' London's financial district.[31]

This aspect of the Laurier boom went hand in hand with the evolving English-Canadian view of the British Empire and Canada's role in it. Canadian imperialists of that era – and Aitken was a very good example of the Laurier boom type – were both strong Canadian nationalists and fervent adherents to the British Empire. They believed that Canada could best achieve national status within a transformed empire that was politically and economically tied together in an imperial federation with preferential tariffs. These imperialists thus saw no conflict between their allegiance to Canada and their British citizenship. Some even saw Canada's role as central to the continuing supremacy of the British Empire, with its centre of gravity shifting from London to the new and vigorous future represented in Ottawa.[32]

However quaint it may seem today, this view was grounded in the economic reality of the time. When Aitken first visited London to promote his bonds and shares in the autumn of 1908, he and his Canadian competitors recognized the immense amount of British capital available for utility promotions and industrial mergers. This 'easy' capital was to stoke the merger wave during the next five years. Indeed, without British capital, the first great Canadian merger wave might have waited until the business cycle upswing of the 1920s, and Aitken might never have promoted the Canada Cement, Canadian Car, and Steel Company of Canada mergers.

Like other promoters, Aitken often chose names that started with 'Canada,' 'Dominion,' or 'Canadian' to denote the transnational reach of the steel, portland cement, and transportation industries that were at the heart of the Laurier boom. The geographical reach of these enterprises was exceeded only by the egos of their financiers. Theoretically, the public issue of securities should have dispersed ownership from a dominating individual or family to a large body of investors. In practice, however, control was often concentrated in the hands of the financiers, who paid themselves out of the voting common stock of the consolidations they created. Their actions were a symptom of the brief domination of finance capitalism, forming as it were a bridge between an earlier age of family capitalism and the emerging age of managerial capitalism.[33]

This intermediate, or bridging stage, in economic history was marked by the development of an international market in industrial securities, the rapid growth and linking of organized exchanges for the trading of securities, and the predominance of promoter-financiers in manufacturing industry. This period also witnessed the apparent supremacy of 'financial' over 'industrial' objectives, at least during the years in which the new enterprises remained dependent on their promoters for raising capital. This period of finance capitalism was relatively short-lived, but it left a lasting impression on the observers of the day.

In Canada, both the first and second industrial revolutions lagged a few years behind those in Germany and the United States but preceded similar developments in such nations as Australia and Argentina.[34] Canada's first industrial revolution came in the form of textile, brewery, flour milling, iron, rolling stock, and farm-implement factories, which began to spring up along the Lachine Canal in Montreal and the communities surrounding Lake Ontario during the 1850s and 1860s.[35] This development was not accompanied by significant changes in finance. Retained earnings and the occasional loan from family, friends, or financial intermediaries were generally sufficient for the relatively modest requirements of single-plant operations manufacturing for local needs.[36]

By contrast, Canada's second industrial revolution produced fundamental changes in industrial financing. Security issues became a critical source of capital, for retained earnings and family wealth were found to be inadequate in meeting the very large capital needs of the enterprises that were springing up in new industries such as steel, precision machinery, portland cement, synthetic chemicals, and electric power generation.[37] As firms became multi-unit operations, the need for security financing became much more pronounced. By 1909, when the inflationary updraught of the business cycle was finally hitting with full force, the country experienced its first sustained merger wave – a decade after similar waves in the United States, Britain, and Germany.[38]

The Nature of Financial Entrepreneurship

Anyone approaching the subject of investment banking in the Anglo-American world before the First World War finds that the institutions themselves were inextricably entwined with the personalities that stood behind them. These investment banks, although they would eventually outgrow their founders to become enduring enterprises with professional management, lived their early years as idiosyncratic vehicles for individual financial operators. The first decade of the Royal Securities Corporation's existence was, for example, so much a product of Aitken's efforts and ambitions that the organization's history necessarily blends into an entrepreneurial history of the man.[39]

Aside from Royal Securities, Aitken's connection with other business enterprises was short-lived. This study is not, therefore, an institutional history of the Montreal Engineering Company, the Canada Cement Company, or the Montreal Trust Company. It is nonetheless a business history of a very particular type, one that focuses on financial entrepreneurship and the organizational and managerial forms that are created or adapted to achieve the entrepreneur's objectives. As Arthur Cole stressed long ago, entrepreneurship is more than an individual phenomenon; it is also an organizational phenomenon, a 'purposeful activity ... undertaken to initiate, maintain, or aggrandize a profit-oriented business unit.'[40]

Personality, emotion, family, and society are thus combined with the factors of business organization, management, and political environment in order to expose the human factors that lie behind investment decision making – what John Maynard Keynes called the 'animal spirits' of capitalism.[41] Managing the Royal Securities Corporation from its creation in 1903, Aitken emerges as a man apparently overreaching, yet ultimately able to conclude all of his financial deals. Aitken's correspondence reveals his mood swings as much as the content of his business deals. His associates and employees during these years experienced a roller-coaster of highs and lows. Some held Aitken's business acumen in such high esteem that they were more than willing to put up with his autocratic and apparently erratic style. As one business associate (whose agreement was unilaterally altered by Aitken halfway through a flotation) put it after complaining about Aitken's mercurial nature, 'I quite appreciate that anybody who sails with you must obey the Captain's orders and submit to any changes in the vessel's course. I want to sail on the next voyage.'[42]

Although most climbed aboard for the next voyage, the captain did change course often without regard to the sensibilities of his crew, and these sudden shifts inevitably led to misunderstandings, outbursts of temper, and even lifelong resentments. Aitken pushed those around him too hard, justifying it with the excuse that he pushed himself even harder. He was often authoritarian, critical, and harsh in dealing with his business associates and employees. Ironically, he often treated rivals better than allies. Aitken could temper his outbursts with occasional flattery, generosity, and self-deprecation but was incapable of such gestures at the peak of any stressful negotiation or in those fragile days preceding a major flotation of securities. At these times, he was excessively direct or unnecessarily brutal. But in more relaxed periods, he employed enough flattery to sugar-coat the most bitter pill.

Beyond such emotions, there were objective calculations behind Aitken's investment decisions. He carefully investigated the businesses he financed. Moving far beyond an examination of past balance sheets and profit-loss statements – for he well knew the limitations of financial accounting during the gilded age – Aitken carefully investigated the plant, equipment, and especially the quality of management. He quickly developed an eye for 'progressive' managers, as he called them, and it must be said that he had a remarkable intuition for finding talented people for his enterprises. The Royal Securities Corporation, for example, brought together Izaak Walton Killam, Arthur J. Nesbitt, and Ward Pitfield. These men and their respective firms were to dominate Canadian investment banking for much of the twentieth century. To this list should be added utility engineers Fred Teele and Carl Giles, and one of Canada's earliest managers of big industry, Frank P. Jones.

While Max Aitken's style of management may have seemed bizarre at times, there was generally a method to his madness. The sticks of criticism and superhuman demands were balanced by the carrots of promotion and profit sharing. The organizational flux within the enterprises was the product of relentless attempts to find the most effective and least expensive system or method to complete a given task. His complaints about excessive advertising or the use of letterhead stationery for interoffice communication were intended to create a lean corporate culture that kept expenses low as a matter of principle.

As the title of this book suggests, business and the making of profit always occur in a particular political context. The vast profits of financial entrepreneurs operating largely in the industrial heartland of central Canada caused anger in rural areas, but the reaction was most organized and effective in the region of recent settlement. Western grain farmers, dependent for their livelihood on volatile climatic conditions and international markets, questioned the fairness of any system that could permit financial middlemen to make millions of dollars almost overnight. Looking back to an earlier era of what they perceived to have been fair capitalism, they regarded as basically immoral the evolving system and the way it allocated profit.[43] This new environment, consisting of immense industrial enterprises, vast railway companies, and the stock and commodity exchanges, seemed to be dominated by banks and high financiers. Western farmers and 'progressives' dedicated themselves to fighting the trusts in order to protect the truly productive members of society.

Aitken profited handsomely from his utility promotions, but it was his consolidations during the first Canadian merger wave that made him a multimillionaire. The farmers in western Canada considered these profits undeserved at best and outright theft at worst. As Aitken explained with characteristic exaggeration to his new friend Winston Churchill in 1911, 'There is an objection to me you must know about. I created all the big trusts in Canada. None of them are bad trusts but the Western Farmers attack me very often and sometimes very offensively.'[44] The attacks were to continue in earnest for the next two years, abating only when the merger movement itself died out, by which time Aitken had begun to move out of the investment banking business altogether. And while he became history as Lord Beaverbrook, his Canadian career as Max Aitken was consigned to the shadows.

2

Circuitous Road to Halifax, 1879–1904

Nothing is so bad as consistency.

Lord Beaverbrook, 'Success,' 1922

Max Aitken [is a] get-rich-overnight financier who, when down on the heel and thoroughly discredited ... was taken hold of and literally lifted out of the gutter by the late John F. Stairs and Mr. Harris.[1]

Thomas Cantley, general manager of the Nova Scotia Steel and Coal Company, writing to a Scottish shareholder in 1910

Although I am very much attached to Halifax, I can readily believe that I might ... achieve better results if I devoted myself to some larger sphere. At the same time I am very much attached to some of our Halifax men.[2]

Max Aitken, writing a Montreal financier to turn down a job offer in April 1904

No single circumstance or event in Max Aitken's childhood foreshadowed his future success and fame. Only in hindsight can one see that certain clues, taken together, suggest his rapid rise in the world of business and finance. Nonetheless, almost all of his biographers have found in his childhood the critical element that produced the iconoclastic businessman, politician, and minister. Aitken himself was the main source of the 'facts' about his youth, and he shaped these facts to fit his own 'rags to riches'

legend – Lord Beaverbrook, the millionaire who had worked his way up
into the centre of British business and politics from the poverty of rural
northern New Brunswick. The truth is that his family, though not rich, was
far from poor – a fact discovered by his most recent biographers.[3] And
although these same biographers readily admit that Aitken reinvented his
earlier years, they nonetheless have selected those aspects of the mythol-
ogy that best support their interpretation of the Beaverbrook story.

It hardly seems useful to attempt yet another full re-creation of Aitken's
youth, given the plethora of existing biographies that have relied on anec-
dotes cultivated by Beaverbrook in his sunset years. Rather, we can use certain incidents from his childhood, particularly those for which some
impartial evidence exists, to sketch out the themes of restlessness and
entrepreneurial inventiveness that pervaded his financial career in Canada. This background will be the entry point for the remarkable decade
that followed – the years in which Aitken used Halifax and Montreal as a
base from which to forge a business empire that would become a symbol of
the new finance capitalism emerging during the Laurier boom. After he
entered John F. Stairs's world in Halifax, in particular, there was a stream
of correspondence between Aitken and his many associates, and this allows
for a detailed and relatively objective reconstruction of one of the most
remarkable financial careers during the gilded age of Canadian finance.

Growing Up in Newcastle

Max Aitken's father was a well-educated Presbyterian clergyman who had
emigrated from Scotland to Canada West in 1865 to take charge of his
first congregation in Maple, Ontario, a town since swallowed by metropolitan Toronto. Here, Rev. William Cuthbert Aitken met Jane Noble, the
daughter of a prosperous store-owning farmer. They were married in
1867, the year Canada West and Canada East joined with Nova Scotia and
New Brunswick to form the new Dominion of Canada. Max was the fifth
Aitken child when he was born on 25 May 1879, just when Sir John A.
Macdonald's Conservative government was implementing its National
Policy of tariff protection against the world, creating a hothouse environment for new Canadian industry. Almost immediately after Max's birth,
his father was transferred to Newcastle, New Brunswick, on the banks of
the Miramichi River.

The Miramichi was forever home to Aitken in his imagination. He
waxed lyrical in his old age about this 'country of rolling forests, with dis-
tant glimpses of hills and valleys and of broad rivers, full of big salmon

running down over rapids past tree-clad islands to meet the great tides sweeping up from the Miramichi Bay.'[4] Commonly known as the manse, the Aitken house was the largest in Newcastle. Even with the four additional children after Max, there were never more than two sharing a bedroom. And if young Maxie, as he was known by the townspeople, felt psychologically confined by his parents' discipline or by his numerous brothers and sisters, his world was wide open outside the manse door.[5] As he recalled in his memoirs, Newcastle in the 1880s was a scattered town 'extending up and down the river for miles and miles, where many small farmhouses stood in the clearings made in the overwhelming mass of dark forest land.'[6]

In these same memoirs, Aitken enjoyed thinking of himself as one of the town's bad boys, and there is supporting evidence that his personality and disposition caused friction both at school and at home. As he entered his teens, he became increasingly restless.[7] His teachers complained about his wandering mind and his impish behaviour. He began to show up late for school, and his marks, previously among the highest in class, dropped precipitously after he turned thirteen.[8] Unable to sit still, he mimicked his teachers behind their backs and taunted his classmates.[9] He was regularly detained after school and his teachers concluded that although he had a 'lively' imagination, he was too restless ever to amount to much.[10] He acted even worse out of school. One of his brothers admitted that Max was 'the devil to live with,' and his eldest sister was so enraged by his conduct on one occasion that she threw him down the stairs.[11] His mother, applying the Victorian belief in physical discipline, felt obliged to beat him occasionally. One neighbour of the Aitken family remembered seeing Max 'quite often with his hand in front of his face, sobbing after being punished by his mother.'[12] No amount of punishment could seem to stop him, however, and his father, consciously directing his children into the professions, feared that he would become the black sheep of the family.[13]

Max hated the discipline and tedium of working for someone else as much as he hated school. His first job was picking the bugs off potato plants, a staple crop in the region. Max and other young boys would walk down the rows of potato plants armed with a stick in one hand, prodding bugs into a can held in the other hand. Paying two cents for each full can of bugs, the work was hard, boring, and uncomfortable. Then, at eleven years of age, Max landed his first respectable job, which paid twenty-five cents a week. Hidden behind a screen, he pumped the organ at his father's church during services and choir practices. This was comfortable work compared with bug picking, perhaps too effortless. Drifting off to sleep one Sunday during the service, Max missed his cue to begin pumping, and the choir had to sing without the accompaniment of the organ. He was fired by his father.[14]

Although Max proved unable to keep a regular job, he excelled at inventing his own business schemes. He took advantage of a soap company's promotional offer of a bicycle by borrowing money from one of his older friends to buy a crate of the soap. He then went from door to door selling it at cost on condition that the wrappers were returned to him. When he had enough wrappers to meet the promotional offer, he turned them in for the bicycle. He exhibited the same creative spirit as a newspaper boy. By enlarging his paper route and subcontracting delivery to a number of other boys, he managed to boost his total earnings even while relinquishing some of his profit per newspaper.[15]

Max also displayed an innate talent for promoting new schemes with the use of other people's resources. At the age of fourteen, while working in the printing department of the *Union Advocate*, Newcastle's weekly newspaper, he started his own weekly called the *Leader*.[16] The newspaper was a promotional vehicle for his 'Leader Publishing Co.,' advertising on the front page his willingness to print letterheads, statements, envelopes, posters, and other outside jobs. The masthead of Max's newspaper blared, 'We Lead, Let Those Follow Who Can,' and he carried a serial story to make up for the *Leader*'s rather pedestrian news about temperance meetings and the travel itineraries of local notables. To maintain the interest of his readership, he ran an essay competition on Newcastle's industries; the first prize was 'a pair of genuine Acme skates,' and 'a beautiful pearl handle' pocket-knife was reported as the second prize.[17] No doubt he convinced the *Union Advocate*'s owner, W.C. Anslow, to let him use the *Advocate*'s printing equipment free of charge, but when Anslow ran short of time and supplies during the Christmas advertising rush, Max was forced to discontinue publication.[18]

Although the paper lasted only three editions, the *Leader* was a grand adventure that kept boredom at bay. The fact that it provided a little extra pocket money was almost beside the point. Max's sister said decades later that he 'did not make money because we were poor. He made money because he liked making money.'[19]

Dick Bennett and the Bad Protégé

Max's closest friend during his youth was Richard Bedford Bennett, a driven young man who eventually achieved his dream of being prime minister of Canada but was unfortunate enough to do so during the very worst years of the Great Depression. Max was ten and Dick Bennett was nineteen when they first met.[20] At the time, Bennett was principal of the small school at Douglastown, two miles downriver from Newcastle. Max was impressed by the young man's large words and ponderous conversation. Unfortunately, these were exactly the qualities that made Bennett appear arrogant to others, and as he had few friends he readily accepted Max's many invitations for Sunday dinner with his family at the manse. It was an unusual friendship, given the difference in age, but Max's parents were only too pleased to see him attracted to someone with education, ambition, and such obvious religious principle, even if it was of the Methodist variety. They were delighted when their errant son began to talk of becoming a lawyer after Bennett announced his intention to attend law school.

Bennett moved to Halifax the following year and entered the Dalhousie Law School. Upon graduating in 1893, he returned to the Miramichi to become a partner in L.J. Tweedie's law firm in Chatham, directly across the Miramichi River from Newcastle.[21] Max's friend and mentor was now larger than life – a real lawyer and a figure to be reckoned with in the community. Bennett responded to Max's hero-worship by encouraging him to follow in his footsteps; he was becoming increasingly concerned about Max's lack of interest in his studies. By this time, Max's high school teacher had written him off as a hopeless case and, trying to minimize his bad influence, had placed him at the front of the class 'to prevent him from annoying the other pupils and distracting their attention to work.'[22]

As soon as the school year finished, Max appeared at L.J. Tweedie's law firm asking for work as a law clerk and articling student.[23] Although Bennett was disappointed by Max's decision to leave school, he convinced Tweedie to hire the youngster.[24] Max began by typing up documents, deeds, and letters, a job that struck him as dull beyond imagination. Meanwhile, in early 1896, Chatham formally became a town and elections were called to choose members for the new town council. Seeing a chance for some needed excitement, Max talked Bennett into putting his name forward as a candidate for alderman, and skilfully if a little recklessly he ran Bennett's election campaign. Bennett was elated when he discovered that he had won by a narrow margin – at least, he was elated until he learned of Max's unreasonable promises to several voters on his behalf.[25]

The excitement of the campaign soon faded, however, and Max found

it harder to cope with the drudgery of law clerking. Bennett's companion-
ship was the only thing he truly desired, and he felt bereft when he discovered that Bennett had decided to move to Calgary in January 1897 to
take up a more promising partnership with Senator James Lougheed,
who desperately needed a partner to help him cope with all the new business being generated in that western Canadian town, which was growing
by leaps and bounds. Aitken was torn between sadness for his own loss
and happiness for Bennett, who was now embarked on a great adventure.
There were, after all, limited possibilities for advancement in Chatham
with Tweedie. Business was sluggish, and since Tweedie was provincial
secretary in the New Brunswick cabinet, he was too busy with provincial
politics to work very hard at his law practice.[26]

Bennett had no compunction about leaving Tweedie, but he was concerned about leaving Aitken behind. Tweedie had already complained to
Bennett about Max's attitude; the boy lacked the obedience expected of
an apprentice employee, and he had trouble concentrating on routine
tasks.[27] Knowing full well that Tweedie would eventually get rid of Max,
Bennett tried to convince his young protégé to resign his clerkship and go
on to law school. Certainly, Max's family could afford the fees. But Max
could not be moved, and as Bennett feared, L.J. Tweedie fired him the
moment he found a new articling student who showed more potential.[28]

It was the summer of 1897, and Max now had nothing to keep him at
home.[29] He wandered to Halifax and Saint John to see the two commercial centres of the Maritimes. After failing the entrance examination to
Dalhousie University, he began to peddle life insurance policies from
door to door to pay his way.[30] He did not do very well in the beginning.
He sold one policy to Sandy Corbett, the owner of a men's clothing store
in Saint John, who felt sorry for the ragged-looking youngster. Max went
back to Corbett's store later to see whether he could buy an inexpensive
suit. Corbett's cheapest suit was eight dollars. Max had only one dollar;
but again taking pity on him, Corbett accepted the dollar as a down payment, the rest to be paid in one-dollar weekly instalments. Aitken took
the suit but could not make the remaining payments. When Corbett
finally confronted Max weeks later in the insurance office he was told:
'It's no use looking for money from me, Sandy. You see that floor? Well, I
slept on that last night and every night for the last week. I didn't even
have enough money for a bed. So I can't pay you a cent. I haven't had
more than $1.50 in a week, and I borrowed that to keep me from starving.
Which is about all it did.'[31] Ever the optimist, Max promised to pay what
he could as things improved, and the following week he sent fifty cents.

But this was the last payment Corbett received until decades later, when Lord Beaverbrook remembered his old debt.[32]

From his new office in Calgary, Bennett heard discouraging news about Max. Realizing that he alone could not convince Max of the benefits of a professional career, he wrote to Rev. William Aitken from Calgary asking for his help in getting Max into university. William Aitken, however, could no longer agree that this would be best for Max, much less possible:

Would a College Course be now a benefit to Max? My deliberate opinion is, that it would not. His nature is such as would never make a first class student. He is too eager to grasp the practical. And now that he has got a taste of business and a liking for the business intercourse of the world, I believe that he could no more set himself down to a course of theoretical study than he could take (or rather think of taking) a journey to the moon. He would do no good at College now: in fact he would be sure to learn indolent habits and suffer harm.[33]

Thanking Bennett for his 'kind interest in Max,' William Aitken explained how his son had benefited from Bennett's example, and he regretted the extent to which the youngster was lost without Bennett, for he too wanted Max to become an educated professional:

Your influence on him, in the past, has I know been very beneficial. Max is the better of having some one near him, to whom he can look with respect and for guidance. It would be selfish in me to express a desire that you had remained in Chatham. I cannot do that – But had you remained there I feel certain that you would have imparted to Max ambitions and energies and moral motives which would have helped him materially in the successes of life.[34]

Early Misadventures

Sometime in November 1897, Max entered the law school in Saint John, but according to his own account he lasted no more than a few days there.[35] Meanwhile, he continued to peddle insurance. By the following spring he had scraped together enough money to travel by train to western Canada to see his old friend Dick Bennett in Calgary and find out for himself whether fortunes were being made in that boom town. If he expected Bennett to arrange a new articling position for him, he was to be disappointed. By this time, Bennett understood that Max did not have the patience or aptitude to become a lawyer, much less to endure four years as an articling student.[36] So Max had to satisfy himself with some small forays

into business with a new-found partner named Jack McLean.[37] These
included purchasing a bowling alley housed in a building across the street
from Lougheed and Bennett's law office. Bennett soon began to distance
himself from his wayward protégé, for Max was increasingly fraternizing
with the undesirable characters who frequented the bowling alley.[38]

Bennett did not warm to Max until the territorial election campaign in
the autumn of 1898. Bennett had committed himself to running for a seat
in the North-West Territories assembly, and Max worked his way back
into his mentor's affections by tirelessly canvassing on his behalf. He cam-
paigned particularly hard in the poorer Mission district of Calgary. Here
he freely dispensed whisky and won over the hard-living inhabitants by
once again making promises that Bennett could not keep. When the
November election was over, Bennett found that he had won quite hand-
ily, and having by then become more tolerant of the seedier side of politics, he was genuinely grateful to Max for his adroit handling of the
campaign. Max, in turn, was overjoyed to have regained Bennett's
approval, however short-lived.[39]

After Bennett's election, Max and Jack McLean sold the bowling alley
in exchange for a stationery and tobacco store, making a small profit on
the trade. Bennett could now see that Max had no intention of ever
becoming anything more than a salesman and trader, a mere 'drummer'
in Bennett's eyes. He was disappointed in Max and embarrassed by his
uncouth friends. Perhaps hurt by Bennett's disapproval, Aitken soon left
Calgary for Edmonton, where he decided to get into the business of servicing the large crews of workers who were extending the railway system
farther northwest. He had learned that Jimmy Dunn, one of his boyhood
friends from New Brunswick, was working with railway promoters in
Edmonton. Dunn, later to become famous as Sir James Dunn of the
Algoma Steel Corporation, was sure to know the railway men with whom
Aitken wanted to do business.

Max had first met Dunn during his family's annual summer vacation
on the Baie des Chaleurs on New Brunswick's north shore. Although five
years older than him, Dunn became both a friend and a rival, in part
because he was so similar in temperament and outlook.[40] Dunn had, for
example, a great deal of difficulty fitting into any one job. He had been a
deck-hand on Lake Superior, an armaments factory worker, and an assistant to a lecturing quack called the 'professor of memory,' with whom he
had toured England. On his return to New Brunswick, he had decided to
become a lawyer by articling for four years in Bathurst. Aitken had introduced him to Bennett, who advised Dunn to go to Dalhousie Law School

rather than waste four years apprenticing. Unlike Max, Dunn followed Bennett's advice, worked his way through school, and started practising law with B.F. Pearson, a prominent Halifax lawyer and business promoter. Pearson had sent Dunn to Edmonton to act as legal adviser for himself and some fellow western railway promoters.[41]

Shortly after he and Max met in Edmonton, Dunn decided that his future lay in the rapidly expanding business of trading and selling securities rather than law, and he moved to Montreal. Max then found a new partner and began shipping meat supplies to the railway work camps. The new business required capital, but Max thought the large profits he would make in getting meat to the camps more than justified an equally large bank loan. However, when unforeseen delays and inclement weather spoiled his supplies before they arrived, his debt became unpayable. In his memoirs, he claimed that it was Dunn's logic – that the 'West must pay tribute to the East' – that convinced him to leave the West and return to the Maritimes.[42] But getting away from his creditors was the real reason. On the way home he arranged to meet one of his older brothers at a recruitment station. The South African War had just begun, and he saw a golden opportunity to escape his recent failures.

Max was nineteen when the Boer War broke out. It is probable that he shared the romantic view of war held by most young men at the time. Moreover, he believed that it was the duty of all Canadians to fight on behalf of the British Empire, a sentiment held by his family and most Protestant British Canadians, particularly Maritimers.[43] But he was not to have the opportunity to prove his commitment to the empire on the battlefield. Afflicted by asthma since childhood – a condition that plagued him his whole life – he was rejected by the recruiting officers, and he underwent the humiliation of seeing his brother and the other 'lucky' volunteers sail away without him.[44]

His dreams of glory shattered, Max moved on to Saint John, where he began to sell insurance. With the money he made, he hired a reluctant Bennett to help him discharge some of his outstanding debts in the West and to get his books and papers recovered from one debtor who was holding his property as a lien.[45] Selling insurance was boring compared to his western ventures, irrespective of how they had turned out financially, and he grew increasingly dissatisfied with his lot in life. Gambling and drinking with the other travelling salesmen dulled but did not eliminate his growing sense of anxiety.[46]

When the new century began, Max was twenty years old. He had been on his own for more than four years but had accomplished little, and nothing much seemed to be on the horizon. According to his memoirs, it was on his birthday in May 1900 that he suddenly resolved to stop wasting his time.[47] Whether this was an overnight conversion or one prompted by the mounting frustration of his successive failures, he did begin to pay more attention to business as he travelled through the Maritimes peddling insurance. While in Halifax, he met and cultivated a friendship with William B. Ross, a prominent lawyer-promoter who was involved in numerous utility and railway enterprises with James Dunn's old principal, B.F. Pearson. In addition to organizing the Halifax Electric Tramway, the People's Heat and Light Company, and numerous other enterprises, Ross and Pearson had been among the original promoters of the Dominion Coal and the Dominion Iron and Steel companies, which were among the largest operations in the Maritimes.[48] When Aitken first met Ross in Halifax, Ross and Pearson were promoting various utility ventures in Cuba, Brazil, and the British West Indies.[49]

Ross told Max how he could get a small block of São Paulo Tramway, Light, and Power bonds from a Montreal broker and sell them on commission. Max eagerly took up the suggestion.[50] Although selling utility bonds was much harder than peddling insurance policies and the profit was no larger, the business gave him a tantalizing glimpse of the newest and most rapidly growing financial business of the day – underwriting securities.[51] Bond selling thus carried hope for the future. If he made enough money in commissions, he could reinvest his earnings in larger blocks of securities at a slightly lower price, thereby increasing his 'spread,' or profit. The larger the block, the greater the spread, and those promoters who underwrote the entire new issue made the largest profit of all.

Max realized, however, that it would take years of commission work to save up enough capital to purchase the large blocks necessary to make a real killing, much less to get in on the ground floor as an underwriter. Too impatient to work his way up the ladder by gradually reinvesting his modest profit in ever-larger blocks of shares, he decided to apprentice under a promoter who was already at the top of the financial pyramid. Although Max thought that Ross and Pearson were both good promoters, he soon realized that the most respected financier in the Maritimes was a man in his early fifties who came from a long-established Halifax merchant family, John F. Stairs.[52]

Apprenticing under John F. Stairs

Aitken's version of meeting John Fitzwilliam Stairs on a train and getting his new job was short and simple: 'We talked. He asked me to his home for "supper" after church on the next Sunday night.'[53] There were other versions of how Aitken came to work for Stairs, and in one of these Aitken asks Stairs for a job while travelling by train to Montreal. Stairs makes no commitment, but on his return to Halifax he discovers 'Aitken busily at work at a desk in the office,' at which point he calls in his bookkeeper demanding an explanation and is informed that Aitken has told everyone that Stairs had 'instructed him to report for work.' Impressed with the young man's boldness, Stairs allows him to remain, and Aitken soon becomes his executive assistant.[54]

Whatever the manner of Aitken's hiring, it is logical to assume that the first meeting on the train may not have been all that accidental. Being in the business of selling insurance and securities to the wealthier classes, Aitken would certainly have known of John F. Stairs. Moreover, Stairs himself may have been observing the progress of the young bond sales-man. Since Halifax was a close-knit community of only 40,000, everyone in the securities business from the lowest bond salesman and broker to the highest bank managers and financiers would at least have known of one another.

One important point remains above speculation. By hiring Max as his personal secretary, Stairs gave Aitken a personal and first-class intro-duction into the world of Canadian high finance.[55] Stairs guided him through the complexities of company promotion, underwriting, and merger promoting while allowing him the freedom to act as a creative agent in his own capacity. Moreover, he also gave Aitken an entrée of sorts into the upper echelon of Halifax society, for the Stairs family repre-sented old money in a society greatly respectful of established merchant families. John F. Stairs's grandfather, William M. Stairs, had founded the provisioning firm of Wm Stairs, Son & Morrow, and John's father, William J. Stairs, had expanded the firm and diversified into industrial and financial enterprises such as the Dartmouth Ropeworks, the Starr Manufacturing Company, the Halifax Gas Light Company, and the Union Bank of Halifax. William J. Stairs eventually became president of both the Union Bank and the Halifax Chamber of Commerce.[56]

As the eldest surviving son, John F. Stairs had been groomed to take over the family enterprises. At the age of twenty-one he became a partner in Wm Stairs, Son & Morrow and at the same time was made general man-ager of the Dartmouth Ropeworks. By the early 1880s, Stairs was adding to his family's wealth by promoting new industry. In 1882 he helped establish Nova Scotia Steel, popularly known as Scotia, a primary steel-manufacturing enterprise at New Glasgow that would eventually become Stairs's single largest interest. Bullish on the industrial future of the Maritimes, he rescued the insolvent Nova Scotia Sugar Refinery of Halifax four years later. Stairs was particularly good at expanding his industrial operations through mergers. In 1890, for example, he consolidated the Dartmouth Ropeworks with six other Halifax and Saint John rope manufacturing firms to create the Consumers Cordage Company.[57] Three years later he merged the Nova Scotia Sugar Refinery with two other Maritime refineries to form the Acadia Sugar Refining Company.[58] In 1895 he consolidated Scotia with a secondary steel complex at New Glasgow, thus creating Canada's first integrated iron and steel company.[59]

Less an industrialist than a promoter and financier, Stairs left his deepest imprint on the financial enterprises with which he was associated. These included old 'family' enterprises such as the Union Bank of Halifax but, more significantly, new financial intermediaries that he was instrumental in creating, such as the Eastern Trust Company in 1893 and the Royal Securities Corporation ten years later. In all these enterprises, Stairs refused to be troubled with the details of day-to-day management. He left these administrative matters to others, especially his younger brother George, who managed the Dartmouth Ropeworks through most of the 1880s and remained manager after John folded the ropeworks into the Consumers Cordage consolidation.[60] Aitken was the eager recipient of the financial knowledge and skills which Stairs had gained over these decades, but like George Stairs he also played the more mundane role of manager, through his position as Stairs's executive assistant and personal emissary.

Stairs also had a permanent influence on Aitken's political ideology, an influence that would find its most extreme expression during the 1911 Canadian reciprocity election and the ill-fated Empire Crusade of 1929–31. In his earlier years, Stairs had been a strong supporter of Sir John A. Macdonald's National Policy of tariff protection. In 1879, the year in which Aitken was born, Stairs had entered provincial politics in a by-election for Halifax County. Hailing his victory as a triumph for the National Policy, the local Conservative newspaper looked forward to his brilliant career in politics.[61]

Stairs's career in politics did prove to be long, but it was hardly brilliant. He successfully ran for federal office in an 1883 by-election, but he was thoroughly drubbed in the general election four years later. He then ran in the 1891 election, but his victory was marred by allegations of bribery, 'treating,' and intimidation. During his early years in office, Stairs was often accused of using his numerous high-level contacts in the Conservative government to further his corporate business interests. It is unlikely that he himself saw any conflict of interest; the National Policy was designed to help Canadian industry, and since he was one of the most important industrialists in the Maritimes, he of all people should benefit from government policy. Nonetheless, he understood the damage of such charges and stood down before the 1896 election in favour of Robert L. Borden, a renegade Liberal who had turned Conservative. Stairs then took over the provincial leadership of the Conservative Party, hoping to defeat the long-ruling Liberals. He failed in this bid, however, and went down to personal defeat in his own riding during the 1897 provincial election.[62]

When Max Aitken arrived in Halifax, Stairs was still the leader of the Conservative Party in Nova Scotia, but with the Liberals in power in Ottawa as well as Halifax, his access to patronage and thus political influence was limited.[63] Stairs's politics were now relegated to the realm of ideology, and like many other Conservatives of the age, he supported imperial federation – a concept with which Aitken had been acquainted since childhood through his family and friends, particularly Dick Bennett, who had been an impassioned zealot on the subject.[64] The dream was of a political and military federation of the so-called white Dominions and Great Britain, bound together by an empirewide protectionist tariff.[65] Having been nurtured in such an environment, it is hardly surprising that Aitken was to become one of the most partisan proponents of a tariff-protected empire during the twentieth century – often to the consternation of his contemporaries and to the bewilderment of his biographers.[66]

The Scotia Group

Stairs's closest business associates, Robert E. Harris and Charles H. Cahan, shared his political creed. Cahan was even for a time the honorary secretary of the Halifax branch of the Imperial Federation League.[67] More than politics, however, it was business that brought together Stairs, Harris, and Cahan. As his projects grew larger during the 1890s, Stairs needed more capital and financial skills than his own family could provide, and he turned to Harris and Cahan. They, in turn, needed the varied business and social connections provided by the Stairs family, for they both had come from modest small-town backgrounds.

Charles Cahan's life was a parable of the great optimism of the age and a striking illustration of the indistinct line that separated business, politics, law, and journalism during the Laurier boom. Cahan availed himself of every opportunity that came his way and created as interesting and exciting a life for himself as could be imagined, eventually taking a run at the leadership of the Conservative Party of Canada in a bid to become prime minister. Born into very limited circumstances in the small and declining coastal community of Yarmouth, Cahan had worked day and night to support himself while getting the marks necessary for an entrance scholarship to Dalhousie University.[68]

Receiving his BA in 1886, he joined J.J. Stewart's newspaper office as chief editorial writer so that he could fund three years of studies at the Dalhousie Law School. Stewart was instrumental in establishing two Conservative newspapers in Halifax, the *Morning Herald* in 1875 and the *Evening Mail* four years later, and his office became the heart of opposition to Premier William Steven Fielding's Liberal government. Like Stewart, Cahan favoured a very aggressive style of writing, which included direct and personal attacks on prominent Liberals in Nova Scotia, relying upon exaggeration on occasion. This approach was so sensational that even some Conservatives, including Sir Charles Tupper and his son Charles Hibbert Tupper, were repelled. On graduating in 1890, Cahan successfully ran for a seat in the provincial assembly and became leader of the Conservative opposition. From the assembly and his newspaper office, he fought the Liberals until his electoral defeat four years later. He expected but did not receive the nomination for John F. Stairs's federal constituency in 1896. Although he was one of Stairs's closest allies, he did not have the support of the Tuppers, and the nomination was given to an ex-Liberal lawyer by the name of Robert Laird Borden.[69]

Although Robert E. Harris's accomplishments were more narrowly concentrated in business and law than Cahan's, he was also a small-town Nova Scotian who made good. The son of a blacksmith, Harris was born into a large family in Annapolis Royal. Since he could not afford to go to law school, he articled for four years in his home town and in Halifax, after which he moved to Yarmouth to practise law during the 1880s. Since Yarmouth was Cahan's home town and since the two men were close in age (Harris having been born in 1860 and Cahan a year later), it is likely that they met at this time.[70]

Appointed king's counsel at the unusually young age of twenty-nine, Harris was noticed by Hugh McDonald Henry while appearing in Halifax on appeals.[71] Henry, a pillar of the Halifax bar, invited Harris to join him and his younger brother, William Alexander (Will) Henry, in their law

practice, an offer that Harris accepted.[72] Almost immediately after his
arrival in Halifax in 1892, Harris became the firm's senior partner when
the elder Henry was elevated to the bench.[73] He began to specialize in the
expanding field of commercial law and was soon acting for various companies, including Eastern Trust, which had been established in 1893 by
John F. Stairs with the help of 'Judge' Henry and W.B. Ross and of which
Harris was eventually to succeed Stairs as president.[74] Harris invited
Cahan to join the firm after Cahan's electoral defeat in 1894, and Harris,
Henry & Cahan, tethered to John F. Stairs's business interests, quickly
grew into one of Halifax's pre-eminent corporate law firms.[75]

Aside from Stairs, these were the men with whom Aitken was to forge
his closest business relationships in Halifax, and he would owe a great
deal of his early training in corporate law and finance to them. He also
gained the benefit of learning two distinct approaches to business from
them. Outward looking and urbane, Cahan was an adventurer who spent
more time in the tropics setting up and running utility ventures than in
his Halifax law firm. Harris, on the other hand, was conservative in his
approach to business, a man of detail who cared less for adventure than
for looking after business at home in Halifax and the Maritimes.

Stairs, Harris, Cahan, and Aitken worked with W.B. Ross and B.F. Pearson in numerous business ventures, but steel and politics separated them.
Stairs's group was closely associated with Scotia Steel, whereas Ross and
Pearson were instrumental in creating Scotia's main rivals, Dominion
Coal and Dominion Iron and Steel. Ross and Pearson were staunch Liberals, and they used their political connections provincially, and after 1896
federally, to promote their coal and steel companies.[76] In fact, when the
bill incorporating Dominion Coal went before the Nova Scotia legislature
in 1893, Cahan unsuccessfully tried to block its passage by accusing
Dominion Coal's promoters of being stock market operators with little
interest in the long-term viability of their enterprise, a charge occasionally laid against his own crowd.[77]

Perhaps Cahan and the Scotia group as a whole need not have worried
about the competition. Both Dominion enterprises were to suffer chronic
financial difficulties, some of them perhaps caused or at least exacerbated by the promoters themselves. According to one account, two-thirds
of the security issue that launched Dominion Coal was promotional
stock* held by the firm's promoters and their brokers, and between

---

*Promotional stock is a reference to the bonus common shares 'given' to the promotional
syndicate, underwriters, and stockbrokers as remuneration for their services, often in lieu
of a cash commission.

$7 and $8 million was wasted during the construction phase.[78] While the evidence supporting this interpretation is sparse, the Scotia group itself believed that the Dominion enterprises were doomed to fail, an attitude quickly absorbed by Max Aitken. When a prominent Boston financial house asked him about a possible merger between the Scotia and Dominion steel companies, he immediately dismissed the prospect as 'unthinkable,' adding that Dominion Iron and Steel stock, which was listed on the Boston Stock Exchange and was widely distributed in the area, was 'intrinsically' valueless.[79] Although Scotia had its own problems, the company was financially more stable than Dominion Iron and Steel, and Aitken took every opportunity to boom Scotia and impugn the Dominion enterprises.[80]

The Scotia men also held an advantage over the Dominion clique in the financial arena, in that they had ready access to the resources of the Union Bank of Halifax, whereas Pearson and Ross did not have their own bank. Aitken quickly realized the extent to which the Scotia group used loans from the Union Bank of Halifax to capitalize their ventures. The Union Bank's officers could hardly deny any request connected to the Stairs.[81] Even with the resources of the Union Bank, however, some ventures were too large for the Scotia group alone. Indeed, Stairs, Harris, Cahan, and Aitken were only too glad to work with Ross and Pearson on projects that did not involve their rival steel and coal companies, a fact that highlights the delicate equilibrium between competition and cooperation during the Laurier boom.[82] Table 2.1 illustrates quite vividly the convergence of interests between the Scotia and Dominion groups.

From Aitken's perspective, the members of both groups shared one characteristic. They were one generation older than himself, which made them a little more cautious and at times more reserved about adopting new ways of doing things. As Aitken gained confidence in himself, he increasingly advocated changes in the way the Halifax clique promoted and financed companies. While he realized that his young age made it difficult for the older men to consider all his ideas seriously, there were important differences among the group. John F. Stairs was the most open to Aitken's suggestions, followed by Charles H. Cahan. Both shared Aitken's sense of high adventure. W.B. Ross seemed to appreciate Aitken's abilities from the beginning.[83] His partner B.F. Pearson held a similar assessment but by the new century was spending less time on business and consequently had little to do with Aitken.[84] Robert E. Harris and George Stairs had daily contact with Aitken but were wary of John F. Stairs's inexperienced assistant and had difficulty accepting his precociously

TABLE 2.1 Corporate overlap between the Scotia[a] and Dominion[b] groups, 1893–1903

Corporation	J.F. Stairs	G. Stairs	R.E. Harris	C.H. Cahan	W.B. Ross	B.F. Pearson
STEEL AND COAL COMPANIES						
Scotia Steel & Coal (1895)	** P	*	* P			
Dominion Coal (1892)					**	**
Dominion Iron & Steel (1899)					**	**
MARITIME INDUSTRIAL COMPANIES						
Acadia Sugar (1893)	**		*			
Consumers Cordage (1893)	**	*				
Rhodes Curry (1893)						**
Canadian Flour Mills (1900)		**				
Robb Engineering (1900)	**					
Robb-Mumford Boiler (1902)	**				**	**
FINANCIAL ENTERPRISES						
Union Bank of Halifax	*	*				
Eastern Trust (1893)	** P		* P		**	
Royal Securities (1903)	** P	** P	**	**		
People's Bank (1903 acq)	**		**			
Alliance Bank (1903 shell)	**		**		**	
MARITIME TRANSPORTATION/UTILITIES						
Halifax and Yarmouth Railway					*	
Nova Scotia Telephone Co. (1887)						**
People's Heat and Light (1893)				**	**	**
Halifax Electric Tramway (1895)					**	**
Nova Scotia Shipping Co. (1902)			**	**	**	**
Elgin and Havelock Ry (1902)	**		**			

TABLE 2.1 *(Concluded)*

Corporation	J.F. Stairs	G. Stairs	R.E. Harris	C.H. Cahan	W.B. Ross	B.F. Pearson
FOREIGN ENTERPRISES						
West India Electric Co. (1897)						**
Havana Street Railway (1899)				**	**	**
Havana Tobacco Co. (1899)					**	**
Cuban Electric Co. (1899)						**
Demerara Electric Co. (1899)		*	*	*	* P	**
São Paulo Traction, Light & Power (1899)					**	**
Trinidad Electric (1901)	** P		**		** P	**
Mexican Light & Power (1902)				**		**
COMPANIES FORMED AFTER 1903						
Rio de Janeiro Tramway, Light & Power (1904)						**
Empire Trust Co. (1905)						**
Commercial Trust Co. (1905)				**	** P	
Shipbuilding and Investment Co. (1905)	**	*			**	*
Brandrum-Henderson (1906)			**			
Camaguey Co. (1906)		**	**	**		
Porto Rico Railways (1906)		**	**	**	** P	
Mexican Northern Power (1909)						*

Source: Various issues of *Monetary Times* and *Canadian Journal Commerce*, 1892–1909, and Beaverbrook Papers, House of Lords Record Office, correspondence, 1902–6.

[a] Scotia group: J.F. Stairs, G. Stairs, R.E. Harris, and C.H. Cahan

[b] Dominion group: W.B. Ross and B.F. Pearson

** Promoted original company or acquisition *or* a director on original board

* Director on a subsequent board or general manager

P President of corporation for designated period

commanding manners. While hungry to learn, Aitken was never the humble student, and his attitude offended the two older men.

As John F. Stairs's personal assistant, Aitken's first job was to sell the bonds of the Trinidad Electric Company. The company had been created in 1901 when Stairs, Harris, Cahan, Ross, and Pearson had acquired and consolidated three utility companies servicing Trinidad's main city, Port of Spain, and its population of 65,000. One firm controlled seven miles of mule tramway, while a second owned one and a half miles of dilapidated electric tramway. The third company possessed the thermal power stations that delivered electricity to the city. With Cahan supervising the reconstruction work in Trinidad, the Halifax promoters issued bonds to pay for a reconstructed coal-fired plant and twelve miles of new electric tramway, together with rolling stock. Aitken canvassed local investors, convincing them that while Trinidad Electric bonds were almost as secure as any government or bank bonds, they would pay a 1 or 2 per cent higher rate of return.[85] This he did so well that Trinidad securities were soon owned by dozens of ship captains, ministers, lawyers, and businessmen throughout Nova Scotia.[86]

Stairs then decided to entrust Aitken with a more complex assignment. The Union Bank of Halifax, of which the members of the Stairs family were the largest shareholders, wanted to acquire the Commercial Bank of Windsor, Nova Scotia. Stairs sent Aitken as his emissary. After more than a week in Windsor, Aitken successfully bought the bank for Stairs and for the Union Bank at an attractive price. Whether he was paid $10,000 for concluding the deal, as he later claimed, or merely one-fifth or even one-tenth of this sum (a more believable figure given his age and the times), it was his first real taste of success.[87] The deal taught him the marvellous profitability of mergers and acquisitions relative to the mere peddling of securities, a lesson he would never forget.[88]

Aitken's new prosperity, in such sharp contrast to his insurance days, was beginning to be noticed. In September 1902, Rev. William Aitken stayed for a number of days with his prodigal son at his rooms in the Roy Building in Halifax. He was elated with Max's newly achieved focus and ambition, doubly so given his earlier misgivings about his son's 'energies and moral motives.'[89] On returning to Newcastle, William Aitken wrote to Max: 'You are doing well – *that* I could plainly see. I sincerely hope that you will go on from prosperity to greater prosperity. You spoke to me declaring your firm belief that *principle and uprightness* are at the root of a manly life. You are quite right. Hold on by them – never let them for a moment leave you and you will be successful in the best sense of the word.'[90]

ROYAL SECURITIES CORPORATION

Limited

BOND DEALERS

HALIFAX, – – CANADA

WE OWN AND OFFER

$192,000

TRINIDAD ELECTRIC COMPANY

First Mortgage 5 per cent. Gold Bonds

Dated June 1st, 1901   Due June 1st, 1931

Interest payable 1st June and 1st December

Principal and Interest payable in Gold at the office of

The National Trust Company

MONTREAL

Total authorized issue outstanding, $720,000

PRICE

PAR AND INTEREST NETTING 5 PER CENT ON INVESTMENT

These Bonds cannot be called before maturity and are offered
subject to previous sale

Trinidad Electric bond prospectus. *Source:* House of Lords Record Office, Beaver-brook Papers, G/19

Material success, in the elder Aitken's eyes, was a reflection of the fact that Max had finally become settled in the Christian moral and spiritual sense. Max himself might have believed this basic tenet of Victorian values; certainly, his upbringing would have encouraged him to do so. In reality, however, he used this Victorian ethos whenever it was useful to him but did not abide by the code when it was inconvenient. This divergence – hypocrisy, if you like – was reflected in the high moral tone in which he later lectured associates and employees for committing the same acts of which he had been guilty in the past.

Royal Securities: Stairs's Final Act

By 1903, business was going so well that John F. Stairs and the Scotia group decided to establish an all-purpose investment banking and stockbroking operation to raise capital for the group's many investments in the Maritimes and the Caribbean. They wanted to issue securities of their newly incorporated enterprises (a risky business by any definition) through a corporation that limited their liability to the amount of capital they had originally invested. An unincorporated brokerage firm was suitable for retailing government or corporate securities in which it had no direct interest, for it was not liable for the financial performance of these entities. It was, however, wholly inadequate for an entrepreneurial investment bank that had to issue, underwrite and retail the securities of companies that it had created.

Three types of incorporated financial institutions were common by the turn of the century: banks (including savings and loan institutions), insurance firms, and trust companies. Insurance companies and banks were highly regulated, and although trust companies were less highly regulated, the common law pertaining to the fiduciary responsibilities of trustees could potentially prevent the institution from making speculative investments, which was the main business envisaged for the new investment bank. A securities corporation, or 'bond house,' on the other hand, would provide the shelter of limited liability while pooling the capital and credit of its shareholders and other financial intermediaries. At the same time, its activities would go largely unregulated.[91]

The only bond house in Canada at that time was the Dominion Securities Corporation, which had been established in Toronto by Sen. George Cox and his Toronto associates in 1901. John F. Stairs had observed how Dominion Securities underwrote and sold the securities of companies connected to the Cox group and how it borrowed large amounts of short-term money (call loans) from many banks at the same time in order to cover the few months between the initial purchase of the issue and its subsequent resale to brokers and investors.[92]

Stairs could see the usefulness of such a vehicle and consequently, in April 1903, the Royal Securities Corporation (RSC) was incorporated under the Nova Scotia Companies Act with a nominal capital of $50,000.[93] All five original shareholders, John F. Stairs, George Stairs, Robert E. Harris, Charles H. Cahan, and Max Aitken, were made directors. John F. Stairs became the new president, appointing Aitken as the RSC's secretary. He did so for two reasons. First, Aitken had displayed some very promising skills in his capacity as Stairs's personal assistant. Indeed, there is some evidence that Stairs may have paid one-half or more of Aitken's original share subscription, a reflection of his faith in his young protégé.[94] Second, Stairs had no intention of personally managing the RSC, and there was no one else available in the Scotia group to run the corporation. George Stairs was too busy managing the Halifax branch of Consumers Cordage; Harris was too occupied with running his law firm; and Cahan by this time was in Mexico working on a new utility venture.

From the beginning, John F. Stairs intended that Scotia should be the RSC's most important client. Just three years before he created the RSC, the steel company's directors had decided to construct a primary-steel manufacturing complex at Sydney Mines, Cape Breton, in order to be closer to newer, higher-quality sources of coal and iron ore. As president and chief financier of Scotia, Stairs was responsible for raising the necessary capital for expansion. In 1901 he organized the issue of $2 million common stock and $1 million bonds. One year later he underwrote and sold another $1 million stock issue. While these issues should have provided sufficient cash, mounting construction costs combined with a drop in Scotia's share prices during the 1902–3 financial recession necessitated the additional sale of Scotia securities. Stairs fully realized this when he created the RSC, and he soon had Aitken underwriting a further issue of $880,000 par value of Scotia common stock.[95]

Since the Maritimes had been saturated with Scotia securities from previous issues, Aitken tried to create a new market for Scotia in Boston. In June 1903 he devised an arrangement with Hayden Stone & Co., a large Boston investment bank, to find new brokers and investors, and to list Scotia on the Boston Stock Exchange.[96] Aitken then attempted to find new underwriters in central Canada, while Stairs pressured his fellow directors to accept large slices of the underwriting in their personal capacities. By the following April, the market was ready and the RSC, along with the Montreal and Toronto brokers whom Aitken had selected, began selling Scotia common stock to long-term investors.[97]

Having placed at least some of the Scotia stock on the Boston market, Aitken had minimized the decline in the price of Scotia common when the RSC and the brokers began to retail the issue.[98] Unfortunately for Stairs and Aitken, however, the cash raised from this issue once again fell short of Scotia's ever-increasing needs. The recession of 1902–3 had stifled the demand for iron, coal, and steel, and, as a result, Scotia's revenues had dropped precipitously. Even more money was needed to meet both operating costs and the last phase of construction at Sydney Mines.[99]

Graham Fraser, the vice-president and general manager of Scotia, suggested that the company limit itself to a $500,000 issue of bonds, taking the rest of what it would need from shareholders by not paying dividends for a few years. At least at first, George Stairs supported Fraser's suggestion, but John F. Stairs and Aitken were opposed. They were sure that the market value of the company's securities would plummet if the board announced that it was not paying any further dividends because the company had so consistently underestimated construction and operating costs and overestimated revenues. This would be tantamount to an admission of managerial failure of enormous proportions, making it impossible to underwrite and sell any Scotia securities for years to come. The majority of Scotia directors agreed. They decided instead to continue paying dividends and to issue $1.5 million of bonds if the RSC could put together a syndicate willing to underwrite the flotation. The decision so infuriated Graham Fraser that he resigned and went to work for the competition, Dominion Iron and Steel.[100]

Stairs was gambling that with Aitken's help, he could convince some of his central-Canadian associates to back the new issue. Despite investor concern over Scotia continually returning to the market as well as Fraser's sudden resignation, Scotia's financial reputation was still good compared with that of Dominion Iron and Steel and the newly established Lake Superior Corporation (later Algoma Steel).[101] In early September 1904, Stairs and Aitken went to Toronto to put together a syndicate for the new Scotia issue. They arrived at the King Edward Hotel and reviewed their strategy once more. They both recognized how much depended on the ensuing negotiations and how little margin they had for error.

When Aitken awoke the next morning, he discovered that Stairs had collapsed from pneumonia. He dropped everything and joined Stairs at the hospital, where he stayed attending the man who had done so much for him. He was eventually joined by Stairs's wife who had travelled from

Halifax fearing the worst.[102] Aitken's vigil was interrupted a few days later by a cable from Harris insisting that he leave Stairs's bedside and proceed with the syndicate negotiations without Stairs. Reluctantly, Aitken returned to the business at hand and put together a group led by W.D. (Will) Ross (no relation of W.B. Ross) and the Metropolitan Bank. They were joined by the Toronto brokerage firm of Osler & Hammond, the Imperial Bank, and the chief shareholders of the Massey Harris farm implement firm, historically one of Scotia's most important customers.[103] The Toronto underwriters were aware, however, of Scotia's weaknesses and asked Aitken whether they could have two representatives on the Scotia board to protect their interests. Aitken not only thought the request reasonable but, given the work he was doing, concluded that he also had a right to be on the board. Thus, on 23 September, he and Will Ross cabled all of the Scotia directors that the underwriting agreements would be signed immediately if the Scotia directors accepted three new nominations for the board.[104]

Harris cabled his protest immediately to Aitken: 'Your proposition about nomination cannot be considered and even its suggestion after agreeing to underwrite without any such condition is calculated to shake everybody's confidence in you. For your own sake withdraw your telegram at once and stick to your agreement.'[105] In the face of Harris's adamant opposition, the Toronto men agreed to underwrite without the directorships, but Aitken refused to do anything further for Scotia, including marketing the issue.[106] He now feared that Stairs was not going to recover, for his pneumonia had worsened and become complicated by heart and kidney failure. Aitken waited and hoped, but he began to despair as Stairs succumbed to the pain caused by his failing heart.[107] With his wife and Aitken by his side, Stairs died on 26 September at the age of fifty-six.[108]

3

Caribbean Adventurer

Examine your profit and loss account before you go out to conquer the financial world, and then go out for conquest – if the account justifies the enterprise.

Lord Beaverbrook, 'Success,' 1922

Aitken travelled back to Halifax in a private railway car with John F. Stairs's body and his widow. He was stricken with grief, but as soon as he arrived in Halifax he immediately set about helping the members of the Stairs family cope with their unexpected loss.[1] They thanked him by inviting him to select John F. Stairs's epitaph and to walk next to the family in the funeral procession to Fort Massey Presbyterian Church.[2] As the procession was forming, J.C. Mackintosh, an established financier and a leading elder in the church, tried to push Aitken out of line and take his place, but George Stairs immediately took Mackintosh aside so that Aitken could resume his position.[3]

The incident was symbolic of Max's immediate loss of status among many within the community after Stairs's death. In their opinion, he had been little more than Stairs's personal secretary, and any authority wielded by him was solely in the capacity of Stairs's representative.[4] Max, already in deep despair over Stairs's death, sank even further when he realized how many of his old associates refused to recognize the fact that although Stairs had conceived the RSC, he himself had been its general manager from the beginning, shaping Stairs's concept into a workable structure. He confided to Will Ross that although he hoped to resume business 'as strenuously as ever,' he feared that his 'own usefulness' had come to an end.[5] He did no RSC work for one week while he thought about his predicament. His close association with Stairs had been of incalculable benefit to him, but he realized that all of his achievements had been ascribed to Stairs. Ironically, if he was to change the Canadian business community's perception of him as Stairs's junior assistant, he would have to prove himself more capable than his deceased mentor.

Emerging from his deep depression, Aitken moved decisively and with an energy born of desperation. In the following months he successfully floated the largest industrial issue ever handled by the RSC. He rebuilt, reorganized, and refinanced the Trinidad Electric Company, after which he purchased control of the Demerara Electric Company. Preferring the higher profits generated by foreign utility ventures relative to Maritime industry, including Nova Scotia Steel, Aitken put his personal stamp on the RSC by setting up new enterprises in Cuba and Puerto Rico. Throughout it all, the fear of failure was his constant companion and a painful spur to success as he suffered from nightmares, insomnia, and recurring bouts of intestinal disorders, culminating in an appendicitis attack.[6]

Acquiring Control

Aitken's first step was to assume John F. Stairs's position as chief financier of the Nova Scotia Steel and Coal Company. This meant reversing his earlier decision not to manage Scotia's selling syndicate. Meanwhile, he did not publicly raise the issue of his eventually being appointed to the board, and he accepted the $10,000 commission fee offered by the Scotia board even though he privately felt that it was entirely 'inadequate for the work and travelling' involved in taking charge of the pooling* committee. His first priority was to prove his ability. Profit would have to wait.[7]

The same reasoning applied to the $172,000 stock issue of the Robb-Mumford Boiler Company, a subsidiary of Amherst-based Robb Engineering Company, one of the most technically sophisticated steam and thermal engine manufacturers in the country. Originally financed by Aitken and the Scotia group, Robb-Mumford had been set up near Boston in 1902. In July 1903 Aitken, along with Harris and John F. Stairs, had personally underwritten the entire issue, but they had been unable to sell it to the investing public because of the sharp stock market downturn of

*A pool was the promoters' combined holdings of securities, which could be used to manipulate prices through well-timed sales or purchases as directed by the pool's manager.

1902–3.[8] Since stock prices had recovered from their previous low by October 1904, Aitken decided that the time was ripe to sell the issue. He mobilized his RSC salesmen and passed on large blocks to various brokers, including J.C. Mackintosh, despite the older man's behaviour at Stairs's funeral.[9] Aitken put his personal feelings to one side, at least for the time being. He had little choice; on top of the Robb-Mumford issue, Aitken had to prepare the RSC for another Trinidad Electric issue in 1904.

Aitken knew that the utility issue, unlike the two industrial issues, would make the RSC a large profit. Indeed, he had become increasingly pessimistic about the future of Maritime industry and began to criticize what he perceived as the deficient management of many local companies, including Scotia.[10] But there was another reason why Aitken wanted to shift the RSC's resources out of Maritime industry and into foreign utility companies. He knew that he could exercise far more control over the destiny of these enterprises than was possible with companies such as Scotia, in which he could not even obtain a seat on the board of directors despite the fact that he had become the company's chief financier.

His first step was to begin to exert more control over Trinidad Electric. For a fee of $12,000 and approximately 1,320 common shares, Aitken agreed to pay off all the utility company's liabilities and buy four new tramcars, to extend the car shed to house the additional rolling stock, and to lay down new rails. Trinidad's general manager was an able American engineer, Fred Teele. Offering him a share of the profits, Aitken asked Teele to oversee the purchase and reconstruction in order to achieve the highest quality at the lowest cost.[11]

Working from early morning until late at night six days a week and scheming on the seventh, Aitken now lived in his office when he was in Halifax. With each successive flotation, his confidence grew. The Scotia issue was sold on time without any irreparable damage to the price of the steel company's stock – no small feat given the number of securities that had already been issued and the persistent rumour that further issues might yet be required.[12] TheRobb-Mumford issue was successfully floated despite the fact that his customers had already been fed full of Scotia bonds. Similarly, Trinidad Electric's securities were all sold, the company's debts were paid, and its rolling stock and track increased. By March 1905, six months after Stairs's funeral, Aitken was just beginning to enjoy the first fruits of his hard work when disaster struck from an unexpected quarter.

The People's Bank Fiasco

When Aitken had acquired the Commercial Bank of Windsor on behalf of the Union Bank of Halifax three years earlier, he had understood that the merger was only a small part of a larger scheme conceived by John F. Stairs. Concerned about the demise of regional banking in the Maritimes and the threat that this might eventually pose to his own power, Stairs had taken the offensive. His plan was to merge a number of the regional Maritime banks with a central-Canadian bank into a larger, more efficient chartered bank headquartered in Halifax; this chartered bank would then be able to compete effectively with the large chartered banks in Montreal and Toronto, as well as with the Bank of Nova Scotia and the Royal Bank of Canada, which had shifted (or were in the process of shifting) their operations to central Canada.[13] For this purpose, Stairs had incorporated a shell company called the Alliance Bank of Canada in 1903, but he had made little progress on the scheme, for Scotia's finances had taken up an increasing share of his time and energy.

Months before his death, however, and with the help of Robert E. Harris, he did manage to buy control of the People's Bank of Halifax. After examining the bank's assets and liabilities, Stairs and Harris had paid $400,000 for $280,000 par value of ordinary shares. These shares were subsequently purchased from Harris and from Stairs's estate in four equal parts by George Stairs, Harris, Aitken, and the RSC. Then in March 1905, just before the Scotia group was about to pour another $500,000 into the People's Bank to raise its capitalization to $1.5 million, they were approached by the Bank of Montreal to see whether they would sell their majority interest at a share price substantially lower than they had originally paid. The reason for the low offer, they were told, was that the People's Bank was about to collapse because of a fraud that had reduced the value of the bank by a figure of between $200,000 and $300,000.[14]

Unbeknown to the Scotia group, the People's Bank officers had made a large loan to one of the bank's directors a few year's earlier, not realizing that the schooners offered as collateral were nonexistent. The bank's chief shareholders and officers had become aware of the problem by the time of Stairs's purchase, but they had concealed the situation because they needed his investment to prevent the bank from collapse. All went well until the beginning of 1905, when the bank's officers discovered a further $100,000 worth of phony collateral. Without informing the Scotia group, they then asked the general manager of the Bank of Montreal, Edward Clouston, whether he would buy the bank before it collapsed.

Clouston agreed but only at a price that reflected the bank's legitimate asset base. At the time, each share was publicly valued at $140, the price originally paid by the Scotia group. The Bank of Montreal would pay no more than $115 per share.

Aitken, Harris, and George Stairs were astonished that the officers of the People's Bank, themselves the victims of a gigantic fraud, had chosen to perpetrate a second fraud on the bank's single largest group of shareholders. They refused to sell their shares at Clouston's price. George Stairs wanted to sue the other directors and officers of the People's Bank for fraud and recover the group's full investment. Harris and Aitken were more inclined to try and cut the group's losses by negotiating a slightly higher share price with the Bank of Montreal. They took the train to Montreal to discuss the situation directly with Clouston, but he refused to reconsider the original deal. In Clouston's opinion, the price offered by the Bank of Montreal was more than fair, given the underlying value of the People's Bank. He reminded the Scotia group of the consequences that would flow from the collapse of the People's Bank. No one would benefit, least of all the majority shareholders standing in front of him. They might win a lawsuit based on fraud and fiduciary duty, but the victory would be a pyrrhic one since few assets would be left in any recovery on the judgment.

George Stairs was too angry to agree, and he marched out of Clouston's office with Harris and Aitken in tow. Clouston decided to recall Aitken, perhaps considering him the least distraught or the most pliable of the group. He explained that the Bank of Montreal could pay only $115 per share, since any higher sum paid to the Scotia group would upset the agreement already reached with all the other shareholders of the People's Bank; but he offered to arrange matters so that the Scotia group would be able to exchange People's stock for Bank of Montreal stock at a rate slightly more advantageous than that offered the other shareholders of the People's Bank.[15] Aitken discussed this compromise with Harris, and both concluded that it was the best deal possible in the circumstances. They then proceeded to convince George Stairs of the futility of a lawsuit. As Aitken explained a few days later in a confidential letter to Will Ross,

Our loss will amount to about $11,000.00 each and the Royal Securities will lose about $11,000.00. This loss will be mitigated somewhat by circumstances, and Mr. Clouston apparently appreciates the way in which we have acted ... I do not think [however] that [the People's Bank's officers] are to be excused for having told

Clouston of the Bank's position before telling us, and for not having been brave enough to come and tell us first, even when things were at their worst. Nothing is known to the shareholders yet, but they will know in about ten days. The loss will amount to about one sixth of everyone's holdings. The bank will simply tell the story of the ... forgeries and frauds and they will not be disgraced in other eyes as they are in ours, since it was only to Mr. Stairs that they grossly misrepresented the position of the Bank's affairs.[16]

For Aitken, the cloud of the People's Bank fiasco had a silver lining. Through it, he had met and impressed Canada's most powerful banker. From the time he was a boy, he had seen Clouston's picture gracing the notes issued by the Bank of Montreal, the country's de facto currency. The man's handsome face and sculpted beard were synonymous with money, wealth, and the power that lay behind the Corinthian columns of the Montreal head office. Although Clouston was known as a cold fish by all who did business with him, Aitken had felt an openness and congeniality that reminded him of John F. Stairs.

For his part, Clouston had been struck by the young man, and on inquiring about him he discovered that because of Trinidad Electric, Aitken was said to have a talent for financing and reorganizing utilities. Perhaps, Clouston thought, he could do the same for the stagnant utility company in British Guiana in which he, Sir William Van Horne (the president of the utility), and some other prominent Montrealers held a large ownership stake. The Demerara Electric Company had been losing money almost from the day it had begun operating in early 1901, and it was time either to abandon the investment or to hire someone to reorganize the enterprise. He decided to ask Aitken whether he was interested in the job.[17]

Chasing Rabbits in the Tropics

Edward Clouston and Sir William Van Horne were members of the inner circle of Frederick Stark Pearson's utility empire.[18] Dr Pearson, as he was generally known, was a brilliant if erratic engineer from New England who had helped revolutionize American cities through electrification. During the 1890s he began to do the same for Canadian cities, starting with Halifax. Meeting B.F. Pearson (to whom he was not related) by accident while on vacation in Nova Scotia, he had helped the Halifax promoter as well as W.B. Ross and their associates amalgamate all the old horse-drawn trolley lines into one electric tramway system by designing the thermal power plant, the track, and the electrical distribution system. Soon afterwards, B.F. Pearson introduced Dr Pearson to such financiers as Clouston, Van Horne, and William Mackenzie, and by 1898–9, Dr Pearson had convinced the central Canadians to help him and his Halifax friends finance some new utility enterprises in Jamaica, Cuba, and Brazil.[19]

When John F. Stairs was invited by Dr Pearson to be one of the investors in a smaller operation – a project in British Guiana that would eventually become the Demerara Electric Company – Charles H. Cahan was sent to the tropics as the Scotia group's scout.[20] Stairs and his associates ultimately decided against the project, but on Cahan's advice they joined with Dr Pearson, Van Horne, B.F. Pearson, and W.B. Ross in establishing the Trinidad Electric Company in 1901. When Dr Pearson and Van Horne dropped out of this enterprise within the first few months, John F. Stairs was left in control.[21]

One year later, Cahan travelled with Dr Pearson to Mexico to help him set up the Mexican Light and Power Company, but once again the Scotia group pulled back from making a joint investment with Dr Pearson and his central-Canadian friends, though Cahan decided to remain with Dr Pearson and oversee construction of the project. Aitken soon began to receive disturbing letters from Mexico.[22] Cahan believed that Dr Pearson suffered from delusions of grandeur and was financially reckless. Pearson was in fact a dreamer, and his faith in the ultimate viability of the Mexican project blinded him to any short-term financial problems, including his enormous overexpenditures during the initial construction phase. Cahan was driven to distraction by Pearson's lackadaisical attitude, and he increasingly took control of managing the project.[23]

Despite Cahan's reports, Aitken still wanted in on the ground floor of Dr Pearson's enterprises. Irrespective of the long-term prospects, the securities generated by the great engineer's projects were in such demand that a short-term underwriting profit was virtually assured. But given the number of more moneyed central Canadians who vied for a piece of Dr Pearson's ventures, Aitken never had a chance. Of necessity, he had to concentrate on the Scotia group's much smaller enterprises.[24] Trinidad Electric was puny compared with Mexican Light and Power, but at least Aitken and the RSC's shareholders made up the inner underwriting circle. In fact, the RSC had made a substantial profit out of the Trinidad Electric flotation and Aitken now wanted to establish a larger utility venture that would be a new cash cow for the RSC.

After asking around, Aitken received an engineer's report on a utility proposition in Matanzas, Cuba, in March 1905. The report had originally been prepared for Dr Pearson, but although Pearson was pleased with the engineer's conclusions, he had considered the venture too small and had turned it over to his purchasing agent and partner in New York, W.P. Plummer.[25] Plummer sent the report on to Aitken and the RSC, hoping that he would get the equipment contracts if a venture was ever launched. On the strength of this report, Aitken organized a promotional syndicate in which each member contributed $100 to fund an investigation of the Matanzas deal from the ground. The members of the syndicate included all the RSC shareholders along with W.B. Ross and B.F. Pearson, as well as Trinidad Electric's chief engineer and manager, Fred Teele.[26]

Almost immediately after this, Aitken set up another promotional syndicate to investigate some more speculative tramway, light, and power propositions in Latin America. The promotional group was a reproduction of the Matanzas syndicate, except that it was incorporated as the Colombian Securities Corporation and included a few more Halifax investors.[27] Aitken then asked one of Colombian Securities' shareholders, A.K. Maclean, a Halifax lawyer and Liberal MP, to travel south and investigate potential utility opportunities in Colombia, Venezuela, and Panamá.[28]

Maclean had only just left for the tropics when Clouston summoned Aitken to Montreal to see whether he could reverse the sagging performance of the Demerara Electric Company. Some of Clouston's fellow investors had come to the conclusion that since far more profitable enterprises were now beginning to be established in Canada, they 'should not be in these foreign enterprises.'[29] Others, such as Clouston and Van Horne, who had active and sizable investments in profitable Mexican and Brazilian utilities, were prepared to keep their money in a revamped Demerara Electric if it was 'under the same management and control as Trinidad.'[30]

Aitken immediately accepted Clouston's offer, seeing in it the greatest opportunity that had come his way since he was asked to be John F. Stairs's executive assistant. If he demonstrated to Clouston, Van Horne, and the other prominent Montrealers – who between them were some of the richest men in the country – that he could revive the moribund company, then he could count on their financial support in all future schemes. Moreover, he was convinced that he could do it by bringing in new management and rebuilding and extending the existing tramway system. His confidence was based in large part on one individual – Fred Teele – Trinidad Electric's chief engineer and general manager.

Before Teele had joined Trinidad Electric in 1901, he had been the chief engineer of the Boston Elevated Railroad Company's power station. As such, he was part of an emerging corps of American engineers who were educated and trained in electric power generating and transmission.[31] Teele's skills went beyond running thermal power plants and tramways, however. He was also a superb manager of human capital, and he had gathered together a competent staff in Port of Spain, including his chief accountant, Fred Clarke. It was Clarke who provided Teele with a detailed statistical picture of Trinidad Electric's operations. Harnessing the abilities of these two men, Aitken was confident that he could turn the fortunes of the Demerara operation around and use its success as a base for future expansion in the Caribbean and Latin America.

Aitken carefully reviewed with Teele what was at stake in the new project, telling him that Clouston had already concluded that Demerara was virtually a lost cause and that Aitken was his last desperate hope. If they succeeded in resuscitating the company, Aitken was convinced that 'there will never be any proposition which we bring out that Mr. Clouston will not back.' Aitken explained that the project's success was a critical test of Teele's 'engineering capacity' as well as his own managerial and financial abilities, and for these reasons they 'must make the undertaking a success.'[32]

Aitken admitted to Teele that Clouston's gloominess was well founded. Aitken had sought out the opinion of H.P. Bruce, the American engineer who had been Demerara Electric's first general manager and was now an independent consultant, to identify Demerara's major weaknesses.[33] Bruce had given Aitken an 'exceedingly pessimistic review of the Georgetown situation. He drew a horrible picture of the sugar market,' the colony's chief export; British Guiana was 'poverty stricken,' and consequently its working classes would be unable to pay the increase in tram fares needed to cover the major repairs required. And although electric lighting revenues could be increased, higher operating costs would more than match any additional revenues because of the very poor condition of the thermal plant.[34]

Realizing how much work lay in store for him and how essential he was to the new project, Teele demanded a substantial salary increase from the Scotia group. Aitken warned him that R.E. Harris and George Stairs would refuse, but said not to worry because he would personally guarantee that the RSC would purchase Demerara shares on Teele's behalf to give him a substantial stake in the future of the company. Not mollified by Aitken's offer, Teele threatened to take another job if he did not

receive a substantial salary increase. Aitken went back to Harris and
Stairs, arguing that they had no choice but to cave in to Teele's demands;
the American engineer was essential to making Demerara Electric a paying proposition. Knowing full well that Dr Pearson had been trying to
hire Teele for his Brazilian operations, the Scotia group finally relented,
and Teele's salary was boosted to $10,000 – more than double Aitken's
own salary of $4,000 as general manager of the RSC. The whole affair left
a bad taste in Aitken's mouth, and he decided to give Teele a little lecture
on the trade-off between long-term gain and short-term sacrifice when
informing him of the salary increase:

I have told you before that I believed we could make more money than you would
have hoped to make by accepting a larger salary from Dr Pearson, J.G. White &
Co. or any other firm of electrical engineers ...

I am giving money and time to the working up of a certain line of promotion;
perfectly willing to wait years for my returns.

I want very much to feel that we thoroughly understand one another; if we do,
I am confident that you will be as loyal to me as I to you, as has been the case in
the working partnership which exists between [W.D.] Ross of Toronto and myself,
for instance ...

I know I made out a good case when I argued for the reasons for giving you
$10,000 salary at once, but I advise you strongly against the method.[35]

Whatever Teele's methods, Aitken's faith in his ability was well placed.
Within a few days of arriving in Georgetown, Teele had diagnosed Demerara Electric's ailments, which seemed to include everything from the
thermal power station to the tramlines, railcars, and accounting staff. He
then interviewed all the important colonial government officials, 'from
the Governor down,' to ensure that they would 'prove quite approach-
able in case we require any legislative action.'[36]

Meanwhile, Aitken was busy raising the capital required for repairs and
reconstruction. The Scotia group and their Maritime associates purchased two-thirds of the equity held by Montreal investors, who had
unloaded their shares at 12 per cent of par. Many felt they were lucky to
get out even at this price. Rather than have his Maritime friends deal
directly with the Montreal owners, Aitken set up a holding company
called the Dominion Trust Co. to purchase Demerara shares.[37] This was
the first of many occasions on which Aitken would use a corporate intermediary of intentionally short shelf life in order to effect an acquisition.
By using such a vehicle, he was able to centralize and thus expedite any

corporate acquisition. Moreover, he could use his position – and he always placed himself in absolute managerial control of his temporary holding companies – to give birth to the new or reconstructed company, thereby conducting the security flotation at the exact time, in the exact amount, and at the place or places that he alone judged best in the circumstances. The transitional holding company also gave him the liberty of choosing the new company's organizational and managerial form, as well as the selection of key staff, as in fact he did with Demerara Electric.[38]

Ownership and control were thereby transferred, but money still had to be raised to pay for Teele's reconstruction of Demerara Electric, and this could only come in the form of new securities. As part of the deal, Aitken had committed the RSC to issue $100,000 par value bonds (to be sold at 60 per cent of par) to fund the reconstruction and reorganization of Demerara Electric. RSC salesmen fanned out through the Maritime provinces, knocking on the doors of investors who had previously bought Trinidad bonds. Happy with Trinidad's regular payment of interest and accepting RSC statements that the company would be completely reorganized along 'Trinidad lines,' they snapped up the Demerara securities expecting similar results.

By the end of 1905 the Demerara work was well in hand. Teele had rerouted the streetcar line, improved office procedures, and replaced many of the staff.[39] Aitken felt free enough to continue his search for the next utility promotion, and he notified W.P. Plummer, Dr Pearson's chief agent and partner in New York, that the RSC was now 'in good shape for a nice little new proposition.'[40] Any venture, he suggested, 'slightly larger than Trinidad, would not be too big for us.'[41] He also informed a separate firm of electrical engineers and contractors in New York, J.G. White & Co., that the RSC was 'open to handle anywhere from $600,000 or even $1,000,000 in the way of an Electric proposition, and we want to be as well-placed as we were in Trinidad for instance, or as we believe ourselves to be in Demerara.'[42]

By this time, A.K. Maclean had returned to Halifax from his Latin American tour with reports on four possible tramway and electric lighting ventures: in Bogotá, Barranquilla, Panamá City, and Caracas. Maclean was entirely opposed to the two Colombian ventures, doubtful about the Panamanian one, and lukewarm to the Venezuelan scheme.[43] Aitken, in turn, was sceptical about the value of Maclean's reporting, which he felt had been too greatly influenced 'by climactic [sic] conditions and physical discomforts.'[44] He preferred the advice of his New York associates, as well as that of Fred Teele, since they were more familiar with tropical conditions. With these men he discussed new propositions, including the

Map 1 Caribbean region, c. 1900. *Source:* Adapted from Colin Rickards, *Caribbean Power* (London: Dennis Dobson 1963), frontispiece.

Central Colombian Railroad (Buenaventura to Cali) project, the Paramaribo (Dutch Guiana) concession, the Guatemala City tramway and lighting venture, and the Quito (Ecuador) proposal.[45]

The last project in particular struck Aitken as promising, though his enthusiasm was not shared by W.B. Ross and R.E. Harris. In an effort to change their minds, he sent them a lengthy report on the proposal and asked whether they would agree to meet with Mr Carbo, the sponsor of the project, who also happened to be the director of public works in Ecuador. Carbo had convinced Aitken that the Quito proposal was at least worth investigating. Aitken admitted that Ecuador was far from Halifax, but he was confident that the securities could be sold in Canada. Moreover, Carbo had assured him that 'the history of Ecuador is better than that of any other South American Republic; the people have not any revolutionary tendencies, and are a farming and pastoral people.'[46]

Aitken wrote to C.H. Cahan in Mexico in a similar vein, adding that both 'Mr. Harris and Mr. Ross do not think very much of going so far away from home; but the situation is that our Corporation can sell the Bonds.'[47] Cahan was sympathetic to Aitken's view, but Ross and Harris could not be moved. Aside from the question of distance from Halifax, they believed that the RSC had its hands full with Trinidad Electric and the new Demerara project. Aitken disagreed. With Demerara rehabilitated, and using Clouston and Van Horne and their central-Canadian capital, he believed that he could easily launch another southern utility project.

Accepting that he could never convince Harris and Ross to investigate the Quito proposition, he cut his losses with Carbo and decided to find a new venture closer to home – in the Caribbean – where Harris and Ross would feel more comfortable. The British West Indies had already been picked over by Canadian utility promoters, but Aitken knew that there were still potential ventures in Cuba, where the Americans had only a few years before broken Spanish control, and he decided to travel there to investigate the possibilities. The trip would do double duty as a honeymoon.

Cuban Honeymoon

With virtually no prior notice to friends and family, Aitken married Gladys Drury on the evening of Monday, 30 January 1906.[48] Gladys was the nineteen-year-old daughter of Colonel Charles Drury, a decorated veteran of the Northwest Rebellion who had also been a commander during the Boer War. He was now the commandant of the Maritime provinces' militia district and was soon to be the first Canadian governor of the military garrison at Halifax.[49] Gladys possessed both poise and social position, and she was very attractive by the standards of the day. Ever since her arrival in Halifax with her family the year before, Aitken had pursued her with all the charm and persuasion he could muster.

Gladys was swept off her feet, but her parents were less than keen about the impetuous young man.[50] Only forty-five invitations were issued for the wedding at St Paul's Anglican Church in Halifax. In the Halifax *Morning Chronicle*'s description of the wedding, no mention was made of Gladys's parents attending the ceremony, though Aitken's mother and brother Traven were present. The best man was James A. Stairs, the eldest son of John F. Stairs, and Gladys's sister, Edith Drury, attended the bride. Gladys wore a 'going away gown of hunters' green' rather than the traditional white, and she was ready to set off on her honeymoon that evening.[51]

Aitken claimed later in life that his marriage to Gladys was the result of a cold-blooded decision to attain stature within the Canadian business community.[52] His shabby treatment of her years later would tend to support this interpretation, and their so-called honeymoon in Cuba reflected the extent to which business took priority over his wife from the very beginning of their life together. When they arrived in Havana, Aitken immediately began to examine potential utility operations. Working on preliminary reports prepared by Dr Pearson (which came through W.P. Plummer in New York) as well as intelligence gathered by Royal Bank managers, from Havana in the northwest to Santiago de Cuba in the far southeast, he concluded that the two best utility propositions were at Matanzas, a seaport only 55 miles east of Havana, and at Santiago, the island's other great seaport, which was about 450 miles from Havana.

After the scenic train ride along the coast from Havana, Aitken and Gladys were joined by Fred Teele in Matanzas.[53] The two men then went off to inspect the proposed tramline route as well as the districts of the city that would be served by the tramway. By the end of the day, they were convinced that a tramway and electric-lighting operation in Matanzas would be a 'profitable undertaking.' The following morning, Aitken wrote to the 'Matanzas syndicate' extolling the virtues of both the venture and the country, using letterhead borrowed from the Matanzas branch of the Royal Bank of Canada: 'The island of Cuba is enjoying wonderful prosperity. The soil is exceedingly fertile, and the country very rich. The future must hold great things in store for Cuba and Matanzas necessarily must share in the general prosperity. The only danger is from yellow fever and as the people become more cleanly in their habits this danger will be eliminated. Except for the buildings Cuba will compare favorably with Canada in every respect barring morals.'[54]

In his opinion on Cuban morals and sanitary habits, Aitken identified with the prejudices of the majority of the North Americans who had been flooding into Cuba since the end of the Spanish-American War to take advantage of American suzerainty.[55] The speed at which North American investment expanded in the early 1900s was not only a consequence of American political control; it was also a product of the active collaboration between Cuba's ruling and commercial élite and the businessmen, promoters, and carpet-baggers who were flooding in from the north. In some cases, collaboration was voluntary, at least for those Cubans who believed that North Americans would bring the island political and economic progress along with new capital. For others, in particular the Cuban property owners who had emerged from the war in debt – their bank accounts devalued and their plantations or other property in ruins – and who chafed at foreigners taking advantage of their sudden penury, collaboration meant little more than a humiliating capitulation.[56]

Without a doubt, Cuba's misfortune was North America's opportunity. In 1904 one American investor crowed: 'Nowhere else in the world are there such chances for success for the man of moderate means, as well as for the capitalist, as Cuba offers today.'[57] Canadian investors had been similarly impressed. As early as 1900, according to the *Canadian Journal of Commerce*, 'Canadian capital and clearer northern brains' were turning Cuba into a 'modern hive of industry.'[58] The Canadians who first arrived, including Sir William Van Horne, B.F. Pearson, and W.B. Ross, invested in utilities, railways, and finance.[59] Aitken arrived relatively late in the scramble, but there remained a few unfilled niches outside Havana.

The first step was to obtain a municipal franchise giving a right of way to construct and operate a tramway and lighting system on a proposed route through a city. In Matanzas, Aitken discovered that Albert Wright, an American lawyer operating out of Havana, had already secured a franchise for a proposed tramway on the choice streets of Matanzas. The American had no intention of constructing anything himself, however. Having followed Dr Pearson's movements in Cuba the year before, including his inspection tour of Matanzas, Wright had been convinced that Pearson or someone else would soon be proceeding with a utility venture in the city. Accordingly, he had selected the most logical streets for a tramway route, and he had made his franchise application accompanied by a $6,200 deposit immediately after Pearson's departure. Wright had been waiting for someone like Aitken to buy out his franchise. His price was $30,000 plus an interest in the new company.[60]

The franchise was solid, but it was not worth the exorbitant price Wright was asking, so Aitken decided to try and circumvent the American lawyer. Since exclusionary franchises were illegal under Cuban law, he decided to use the threat of obtaining an alternative tramway franchise to deflate Wright's bargaining leverage and force him to sell out at a much lower price.[61] He contacted another lawyer in Havana to begin the franchise application process and then prepared to make the twenty-five-hour journey to Santiago with his wife and Teele, leaving the American lawyer to squirm in the meantime.[62]

From a technical point of view, the Santiago proposition turned out to be superior to the Matanzas proposal. First, the city was the second largest in Cuba and appeared to have tremendous potential. Second, the layout

of the proposed tram route on an existing franchise owned by local interests was preferable to Wright's franchise in Matanzas. Finally, the price
being asked for the franchise as well as for the existing thermal-power
lighting plant was reasonable. By the time they had finished their initial
inspection, Aitken and Teele were satisfied that Santiago would be the
RSC's next utility venture, and after negotiating and signing some provisional agreements, they decided to leave Cuba as quickly as possible. Aitken was anxious to return to Canada in order to set up the promotional
syndicate for the new venture, while Teele had to return to Georgetown
to wind up Demerara's reconstruction before taking on the Santiago
project.

On their return to Havana, Aitken and Teele stopped over in
Camagüey, a small inland city of about 35,000 inhabitants.[63] Aware that a
local Cuban utility owner wanted to sell out, they made a hasty visit to the
existing power plant, where they found modern and well-installed equipment.[64] But what they saw did not change Aitken's mind. Camagüey and
Matanzas were put on a back burner, along with Quito, Panamá, and
Guatemala City, as the RSC forged ahead with the Santiago venture.

The Camaguey Company

Returning to his Halifax office in early March 1906, Aitken immediately
began work on the Santiago proposition.[65] Just as the banking and underwriting syndicates were being formed, however, he received discouraging
news from Cuba. The Santiago people, having received a better offer
from another utility promoter, had cancelled the provisional agreements.[66] Aitken decided that he had to return to Cuba immediately to try
and rescue the deal, and this time he would travel with his own lawyer to
make sure that all agreements in principle could be transformed into
binding contracts. He picked H. Almon Lovett, a senior barrister who
had only recently left B.F. Pearson's Halifax law firm to join Harris,
Henry & Cahan. Through his close association with Pearson and W.B.
Ross, Lovett was experienced with utility franchises as well as with the
drafting of purchase agreements in utility acquisitions. Before setting out,
Aitken cabled Cuba, arranging to meet with the Matanzas and Camagüey
representatives in case he could not save the Santiago deal.[67]

Aitken arrived in Santiago to discover that the situation was even worse
than he had feared. The owners were now demanding a controlling position in the new utility company. In addition, the local government had
rewritten the tramway franchise, redirecting what would have been profit
into lower-cost service. Aitken concluded that both the local government

and the franchise owners were 'very unsafe,' and in the end he was relieved that the deal had unravelled at this early stage rather than after the RSC had committed a large amount of capital, along with its reputation.[68]

Aitken then travelled to Matanzas, where he found that he was faced with a problem more serious than an active local government or a costly franchise. The source of the trouble was one Mendoze Capotte, the owner of the lighting plant in Matanzas. On his first visit, Aitken had made it clear that he had no intention of purchasing Capotte's antiquated thermal-power plant. Instead, he would build a modern and well-equipped plant to service the new tramway and lighting operation. Capotte warned Aitken that he had the political clout to force the purchase, but Aitken did not believe him and approached the municipality directly after bribing a local politician. He then asked the municipality not to require him to purchase Capotte's lighting plant and equipment in the tramway and lighting franchise. The municipal officials, on instructions from their political superior, did what was asked. But when Capotte discovered what had happened, he used his influence in the central Cuban government to have the Matanzas agreement declared illegal. Faced with the prospect of paying for a power plant that was worth little more than its value in scrap metal, Aitken decided to pay another visit to Camagüey.[69]

Although smaller than Santiago and farther away from Havana than Matanzas, the picturesque city of Camagüey was no longer a backwater, in large part because of Sir William Van Horne's decision to make it the headquarters for the Cuba Company Railway.[70] Van Horne had incorporated the Cuba Company in 1900, while the dust from the Spanish-American War was still settling. Raising millions of dollars in the United States, he had then built a railway that crossed the length of Cuba from the north coast near Havana to Santiago in the far southeast.[71] Camagüey had proportionately fewer North American businessmen than Havana or Santiago, but its expatriate business community was predominately Canadian.[72] Two years earlier, the Royal Bank of Canada had set up a branch there, and its business had expanded so rapidly that it had begun to construct an ornate new building.[73] In fact, Aitken had received most of his advance information about the city's utility prospects from Royal Bank managers in Havana and Camagüey.[74]

He was reassured by what he saw. The city's power plant was one of the most modern in Cuba. There were no legal difficulties with the tramway franchise. Most of the tramway line had already been laid by the local power plant company, which owned the recently constructed lighting plant in Camagüey. The Puerto Príncipe Electric Light Company[75] was owned by Roberto A. Betancourt, a businessman from a family that was prominent in local business and politics but had suffered losses during the Spanish-American War. Whatever the reasons prompting him, Betancourt threw himself into selling his family's company with great enthusiasm. He had already entered into discussions with a syndicate from New Haven, Connecticut, but also welcomed any offers from other parties, including the RSC.[76]

Aitken went out of his way to charm Betancourt. He preferred the Cuban gentleman to the men with whom he had tried to deal in Santiago and Matanzas. Betancourt appeared to have integrity as well as social standing, and judging from the way he ran the power plant, he was also a fairly good manager. Although Aitken intended to purchase control of the old company, he wanted Betancourt to remain as general manager and shareholder in the new utility venture. When Betancourt threw in some of his family's land for real estate development as a sweetener, he and Aitken finalized the terms of the purchase on the spot, Almon Lovett drafting the contracts.[77] But just when Aitken was on the verge of signing the final agreement, his nerves got the better of him and he drew back. Realizing the enormity of the step he was about to take and losing confidence in his own judgment, he cabled Teele for a second opinion: 'Would you advise the purchase of Camaguey light, property, and tramway franchise, $300,000.'[78] Teele was annoyed that he had not been given the chance personally to consider the project in any detail, and in his reply to Aitken he complained:

I really think it was a bit unfair on your part to ask me to express an opinion regarding Camaguey, without my having the slightest idea as to what the output of the present plant was, the number of lights it supplies, its present capitalization, etc., also the size of the city, the mileage of the track required, and cost of construction, the cost of coal to the power station ...

As you will remember, we were in Camaguey less than 24 hours [on the previous trip], as we arrived two hours late, only went across the city once, and during that time obtained no data whatsoever, the only real information being gleaned from our visit to the power stations which showed that the machinery was of the latest type and well installed.[79]

Aitken knew full well that Teele could offer no useful advice. He had simply lost confidence in his own intuition, his sense that the new venture would be a money maker, and had momentarily stepped back from the precipice of action. Now he did his best to brace himself and sign the final contract. Afterwards he instructed Lovett to return to Canada and incorporate the Camaguey Company, Limited.[80]

The bond issue had to be sold quickly, since Aitken had planned a leave of absence for Teele from Trinidad Electric in the autumn in order to lay out Camagüey's tramway lines. Although Betancourt was to be the general manager of the new company, and although his chief engineer of many years, Carl Giles, would continue to run the power plant, Teele would have to construct and manage the new street railway – at least in the beginning – since neither Betancourt nor Giles had any previous experience with electric tramways.[81]

By the first week of June 1906 the RSC had sold about $347,000 worth of Camaguey Company bonds. As the market could not immediately absorb further bonds, Aitken suspended selling. He was more than pleased with the results, for more bonds could be gradually issued later in the year or even the following year as the tramway construction proceeded. In the meantime, the electric lighting contract was clearing about $3,000 a month, which meant that interest on the bonds already sold could be covered in perpetuity even if the urban railway never earned a dime.[82]

By this time, Teele had done a remarkable job of reconstructing and reorganizing Demerara Electric, and Aitken was 'beginning to shout "success"' to those who had been dubious that the Demerara company could ever be made to pay.[83] Extrapolating from the figures for May, it looked as if net profits for 1906 could be as high as $50,000, so Demerara would not only be able to meet its bond interest but could also pay a dividend on its common stock for the first time in the company's history.[84] This remarkable turnaround gave Aitken the confidence and the financial backing he needed to promote yet another utility project.

The Porto Rico Railways Company

Aitken's next destination was Puerto Rico, another spoil of the Spanish-American War. The economic consequences of war and U.S. occupation were of the same nature as in Cuba, but in Puerto Rico the American commercial and industrial penetration was more strongly felt, simply because the island's economy had been tied more closely to Spain before the war.[85] Now, under the American-dominated civilian government created under the Foraker Act of 1900, U.S. direct investment in banks, sugar plantations, industries, and utilities flowed in, facilitated by laws that discriminated against the local commercial élite. Less than one decade after passage of the Foraker Act, 142 foreign corporations with a total capital of almost $300 million were competing with 119 domestic corporations (and not all of these were locally owned) that had a total capital of less than $22 million.[86]

One of the first North American firms to obtain a toehold in Puerto Rico was the eminent New York engineering firm of J.G. White & Co. The fighting between American and Spanish troops had barely finished before the firm purchased an interurban steam railway connecting the capital city of San Juan with the wealthy district of Rio Piedras, a distance of seven miles. One month after the purchase, in December 1898, J.G. White & Co. incorporated the San Juan & Rio Piedras Railroad Company, a New York company that was the shell for the Puerto Rican operations.[87] The firm later purchased a lighting plant and tramway service in the city of San Juan as well as two franchises: a possible water power at Comerio Falls on the La Plata River, about 15 miles from the capital city, and a potential interurban steam railway line connecting the town of Caguas, twenty-five miles from San Juan, with the town of Rio Piedras. In March 1906 Aitken was asked whether he was interested in purchasing all these properties in a package deal.[88]

Aitken had come to know J.G. White & Co. through equipment purchases for his operations in Trinidad and British Guiana. Immediately after his return from Cuba with the Camaguey contracts in hand, he travelled to J.G. White & Co.'s head office in New York to review their proposal. He carefully examined the accounting and engineering data. Impressed with what he saw, he entered into a provisional purchase agreement that was subject to his personal inspection in Puerto Rico the following month.[89]

It was evident to Aitken that the project would be too large for the RSC alone in terms of both construction and finance. Teele was spread too thin on account of his work in British Guiana and Cuba; he could not possibly oversee a construction project that was larger than the Demerara and Trinidad operations combined. Moreover, the Puerto Rican operation necessitated the construction of a hydroelectric power plant, and since Teele's experience was limited to coal-fired thermal plants it would be of less value.[90] Aitken realized that the project's construction would have to be contracted out. J.G. White & Co. seemed perfect for the work; the firm had the engineering expertise, the equipment, and the intimate knowledge of local conditions.

At least $2 million in cash needed to be raised for the initial phase of construction. Since the RSC did not have the resources to act as the sole

house of issue as in previous flotations, Aitken would have to find some
partners for it. Here J.G. White personally stepped in. He suggested that
his company, experienced in the ways of utility finance, would be more
than happy to sponsor the issue along with the RSC. Aitken agreed but on
the condition that he, as representative of the RSC, would be the manager of the promotional syndicate. With one more Canadian firm, perhaps A.E. Ames & Co. of Toronto, he would have a banking syndicate
strong enough to carry off the issue, at least in Canada. However, it was
unlikely that Canadian investors would be able to digest such a large issue
at one sitting; Aitken knew that he would have to make a market for some
of these bonds in Britain.[91]

After the meeting in New York, Aitken immediately travelled back to
Canada to convince his Halifax associates as well as Will Ross and A.E.
Ames of the merits of the deal. He suggested that they accompany him to
Puerto Rico to see the properties for themselves,[92] and both Ross and
Ames agreed to go. They sailed with him to San Juan that July. Meeting
up with Fred Teele, the party reviewed the properties with Philip G. Gossler, who was vice-president of J.G. White & Co. and the founder of the
Canadian White Co., the firm's subsidiary in Canada. Determining that
the operating expenses of the existing electric tramway and steam railway
systems were excessive, Teele suggested a number of administrative
changes that could reduce these costs. Most important, the group as a
whole concluded that Comerio Falls could support a hydroelectric plant
capable of generating sufficient power for the tramway, the interurban
railway, and the lighting system for San Juan.[93]

Despite the daunting size of the project, Aitken finalized the purchase
agreement on behalf of the RSC.[94] He called the new enterprise the
Porto Rico Railways Company. The word 'Porto' was used because Puerto
Rico's first military governor had ordered the name of the island changed
from Puerto Rico to Porto Rico, and Aitken automatically adopted the
Americanized version (which would remain the name of the island until
1932) in his corporate charter.[95]

Impressed by the project, A.E. Ames agreed that his firm would join the
RSC and J.G. White & Co. in the promotional syndicate. J.G. White and
Philip Gossler were similarly enthusiastic about Aitken's financial plans
and the extensive construction work that these would fund. No one could
have foreseen the stormy weather that lay ahead. In months, financial
markets throughout the world would be increasingly squeezed for liquidity. In little more than a year, this liquidity crisis would produce a panic
on Wall Street and a stock market crisis that immediately spread to Can-

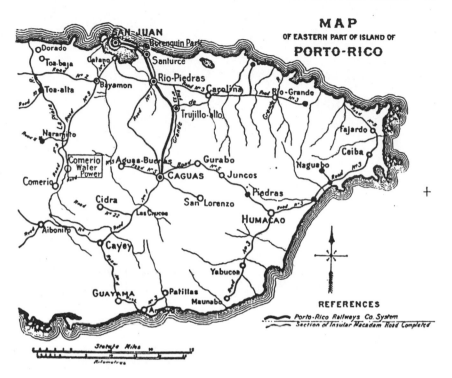

Map 2 Eastern part of Puerto Rico, showing Porto Rico Railways route, 1907.
Source: Adapted from *Annual Financial Review* (Canadian), 8 (April 1908), 454;
originally part of Porto Rico Railways bond prospectus and 1907 annual report.

ada. Securities of any kind would be almost impossible to sell, and Porto
Rico Railways would find itself chronically short of money for construction. To make matters worse, J.G. White & Co.'s response to the financial
crisis was to double its construction fees, putting an intolerable burden
on Aitken and the RSC.

Although Aitken could not have predicted this in the summer of 1906,
the problems he faced in financing Porto Rico Railways would transform
the RSC from a follower into an innovator. On the financial end, the RSC
would soon become an international investment bank with a foothold in
the financial capital of the world, the City of London. On the operational
side, Aitken would create the Montreal Engineering Company so that
purchasing, consulting, and construction services would be internally
provided to the RSC's growing family of utility enterprises.

4

Building the Royal Securities Corporation

Royal Securities Corporation was Me.

Lord Beaverbrook's statement in his autobiography 'My Early Life,'
published shortly after his death in 1964

I am sure that it is only a matter of time when we shall have to open an office here.

A.J. Nesbitt, writing to Aitken from the Savoy Hotel, London, 26 June 1907

Aitken was able to finance his new projects in Cuba and Puerto Rico because he personally shaped an investment bank that could issue, underwrite, and retail the growing number of securities created by these enterprises. By the time of his first visit to Cuba, he had already acquired a talented managerial and sales staff as well as branch offices in Montreal and Saint John. Ambitious young Maritimers such as Izaak Walton Killam and Arthur J. Nesbitt aggressively built up a new clientele of individuals and institutions prepared to invest in Aitken's new ventures. Good staff and new customers were essential if Aitken was to overcome the factors of supply and demand that constrained him.

On the supply side, Royal Securities' modest nominal capital of $50,000, one-fifth the original capitalization of the Dominion Securities Corporation, meant that the firm was heavily dependent on borrowed money. Most of this came in the form of short-term loans (known as 'call loans') from various Canadian banks. Call loans were risky because any major reduction of a bank's reserves – during a stock market panic, for example – would trigger calls on outstanding loans at the precise time that a bond house such as the RSC would be suffering from a cash shortage. As a consequence of its reliance on borrowed money, particularly call loans, the RSC was overly sensitive to any financial downturn. Nonetheless, Aitken's larger ventures in Cuba and Puerto Rico required large amounts of borrowed money, and as the RSC's debt load rose, so did the possibility that even a small miscalculation on Aitken's part would result in the firm's failure. There was only one effective way to reduce this debt load (and thus the RSC's vulnerability) and that was to bring in cash by selling securities.

On the demand side, the limited Maritime market simply could not absorb the volume of securities Aitken was creating through his new utility enterprises. He had to develop a market beyond Nova Scotia and New Brunswick. He had already begun to do this with the opening of the first RSC branch office in Montreal in 1906, but even the pan-Canadian market was shallow and could easily be plugged. So Aitken had to time his flotations strategically in order to avoid issuing securities just after similar securities had hit the market; two public utility issues within the same month, for example, would exceed investors' demand within the Canadian market.[1] From the time he began to explore Cuba and Puerto Rico for new utility ventures, therefore, Aitken knew that Canadian investors alone could not digest all the securities he would have to issue.

Aitken immediately looked to Britain, where for decades investors had absorbed ever-larger amounts of public and private securities from around the world. The advanced industrial nations of Europe became creditors on a huge scale during the age of high imperialism, but Great Britain's massive investment in overseas securities put it in a league of its own. Between 1870 and 1913, Britain devoted 5.2 per cent of its gross national product to foreign lending, while Germany and France, the two other major creditor nations of the world, averaged a rate of 2 to 3 per cent of national product.[2] The United States and Canada were the two largest recipients of portfolio investment from Britain during this era, the United States being the single largest destination until the turn of the century.[3] From 1902 until the First World War, in the 'last great surge of British lending,' Canada replaced the United States as the single largest borrower, 'absorbing perhaps a third of British lending,' a reflection of Canada's remarkable economic growth during the Laurier boom.[4] Aitken and other Canadian financial promoters began to invade the city of London in order to make a market for their securities, thereby directly facilitating the flow of British capital to Canadian business.[5]

Aitken's New Team

Almost immediately after Stairs's funeral in 1904, Aitken came up against the institutional limitations of the RSC. He was generating so much work that he could not possibly perform all his daily office functions and oversee staff while also negotiating underwriting syndicates, monitoring selling agreements, and examining potential new issues. He needed more salesmen to handle all the securities generated by his new issues. He required a full-time accountant to manage the increased daily flow of money in and out of the RSC and to provide the data necessary to compare the profitability of the various issuing, underwriting and retailing transactions of the firm. And as he was now spending more time in Toronto, Montreal, Boston, and New York than in Halifax, he needed a full-time manager he could rely on to handle the day-to-day business – someone who would make the daily bank deposits, respond to correspondence, draft and sign underwriting agreements, supervise the brokers handling RSC issues, and oversee the new permanent staff. In addition, Aitken needed to set up a branch office in central Canada in order to enlarge the market for his securities.

For his new office manager in Halifax, he chose Blake Burrill, a young man from Yarmouth, Nova Scotia, who had been highly recommended by Aitken's business associate A.K. Maclean.[6] Coming into the office in December 1905, Burrill replaced Aitken as secretary, and Aitken moved up to vice-president and managing director. Burrill was given an annual salary of $2,000, one-half of what Aitken himself was receiving, and he performed his new duties meticulously. Now that Aitken could concentrate on creating new business rather than conducting existing business, he soon come to consider Burrill 'indispensable.'[7]

On the recommendation of Burrill, Aitken hired Gerald Farrell to manage the RSC's new sales staff. Twenty-six years of age – the same age as Aitken – Farrell was vivacious and ambitious, a veteran of the Boer War, an active sportsman, and a man about town. His father, Edward Farrell, had been a famous Halifax physician, professor of surgery, and founder of the Halifax Medical College. He had also been the anti–National Policy Liberal politician who, with Alfred Gilpin Jones, had run against John F. Stairs and Thomas Edward Kenny in the infamous 1891 election and had lost – and lost again in the subsequent by-election after having the first declared void because of Conservative vote tampering. Despite these political differences, the Farrell name stood for an established and moneyed Irish Catholic family known throughout the province.[8]

In Gerald Farrell, Aitken thought he had found the ideal person to manage the future central-Canadian office. Whereas Burrill was a competent and reliable employee, Gerald Farrell was entrepreneurial, someone who could build up the RSC in central Canada. As Aitken soon discovered, however, Farrell was impossible to control. Although he was an excellent salesman, he was also a *bon vivant* with a weakness for the high life in the big city. In Farrell's first three months with the RSC, Aitken caught him making two unnecessary trips to Boston and Philadelphia. He told Blake Burrill that Farrell might indeed have 'his good points' but was 'too great a source of worry and annoyance to put up with.'[9] He threatened to sack Farrell, but Burrill begged him to give Farrell another chance. Aitken relented but decided that Farrell would have to continue travelling through the Maritime countryside supervising the sales staff, rather than being made manager of the proposed branch office in Toronto or Montreal, the job Farrell really wanted.[10]

As far as Aitken was concerned, the new office would be instrumental in absorbing an ever increasing stream of securities spawned by his promotions.[11] He had managed to build up a small client base in central Canada but had been hindered by the lack of a branch office.[12] The real question was whether the new office would be located in Montreal or Toronto. Aitken first considered Toronto, primarily because of his connection to Will Ross, the general manager of the Metropolitan Bank. Born ten years before Aitken and raised in New Glasgow, William D. Ross was son-in-law to Senator James D. McGregor, who had almost succeeded John F. Stairs as president of Scotia. Joining the Bank of Nova Scotia at fourteen years of age, Ross had quickly worked his way up. He had moved to central Canada in 1897 and left the Bank of Nova Scotia in 1901 to become deputy minister of finance in the Laurier government. When A.E. Ames and his associates incorporated the Metropolitan Bank the following year, they hired Ross as the new assistant general manager.[13] During the financial downturn of 1902–3, Ames found himself bankrupt, and Ross worked day and night to pull the bank 'out of a nasty hole.' He succeeded and was made general manager of the Metropolitan Bank for his efforts.[14]

Aitken had first met Ross while acting as John F. Stairs's personal secretary. Their relationship quickly matured, for the Scotia group and the RSC were borrowing increasing amounts of money from the Metropoli-

tan as bridge loans for Scotia at the same time as Ames and other prominent Toronto businessmen were beginning to buy Scotia securities on a
regular basis. The RSC found itself placing the orders through Toronto
brokers and investment middlemen, generating profits that could have
flowed to Aitken and the RSC if only he had had his own brokerage firm
in Toronto executing the orders. In fact, in the months preceding Stairs's
death, Aitken had entered into a tentative partnership with Will Ross and
Edward Cronyn (a Toronto broker who was then working for Aemilus
Jarvis & Co.) to divert these profits back to himself.[15] Aitken and Ross
were to be Cronyn's silent partners, and Aitken purchased a seat on the
Toronto Stock Exchange for $9,000 in Cronyn's name. Since Aitken and
Ross both knew and trusted each other but had little knowledge of Cronyn, Aitken sent some RSC stock orders to Cronyn for execution to 'know
absolutely Cronyn's way of dealing.'[16]

Unaware that he was being closely observed in the Toronto Stock
Exchange, Cronyn could not avoid the temptation of making a little
money for himself. He put his sell orders on behalf of the RSC in a manner that pushed down the price of the stock, and he then repurchased
the stock on his own account at the artificially low price. Incensed, Ross
and Aitken sold the seat on the Toronto Stock Exchange and refused to
consummate the partnership.[17] The Cronyn episode serves to illustrate
Aitken's double standard; he had seen nothing wrong the year before
when he had manipulated Scotia stock to make a little money for himself,
but the same behaviour was somehow unacceptable for those who worked
with him.

With the failure of the Toronto deal, Aitken attempted a slightly different arrangement in Montreal the following autumn, just weeks after John
F. Stairs's death. He convinced two Montreal brokers, A.P. Christmas and
F.M. Manley, to join him in a new brokerage firm that would act as the
RSC's exclusive distributor in central Canada for six months. If the RSC
was satisfied at the end of this period, it would consider starting a new
firm in Montreal with Christmas and Manley in charge. Aitken put up the
entire capital of $10,000 in order to be the controlling partner with the
right to dictate the timing and prices for all sales.[18] Almost immediately,
however, Christmas and Manley ran afoul of the original agreement when
the central-Canadian tombstone* for a Scotia steel issue showed the new

*Tombstone was (and remains) the customary term for a one-page prospectus that adver-
tised, in any financial periodical, the terms of the security issue and the names of the financial houses supporting the issue.

partnership as the main sponsors rather than the RSC. Aitken feared the reaction of the central-Canadian underwriters, who felt they deserved preferential treatment for helping float Scotia securities in the past. They 'would have been right glad to have got the chance of offering the Scotia Consolidated [bond issue] in Montreal,' Aitken explained to Christmas, and now they 'will raise a perfect storm' because 'we passed over their heads and dealt with you, who had no claims upon the Scotia Company.'[19]

These early experiences in Toronto and Montreal convinced Aitken of the necessity of setting up his own RSC branch office. The manager of the office would have to be someone entrepreneurial enough to find an opening in Canada's financial establishment yet manageable enough to be sure of following Aitken's general policy. After his disappointment with Farrell, Aitken had discovered a salesman from Saint John, New Brunswick, a wholesale goods drummer his own age whom he thought perfect for the job.[20] According to his account many years later, he met Arthur J. Nesbitt at the Halifax Hotel:

The imaginative genius of this promising young man appealed to me. At two o'clock in the morning, after he had gone to bed, the notion of engaging him for the Royal Securities Corporation occurred to me. There was no telephone service in the rooms in those days. So I sent a message to him, asking if he would join me. He replied that he was in bed, and that it was late. He would like to have stayed where he was. But I persisted, and he came to me. We talked about the wholesale dry goods business and other subjects. When he was exhausted, I asked 'How much are you getting?' He said: '$2,100.' I said: 'I will give you $1,800, if you will go to Montreal and open up there a branch of the Royal Securities Corporation.'[21]

Nesbitt, who was probably surprised and no doubt a little flattered by Aitken's attention, despite the somewhat lower starting salary, agreed to join the RSC the following week and was sent to Montreal, where he opened the new office at the end of December 1905.[22]

Meanwhile, Aitken had selected his youngest employee, Izaak Walton Killam, to work at another RSC branch – in Saint John, New Brunswick – under the direction of Horace Porter, the man he had hired to manage the new office. Killam would ultimately become the heir to Aitken's business empire and one of the most commanding financiers in Canada. Born in Yarmouth, Nova Scotia, in 1885 into a merchant and shipowning family, he had become a clerk in the Yarmouth branch of the Union

Bank of Halifax at the age of sixteen. Two years later he was transferred to the Halifax head office. Aitken first saw the tall 'wide-eyed lad' when making the daily RSC deposits just before Blake Burrill took over these duties.[23] After being told by the manager that Walton Killam was 'the best man in the Bank,' he lured Killam away with a salary of $1,500 per year. This was considerably more than a bank teller's pay, but Aitken's intuition was that Killam had the potential to become a great investment banker.[24] This proved accurate in the long run, though Aitken had cause to question his judgment within the first year of Killam's employment.

While he was a salesman operating out of the Halifax office, Walton Killam lived up to Aitken's expectations, but when he moved to Saint John he began to adopt a more relaxed approach to selling securities. Farrell, on his rounds as sales manager, noted that Killam needed 'working up a bit,' that he showed up to work late and then sat 'in the office too much,' not bothering himself with chasing prospective investors. While he was generally 'behaving himself all right' and 'making a good impression on the clients who came to see him,' he definitely needed 'to get a hustle on.' What he most needed, Farrell suggested, was 'a good blowing up, one like I get from your Royal Highness occasionally.'[25]

Reluctantly, Aitken came to the same conclusion, blaming Killam's growing idleness on two factors.[26] His starting salary had been too high, and he had become addicted to the club life of playing bridge into the early hours of the morning. Moreover, Killam was getting into the bad habit of returning cash to investors who were unhappy with the performance of certain securities; Aitken had to remind him of 'the necessity of viewing matters from the Corporation's standpoint, and not from that of your clients.' While he was prepared to buy back securities from dissatisfied RSC customers as a last resort, Aitken naturally felt that it was bad business for the RSC to encourage repurchase as a routine procedure.[27] To take care of this problem, Aitken cut Killam's salary in half, making the rest of his income dependent on commissions.[28] Many years later, Aitken claimed that 'a change came over him the very next day. The bridge table was forsaken; the Club life was forgotten.'[29]

The Structure of High-Risk Financing

With office managers such as Nesbitt, Burrill, and Porter, and salesmen such as Killam and Farrell, Aitken was free to concentrate on the business of investment banking; that is, the business of promoting companies, arranging consolidations, and issuing securities that were the fountainhead of profits for the RSC and himself. To unlock the mysteries of security financing during the Laurier boom, we must first understand the use and distribution of common stock. Since the various stages involved in manufacturing, distributing, and retailing regular consumer goods are better understood, we can start with this simple analogy in order to draw out the similarities and differences between finance and the so-called real economy. Although the explanation is based on past events, the principles underlying company promotion and securities underwriting and retailing remain largely valid in today's world of high finance, and they are particularly applicable to what became known as junk bond financing during the 1980s.

The Camaguey Company, for example, was a typical high-risk utility promotion that created a par value of $1.3 million of securities. Of that amount, $600,000 of bonds were sold to investors at their face value (in other words, par value) to raise the cash necessary to purchase Betancourt's property ($300,000 for the power plant alone) and Camaguey's new cars and equipment, to construct Camaguey's tramway system, and to enlarge the existing power plant.[30] The remaining $700,000 represented the face value of common stock that was earmarked as a bonus to promoters and underwriters, as well as to the investors who purchased the bonds.

Camaguey's promotional syndicate was made up of the RSC and its chief associates, including Aitken, Harris, George Stairs, W.B. Ross, Will Ross, H.A. Lovett, and T.G. McMullen.[31] These promoters each put up $200 in order to cover the costs of investigating the Camaguey proposition, which included paying for Aitken and Lovett's trip to Cuba and the legal fees for incorporating the new utility. In many investigations this money would be lost, but as the syndicate had decided to go ahead with Camaguey, all syndicate members were entitled to a return in the form of common stock as the 'creators' of the utility – just as a manufacturer producing consumer goods receives remuneration. Similarly, the promoters negotiated the prices at which the bonds were 'sold' to underwriters, brokers, and investors – just as manufacturers might negotiate prices with their wholesalers and suggest prices to retailers.

Underwriters can be likened to wholesalers because they purchase bonds (goods) in large lots, reselling them to brokers (retailers) in smaller lots and at a higher price. There are two important differences, however. First, unlike manufacturers, who rarely do their own wholesaling, the promoters of the time often acted as their own underwriters; in the Camaguey case, for example, Aitken, Harris, Stairs, and the RSC were

both promoters and underwriters. They were joined by Teele, Betancourt, and Van Horne as well as by Herbert Holt and E.L. Pease of the
Royal Bank.[32] Second, the underwriter agreed to pay for the bonds only if
the issue was not sold within a given period to brokers and investors,
whereas a wholesaler generally pays immediately for the goods irrespective of whether they are then sold to retailers and ultimately to consumers. Nonetheless, both underwriters and wholesalers perform one
common function. They assume the risk of the market, absorbing the
securities (goods) in any given issue (production run). In this way, the
promotional syndicate (the manufacturing firm) is able to sell its bond
issue (output) before it is marketed to the general public.

Brokers (retailers) buy in small lots and market the securities (goods)
to investors (consumers). Brokers are similar to retailers in that they have
a personal relationship with the investor (consumer), thus allowing them
to market the particular bonds (goods) in the most effective manner possible; but they are dissimilar in that they price their sales to investors
according to the terms set by the promotional syndicate rather than by
the underwriters. Investors, like consumers, however, hold the promotional syndicate (in particular, the investment bank behind the syndicate)
to be the guarantor of the quality of the securities. Although this does not
imply direct legal liability – as in the case of a manufacturing firm, which
automatically assumes legal liability for the product manufactured – the
RSC's reputation among investors hung in the balance on every security
issue.

During the gilded age, the remuneration paid to promoters, underwriters, and brokers was allocated according to the degree of risk and
could come in one or more of the following forms: (1) a lump sum cash
payment; (2) a commission based on a per cent value of the entire issue;
(3) an amount representing the difference, or 'spread,' between the purchase price and the selling price of the securities; or (4) an agreed
amount of free, or 'bonus,' common stock received by the syndicates with
their allotment of senior securities – bonds or preference shares.

Brokers received almost all of their profit on the spread between their
purchase price and the price at which they marketed the securities. Promoters and underwriters, on the other hand, could receive a lump sum
or percentage commission but were generally paid with bonus common
stock, the currency of choice in the high-risk flotations of the Laurier
boom. These common shares were worth almost nothing at first because
they were based on the future earning power of a utility enterprise that
had not yet been constructed or reorganized. They gained value only

slowly, after the utility was operating and beginning to generate a regular profit, thereby creating some demand among investors for the common stock.

Since bonus stock took at least a few years to fight its way to par value, this was a high-risk but potentially high-yield form of profit. In the Camaguey Company issue, for example, promoters received a 100 per cent stock bonus ($600,000 face value), of which they were prepared to give up 50 per cent to the underwriters for insuring the issue of the $600,000 worth of bonds within a certain period of time, keeping in mind of course the significant overlap of promoters and underwriters. The underwriters, in turn, agreed to give up 25 per cent of their stock bonus to brokers, who needed them as an incentive to 'sell' investors on Camaguey bonds, so every bond investor received a 25 per cent stock bonus. The extra $100,000 of bonus common stock was earmarked for incidental expenses, including a $45,000 finder's fee paid to the superintendent of the Royal Bank at Havana and the Royal Bank manager at Camagüey.[33]

Despite the RSC's small capital base, Aitken had managed to fund the RSC's expansion by reinvesting almost all of its profits back into the corporation – his appetite for expansion and therefore profit being insatiable. To boost profits as of January 1905, he decided that the RSC would receive a 10 per cent stock commission as a fee for any issue handled by himself. The fee was more than justified, he argued, by his expertise in organizing and managing promotional and underwriting syndicates. Through Aitken's 10 per cent policy, the underwriters were in effect being forced to give up a margin of their profit to the RSC, which now gained the prospective benefit of greater future profit, as well as having immediate collateral for call loans in cases where Aitken could convince the banks to accept common stock (deeply discounted, of course) as security on advances.

Among Canadian bond houses, the 10 per cent policy appears to have been unique to the RSC. Few underwriters liked the policy including RSC president George Stairs, who in his capacity as underwriter grumbled that the arrangement seemed overgenerous to the RSC.[34] Nonetheless, most of the underwriters eventually accepted Aitken's policy, though Harris was still complaining one year later that 'the Royal Securities Corporation is getting far too much and the underwriters far too little.'[35] Aitken explained to Harris that the policy was intentionally generous, because 'our ambition is to build up a very big Company and this can only be done by the directors of the Royal Securities Corporation recognizing the services of their officers who grab everything in sight.' Moreover, 'any disposition on the part of the directors to allow their officers to be at all generous in relinquishing profits or possible profits ... would tend to lower the moral [sic] of the entire staff.'[36]

Fed Up with Halifax

By 1906 the RSC had doubled its authorized capital to $100,000, and it issued 500 shares to raise fresh capital for the company.[37] At this time, Aitken, Cahan, Harris, and George Stairs contributed pro rata shares of the $25,000, paying a par value of $100 for their additional RSC shares.[38] They then sold the remaining 250 shares to outsiders at twice the par value, a more accurate reflection of the RSC's underlying value.[39] This issue should have raised a total of $75,000 – fresh capital that was desperately needed by the RSC. In actual fact, the $50,000 that came from the new shareholders went back into the pockets of the RSC shareholders as a dividend, so the RSC netted only $25,000 out of the transaction. Although personally benefiting from the dividend, Aitken had argued in favour of putting all capital gains back into the RSC, but he was outvoted by Harris and George Stairs.[40]

The new RSC shareholders included the RSC's senior management, Blake Burrill and Gerald Farrell. Aitken supported Burrill and Farrell in their application for shares because he thought that shareholding was the most effective way to inculcate loyalty among employees. He made it clear to all his employees that the route to promotion was within the organization, and he promised he would not bring in 'new men' and 'promote them over the heads' of existing employees. Offering them shares in the RSC was Aitken's way of rewarding and keeping his senior people.[41] He also wanted some new shareholders who would be under his sway in order to dilute the influence of Harris and George Stairs on the RSC's general policy, so he invited three friendly associates, Will Ross, H. Almon Lovett, and W.B. Ross, to take up shares. Harris, who had become president of Scotia, was particularly opposed to W.B. Ross becoming a shareholder because of Ross's position on the board of Dominion Iron and Steel. For his part, Ross had a low opinion of both Harris and Scotia, and he only wanted to become a shareholder because of his faith in Aitken's abilities.[42] Aitken got his way in the end, however, and W.B. Ross ultimately became a shareholder in the RSC, along with Will Ross and Almon Lovett.

As far as Aitken was concerned, of course, the $25,000 of capital that

RSC had gained from its new shareholders was a mere drop in the bucket. He needed substantially more capital for his projects in Cuba and Puerto Rico, and he dreaded the thought of leveraging the RSC any further. He felt himself a prisoner to the vagaries of his bankers as well as to the fluctuations of the market for call loans. By the summer of 1906, Aitken was becoming increasingly testy about the RSC's debt load and the actions of his bankers. He poured out his woes in a long letter to Will Ross:

Although the earnings of the [RSC] will always be capitalized, still I think our shareholders should provide us with much more money than is at present at our disposal. We are continually calling upon our bankers to make us advances on slight margins. Unfortunately we are compelled to do this by reason of our very large operations. Frequently we use large sums of money in unnegotiable securities and in securities on which our bankers will not readily advance us. For instance new issues such as Amherst Foundry, Camaguey Bonds etc. etc. Of course after a time the banks get used to these securities and take them readily enough. But at first it is hard to get them to advance.

Reminding Ross that the RSC's liabilities invariably amounted to more than $1 million, he pointed out that he had to spend too much time 'financing the business of the Corporation with insufficient funds' and 'asking favours' of bankers. In his opinion, the RSC could not get along one day without the 'considerable attention' he devoted to these 'banking arrangements.'[43]

Then there was the matter of his salary. Aitken confided to Will Ross that he was leaving for New York to discuss an offer he had received from J.G. White & Co., the utility engineers and financiers. He had waited patiently since John F. Stairs's death for George Stairs and R.E. Harris to give him a salary increase, but in the end he had been obliged to raise the matter himself. When he had asked that his salary of $4,000 be doubled in recognition of his numerous successes, Stairs had tried to avoid the issue by telling him all the reasons he should remain in Halifax, 'utterly' missing the point that he was being 'starved out of the place.' Harris told Aitken that he would have to restrict himself to RSC business if he expected any salary increase – an important consideration for Harris, since Aitken had just started up a trust company that was competing with Eastern Trust, a company in which Harris had a large interest.

This advice infuriated Aitken. Receiving 'a very fine salary himself' from Scotia, Harris made money on his own behalf from more than a dozen different businesses, including his law firm and the RSC. Aitken was particularly upset by Harris's insinuation that he had made some extra profit for himself in the Camaguey promotion, when in fact he had turned over his entire bonus common stock to the RSC. 'You can hardly appreciate how much hard work I have done upon this job,' he complained to Will Ross, 'and when I consider that my remuneration thereto amounted to about $332 a month, you cannot wonder at my jacking up.'

Aitken went to New York, but finding it 'hard to pull up stakes,' he decided against the move. He may have soon received a larger salary from Harris and Stairs, but his insistence on doubling the RSC's capital continued to fall on deaf ears for the time being, and he was forced to continue soliciting bank managers for loans and convincing them to take what they considered speculative securities as collateral. To put the RSC under his complete control, Aitken now realized that he would somehow have to shake Harris and Stairs out of the company.

Making a Market in Britain

Bank advances, supplemented by the 10 per cent policy, could not entirely compensate for the RSC's lack of capital. The difference had to be made up somehow, and Aitken was forced to economize in every possible way. This could be seen in his incessant demands that letterhead stationery never be used for in-house communication, that envelopes be reused, that advertising expenses be limited, and that travelling expenses be kept to a minimum. By 1906, the RSC had approximately a dozen full-time employees, and all were subjected to Aitken's continual scolding. To their consternation, no expense seemed too small to escape his notice; each employee received critical commentaries on expenditures in the form of long written complaints from Aitken.[44] Even the RSC's accountant, who supplied Aitken with the ammunition for most of his letters, was not exempt: 'Referring to Halifax Expenses for ... August,' wrote Aitken, 'I note that Postage amounted to $35! Is not this figure excessive? I note that Exchange amounted to $37.47 which seems to be excessive. The Telegraph accounts amounted to $33.38; were all personal telegrams paid for by the individuals, or at least charged to their accounts?'[45]

As manager of the Saint John office, Horace Porter was required to send regular reports to Aitken, who then castigated him for his 'extravagant' use of office stationery: 'I note that your correspondence to me is written on our letter paper, and that instead of using a following sheet you use a second sheet with our heading engraved thereon. We supply our offices with cheaper quality of paper for Inter-Office correspondence, and I have to request that you use paper of this description in addressing me.'[46] Nesbitt, in particular, was reproached for his spendthrift ways. His Montreal office had cost the RSC exactly $2,555.21 in its first six months of operation. According to Aitken, this was 'at least $1000 in excess of the cost of conducting our St. John office,' and he told Nesbitt that he expected a 'smaller expenditure for the balance of this year.'[47] 'I note,' Aitken continued, 'that you paid the Sherbrooke "Record" $12.60 for advertising. Do you consider it advisable to continue this payment? Are you securing any business from Sherbrooke?'[48] Some of Nesbitt's expenses were unavoidable if he was successfully to open up the central-Canadian market to the RSC's new Camaguey and Porto Rico issues, yet Aitken continued to press him to keep his expenses down.

The financial constraints on the RSC also meant that further expansion into the British market would have to be done on a shoestring. Aitken devised a private joint venture that would not draw on the limited capital and human resources of the RSC. His plan was to select an individual not employed by the RSC who would sail to Britain and attempt to interest brokers in various RSC securities, especially the new utility issues. Aitken would join his partner a few weeks later, and the two would canvass houses in London, Birmingham, Manchester, Edinburgh, and Glasgow. Together, they would personally bear all expenses and share in all profits.[49]

Aitken's partner was James Harding, a long-established wholesale merchant in Saint John, who often underwrote and sold securities on the side. In the past, Aitken had occasionally sold him small lots of securities which his own salesman had been unable to retail. Harding was considerably older than the other RSC salesmen. This was a disadvantage in Canada, where investors were more forgiving of the pushiness of young men, but Aitken believed that it could be an advantage in Britain, where brokers and jobbers were less receptive to brash young salesmen and more respectful of age and experience. This venture would be the first step towards creating a potentially limitless market for RSC securities, as well as a permanent office in Britain: 'I cannot too highly impress upon you,' Aitken explained to Harding, 'the desirability which I think exists for establishing a business in England: I think we will work out together pretty well, and in that event, I believe an office in London or elsewhere is going to be a very valuable property.'[50]

On his arrival in London in September 1906, Harding discovered that no broker was willing to discuss the Camaguey issue. A bloody insurrection against the American-supported government had broken out in

Cuba just weeks beforehand, and as the rebels took control of much of the island, British investors began to recoil from the prospect of any Cuban speculation. Harding tried to downplay the Cuban revolt, but the British brokers and their clients had read about the success the rebels were enjoying and had concluded that Cuban investments were now unsafe. Harding was accordingly forced to concentrate his efforts on the Porto Rico Railways issue.[51] He started with Foster and Braithwaite, one of the largest and longest-established houses in the City. He managed to procure an interview with one of the firm's senior brokers, but while Braithwaite politely acknowledged that everything 'appeared all right' in the prospectus, the firm refused the business on the grounds that the British market was not buoyant enough just then to introduce a new utility issue.[52]

However, Braithwaite did give Harding a letter of introduction to W.M. MacLeod of Fielding & MacLeod, another well-respected brokerage house in the City. When Harding arrived with his Porto Rico prospectus, MacLeod took a copy after a brief interview, but a few days later he returned the prospectus, citing 'too much business' as his reason for refusing to take the issue.[53] Undeterred, Harding continued to knock on doors, but with no better result; and although he had letters of introduction to the most important firms in Glasgow, including William Jacks & Co. and Fergusson, Guthrie & Co., his trip to Scotland turned out to be equally fruitless.

'It is most infernally discouraging,' Harding wrote to Aitken, 'when you think you have got things to entice everybody, to find such a lack of interest.' The British financial community was close-knit – 'clubby,' in Harding's words – and he soon realized that the more brokers he called on, the more difficult it would become to place the RSC issues: 'One difficulty is that in London, you cannot approach two Brokers at the same time. You would hardly conceive that it would be possible, but if you did so it would be well known in a very short time, and both would turn you down very quickly. Then again, to have one Broker place a thing before some Clients and then afterwards someone else to try it, they say 'Oh! that is on the Market. Other Brokers have had this before,' which rather gives it a black eye.'[54]

In addition, the London and Glasgow houses felt that partial issues were not sufficiently profitable to bother with. Aitken had earmarked $100,000 of the Porto Rico bond issue for the London market, but Harding judged that $500,000 was the minimum size needed to interest the London brokers. Moreover, they preferred entire issues with a value in excess of $1 million.[55] Harding nevertheless stayed on in the hope that things would improve after Aitken joined him. He found that some of the British brokers, never having heard of the RSC, had expressed a desire to meet the RSC's managing director. In such cases, only Aitken himself could convince the brokers of the investment quality of the issues, a decisive factor in a society in which investors almost automatically accepted the recommendations of their brokers – unlike their counterparts in the United States and Canada.

Aitken was about to sail for England in late September when he was suddenly hospitalized.[56] It turned out to be an attack of appendicitis. He had been working day and night since John F. Stairs's death two years earlier, and his health was visibly deteriorating. The previous summer he had been bedridden for weeks with a painful stomach and bowel condition.[57] This had been followed weeks later by insomnia and heart pains, confining him to bed once again.[58] Aitken had begun to believe he was suffering from heart disease, but Dr Curry, his physician in Halifax, argued that his condition was 'wholly brought about by overwork and hallucinations' caused by 'too great business strain' following Stairs's funeral.[59] Aitken had become a hypochondriac. Nonetheless, as everyone around him observed, the immense stress caused by his frantic pace was having a deleterious impact on his physical health. Gerald Farrell spoke for many in the RSC when he wrote, 'Although it seems unkind to say so, I was very glad that you had this attack of Appendicitis, as you certainly were not well and the fact of your having an operation would give the doctors a chance to discover what was the matter, and probably would frighten you sufficiently to make you live a little more regular life in the future than you have done in the past.'[60]

Aitken cancelled his trip to Britain, and he remained sick for the rest of the autumn. Meanwhile, although Harding could not place any portion of the first Porto Rico bond issue in Britain, the RSC was able to sell the remaining bonds (now accompanied by a 50 per cent stock bonus) to Canadian investors. Aitken, against his doctor's orders, was dictating business correspondence from his hospital bed, and he suggested in one such letter that Harding reduce his prices and try to push Trinidad Electric among the 'West India crowd' in London.[61] He then wrote to Kitcat, Mortimer & Aitken of Threadneedle Street in the City, enclosing a Porto Rico prospectus – but with no better response than Harding had received when calling in person.[62] To save on expenses, Harding closed up the small office he had used as his base of operations since his arrival in England, but he continued to knock on doors.

Not until three months later did he give up completely and return to Canada.

Harding and Aitken had lost about $3,500 in the venture, but Aitken had obtained some very valuable information concerning the British capital market and was not nearly as disappointed as Harding.[63] In fact, even before Harding's return to Canada, Aitken had decided that the second Porto Rico flotation, slated for May 1907, would be made primarily in Britain, either by himself or by Nesbitt.[64] Almost $1 million of securities needed to be sold, an amount that was far too large for the Canadian market, particularly so soon after the first Porto Rico issue.[65] He instructed one of his syndicate partners, A.E. Ames of Toronto, to prepare an experimental prospectus, drafted 'from the English point of view ... erring, if at all, on the side of fullness' and with sterling currency conversions 're-cast to comply with English requirements.'[66] He sent a draft of the 'English' Porto Rico prospectus to E. Mackay Edgar, a Montreal broker with close connections to the London merchant bank of Sperling & Co., to whom Edgar was to forward the prospectus.[67] Finally, in May 1907, Aitken decided that he would send Nesbitt to London to place the Porto Rico securities if it turned out that Sperling & Co. would not take the complete issue. While in England, Nesbitt could also sell Camaguey, Trinidad, Scotia, and other RSC securities.[68]

Nesbitt spent the next ten months in Britain and on the Continent trying to create a market for Porto Rico, Camaguey, and other RSC issues. Displaying tremendous energy, he successfully obtained interviews with some of the largest investment banking firms in Britain, including Chaplin, Milne & Co., C.J. Hambro & Son, and Arburthnot Latham, as well as the smaller London houses specializing in Canadian issues, such as Robert Fleming & Co., Dunn, Fischer & Co., and Sperling & Co. Following the trail of another young salesman who had recently sold $600,000 of utility bonds to various Swiss banks for Dunn, Fischer & Co., Nesbitt travelled to Geneva and Zurich.[69] He also tried to sell his Porto Rico bonds to the Banque Centrale Anversoise in Belgium and the Deutsche Bank in Germany.

Nesbitt failed in all these attempts, but on his return to London he received a few promising inquiries, and by the end of 1907 he was selling substantial blocks of Royal Securities' bonds and shares. The timing could not have been better: the North American capital market had shut down completely in October 1907 as a major financial panic swept the United States, causing collateral damage to the Canadian capital market in the process.[70] The British market now became essential to the RSC's survival. Porto Rico Railways could not raise a dime in North America after mid-October, so Aitken did whatever he could to accommodate the needs of his new British investors, including arranging dividend payments through a London-based bank and issuing regular reports on the company's performance.[71]

By this time, Aitken had transferred his permanent residence from Halifax to Montreal, the financial and industrial hub of Canada. The move was probably inevitable, but the timing was determined by two factors. In the early spring of 1907, he had acquired control of the Montreal Trust and Deposit Company, and his position as general manager and vice-president required that he reside in Montreal. At the same time, he created for the RSC a purchasing and engineering department (soon to be known as the Montreal Engineering Company), which he had decided would be managed out of the Montreal rather than Halifax office. Both moves were part of Aitken's plan to break away from the control of his more conservative Halifax associates, allowing him to become Canada's premier investment banker.

5

The Montreal Engineering Company

Where were the office towers of top and middle managers, the vast engineering and research departments, the ships steaming down the St. Lawrence laden with turbines, generators, telecommunication equipment, and motors? No organic connection was forged between the nominal home of the utilities and their host countries. Canada was not the primary source of equipment, management, or engineering services.

Christopher Armstrong and H.V. Nelles, 'Southern Exposure,' 1988[1]

The Royal Securities Corporation was already moving beyond the traditional functions of an investment bank when in 1907 it launched the Montreal Engineering Company, thereby providing its family of utilities with a competitive edge through systematized cost accounting as well as purchasing, construction, and engineering advisory services. The first company of its type in Canada, Montreal Engineering was to underpin Royal Securities' resurgence under Walton Killam in the years following the First World War, a resurgence that culminated in the creation of the International Power Company in 1926, a holding company that consolidated the RSC's ownership of utility companies throughout the Americas, including those controlled or created by Aitken before the war.[2]

Montreal Engineering was a milestone in Canadian business development. It represented the first attempt by a Canadian utility entrepreneur to overcome the problems experienced by enterprises whose financial and legal head offices were geographically detached from their operating bodies. Montreal Engineering provided the RSC utilities with a head office that could contribute operational skills and engineering knowledge. It systematically collected information from the far-flung utilities so that their diverse experiences could be accumulated and general lessons learned and used as a basis for suggesting operational changes. Moreover, Montreal Engineering paid a liberal fee for its services, thus directly benefiting Max Aitken and, later, Walton Killam.[3]

Before the creation of Montreal Engineering, the RSC's utilities were little more than free-standing companies – firms whose operations were entirely located abroad, even though their head offices were in Canada. Mira Wilkins, the business historian who first propounded the concept, suggests that the free-standing company be thought of as a sub-category of multinational enterprise because of its rather particular attributes.[4] Unlike 'typical' multinationals, free-standing companies did not grow organically from a well-established domestic base; they were created solely in order to operate in host nations, and control was exercised by a board of directors resident in the home country.

Since the company was necessarily managed at the locus of its operations, with little or no management function required in the home country, the head offices of free-standing companies were skeletal affairs compared with the enormous head offices of more typical multinational enterprises. The head offices of English free-standing companies were often 'little more than a brass nameplate in the City.'[5] Similarly, the head offices of Canadian utility free-standing companies were located in law offices or bond houses in Montreal, Toronto, or Halifax. For example, the head office of Mexican Light and Power, Mexican Tramways, Barcelona Traction, and Brazilian Traction was a room in the Toronto law firm of Blake Cassels.[6] Before the creation of Montreal Engineering, the RSC's Halifax office doubled as the financial and legal headquarters of Aitken's utilities.[7]

Wilkins argues that the absence of a real head office produced the most prominent characteristic of free-standing companies – their propensity to fail. She suggests that such firms could not effectively transfer hard-won experience from their operations in host countries to their head offices at home and thus make consistently sound decisions over time.[8] D.G. Paterson, in his study of early British direct investment in Canada, found that the geographical separation between the legal-financial process and the administrative-operational aspects, combined with the firm's (defined as the shareholders, particularly their representatives on the board of directors) lack of knowledge of local conditions, resulted in relatively poor decision making and the consequent failure of many of the British free-standing companies operating in Canada.[9]

In their study of Canadian-controlled foreign utility enterprises, Christopher Armstrong and H.V. Nelles maintain that the Canadian free-standing utility enterprises operating in Latin America and the Caribbean lacked the head office support and strength of the American and European utility multinationals that emerged after the First World War. It was almost inevitable, therefore, that the Canadian free-standing utilities would lose ground to their more integrated multinational rivals, for instance, General Electric's utility holding company EBASCO (Electric Bond and Share Co.). EBASCO grew out of an electrical equipment manufacturing company and thus began life with a related affiliate that manufactured electrical equipment, thereby giving it an edge in providing managerial, engineering, and purchasing support to its family of operating utilities.[10] The Canadian utilities, in contrast, were essentially financial creations, their real horizons determined by the individual abilities of their small complement of engineers and managers in the host countries.[11]

From New York to Montreal

From the time that the RSC was organized, Aitken had received complaints from both Trinidad Electric's general manager and its accountant about the excessive price that Dr Pearson's New York partner, W.P. Plummer, was charging for operating equipment. As well as being the linchpin of Pearson's utility promotions throughout the world, Plummer acted as a utility equipment consultant and purchaser.[12] Through Pearson's influence, he played a key role as a middleman between the Canadian utility firms and major electrical equipment manufacturers such as Westinghouse and General Electric. Demerara Electric and Trinidad Electric placed the majority of their requests for new equipment through Plummer, as well as their requests for components to repair existing facilities. Plummer then placed the orders with the most appropriate and (presumably) lowest-cost manufacturer. Sometimes the decision to order or repair plant and equipment required engineering advice, in which case there was an additional fee to be paid for the Pearson organization's consulting services.[13]

These service and consulting fees were hidden in the equipment prices charged by Plummer, and Aitken suspected that the RSC utilities were being charged more than the services warranted. By 1906, moreover, complaints about equipment arriving late or damaged had begun to accumulate. As the RSC was operating four separate utilities in the Caribbean, Aitken decided that it was time to dispense with Plummer's middle-man services. At first, he thought it would be more cost-effective to have Trinidad's accountant, Fred Clarke, move to New York and set up a small office as the in-house purchasing agent for the RSC. W.B. Ross, the president of all four utilities, approved the scheme, admitting that he had 'never been satisfied with Plummer.'[14]

Just as quickly, however, Aitken changed his mind about locating in New York; instead, he decided, the new department would share office space with the RSC in Canada. Although New York was closer to the firms that manufactured electric utility equipment, Aitken wanted to forge a permanent connection between the RSC and the new purchasing arm that would eventually strengthen his utility empire as a whole. After all, the RSC was responsible for financing all the equipment purchased by the West Indian utilities, and if Aitken's organization could exert more control over costs, this would allow the RSC to forecast with greater precision the amount of funds that would need to be raised. For this purpose Aitken wanted an accountant, such as Clarke, who was experienced enough in the utility business to be able to place equipment orders at the lowest possible cost and make projections concerning future capital replacement.

To accomplish these tasks, however, Clarke would need privileged access to administrative, financial, and operating information from all four utility companies. Aitken knew exactly how to achieve this; he planned to have Clarke appointed secretary in all the utility companies.[15] Aitken said to Teele that once Clarke moved north, 'I shall place all matters of official correspondence between yourself and the Corporation in his hands; also all matters of ordering and keeping track of detail; also all matters of accounting re Expenses, etc., as that [sic] there will be a certainty of its being done thoroughly.'[16] From Trinidad, Clarke wrote to Aitken about this 'splendid plan' for an engineering and purchasing department within the RSC and said he felt that the experience Teele and he had 'found in the tropics' would be of 'great assistance' to the new organization.[17]

Although Aitken had cleared his idea with W.B. Ross, the titular president of Trinidad Electric, he removed Clarke from Trinidad Electric without conferring with any of the other Trinidad officers or members of the board of directors in Halifax – indeed, without even informing them. Not surprisingly, some of them objected. Col. Frederick Oxley, the fifty-three-year-old chartered accountant in Halifax who was the secretary of Trinidad Electric, complained to fellow board member Robert E. Harris about Aitken's precipitate action.[18] When the criticism finally reached Aitken's ears, he dispatched an unapologetic explanation to Harris:

I have heard of Mr. Oxley's complaint through another source, and understand the nature of this complaint to be to the effect that I am using the Trinidad Company for the purpose of building up other organizations. I want you to know that in Clarke's case I have simply offered better terms than Trinidad is paying.

Royal Securities Corporation interests rank before all other interests to me, and with my Directors' consent, I continue to pursue my reprehensible policy of taking suitable men from wherever I may find them, until the Corporation shall have a surplus of at least ten times its capital, when that time comes, I can afford to carry on the business in a manner which will suit the public as well as the Directors ...

Would it be asking too much of you to advise Mr. Oxley of my way of looking at this thing. I am sure he does not understand the situation.[19]

Harris had no intention of convincing Oxley of Aitken's point of view, since he himself felt that Aitken's action had lacked proper corporate authority. Moreover, he was aware that Aitken's plan for the RSC would eventually include engineering services to complement the purchasing department, and he immediately wrote back cautioning Aitken against trying to take Teele away from Trinidad Electric for this purpose.[20] Aitken had indeed earmarked Teele to be the new department's chief engineer, but in view of Harris's strenuous opposition he decided to come up with an alternative plan, which soon proved superior to the original. A few months earlier, when Roberto Betancourt's chief engineer, Carl Giles, had decided to leave the Camaguey Company, Aitken had immediately hired him. Giles had become increasingly fatigued with the tropics and yearned to move back north. After observing Giles's work in Cuba, Teele had advised Aitken that the American engineer was a 'particularly valuable man' and should be kept within the RSC organization if at all possible.[21] With Giles, Aitken now had a full-time engineer in his new department, and at the same time he had mollified Harris.

Aitken wanted the new department to perform four basic functions: Giles would provide engineering advice to all RSC utilities; Clarke would take care of all purchase orders, calling on Giles's expertise when necessary; Clarke would extend the managerial accounting system he had developed for Trinidad (and was now instituting for Demerara) to Camaguey, Porto Rico Railways, and all other utilities that came within the domain of the RSC; and both Giles and Clarke would provide regular and systematic financial auditing services for all the utility companies, including the auditing of accounts submitted by other construction contractors and subcontractors. After the department had succeeded in providing all of these services effectively, it could add utility construction to its list of services.

Without consulting his fellow RSC directors, Aitken decided that Clarke and Giles would operate out of RSC's Montreal branch office rather than the Halifax head office. The decision was sensible, since many of the RSC's new utility securities were now being sold in Montreal. Moreover, the office was located near the largest electrical equipment firms in Canada, including Canadian White Co. and Canadian Fairbanks of Montreal, Canadian General Electric of Hamilton, and Canadian Westinghouse of Toronto.[22] The arbitrary way in which the decision was made may simply have reflected Aitken's lack of concern for the sensibilities of his fellow RSC directors, including the RSC's president George Stairs and his fellow vice-president R.E. Harris. More likely, however, his behaviour was purposely calculated to irritate both men, particularly Harris, enough to force a parting of the ways.

Struggling with the Halifax Directors

Giles's first job was to act as consulting engineer for a very small power and lighting company which the RSC had recently refurbished in Dartmouth, Nova Scotia. Giles carefully inspected the new plant, suggesting ways to lower operating costs over the long term. Both Aitken and the general manager of the Dartmouth Electric Company immediately accepted Giles's counsel on how the company could best protect itself when purchasing an expensive new turbine engine manufactured by the Canadian Fairbanks Company. Aitken then accompanied Giles to the Fairbanks plant to see whether the manufacturer would let Giles inspect the engine at the plant before shipment to Dartmouth. The president of Canadian Fairbanks was taken aback by the request but agreed when told that he would receive payment in full immediately following the inspection.

The turbine purchase completed, Aitken suggested an even closer collaboration between the RSC's purchasing and engineering department and Dartmouth Electric. He recommended that Dartmouth Electric's engineer should 'acquaint Mr. Giles with the whole situation in Dartmouth, so that he will always be able to call upon Mr. Giles in a consulting capacity.' He advised Giles to write a thorough report on the 'general physical condition of the Dartmouth plant, with recommendations for extensions and improvements,' a copy to be given to the general manager of Dartmouth Electric and the original to be filed with Royal Securities.[23]

Meanwhile, initial results from the purchasing department appeared good. Since the RSC was well known and had an established credit rating, equipment manufacturers preferred to deal with it rather than with the individual utility companies.[24] By May 1907, Aitken was confident enough to end the six-year relationship with W.P. Plummer, who received the terse notification that all purchasing for RSC's utilities would henceforth 'be done by the Royal Securities Corporation, Engineering Department.'[25] By this time, Clarke had systematized the books of all the RSC utilities and was in the process of preparing monthly statements, which would soon be used, albeit quite selectively, by Aitken in his bond prospectuses.

Instrumental in this scheme was Clarke's access to all company information, and Aitken ensured that Clarke was made secretary of the Camaguey and Porto Rico companies so that he could properly fulfil his role relative to the engineering department. The Trinidad and Demerara companies were a different matter. Colonel Frederick Oxley was secretary of both companies, and he had no intention of resigning his post and giving up the annual stipends that went with the positions. Aitken wanted to replace him at all costs, however, and began to use the purchasing and engineering department's location in Montreal as his key argument for ousting Oxley, who spent almost all his time in Halifax.

The battle lines were drawn. Fred Teele and W.B. Ross, complemented by the Demerara shareholders resident in Montreal, including Sir William Van Horne, Edward Clouston, and George Drummond, supported Aitken's proposal.[26] On the other hand, Oxley knew that he could rely on Robert Harris and George Stairs to defend his position. By now, Harris and Stairs knew that their earlier suspicions were correct – namely, that Aitken, through the purchasing and engineering department, was in the process of gradually transferring RSC's head office from Halifax to Montreal. If he succeeded, it would be only a matter of time before most or even all of the RSC's utilities would also move their head offices from Halifax to Montreal.[27]

Harris in particular was infuriated when Aitken put forward a proposal to form an executive committee to permit more rapid decision making by the RSC board. Harris and Cahan (who was in Mexico almost all the time anyway) were the only two directors to be excluded from the RSC's executive committee.[28] Since Harris's profitable law firm and most of his business interests were rooted in Halifax or the surrounding area, he had no intention of leaving. At the same time, these interests had become increasingly tied to the RSC and its various spinoffs, and he feared the impact on his own interests if the RSC's centre of gravity shifted to central Canada. For Harris, therefore, defending Colonel Oxley was an essential issue in the power struggle between himself and Aitken.

By the summer of 1907, Aitken had intensified his campaign to replace Oxley with Clarke. He threatened that in his role as managing director of the RSC, he would refuse to raise further money for the utilities unless Harris acceded to his wishes. In 'view of the amount of money' already invested in Demerara Electric, plus the fact that he was about to raise another $25,000 for the purchase of a new turbine, Aitken argued that the RSC was 'entitled to the Secretaryship of the Demerara Company in our Engineering Organization at Montreal.' Moreover:

It would be a great convenience that the Secretaryship should be here if the work is to be done without cross purposes between here [Montreal] and Halifax and Demerara [British Guiana]. Also you understand of course that our Engineering Organization here, headed by Mr. Giles, is at the present time carrying out the plans and specifications in connection with the Turbine without any charge to the Demerara Company.

I do not like to do anything to take the Secretaryship away from Mr. Oxley, but feel that it is in the interests of the operation of the Demerara plant and also that if we put up the additional money we are entitled to the remuneration.[29]

But Harris could not understand why it was necessary to put up $25,000 more for the new turbine for Demerara. In his opinion, enough money had been raised out of the bond issue to cover the expenditure, though Aitken never bothered to tell him anything, he said. Harris refused to make any decision on the locus of head office until he had the information he said he deserved as a company director. Complaining that it was 'unsatisfactory discussing such matters' by letter, he demanded that Aitken come to Halifax and discuss the issues with the board. 'If the management is to go to Montreal,' he added, 'it will of course mean that the Directors here [in Halifax] must resign.'[30]

Aitken refused to deal with the main points raised by Harris. Instead, he suggested that Harris might be able to remain on the board even if management was 'removed to Montreal.'[31] Harris rejected Aitken's logic, but his response was guarded since he was unsure of the position of his fellow Demerara directors in Halifax. While George Stairs professed support for Harris's position that the secretaryship should remain in Halifax, he had an annoying habit of avoiding confrontation by agreeing with everyone when he was in their presence. More disturbing was the news that W.B. Ross, David MacKeen, and other Halifax directors were openly supporting Aitken's position.[32]

Harris was correct in one very important respect, namely, that there was no need to raise new capital for the turbine. Aitken was using a fabricated cash shortage as a pretext to place the secretaryship in Clarke's hands. Moreover, he had purposely withheld information concerning Demerara's reconstruction costs from Oxley and the Halifax directors of Demerara. From the beginning, Aitken had received financial information on Demerara's reconstruction directly from Teele. After Aitken had reviewed the information and made his comments, Teele sent an appropriately optimistic or pessimistic report to Oxley.[33] So even though Harris thought that there was plenty of money left from the bond issue to finance the turbine purchase, he was unable to confirm it because he was being kept in the dark about the company's finances. As officers and directors of Demerara, Oxley and Harris should have been entitled to the financial data necessary to calculate the amount of cash still available for the turbine, and Harris had every right to block Clarke's appointment until he had that information. Nonetheless, Aitken could sense that Harris's position was weak, and he pushed his case by sending a letter to Harris with a copy to George Stairs and W.B. Ross:

I know that the best interests of the Demerara Company are served by having the Secretary's office in Montreal and by carefully watching every detail, which is now being done by the most efficient Engineering Organization which we have established. Mr MacKeen recognizes this, as also does Mr. [W.B.] Ross. You state that Mr. Stairs has the same view of the matter as yourself, but I am inclined to think that Mr. Stairs believes in Montreal as a Head Office of the Demerara Company.[34]

Within months, Demerara's head office was moved to St James Street in Montreal and Fred Clarke replaced Colonel Oxley as secretary. Harris had lost the battle – but not the war. He shifted his ground and redoubled his efforts to keep Trinidad Electric in Halifax and within the control of the Halifax directors. In this skirmish he was partially successful; Trinidad's head office stayed in Halifax and Oxley remained its secretary.[35] However, Aitken continued to exercise some control through the purchasing and engineering services which he delivered to Trinidad from his new base in Montreal. Harris and Oxley fought against this control but were unable to break it until 1910, when Aitken left Canada for England.[36]

Consolidating Control

In the autumn of 1907, Aitken formally incorporated the Montreal Engineering Company.[37] Although no longer a department of the RSC, Montreal Engineering remained the operational arm of the corporation's utility ventures. Through Fred Clarke, all operating and financial information concerning Demerara Electric, Camaguey, and Porto Rico Railways was forwarded directly to Montreal Engineering.[38] This information was used, first and foremost, to determine the performance of the various companies and to make projections concerning future revenues and costs. Financial data that were used to generate the utilities' annual reports were also employed in drafting Royal Securities' tombstones and circulars advertising the sale of securities. Finally, Aitken used his unrestricted access to this wealth of accounting information to exercise control over the enterprises themselves by releasing only what he wanted directors and shareholders to know at any given time.

Never needing to lie overtly about the figures, Aitken could create optimistic or pessimistic reports simply by a selective use of the available data.[39] This skill, so well honed through Montreal Engineering, was to be employed by him in the service of war propaganda during the First World War, initially in his capacity as Canada's chief representative at the front and later as Britain's minister of information. From the experience he gained in advertising and promoting his business ventures, Aitken would become the twentieth's century's first chief of mass propaganda.[40]

Meanwhile, in 1907, the head offices of the Camaguey and Demerara companies, as well as their related holding and subsidiary companies, were formally transferred to Montreal, where they joined Porto Rico Railways.[41] W.B. Ross and Aitken turned over to the company all the fees they received as officers and directors in the utility companies 'under the management of Montreal Engineering,' and in return they were paid a salary of $300 per month by Montreal Engineering for 'their services as Officers of the various Electric Companies.'[42] The operational headquarters of the RSC utilities were instructed to forward copies of all interoffice correspondence direct to Montreal Engineering.[43] In the special case of Trinidad Electric, Clarke had some initial difficulties obtaining information, but these were soon surmounted; in October 1907 W.B. Ross, in his capacity as president of the company, instructed his Trinidad staff to for-

TABLE 5.1 Comparison of RSC utility companies, 1909 (Cdn $000)

	Trinidad Electric est. 1901	Camaguey Company est. 1906	Demerara Electric est. 1899	Porto Rico Railways est. 1906
Assets	2,076	1,383	1,061	6,651
Paid-up capital	1,164	700	425	3,500
Bonds issued	720	600	530	2,942
Gross earnings	209	134	135	409
Operating expenses	93	75	73	215
Per cent of expenses to earnings	43%	56%	54%	53%
Bond interest	36	30	33	148
Net earnings	80	58	23	194
Stock dividends	44	28	–	3

Source: *Annual Financial Review* (Canadian), 10 (Apr. 1910), 478–81, 530–2, 550–1, 566–7

ward copies of all interoffice correspondence to Montreal Engineering.[44] Nonetheless, Trinidad remained the odd man out, and decision making remained divided between Halifax and Montreal as well as between Canada and Trinidad. Monitored by Montreal Engineering, the Halifax directors continued to make all the key decisions, while the management in Trinidad used this divided authority to retain greater managerial autonomy. The situation continued for years, and Trinidad Electric was one of the few Canadian utility companies operating abroad that managed to escape 'the net of the holding company,' including Walton Killam's own International Power Company, during the 1920s.[45]

Carl Giles and Fred Clarke, as president and secretary, respectively, of Montreal Engineering, concentrated wholeheartedly on building up the company which they began to regard as their own, despite Aitken's control and ownership. At first, they worked closely with another Montreal Engineering employee – Traven Aitken, the boss's brother. A few years older than Max, Traven had been practising law in Newcastle but had grown bored with being a small-town lawyer.[46] Aitken offered him the more exciting prospect of investigating and preparing utility franchise agreements throughout Canada and the West Indies. The idea was fine – Montreal Engineering could have used a consulting lawyer to supplement its engineering and accounting services – but Traven was too struck with wanderlust to be of much use to Montreal Engineering. After putting up with long absences, including one trip to check out a gold-mining proposition in the United States, Aitken asked Traven to 'take more interest in the business affairs of the Corporation' and hoped that he 'would come to a frame of mind where the Corporation's interests predominate.'[47]

Despite Max's exhortations, Traven refused to change his ways, and Aitken eased his brother out of Montreal Engineering within two years.[48] Although Aitken was always susceptible to appeals for money by family, friends, old acquaintances, and even strangers who had known his parents, he had much more difficulty with exercising nepotism in his own business empire. While he was willing to give family members a job, he was not prepared to allow anyone, even his brother, to tear down what he had built up. Traven was a liability. Aitken was prepared to indulge Traven in his adventures by providing money that he knew would be squandered, but he was not prepared to allow him to cause harm to Montreal Engineering, and he criticized him only slightly less than nonrelatives for his peccadilloes on the job. The same applied to his wife's younger brother Victor Drury, whom he hired a few years later. Although Drury remained with the RSC for years, eventually rising to the position of vice-president, he did so on the basis of his business abilities and willingness to work extremely hard rather than because of his familial connection to Aitken.

While Montreal Engineering's services were generally considered superior by the management of the Caribbean utilities, the company did receive criticism from one source: Trinidad Electric. Since Teele was absent from Trinidad for long periods, working in Cuba and British Guiana, the directors appointed S.D. Harding as the new acting general manager early in 1907. Both Harding and Colonel Oxley led a chorus of complaints against Montreal Engineering for late deliveries of equipment. In Aitken's opinion, both Harding and Oxley were 'considerably prejudiced against this purchasing from Montreal,' and he wrote to Trinidad asking Harding to provide Montreal Engineering with more constructive criticism:[49]

I have inquired of Mr. Giles concerning the purchases, and he has satisfied me that difficulties in the future will be minimized.

I note that it is your opinion that the Purchasing Office will not be successful in Montreal. If such proves to be the case, said office will be transferred to New York. At present we find it satisfactory in Montreal.

I am of the opinion that the difficulties can be minimized if all the persons interested work together for the benefit of the companies with which they are concerned and for the benefit of the Purchasing Agent. I am perfectly satisfied with the prices which are being secured, and will welcome criticism from you and other Managers.[50]

By early 1908, Giles and Teele had reduced the shipping time from Canada to Trinidad. Moreover, compared with what Dr Pearson's organization charged, they had brought down the cost of most of the equipment and other accoutrements shipped from North America to the tropics.[51] To demonstrate this, Giles distributed a list illustrating the difference between prices being paid for material by Montreal Engineering and those that had been paid by W.P. Plummer the previous year on behalf of Trinidad Electric. Giles pointed out that while 'there had been a general advance in prices during the past year,' Montreal Engineering's prices on average were 'considerably less' than Plummer's.[52]

Keeping Down Construction Costs

From 1907 until the end of 1908, the most valuable service of Montreal Engineering to the RSC and Aitken may have been keeping construction costs in Puerto Rico under control. Aitken's relationship with J.G. White & Co., the construction contractors-cum-partners in the Puerto Rican venture, had started off on a promising note. When Aitken had first considered the Porto Rico project in 1906, he knew that J.G. White & Co. was one of the most respected traction engineering and construction firms in the world. 'One of the very best features' of the Porto Rico project, he boasted, was that the project was prepared and all costs 'estimated by that firm.'[53] By January 1907, however, the relationship had become strained, for Aitken had discovered that J.G. White & Co. had spent about $500,000 more than its original estimate of $450,000 on the San Juan–Caguas interurban railway construction. Since the construction contracts between the RSC and J.G. White & Co. were on a cost-plus basis, this meant that the RSC was stuck with paying for all cost overruns, and on this occasion it did so in part by selling an additional $300,000 of bonds.[54]

Despite warnings from Aitken, construction costs continued to rise above estimates until finally, in April 1907, he threatened to resign as managing director of Porto Rico Railways unless the construction contracts permitting cost overruns between the RSC and J.G. White & Co. were changed. Not willing to test whether Aitken was bluffing, J.G. White agreed to renegotiate the original conditions of the contracts. Under the new terms, J.G. White & Co. was obliged to complete the construction of

TABLE 5.2 Comparison of Montreal Engineering's new prices with W.P. Plummer's old prices: Equipment for Trinidad Electric, 1907–8

Utility equipment item	Old price	New price
Cleats, GE[a] or WE[b]	$12.75	$11.50
Cutouts, WE ea.	0.098	0.093
Cutouts, GE ea.	0.12	0.114
Armature repairs, ea.	49.50	52.00
Fans, 'Shedd' oscillating, ea.	11.25	11.25
Globes, opal inner, doz.	1.32	1.13
Globes, clear outer, doz.	4.75	4.50
Boiler tubes, 4″, per ft.	0.31	0.286
Meters, WE 5 a.	9.00	9.14
Meters, WE 10 a.	9.75	10.24
Lamp shades, 7 in., doz.	1.00	0.50
Sal ammoniac, per charge	0.04	0.03
Switches, H. & H.	0.19	0.161
Controller segments, GE, C.	10.70	10.14
Key sockets, C.	12.00	11.88
Screws, $2\frac{1}{2}''$	0.272	0.19
Screws, 2″	0.257	0.18
Screws, $1\frac{1}{2}''$	0.18	0.13
Tape, Manson, 1 lb.	0.50	0.55
Waste, no. 1 white, 1 lb.	0.085	0.08
Wire, Phillips no. 8	19.50	16.55
Wire, Phillips no. 10	20.50	17.55
Wire, Phillips no. 14	21.50	19.55
Wipers, 13″ × 15″ silk, gr.	6.50	–
Wipers, 15″ × 15″ silk, gr.	–	5.85

Source: Beaverbrook Papers, House of Lords Record Office, A/96, Carl C. Giles to Max Aitken, 3 Apr. 1908
[a] GE refers to products manufactured by the General Electric Company.
[b] WE refers to products manufactured by the Westinghouse Company.

the interurban railway before the end of the year and to do so 'without unnecessary cost' or 'be put off the job.'

Aitken had taken the precaution of having one of his own lawyers, W.N. Tilley, help him prepare a contract that not only protected Porto Rico Railways (and thus the RSC) but also created a legal minefield for J.G. White & Co. A member of the original underwriting syndicate put together by Aitken and A.E. Ames, Tilley was a powerful Toronto lawyer in the firm of Thomson, Tilley and Johnston. Since he and his senior law partners had a large financial stake in the future profitability of Porto Rico Railways, he was suitably motivated to help Aitken snare J.G. White &

Co. in an intricate legal web. The renegotiation took several days, Aitken threatening to walk out on a number of occasions if J.G. White & Co. did not sign the exact text prepared by himself and Tilley. In the end, the New York firm agreed that its construction expenses could 'not exceed $80,000 [on the interurban railway] and any penalty from failure to complete by December 31st [1907], must be borne by them.'[55]

Unfortunately for Aitken and his associates, the renegotiated contract did not improve J.G. White & Co.'s performance.[56] Aitken ordered that J.G. White & Co.'s requisitions for construction supplies as well as disbursements be carefully monitored by Montreal Engineering.[57] Clarke, as secretary of Porto Rico Railways, had automatic access to all the information necessary to audit J.G. White & Co.'s performance on behalf of Montreal Engineering, and the RSC and Aitken began to use Montreal Engineering's analysis as ammunition against J.G. White & Co. White himself became so exasperated with Aitken's accusations and what he considered Aitken's unfair use of the renegotiated contract against his engineering firm that he asked for another long meeting in New York in order to 'go over with you all points of difference and endeavor to clear up and eliminate all differences which have caused friction or annoyance' in the relationship. White went on to say:

While I understand that an individual or a company may, temporarily, gain by resorting to unfair technicalities, yet, in the long run, I believe that such business methods do not result to the permanent advantage of those employing them. These methods necessarily result in loss of friends and unwillingness on the part of those who at all value their own peace of mind to do business with the people resorting to such methods, and, in the long run, an amount of friction, expenditure of time and exhaustion of nervous energy out of all proportion to the temporary advantages gained.

When we first discussed with you the Porto Rican situation and other business, both Mr. Gossler and myself believed that it would be possible for you and ourselves to co-operate harmoniously along reasonable and equitable lines and, during a period of years, to do a considerable amount of business which would be of mutual advantage to yourself and friends and to our company. For many months past there has been an amount of friction which seems to us to have been quite unnecessary.[58]

Aitken would have none of it. He pointed out that Giles and Teele had monitored too many accounts submitted by J.G. White & Co. that were 'not properly chargeable to the Porto Rico Railways Co.' and they had too much evidence of J.G. White & Co.'s 'incompetence' and 'inefficiency' in construction.[59] Besides, construction costs had now so far surpassed the original estimates that unless the RSC raised a further $500,000, construction would have to be stopped immediately. Aitken adamantly insisted that he had not 'resorted to unfair technicalities.' J.G. White & Co. had so consistently exceeded its own estimates by such enormous margins that, in his opinion, there was nothing left but for the firm to admit its bad faith. When White refused to acknowledge this fact, Aitken surprised everyone by tendering to him his letter of resignation as vice-president and managing director of Porto Rico Railways. At the end of the letter, he added one rather premeditated balm: 'In washing my hands of the Porto Rico situation, I can only say that, although I have been the guardian of many dollars spent on account of construction, and although I have had to deal harshly and sometimes violently with contractors here and there, I have never had so hard a task on account of my personal friendship for you.'[60]

J.G. White, who was also a shareholder in Porto Rico Railways by virtue of his firm's participation in the promotional syndicate, would have welcomed Aitken's departure, but Aitken's Canadian associates were furious and demanded that he retract his resignation. W.B. Ross wrote:

With regard to your resignation as Vice-President of the Porto Rico Railways Company, while this may seem to you a very easy way out of the situation, I consider it unfair to your associates and unfair to yourself. It would be time enough to allow differences of opinion between yourself and the Whites ... to cause your present action after their contentions were sustained by the Board and yours overruled. If the Board sustains you in your management and contentions I should say that it would be rather a strange procedure for you to resign. No man can gain in the long run by quietly and willingly withdrawing from a position which he believes has been taken in the best interest of all concerned.

I had hoped that after our last trip to New York that things would run smoothly, and that you, knowing you had the confidence of the Canadian interests, would overlook in a measure all the criticisms of the New York people.

All I have to say in conclusion is that as far as the Canadian interests are concerned the Porto Rico proposition is yours. You conceived it; you promoted it and up to date you have financed it, and whether you make a dollar out of it or not, having put your hand to the plough, I cannot see how in justice to yourself you dare turn back.[61]

Aitken accordingly withdrew his resignation, but he did so on the condition that J.G. White & Co. accept yet another renegotiation of the construction contracts in New York.[62] This time Giles was present and acted as Aitken's key witness in pointing out J.G. White & Co.'s failings.[63] At the end of the two-day session, each side agreed to appoint an engineer and to delegate these two experts to argue over the details. If the engineers found themselves deadlocked over any issue, they were to seek final resolution from an arbitrator who was satisfactory to both sides. Naturally, Aitken arranged for Giles to be appointed the Canadian representative.[64]

At the same time, Aitken increased Montreal Engineering's surveillance of J.G. White & Co. as it began construction of the Comerio Falls hydroelectric project. Giles carefully checked the Comerio's engineering plans drafted by J.G. White & Co., as well as equipment being ordered for the project.[65] Then, in October 1907, Aitken abruptly dropped everything concerning the dispute with J.G. White & Co. into the lap of his Montreal Engineering Company staff. After months of being the chief protagonist in the battle, he had found that a much more pressing problem demanded his attention. A financial panic was sweeping Wall Street. With the panic spreading to Canada, Aitken's securities corporation and his trust company were both directly threatened.

6

The Takeover and Transformation of Montreal Trust

It is not impossible that the American type of trust company may [yet] find a foot hold in Canada.

Ernest Heaton, 'The Trust Company Idea,' 1904

I think Trust Companies in Canada are doing about as impecunious and uninteresting a class of business as can possibly be transacted, and [they] will never improve their class of business, because the Banks will not allow them.

Max Aitken replying to request by U.S. trade journal 'Trust Companies' to write an article on trust company development in Canada, 10 November 1909

Max Aitken's meteoric rise as a trust company manager in five short years reveals the extent to which he was a financial innovator. In 1905 he had started the Commercial Trust Company of Halifax. By 1907 he had acquired a controlling interest in the moribund Montreal Trust and Deposit Company, and within months he turned it into one of the most aggressive financial 'department stores' in the country. He risked incurring the wrath of the powerful chartered banks by taking deposits and then using these funds to offer call loans, which customers, particularly stockbrokers, preferred to the time loans offered by the banks. Soon he was acquiring funds in the United States as well as Canada and relending the money as call loans to brokers in Montreal and New York. Montreal Trust also gave the RSC special access to funds that provided Aitken with bridge financing for security flotations.

As Montreal Trust became more involved in commercial and investment banking, it also became more vulnerable to the business cycle. Seven months after Aitken took it over, a financial panic swept the United States, bringing down numerous banks and trust companies in its wake. The Panic of 1907 reverberated in Canada by pushing down share prices, squeezing liquidity out of the capital market, and producing an industrial recession that persisted through most of 1908. Having previously deposited Montreal Trust funds with one of the threatened American trust companies, Aitken went to New York during the height of the panic, where he personally witnessed J.P. Morgan's efforts to prevent an unprecedented run on trust company deposits from destroying the American financial system.

In the end, Montreal Trust not only weathered the storm of 1907, but after less than a year under Aitken's management it was challenging the largest trust companies in the country. The following year witnessed even more rapid growth and higher profits, but the trust company's performance, particularly in the new bond department, fell below Aitken's expectations. Moreover, he had grown bored with directing the more traditional side of a trust company and had begun to delegate many of his managerial functions to his new corporate secretary. Aitken then began to search for a chartered bank that would be interested in purchasing the trust company. Meanwhile, he concentrated on the business of investment banking. One year later, he sold Montreal Trust to Herbert Holt and the Royal Bank of Canada at a substantial profit. By this time, he had already begun the business that would bring him his largest profits and greatest notoriety – industrial merger promoting.

Aitken's First Venture in Halifax

The decision to establish a trust company in Halifax had been part of Aitken's desire to spread his wings beyond the confines of the Scotia group after John F. Stairs's death. Although the Scotia group was connected to Eastern Trust through John F. Stairs and, after his death, through Robert E. Harris's directorship on that company, not one of the Royal Securities Corporation's directors was numbered among Eastern Trust's president and three vice-presidents in 1905.[1] Moreover, the benefits derived from the linkage, such as they were, all ran in one direction. While Eastern Trust received fat fees for acting as trustee for the mortgages underlying the RSC's bond issues and for acting as transfer agent and registrar each time the RSC's share issues were sold and dividends on the shares were passed, the RSC received no new business in return.[2]

Shortly after John F. Stairs's death, Aitken carefully considered whether he could set up his own trust company through which he could funnel all RSC business. Since W.B. Ross had been involved in Eastern Trust at its formative stage and therefore knew something about the business, Aitken asked his opinion on a new trust company.[3] Ross was enthusiastic. Like Aitken, he believed that there was room for more than one trust company in the Maritimes. Aitken was not the first entrepreneur to consider challenging the regional monopoly of Eastern Trust. His old friend James Dunn, who was now established in the securities business in Montreal, had sent one of his associates to Nova Scotia in 1903 to scout the possibility of setting up a new trust company.[4] Dunn gave up the idea when he moved to England a short time later, but some Maritime investors established the Empire Trust Company only a few months after Aitken and W.B. Ross incorporated the Commercial Trust Company in January 1905.[5]

Although Aitken was the principal behind the Commercial Trust Company from the beginning, as well as the single largest shareholder, he cloaked his interest behind the unassuming office of vice-president.[6] As president, W.B. Ross became the titular head of Commercial Trust, just as George Stairs was then the figurehead president of the RSC. However, as in the case of Trinidad Electric (and soon also of Demerara Electric, the Camaguey Company, and Porto Rico Railways), Ross expected Aitken to run the company as the de facto general manager. Commercial Trust's new board of directors brought together lawyers, politicians, industrialists, and financiers from Nova Scotia, including Almon Lovett (of Harris, Henry & Cahan), A.K. Maclean (a Liberal MP), D.W. Robb (president of Robb Engineering), and J.J. Stewart (founder and publisher of the Halifax *Herald* and president of the Acadia Loan Corporation and the People's Bank of Halifax).[7]

Serious work did not begin until the autumn of 1905. Aitken first targeted companies that were carrying on their trustee and transfer agency business without the help of a trust company, and he convinced them that he could remove the fuss and bother for a modest fee while delivering a superior service.[8] He then attempted to raid clients from Eastern Trust. His strategy with Trinidad Electric was typical of how he went about this. As managing director of Commercial Trust, he 'negotiated' with W.B. Ross, in Ross's capacity as president of Trinidad, to have the utility's transfer agency moved from Eastern Trust to Commercial Trust. In an executive meeting of Trinidad, Ross then put forward a resolution endorsing the change, which B.F. Pearson, in his capacity as a director of Trinidad, seconded. Finally, the resolution was sent out in duplicate to each director asking for his consent.[9]

The scheme failed only when Robert E. Harris convinced enough Trinidad directors to stick with Eastern Trust. As a director of both Trinidad Electric and Eastern Trust, it was perhaps inevitable that Harris would oppose the change. But the fact that his law firm received most of Eastern Trust's legal business, not to mention his personal ambition concerning the presidency of Eastern Trust (and he did in fact become president three years later!), gave Harris every incentive to defend Eastern Trust against incursions by the newcomer.[10] Despite his best efforts, however, Harris could not prevent Aitken from securing new industrial and utility business during the following months; in little more than a year of operating, Commercial Trust was doing corporate transfer and trustee business for ten companies, including Robb Engineering, the Robb-Mumford Boiler Company, Amherst Foundry, Victor Wood Works, Maritime Heating, Demerara Electric, the Camaguey Company, and Porto Rico Railways.[11]

Aitken knew from the moment he conceived Commercial Trust that he would have to do battle with Harris. Indeed, he seemed to relish the opportunity to even the score, for he considered that Harris had mistreated and betrayed him after John F. Stairs's death. One incident in particular rankled. After Stairs's funeral, Aitken had supported George Stairs to be Scotia's new president, a choice favoured by all of the Scotia directors, but after months of deliberation and to everyone's surprise, Stairs had declined the presidency on the grounds of poor health. His decision precipitated a crisis within Scotia, dividing the New Glasgow directors, almost all of whom supported Senator James D. McGregor of New Glasgow, from the Halifax men, who thought McGregor incompetent and held that the RSC had the right to nominate the new president, given its extraordinary efforts in financing the company.

Aitken supported Harris's bid to become president on the understanding that if Harris succeeded he would place Aitken on the board. Since it would have been unseemly for Harris to support his own candidature, Aitken did it for him by undermining McGregor in an underhanded negative campaign that was worthy of a modern election.[12] When Harris was finally installed as president in March 1905, Aitken eagerly anticipated his reward. He was still waiting months later. When at length he realized that Harris had no intention of carrying out his end of the bargain, Aitken consciously decided to channel his anger towards Harris by attacking

Eastern Trust and Scotia, and eventually ripping apart the Scotia group itself.[13]

Running a Trust Company

Within ten months of beginning operations, Commercial Trust had enough business to warrant increasing its capital from $25,000 to $50,000, charging a premium on the stock purchased by new shareholders.[14] By June 1906, Aitken had secured Commercial Trust's largest contract: a trusteeship for the Toronto and Belleville Rolling Mills' $70,000 mortgage, for which Commercial Trust would be paid an annual fee of $3,500.[15] This was 'the first business which the Commercial Trust Co. has received in Upper Canada,' he told Arthur Nesbitt, 'and I am very proud of it.'[16]

Not all went smoothly, however. Most of Aitken's time was devoted to running Royal Securities, so he needed to be able to delegate at least the most routine duties to Commercial Trust's small staff. Early on, he had brought in Edward G. Kenny as corporate secretary to run the daily business. His hope was that Kenny would eventually take on the more difficult management tasks and grow into the position of general manager. Edward's father, Thomas E. Kenny – the great Halifax merchant and shipbuilder who was president of the Royal Bank of Canada – had shared John F. Stairs's business and political vision. Raised within the bosom of wealthy merchant families, both believed passionately in the National Policy, and their business interests eventually became pan-Canadian in scope; they even held stock in each other's enterprises. They ran together on the National Policy Conservative ticket in 1887, and again in 1891 and 1892, for the county seat of Halifax, which during the nineteenth century carried double representation.[17]

Through his family, Edward Kenny had superb connections, but he suffered one major defect. Because of the Kenny family's great wealth, Edward had never needed to work particularly hard, and although he was twenty years older than Aitken he had little direct business experience.[18] Aitken found that he had to provide Kenny with detailed instructions about the most mundane trust company tasks:

In all Companies where you are transfer agent or registrar for stocks, certain stock lists must be sent out immediately on the day the books are closed, for payment of dividends. These times occur regularly, and should be attended to with the greatest possible care. These lists should not be sent to the Royal Securities Corporation, but ... direct to the Companies for whom you are acting, and one of your principal duties as registrar and transfer agent is to see that companies are relieved from duties of this nature, rather than heap difficulties upon them.

If Kenny continued in this manner, Aitken went on, Commercial Trust's corporate clients would no doubt 'withdraw their business under the plea that there is more trouble with transfer agents than there would be if the books were written in their own offices.'[19]

Each week Kenny was required to send him a detailed summary of the week's activities, to which Aitken responded with similarly detailed advice and criticism undiluted by words of encouragement. At one point he would encourage Kenny to seek out the business of solicitors, since they were capable of bringing new business to the firm, and at another would discourage him from seeking legal advice on trust legislation as an 'unnecessary' expense.[20] Later, to confuse matters further, Aitken advised Kenny to avoid 'antagonizing' lawyers who regularly brought business to the trust company or who could potentially do so.[21]

In the face of Aitken's constant criticism Kenny's performance worsened. By the late autumn of 1906, just one year after he had become secretary, Kenny began to suffer what would now be called a nervous breakdown. Realizing at last that the job was simply too demanding for Kenny, Aitken transferred an RSC salesman by the name of J.F. Hobkirk to Commercial Trust, ostensibly as Kenny's assistant but in reality as his replacement. They, along with a typist and receptionist, made up the entire staff of the trust company.[22] Hobkirk turned out to be better than Kenny at running the day-to-day affairs of Commercial Trust, but even he was watched like a hawk by Aitken. One day, when Aitken discovered that Hobkirk had left work shortly before 6:00 PM, he sent a formal warning:

My opinion is that if you are to contribute to the success of this Company it will be necessary for you to arrive at the office at 9 o'clock in the morning and stay there until 6 o'clock at night, unless you are engaged elsewhere in the prosecution of the Company's business.

I explained to you that the success of this Company is entrusted to your care for a time. If success attends your efforts then your own advancement must result. If you do not give the business absolutely all your time and thought I can only anticipate one result.[23]

Despite these difficulties with staff, Aitken's new trust company began to soar. Harris complained about Commercial Trust's unseemly aggressiveness and its propensity to take on a more speculative class of business that should be outside the purview of trust companies. In his view, trust companies were intended to perform trustee functions, functions which Eastern Trust had not, at least recently, strayed beyond.[24] As a corporate lawyer, Harris thought in terms of the fiduciary obligations that went with being a trustee of personal or corporate funds, and how conflicts of interest might arise if the same institution lent these funds to brokers and other stock market operators on a call loan basis. Was it proper for an institution that did not face the onerous reserve requirements of a commercial bank to enter into what could only be described as a general banking business?[25]

Aitken on the other hand thought in terms of the tremendous advantages of a single institution combining trust and banking services. The notion of a universal or 'mixed' bank might not have been familiar to Aitken, but he felt instinctively that the combination was a potent one, as had already been discovered by many trust companies in the United States. Following the American scene through books and magazines as well as with frequent trips to Boston and New York, Aitken began to question the reasons for the conservatism of Canadian high finance.[26] While trust companies in Canada adhered closely to the core trustee activities in which they had been given a legislative monopoly, the vast majority of American trust companies were competing with commercial and private banks in making loans, receiving deposits, and underwriting securities. By the turn of the century, these trust companies had become a central feature of the New York capital market. They provided liquidity to brokers on the call loan market and underwrote many of the industrial securities that buoyed the great merger movement. Most of these trust companies did not even bother with the administrator, trustee, and transfer agency businesses that were a staple of the Canadian companies. They paid interest on all their deposits, whereas the banks paid no interest on most of their accounts in return for providing cheque-clearing services – an activity from which the trusts were barred. The trusts carried a lower percentage of their assets in cash because, unlike the commercial banks, they were not required to maintain reserves on deposits. This allowed them to invest a larger percentage of their assets in remunerative (interest-generating) investments. As a result, trust companies held a whopping one-quarter of all deposits in New York by 1900.[27]

Aitken wanted to emulate certain features of the American system. He saw no reason why he should not lend trust company funds, at least those funds held outside trusteeships. Why not increase those funds, moreover, by enticing deposits through the payment of interest? Although most Canadian trust companies would not touch the business, probably out of fear of retaliation from the chartered banks, at least one Canadian firm, the Imperial Trusts Company in Toronto, was advertising its willingness to pay 4 per cent per annum on deposits.[28]

Nonetheless, Aitken stepped tentatively at first. During Commercial Trust's first full year of business, almost all its revenue came from corporate trust and transfer agency business, though it also took on the most traditional types of trusteeship: acting as executor, administrator, and trustee for individuals and estates. The work was performed so well that before the end of 1906, Commercial Trust was appointed to act as trustee of all funds and investments under the control of the Supreme Court of Nova Scotia.[29] An even more telling barometer of Aitken's initial cautiousness is the manner in which money entrusted to Commercial Trust was reinvested. Approximately 90 per cent of the funds held by Commercial Trust in 1906, about $210,000, was deposited with commercial banks, earning a very modest return of 3 per cent. Only 10 per cent, or about $25,000, was loaned out on the riskier but more remunerative call loan market. Commercial Trust took no deposits at all at this stage.[30]

Even with conventional trust accounts acting as a brake on its overall profitability, Commercial Trust yielded a net profit of 14.5 per cent on its original capital investment for 1906. Aitken planned to expand his call loan business in the coming months; more significantly, he was at last ready to begin accepting deposits. Certainly, the trust company now had one very constant customer in Halifax. With new cash flowing in, Commercial Trust was able to provide much-needed liquidity to Royal Securities through call loans, thereby reducing its dependence on the commercial banks. Aitken calculated that by opening a branch in Montreal, Commercial Trust could similarly lubricate the RSC's rapidly expanding business in central Canada.[31]

Swallowing a Big Fish

Since Arthur Nesbitt was already in Montreal running the new RSC branch office on St James Street, Aitken asked him to scout out the possibilities for a Commercial Trust branch in the city. The location made sense for at least two reasons. First, according to the legislation in Quebec and Ontario, only trust companies with a provincial base were permitted to act as trustees and transfer agencies for the bonds and shares sold in those provinces. Since an ever-growing number of central Canadian investors were purchasing the securities spawned by the RSC, and since these bonds and shares were beginning to trade on secondary markets, Aitken would need a central-Canadian trust office in addition to his Halifax office if he was to capture this new business. Second, although the Montreal Stock Exchange – considerably larger and more active than the Toronto Stock Exchange – provided powerful incentives in favour of choosing Montreal over Toronto, there was also a significant tax advantage. Quebec's stamp tax was imposed on all sales of stock transferred within Quebec. As Aitken observed, 'With our [Commercial Trust] offices in Halifax and Montreal, transfers of stocks for which we act can be made at either office,' thereby avoiding the tax.[32]

Nesbitt asked for advice from Thomas Fyshe, the general manager of the Merchants Bank of Canada, who said that Commercial Trust would need more capital as well as a couple of prominent Montreal directors in order to do well in the city. Not understanding the personalities involved, Fyshe suggested that Commercial Trust merge with Eastern Trust in order to combine resources before trying to set up a branch in Montreal.[33] Aitken could not accept this suggestion but knew that Fyshe's more general advice was correct. To be successful in Montreal, Commercial Trust would have to have substantially more capital as well as central-Canadian directors and officers. He devised a unique solution.

At the time, there were three trust companies operating in Montreal: Royal Trust, controlled by the Bank of Montreal; a branch of the National Trust Company, controlled by the Cox group in Toronto and linked to the Canadian Bank of Commerce; and the Montreal Trust and Deposit Company, the smallest and weakest of the three, in part because it was not connected to a chartered bank.[34] Aitken's scheme was to promote a merger between Commercial Trust and Montreal Trust, through which he would exert managerial control – a very small fish trying to swallow a much larger one, since Montreal Trust was capitalized at ten times the size of Commercial Trust.[35]

As illustrated in table 6.1, Montreal Trust was one of the first trust companies established in Canada. Incorporated in 1889 as the Montreal Safe Deposit Company, its main business was the 'safekeeping and storage of jewelry, plate, money, specie, bullion, stocks, bonds, securities, papers and documents and generally all valuables of any kind.'[36] One year later, the company assumed trust powers and was renamed the Montreal Trust and Deposit Company. Its first president was Sir Donald Smith (later Lord Strathcona) of Canadian Pacific Railway fame, who was also president of the Bank of Montreal. The real brains behind the company, however, was

TABLE 6.1 First Canadian trust companies: Branches by 1904 and size by 1908

Name	First year operating	Head office	Branches by 1904	Paid-up capital by 1908	Assets[a] by 1908
Toronto General Trusts	1882	Toronto	Ottawa, Winnipeg	$1,000,000	$1,089,718
Montreal Trust and Deposit	1889	Montreal	none	500,000	927,359
Imperial Trust Company of Canada	1889	Toronto	none	99,675	168,739
Royal Trust Company	1892	Montreal	Winnipeg	700,000	N/A
Eastern Trust Company	1893	Halifax	Saint John	600,000	658,000
Canada Trust Company	1893	London, Ont.	none	200,000	275,000
Trusts & Guarantee Corporation	1897	Toronto	Brantford, Calgary	1,154,485	[5,038,163]
National Trust Company	1898	Toronto	Montreal, Winnipeg, Edmonton, Saskatoon	1,000,000	1,621,143

Sources: Capital and asset figures for Eastern Trust from *Annual Financial Review* (Canadian), 10 (Apr. 1910); other data derived from ibid., 9 (Apr. 1909); Ernest Heaton, *The Trust Company Idea and Its Development* (Toronto 1904), 44; and E.P. Neufeld, *The Financial System of Canada: Its Growth and Development* (Toronto 1972), 294–5

[a] Asset figures exclude trust funds (value of estates, etc., under administration, trust funds in bank) except in the case of the Trusts and Guarantee Corporation, where trust funds could not be separated from the company's other assets and liabilities.

a Montreal stockbroker, Alexander Strathy, whose idea it was to put Sir Donald on the board in order to gain the patronage of the largest bank in the country. Strathy directed Montreal Trust into the emerging corporate trustee and stock transfer business, and in 1899 Montreal Trust was appointed the clearing-house for the Montreal Stock Exchange. This marked the zenith of Montreal Trust's early development. Later that year, Strathy was struck down by a brain tumour. His unexpected death coincided with Smith's resignation from the presidency and the Bank of Montreal's forging of a much closer relationship with the Royal Trust Company, which promptly moved its operations to the ground floor of the Bank of Montreal's head office. From that time forward, the Royal Trust board was dominated by Bank of Montreal directors, including Edward Clouston, who became vice-president of both institutions in 1905.[37]

By 1907 Montreal Trust had slipped to third place in its native city, behind Royal Trust and the Montreal branch of National Trust, in part because it had languished under four indifferent presidents after Sir Donald Smith's departure. The current one was Richard Wilson-Smith, a fifty-four-year-old investment broker and insurance company president and a one-time mayor of Montreal. Like his three short-term predecessors, Wilson-Smith seemed unconcerned about Montreal Trust's lack of direction. This was partly because he was distracted by his many other business interests. In addition to being president of the Canadian Accident Assurance Company and a director of the Guardian Fire Assurance Company, he owned and edited the *Insurance and Financial Chronicle*, which he had founded in 1882.[38]

In mid-February 1907, Wilson-Smith wrote to Aitken asking whether Commercial Trust would be prepared to act as Montreal Trust's agent in Halifax. Referring to the 'large amount of deposits' that could 'be captured from some of your wealthy citizens,' Wilson-Smith asked Aitken whether he would be prepared to sell control of Commercial Trust in order to provide Montreal Trust with a branch office in Halifax.[39] Declining the offer, Aitken set out his ambitious goals for Commercial Trust, explaining that he would soon be establishing a branch in Montreal, where he would compete directly with the central Canadian trust companies, including Montreal Trust. Commercial Trust's new branch would first take over Trinidad Electric and Nova Scotia Steel's stock transfer business in central Canada, followed by a 'vigorous canvass' calculated to take over the business of all Maritime companies listed on the Montreal Stock Exchange while also pursuing trusteeships and transfer agencies from central-Canadian companies.[40]

Aitken added that Commercial Trust would be setting up a real estate department, since no trust company was yet servicing the needs of the professional property investor in Montreal.[41] He said he had found that the 'buyers and sellers of Real Estate' would be eager 'to place their business in the hands of properly equipped Trust Companies, in preference to individuals who all too frequently turn out to be irresponsible.' Fees would not be restricted to sales, however; he also envisaged the trust company entering the general business of property management, including the collection of rents on the new apartment buildings that were beginning to grace Montreal's skyline. Aitken even cheekily suggested to Wilson-Smith that since the older man and his associates held a great deal of real estate in Montreal, he should expect 'very considerable support' from Aitken and his friends in this new field; besides, Montreal was a large city with 'room enough for more Trust Companies.' Finally, he urged Wilson-Smith to forget about opening a new branch office in Halifax and to let Commercial Trust act as Montreal Trust's agent in Nova Scotia.[42]

This letter was vintage Aitken – audacious, bordering on the reckless, and not a little misleading. In reality, Aitken had no intention of having Commercial Trust act as Montreal Trust's agent. His letter to Wilson-Smith was really an effort to puff the share value of Commercial Trust in anticipation of a consolidation. He wanted to merge the two companies and thereby gain managerial control of an adequately capitalized institution with a foothold in both central Canada and the Maritimes. When Aitken finally got around to revealing his true intent a few days later, Wilson-Smith was incredulous. Incapable of understanding how a merger with such a small company could possibly be in Montreal Trust's interests, he summarily dismissed the proposal.[43]

Aitken then appealed to Wilson-Smith's private interest by including him in the merger syndicate and giving him an immediate $5,000 profit if the merger was consummated. The bribe worked its magic. Overnight, Wilson-Smith became convinced of the merits of the proposed merger and began to sell the idea to his fellow directors and shareholders. Aitken also offered Montreal Trust's shareholders an inducement to sell: he would pay 10 per cent above par for Montreal Trust's shares, a generous offer in view of the trust company's dismal profit the year before.[44] Montreal Trust's directors immediately voted in favour of proceeding with the merger discussions.

By this time, Aitken had already set up a syndicate of mainly Halifax financiers in order to help him acquire control of Montreal Trust. In addition to W.B. Ross, George Stairs, Charles Cahan, and Almon Lovett, the Halifax syndicate was supplemented by Will Ross and the Metropolitan Bank of Toronto. By 20 February 1907, Aitken had framed the preliminary contractual terms for the merger, by which the RSC was to lend Wilson-Smith $50,000 to purchase 500 shares of Montreal Trust at par. The Halifax syndicate agreed to repurchase these shares at $110 per share (thus putting $5,000 into Wilson-Smith's pocket) and to purchase another 2,135 shares at 110 per cent of par in order to give the syndicate majority control. The total bill came to $289,850, of which $250,000 was borrowed from the Metropolitan Bank by the RSC on behalf of the syndicate. The balance of the purchase price, almost $40,000, was supplied by the RSC out of its own funds.[45]

This cash purchase of Montreal Trust by the Halifax syndicate was accompanied by a simultaneous cash purchase of the Commercial Trust Co. by the existing shareholders of Montreal Trust. Wilson-Smith tried to convince his fellow directors and shareholders to purchase Commercial Trust's 550 shares at a little more than $118 per share. After some haggling, Montreal Trust made a counter offer of a fraction less than $113 per share, which was accepted in March 1907.[46] Since Aitken owned 200 of these shares, he reaped a gross profit of $22,500 in this single transaction, every dollar of which was reinvested in Montreal Trust stock.[47]

He had no trouble convincing Commercial Trust's directors and shareholders of the benefits that would flow from the merger, since W.B. Ross, the president and largest single shareholder aside from Aitken, was a key member of the RSC syndicate. Nonetheless, the smaller Halifax shareholders had to be given some assurance that the deal was in the company's best interest. Aitken told the Halifax investors that he, as general manager and second vice-president, and W.B. Ross, as the proposed first vice-president, would run the new company as profitably as they had managed Commercial Trust, and he promised to push the sleepy Montreal crowd out as quickly as possible.[48] Convinced by Aitken, the Maritime shareholders exchanged their shares for Montreal Trust stock and rode along with Aitken on his new adventure.[49]

Before agreeing to consummate the merger, Aitken insisted that the board must remove the existing general manager, John M. Smith (whom he viewed as entirely incompetent), before he would assume his new duties. However, the Montreal board members refused to sack Smith, whereupon Aitken threatened to walk away from the merger.[50] Two weeks of frantic negotiations between Montreal and Halifax then took place. Finally, the Montreal directors agreed to a face-saving compromise.

Smith would be kept on as nominal manager of the Montreal branch on the express understanding that Aitken would 'have absolute jurisdiction over the staff.'[51] To avoid further problems of this sort, Aitken demanded, and the board agreed, that all of Montreal Trust's other employees would resign before the transition so that he could select at his leisure those whom he wanted to keep.[52]

By May 1907 the details of the merger had been worked out – including the condition that Aitken, as the managing director, would permanently reside in Montreal after the transition. It was also understood that W.B. Ross would become first vice-president as soon as he moved to Montreal. Cahan, although living in Mexico most of the year, also took the opportunity to change his Canadian domicile from Halifax to Montreal. To entice Almon Lovett into joining the Maritime exodus, Aitken offered him the position of corporate counsel for the new trust company consolidation if he would leave Halifax.[53] Under the headline 'Montreal Gains Three Good Halifax Men,' the move made the front page of the Halifax *Herald*.[54] Aitken received private letters bemoaning his move but wishing him well.[55] A.E. Collas, a wealthy Halifax businessman and regular underwriter in Aitken's ventures wrote: 'I am sorry to learn that you and Mr. W.B. Ross are likely to be taking up your abode in Montreal. Halifax cannot afford to lose its progressive men.' Clearly, Collas hoped that there was still a chance that Aitken and Ross would change their minds.[56]

The move damaged the Scotia group, creating a barrier between Aitken and Cahan in Montreal and Harris and George Stairs in Halifax.[57] On the other hand, Edward Clouston and Sir William Van Horne welcomed Aitken's move. He had made them money in the past; now he would be in a position to make them even more. Van Horne immediately sent a letter of welcome to Aitken in Halifax, expressing his pleasure 'at the prospect of having you here in Montreal' and his desire 'to turn some business your way' and 'to be of use to you in any way I can.' Van Horne suggested that Aitken visit him at home as soon as he had a chance and, if he had time, to come to lunch the following Sunday: 'We always have an open table that day for friends who may drop in.'[58]

Revitalizing Montreal Trust

As part of the merger deal, Aitken had obtained Wilson-Smith's commitment to retire from the presidency by the end of the year – sooner if Aitken could find a suitable replacement. Aitken wanted one of Montreal's top financiers, a bank president or a manager-cum-entrepreneur of the calibre and reputation of Sir William Van Horne. While Wilson-Smith had some stature in the Montreal community by virtue of his work in politics and insurance, he lacked connections to the large chartered banks and was far from the pinnacle of the Canadian financial élite. Within weeks of taking over, therefore, Aitken approached Sir Montagu Allan, president of the Merchants Bank of Canada, about the possibility of his presiding over Montreal Trust.[59] Sir Montagu was receptive to the idea but stipulated that the RSC syndicate would first have to sell him a large block of Montreal Trust stock. Since it was clear from this response that Sir Montagu would not be satisfied with being a mere figurehead, Aitken decided to look elsewhere for a presidential ornament.

He could not find the ideal candidate on the existing board or within his immediate circle. For instance, Robert Archer was 'a Director of the City & District Savings Bank, and very highly thought of, but narrow-minded as a man can be' and 'conservative beyond measure.' S.H. Ewing, vice-president of Molsons Bank and Sun Life was 'about 75, and weak as water.' Then there was the millionaire F. Orr Lewis, 'one of the most heartily disliked men in Montreal.' Finally, there was George E. Drummond, who 'would run the Company as an auxiliary' to his family's iron and steel businesses. The best of the lot was Frank W. Ross, the president of Dominion Coal and a director on the boards of numerous financial institutions, but he lived in Quebec City and therefore was unavailable. In the circumstances, Aitken preferred to have W.B. Ross as president if he could be convinced to move from Halifax to Montreal, but even he was 'not sufficiently well known in Montreal to give us that prestige and standing which we need.' Aitken suffered from the same problem, but he never once considered taking on the presidency, preferring to run the company behind other men. He decided to delay his decision for a few months in the hope that the perfect candidate would appear.[60]

Aitken relished his new life in Montreal. In his first month there he wrote to Almon Lovett in Halifax: 'I find there is more of interest in Montreal in a few days than in many weeks of Halifax Life.' Aitken was not referring to Montreal's cultural amenities – only after he moved to England would he spend much time on nonbusiness pursuits; he was speaking of its position as the country's financial metropolis. Toronto was growing fast, but it remained outclassed by Montreal in business. Although the great commercial towers springing up from St James Street to Drummond and St Catherine were mainly the purview of a dour Anglo-Scots élite, there were enough prominent French-Canadian, Jewish, and other non-WASP businessmen to give the city a cosmopolitan flavour that was entirely lacking in such regional centres as Toronto and Halifax. Most important, there seemed room here for a young and ambitious outsider. From his lofty prospect on St James Street, where he worked for the RSC two or three hours in the early morning, and his office on Place d'Armes, where he spent the rest of the day working for Montreal Trust, he began to wonder why he had spent so long 'trying to do business from Halifax.'[61]

Through Aitken's direction over the next two years, Montreal Trust was to fight its way out of the pack of medium-sized trust companies and begin competing with the front runners. Aitken had, of course, observed how Royal Trust and National Trust had benefited from being harnessed to the established commercial banks and their associated financial clusters in Toronto and Montreal. He felt that there was even greater potential in a combined trust company and investment bank. Royal Securities was a potentially inexhaustible source of corporate trustee business. All of the trusteeships, transfers, and dividend disbursements created by securities issued by the industrial and utility firms in the RSC orbit would be funnelled to Montreal Trust. The benefits of the linkage would, of course, also flow in the other direction. As Montreal Trust moved into the business of banking in the sense of receiving deposits and advancing call loans, the RSC would directly benefit from privileged access to these funds.

There was one further advantage that Aitken noted. It had long irked him that in 'much the same way as the country grocer was compelled to carry sugar,' the RSC had to carry a supply of unremunerative municipal bonds in order to satisfy its smaller clients.[62] Aitken disliked putting the RSC's scarce capital into municipal bonds when so much profit lay in issuing (rather than retailing) his own utility and industrial securities. Trust companies, however, could not avoid investing in large blocks of low-risk (and correspondingly low-yield) municipal bonds because of their fiduciary obligations regarding the secure investment of trust funds. Aitken thus sold the RSC's municipal bond business to Montreal Trust on the understanding that RSC salesmen could always act as Montreal Trust's agents in selling these bonds to long-standing RSC clients. This bond division of Montreal Trust soon evolved into a bond department carrying a vast array of both low- and high-risk securities.

For the first time in its history, Montreal Trust began to accept deposits. Paying 3 per cent interest compounded quarterly, Montreal Trust brought in $100,000 in deposits by May 1907. To attract even more funds (and to divert corporate funds held at chartered banks), Aitken decided

TABLE 6.2 Comparison of average end-of-quarter call loan rates, 1902–13

	Quarter[a]			
	1st	2nd	3rd	4th
Montreal rate	5.3	5.3	5.4	5.6
New York rate	3.5	2.5	3.9	7.2[a]
London rate	2.7	1.7	2.2	2.8

Source: George Rich, 'Canadian Banks, Gold and the Crisis of 1907,' *Explorations in Economic History* 26, no. 1 (Apr. 1989), 155

[a] As a consequence of the extraordinary demand for credit by the American grain companies moving crops to domestic and overseas markets following harvest, and by farmers awaiting final payments, interest rates invariably spiked upward in the fourth quarter.

to increase the rate to 3.5 per cent, 0.5 per cent above the maximum rate allowed by the Canadian Bankers' Association.[63] While ostensibly prohibiting trust companies from engaging in the 'business of banking,' Canadian federal and provincial law (unlike American law) distinguished between borrowing funds, which banks were empowered to do, and holding funds in trust, which trust companies were permitted to do. This legal obfuscation created a loophole that could easily be used by an adventuresome trust company manager such as Aitken.[64]

The trust company also moved aggressively into the call loan business. Here again, Canadian law drew an imaginary distinction between lending funds and returning funds held in trust. Taking advantage of the vagueness of the law, Montreal Trust and a few other firms began to crowd the banks by moving into the commercial loan business. Nonetheless, the amount of money made available for securities investing through call loans by Canadian trust companies was minuscule relative to what was happening south of the border. American trust companies had been so active in the call loan market that the availability of short-term loans had increased dramatically after 1900, while the rate of interest on such funds declined. The end result was a higher and more stable rate of interest for call loans in Canada than in the United States, and accordingly a chance to profit on the discrepancy between the two markets. To take advantage of the situation, Aitken negotiated an arbitrage arrangement with the Trust Company of America in New York, whereby Montreal Trust would borrow funds on call, relending these same funds at a higher rate in Canada. As the call loan interest rate on the Montreal Stock Exchange was

TABLE 6.3 Montreal Trust, capital, earnings, profit, deposits, and loans, 1906–9 ($ Cdn)

	1906	1907	1908[a]	1909
Paid-up capital	415,113	500,000	500,000	500,000
Earnings	19,163	47,329	58,563	63,945
Percentage return on capital	4.6%	9.5%	11.7%	12.8%
Undivided accumulated profits	3,038	50,368	75,972	109,417
Deposits			345,876	917,329
Call loans			459,580	808,118[b]
Time loans			66,927	212,514

Source: Derived from Montreal Trust Company, minutes of board meetings and shareholders meetings enclosing company annual reports dated 30 Nov. 1908 and 30 Nov. 1909
[a] Only eleven months; fiscal year changed to end in November
[b] Of this amount, $425,000 of funds were lent on the New York Stock Exchange call loan market and $383,118 were lent on the Montreal Stock Exchange call loan market.

always above 5 per cent, Aitken calculated that he could charge 0.5 per cent less than the market rate and still make a profit.[65]

Trust company legislation required that all 'loans' issued by trust companies had to be secured by collateral. This posed little problem in terms of loans made to brokers, who pledged the securities they were purchasing (or had previously purchased) as collateral for their advances. The real question was whether trust companies were legally prevented from giving loans on time. Aitken was careful in this regard, but he could see no reason why Montreal Trust should not advance loans over definite time periods, provided that the trust company acquired ownership of a stipulated amount of the debtor company's share capital or bonds as security. Carefully and without fanfare, Montreal Trust began to give loans on time to some of its corporate clients. As shown in table 6.3, time loans had grown to 25 per cent of Montreal Trust's total loans by 1909.[66]

Aitken also succeeded in immediately establishing a real estate department within Montreal Trust, and he began to provide services never before obtainable in Montreal. As a trustee, Montreal Trust began to look after real estate that was subject to various trust provisions. As an agent, the company supervised numerous small properties, and it was immediately appointed the agent for a highrise office building as well as for 'the largest Apartment House in Montreal.'[67] The company's trustee and transfer agency business also expanded rapidly; every month saw the firm appointed as a trustee or transfer agent for new companies. As well, although Aitken was sceptical about the profitability of the safe deposit department, he invested a little more in the facilities, and after a year he was bragging that Montreal Trust's safe deposit business was the 'largest in Canada' and – contrary to his expectations of this backwater of trust business – surprisingly profitable.[68]

These changes brought prompt results. Within the first four months of 1907, Montreal Trust was posting a 25 per cent gain in the volume of business and a 33 per cent gain in income compared with the same period in 1906.[69] However, Aitken was beginning to upset the delicate equilibrium that had so recently been established among the so-called four pillars of finance – banking, insurance, securities, and trust services. Federal and provincial regulatory legislation gave the financial institutions supporting each pillar the exclusive right to engage in their core services while prohibiting cross-sectoral competition.[70] One of the objects of this legal demarcation was to minimize conflicts of interest so that funds deposited in trust, for example, would not be re-lent or invested for speculative purposes. It was also thought that this segregation of financial institutions would reduce self-dealing by corporate officers and directors, who had privileged access to their institution's funds.

Nevertheless, the web of federal and provincial legislation (occasionally intersected and complicated by common law) underlying the four pillars did little to prevent conflicts of interest in the close-knit Canadian business community. Instead, it encouraged affiliations of legally independent but incestuously connected financial institutions, in which corporate conflict of interest reigned supreme and self-dealing was the norm rather than the exception. Sen. George Cox's Toronto group, for example, covered all four pillars of finance by controlling the Canadian Bank of Commerce, Canada Life, Dominion Securities, and National Trust.[71] In Montreal, where the Anglo-Scots business élite sat on the boards of the Canadian Pacific Railway and the Bank of Montreal, Royal Trust drew nine of its sixteen directors from the board of the Bank of Montreal.[72]

During his lifetime in Halifax, John F. Stairs had managed to cover two of the four pillars through Eastern Trust and Royal Securities. His father and brother had a close affiliation with the Union Bank of Halifax, but Stairs had attempted to secure the third pillar by other means – the stillborn Alliance Bank and the disastrous People's Bank purchase. Like Stairs, Aitken was uninterested in insurance but very interested in the business of deposit banking as a potential source of investment capital. Unlike Stairs, however, he did not have direct access to bank capital, and while the RSC was given some preference at the Union Bank, Aitken knew that his rupture with George Stairs and his move to Montreal would work against him.[73]

Aitken's alliance with the Metropolitan Bank, first forged by John F. Stairs, gave him his best access to capital, but even this was limited by the Metropolitan's $1 million capitalization, which was tiny by Canadian chartered bank standards. Always compensating for his bank's frailty, Will Ross never allowed Aitken to borrow as much as he was continually demanding. And since Aitken was not a board member or a controlling shareholder, there was little he could do except whine to Will about the fact that the RSC was receiving no 'more consideration than the ordinary customers of the bank.'[74]

As the managing director and largest shareholder of Montreal Trust, however, Aitken could do what he liked in terms of giving the RSC preference for call loans. Moreover, he could eventually re-employ funds deposited with Montreal Trust as bridge loans for issuing and underwriting securities, a common enough practice in the United States.[75] The connection benefited Montreal Trust as well, and just months after the takeover, Aitken admitted that the company was 'making progress far beyond' even his expectations. He had found new business everywhere and was amazed that there was nobody else 'looking for it except myself.' He had only one problem; the days were 'not long enough.'[76]

The Panic of 1907

Montreal Trust's general business continued to expand during the summer and early autumn of 1907. But as credit became dearer and short-term interest rates climbed in response to a general contraction of the money supply in the United States, Aitken became increasingly concerned about the ability of some of his debtors to repay if they were called on to do so. The problem was compounded by the fact that some Canadian brokers assumed that call loans were in fact perpetual loans, good for as long as they paid interest. Aitken disliked this attitude, especially when money was becoming scarce. He preferred the way the call loan business was conducted in the United States, where a call loan was understood to be capable of being called in at any time at the discretion of the lender. If brokers in Canada wanted money on time, he argued, they should go directly to a bank and get a time loan.[77]

Aitken of course was not in the habit of taking his own advice; the RSC itself had borrowed extensively on call and could not have paid off all its outstanding loans at the same time if required to do so. Meanwhile, as Aitken heard his friends in the United States talk of an impending crisis, he became increasingly worried. In March 1907 he watched with concern as the U.S. stock market suffered a sharp decline. Dependent as he was on a bullish market for his successive Camaguey and Porto Rico flotations, he was worried that stock market prices would also fall in Canada. Already, short-term interest rates were soaring in Canada, following the same pattern as in the United States. By late April there were widespread complaints about 'tight' money as the call loan rate of interest rose to 7 per cent. Aitken told one friend, 'I would not buy gold dollars today if I could not put them in circulation tomorrow,' adding that even if the banks would lend him money, he would not take it.[78] The RSC's existing loans were enough of a problem. Even friendly banks such as the Metropolitan were demanding some of the money they had lent to the RSC on call.[79]

Aitken worked assiduously to reduce the RSC's debt load. Nonetheless, bridge loans were an essential part of doing business for an investment bank. To lessen its vulnerability to action by the banks, Royal Securities began to rely on loans from Montreal Trust. As Aitken explained to W.B. Ross, he had no compunction about exercising his influence in this respect: 'Money is very tight with the R.S.C. and as you know it is *not* my policy, so long as I administer the affairs of the Montreal Trust and Deposit Co., to deny any money whatsoever to the R.S.C.'[80]

In good times, underwriting was a sure thing, but when shares could not be floated, underwriters had to pay real cash for the portion of the issue they guaranteed. As market conditions continued to deteriorate, Aitken temporarily suspended further Camaguey and Porto Rico issues.[81] Instead, he ordered Blake Burrill to call on the guarantors to pay the first 20 per cent of their underwriting to the RSC. Aitken told Burrill to write personal letters to each, 'informing them that our operations in San Juan and in Cuba are large, and that we cannot borrow a dollar of money even on $5 of security, and that every loan must be liquidated to the Corporation.' Burrill was instructed 'to assume an absolutely stony heart' in collecting the overdue amounts. Aitken was not going to allow the other commitments these gentlemen faced to take precedence over their agreement with the RSC.[82]

In May 1907 the Halifax branch of the Bank of Montreal called in a total of $41,000 of call loans to the RSC. The 'best arrangement that I could make,' Burrill told Aitken, 'was to pay $10,000 cash,' reducing 'our bank account here' to $13,000.[83] By summer, Aitken himself believed that

TABLE 6.4 Camaguey underwriting syndicate: Subscriptions, payments received, and payments overdue, September 1907

Name	Total subscriptions	Payments received	Payments overdue
Robert E. Harris	$ 37,500	$10,333	$ 4,667
T.G. McMullen	37,500	7,500	7,500
W.B. Ross	35,400	10,333	3,827
H. Almon Lovett	10,900	2,180	2,180
George Stairs	9,300	2,790	903
Blake Burrill	3,700	0	1,480
Total	$134,300	$33,136	$20,584

Source: Beaverbrook Papers, House of Lords Record Office, A/48, Aitken to B.G. Burrill, 6 Sept. 1907

the market would soon collapse. He put even more pressure on his salesmen to liquidate the RSC inventory before the storm hit with full force. 'There is going to be an abnormal demand for money, high interest rates and many securities will be pressing for sale,' he predicted.[84] Slashing the RSC's profit, he cut his bond prices by at least three points and increased profit margins to commission salesmen in order to get rid of the RSC's excess inventory of securities as quickly as possible.[85]

Arthur Nesbitt was dispatched to Britain in an attempt to unload the RSC's glut of utility securities. By late summer, Nesbitt had managed to sell enough utility securities to earn himself a $1,000 bonus, but not quite enough to compensate for the collapse of sales in Canada.[86] Aitken was forced to demand a further 20 per cent payment from the Camaguey underwriters in September. He himself (as well as the RSC in its corporate capacity) had managed to come up with the money, but none of the other underwriters paid their 20 per cent, and some were still in arrears on the earlier demand. Aitken summarized what each still owed and sent a copy to each underwriter threatening to shut down construction in Cuba if he did not receive immediate payment. The RSC, he reminded them, had 'advanced a large sum of money on account of Construction and the purchase of materials,' and he added, 'We are not in a position to secure any advances whatsoever from our Bankers.'[87]

Aitken cut prices again and pressed his salesman even harder to unload securities in order to prepare for the coming storm. Historically, financial crises are generally unexpected, but the panic that began in October 1907 had been awaited for months, not only by Aitken but by many other

North American and European financiers. The precipitating event, an attempted cornering of American copper shares, was insignificant enough, but the American capital market was in such a nervous and constricted state that the system as a whole appeared headed for a breakdown. Knowing that the Knickerbocker Trust Company of New York was connected to the ill-fated copper syndicate, depositors began to line up outside the main Manhattan branch to demand their money back on Friday, 18 October. After the weekend the run quickly spread to numerous other trust companies and banks in New York, and by Tuesday it had hit the Trust Company of America, with which Montreal Trust had a large deposit.[88]

That very day Kingsbury Curtis, a New York lawyer who had close connections with the Trust Company of America and also had connections with Aitken through the Porto Rico Railways promotion, cabled him to take the overnight train to New York.[89] Aitken left immediately, intending to withdraw Montreal Trust's deposit,[90] but when he arrived the following Wednesday evening he saw that he was too late; an immense queue had already formed in front of the Trust Company of America's head office. Making a virtue of necessity, Aitken straightway wrote a letter to the besieged trust company's president, expressing his 'regret at the unreasonable and destructive run on the Trust Co. of America' and promising that Montreal Trust would not make a withdrawal 'until you completely recover from the temporary set back.'[91]

The next day Aitken witnessed J.P. Morgan's attempt to save the Trust Company of America in order to prevent a run on all trust companies and banks, including his own. With only a little exaggeration, Aitken described it as the most serious run ever faced by a financial institution, given the fact that it had '14,000 depositors with balances of less than $5,000' and that almost all were lined up to withdraw their money. Morgan saved the day, in Aitken's view, by personally running 'up and down the line of depositors soliciting them to return to their homes and assuring them that the Company would meet its obligations.' Since Morgan was not a director of the trust company, 'his representations seemed to have great weight.'[92]

J.P. Morgan was the toast of financiers throughout the world, for all had felt the shock waves from New York. Although probably none except Aitken had actually witnessed Morgan's performance, the money men of Toronto and Montreal had good reason for cheering J.P. Morgan, for they had been even more adversely affected by the Panic of 1907 than their European counterparts.[93] Canada suffered a 5.5 per cent contrac-

TABLE 6.5 The international liquidity crisis of 1907: Impact on money growth rate, real output growth, and the stock market

Country	Deviation from trend of average annual monetary growth rate (peak to trough)	Deviation from trend of average annual real output growth (peak to trough)	Stock market crisis
United States	−1.7 (12/04 to 12/08)	−14.7 (5/07 to 6/08)	yes
Canada	−9.7 (1/06 to 10/07)	−6.7 (12/06 to 7/09)	yes[a]
Great Britain	−1.6 (1906 to 1907)[b]	−4.7 (6/07 to 11/08)	no
Germany	−17.1 (1906 to 1907)[b]	−2.2 (7/07 to 12/08)	yes
France	−3.4 (1906 to 1907)[b]	−0.6 (7/07 to 2/09)	yes

Source: Derived from Michael D. Bordo, 'The Impact and International Transmission of Financial Crises: Some Historical Evidence, 1870–1933,' *Rivista di storia economica*, 2nd ser., 2 (1985), 53–9
[a] Based on decline of common stock prices in Canada as observed in the *Annual Financial Review* (Canadian), vols. 6–8
[b] No monthly data available

tion in its money supply from September to December 1907, a precipitous fall in stock market prices, and a decline in industrial investment that would persist through most of the following year.[94]

Despite this, the country was spared the collapse of banks and near-banks that shook the American financial system to its knees. This was partly because Canadian trust companies, unlike their American counterparts, generally shunned the lucrative but risky stock market call loan business. Montreal Trust was the major exception to this rule. As a highly credit-leveraged financier, Aitken had faced danger on all fronts simultaneously, and had he not battened down his business hatches just in time, he would have lost everything.

He had indeed 'foreseen this financial stringency' and 'carefully gathered together all' his financial and human resources.[95] He had done this in various ways: by using Montreal Trust to provide extra liquidity for Royal Securities just as the banks began to call in their short-term loans; by selling off securities at bargain prices and reducing the RSC's debt load to a manageable amount; and by dispatching Nesbitt overseas, creating a release valve for excess securities that were no longer selling in Canada. Aitken had passed with flying colours the most important test any financier can undergo – a general market collapse.

The experience left an indelible mark on the way he ran his financial affairs from then on. Having personally witnessed the fragility of the banking system, he remained forever sensitive of the importance of reinforcing the confidence of investors in his financial ventures, and he was always able to pinpoint the danger signals when the system itself was heading for a breakdown. During 1928 and the early part of 1929, for example, Aitken sold most of his common stock, some of which he had held since before the First World War, and placed his gains in bonds and other more secure investments. He thus remained rich while many of his friends struggled during the Great Depression of the 1930s.[96]

In just four years – from the day he was made corporate secretary of the RSC to the day he watched J.P. Morgan attempt to save the Trust Company of America – Aitken had become one of the most aggressive and powerful young lions in Canadian finance. In his new lair in Montreal, he was viewed with a mixture of envy, jealously, suspicion, fascination, and, occasionally, grudging respect by many of the old-time residents. Normally taciturn tongues wagged when he was observed in the friendly company of the two most august members of the business establishment, Edward Clouston and Sir William Van Horne. Aitken was too intuitive not to notice, and he relished being at the centre of a story that he himself was creating as he went along.

Meanwhile, a few of his old associates in Halifax were waiting for him to fall on his face. Robert E. Harris, in particular, was fond of telling anyone within earshot that Aitken had grown too big for his breeches and had become a sharp operator. Other than looking for an opportunity to strike back at Harris, there was little Aitken could do except continue to demonstrate his utility to his associates in Montreal and Toronto. Through such new ventures as his Montreal Engineering Company and Montreal Trust, he had increased their profits and made a believer of many of them, even if they heard a discouraging word or two from disaffected individuals such as Harris. Aitken's power and influence were beginning to eclipse that of his old associates in Halifax, and he hoped that his reputation would in time become less of a hostage to his enemies.

7

Hubris and the Young Financier

I see you are centering everything in Montreal, so that after a while Halifax will be but a branch office.

George Stairs, writing to Aitken in May 1907[1]

The principle involved is briefly this. If your associates are surprised and concerned at your conduct, either your conduct is in error or your associates are not desirable.

Aitken, writing to Arthur J. Nesbitt in December 1907[2]

As the American economic historian Jonathan Hughes pointed out many years ago, there is much more than the profit motive at work in entrepreneurial behaviour.[3] In Aitken's case, a powerful mixture of pride, insecurity, confidence, and vindictiveness drove him forward more than any simple desire for economic gain. His wish to break free of Halifax and the Scotia group, striking back at Robert E. Harris in the process, prompted his trust company ventures as much as his desire for profit. While his survival instinct crowded out concerns about his position in the food chain during the Panic of 1907, he returned to these more complex motivations after the danger had passed.

The possession of control, authority, or influence over others is the most general definition of power. Money confers a certain amount of power, but reputation and prestige are also required if power is to be exercised systematically over time. In a sense, prestige is to power what credit is to cash. Thus, the more prestige Aitken could obtain, the less he had to draw on his own money to accomplish his goals. A steady stream of profit provided the cash, but Aitken lacked the prestige that would give him the amount of power he so desperately wanted.

Unlike overnight underwriting profits, prestige takes more than a few years of experience as a financier to accumulate. Aitken was still viewed as a young pup by many he dealt with, and consequently he was not given the credit he felt his business accomplishments deserved. Even worse, when he tried to force others to respect his abilities by outmanoeuvring them on the field of battle, he more often generated long-lasting bitterness rather than grudging respect, much less prestige of any type. In fact, his reputation actually suffered, because of the allegations of sharp practice that inevitably accompanied his victories over older and more established business figures.

If Aitken could not immediately gain the respect of his older associates, at least he had the respect of the young men who worked for him. He was an exciting boss and his employees were motivated by his vision, captivated by his novel ideas, and buoyed by his optimism for the future. But Aitken was also an exasperating boss. An emotional volcano, he could erupt at any time, demanding more than was humanly possible and criticizing the smallest detail. He was, in other words, the devil to work for, and many who did work for him eventually had to leave – often with very harsh memories of their experience.

Divide and Conquer

The year 1908 began on an optimistic note. Athough $50,000 of senior securities in the possession of the RSC had to be written off – a casualty of the panic – the corporation still came out of 1907 with a net profit of $5,000, while its appendage, Montreal Engineering, showed a return of 100 per cent on its capitalization.[4] Miraculously, Montreal Trust showed a profit of $47,329 (9.5 per cent on its total capitalization) during 1907. This strong performance in difficult circumstances gave Aitken the authority to replace some of the dead wood on Montreal Trust's board with stronger and potentially more useful men, including William Molson Macpherson (president of Molsons Bank) and Frank W. Morse (vice-president and general manager of the Grand Trunk Pacific Railway).[5]

Meanwhile, W.B. Ross had changed his mind about moving to Montreal on a permanent basis and Aitken was forced to look for a new vice-president. The man he steered into the position was the board member and millionaire George E. Drummond, a native of Ireland, who at an early age had emigrated with his family to Montreal.[6] In 1881, Drummond, along with his younger brother Thomas and a third partner T.J. McCall, had founded Drummond, McCall & Co., iron and steel merchants. Their interests increased with time to include mining and manufacturing as well as holdings in enterprises such as Demerara Electric that were typical of wealthy Montrealers like the Drummond brothers. As vice-president and later president of the Lake Superior Corporation, Tom Drummond was busy trying to rescue the troubled steel conglomerate at Sault Ste Marie while George Drummond, one-time president of the Canadian Mining Institute and the Canadian Manufacturers' Association, ran Drummond, McCall. Despite his reservations about Drummond operating Montreal Trust as an adjunct to the family's iron and steel interests, Aitken did well in securing George E. Drummond as vice-president.[7]

Aitken had also found an extremely competent new corporate secretary, V.J. Hughes, to whom he could increasingly entrust the daily management of the trust company.[8] By spring, the country's money stringency was beginning to lift, and Montreal Trust seemed to be 'running along [so] very smoothly' that Aitken felt he was 'almost without a job.'[9] Most of his ambitions for Montreal Trust had been achieved. One problem gnawed at him, however. Because it was now a paying proposition, 'his' trust company was a tantalizing prize for other aggressive financial men, and he wanted more effective control over the company in order to discourage any takeover attempt.

Aitken indirectly controlled $300,000 par value of Montreal Trust's stock through the investors who had joined him in the original purchase. Of this amount, the original Halifax syndicate directly owned $169,000 in shares, $70,000 of which Aitken personally held and $12,000 of which the RSC owned. The last $200,000 of stock remained in the hands of the company's old Montreal shareholders.[10] If a large contingent of the Montreal or Halifax men decided to sell their shares – which was now a real possibility, since the shares had appreciated by approximately 20 per cent in little more than a year – Aitken might lose control of Montreal Trust. This would be particularly galling given that he was responsible for the trust company's higher share value.[11]

Aitken's scheme was simple. Without sinking more money into Montreal Trust, he could centralize ownership by having the RSC purchase all the shares held by Halifax syndicate members and himself, thereby more than doubling his ownership control overnight. However, this suggestion was opposed by the RSC president George Stairs, who questioned Aitken's motives. Stairs thought that Aitken was using the scheme as a pretext to move the RSC's head office from Halifax to Montreal. From the day Aitken had moved to Montreal to begin running Montreal Trust, his actions had been accurately interpreted by Stairs as an attempt to shift the RSC to Montreal and remove him as president in the process.[12] Harris was even more distrustful of Aitken than Stairs was – and for good reason. Aitken was doing everything he could not only to remove Harris's influence from RSC affairs but to undermine his business interests outside Royal Securities.[13]

Employing the tactics of divide and conquer, Aitken tried to drive a wedge between Stairs and Harris. Telling Stairs of the many ways in which Montreal Trust would benefit from being tied to the RSC, Aitken begged him to seek advice from W.B. Ross and Almon Lovett (who, like Stairs, were shareholders in both the RSC and Montreal Trust), rather than from Harris who, as Aitken put it, 'only sees out of one small window; viz, the Eastern Trust Company.' Then, claiming that he was incapable of 'serving two masters' at the same time, he threatened to quit the RSC unless Stairs endorsed his holding company plan.[14]

Despite Aitken's special pleading and threats, Stairs refused to break ranks with Harris. In one last-ditch effort, Aitken travelled to Halifax to convince Stairs of the merits of his plan.[15] Again, Stairs resisted. Aitken now only had two options: to retreat or to carry out his threat. He chose the latter when Stairs and Harris suggested that the time had come to wind up the company. Neither had the time to manage the company on a full-time basis – Harris had his law firm and the presidency of Scotia, while Stairs was busy managing the Halifax branch of Consumers Cordage – and they preferred to sell out if they could not keep the RSC in Halifax. At a minimum, they had expected to be kept informed of developments at regularly held directors' meetings.

Aitken had discontinued board meetings after his move to Montreal, and the Scotia men had become increasingly fatigued by their efforts to remedy the situation. Months before, Harris had warned Aitken, 'We are getting into a bad way of doing business without holding a meeting of the Directors, and it will lead us into no end of trouble.'[16] Aitken's reply had been less than reassuring. He told Harris that while he 'did not mean to usurp more than a due amount of authority,' he nonetheless felt that he had to 'act in a very arbitrary manner to secure efficient results from an organization such as [he was] endeavoring to build up.'[17]

Even more than his words, Aitken's actions had pushed Harris and Stairs towards confrontation. It was only weeks after his failed attempt to exclude Harris from the RSC's decision making that Aitken hatched his plan to have the RSC purchase the Halifax syndicate's block of controlling shares in the Montreal Trust Company. In the circumstances, Harris and Stairs could hardly have come to any conclusion other than that Aitken was doing his utmost to break his links with Halifax and the Scotia group.[18]

Shaking Out the Royal Securities Corporation

Winding up the RSC seemed the only option until Gerald Farrell, the firm's sales manager, offered to purchase the company's name. Harris and Stairs agreed – on condition that all its assets first be liquidated and the cash distributed to the small circle of RSC shareholders. Aitken also concurred but inserted his own rather peculiar proviso. Montreal Trust would keep possession of all the RSC's old office correspondence for a period of two years, after which it would be returned to the RSC's custody.[19]

The logic behind this unusual condition must be inferred. Despite Farrell's rocky start at the RSC, Aitken had gradually come to respect his abilities as a sales supervisor. Yet some residue of mistrust remained, and Aitken obviously preferred to keep RSC's secrets to himself as a precaution against future embarrassments. He may also have wanted to ensure that the correspondence would not be destroyed if the company was later liquidated. It is even possible that Aitken fully intended to repurchase the RSC within the two years and was simply ensuring that all the valuable material contained in five years' worth of correspondence would be preserved for his later use. Information was power, and Aitken was never one to underestimate the immense value of this type of documentation.[20]

Aitken set up two separate promoting companies to fill the vacuum created by the sale of the RSC. The first was the Utilities Securities Company, which was organized on 2 March 1908 with a nominal capitalization of $100,000. It was created as a venture capital vehicle to promote new utility companies in the Caribbean and Latin America. Aitken purchased a majority of the shares for himself and then invited his most trusted and reliable associates – Will Ross, Almon Lovett, Fred Teele, Fred Clarke, and Carl Giles – to become shareholders. He would thus be surrounded by men who had shared his vision of a utility empire run from Montreal through the RSC and Montreal Engineering. With the exception of W.B. Ross, for whom he had reserved some shares, Aitken had no intention of asking any of his old Halifax associates to join his new company.[21]

Aitken then incorporated the Bond and Share Company and immediately reserved shares for his RSC securities men such as Arthur Nesbitt and Walton Killam.[22] Bond and Share was designed as an investment bank that would concentrate entirely on promoting and underwriting, leaving the retailing of securities to outside brokers and bond houses. Operating from its base in Montreal, Bond and Share was to play a pivotal role in the promotion of the Canada Cement Company the following year; but Aitken was too occupied with running Montreal Trust to make much immediate use of his new investment shell, apart from having it hold his Montreal Engineering shares temporarily. In the meantime, he asked Nesbitt to start up a new bond department for the trust company, and Killam was sent to Halifax to represent Aitken in the RSC's liquidation.

Under Aitken's instructions, Killam began to sell off the RSC's inventory of senior securities, together with all the common stock that had accumulated as a consequence of the corporation's 10 per cent policy on underwriting.[23] At the same time, Killam was instructed to figure out whether W.B. Ross was now in league with Harris and George Stairs. Aitken told him:

I cannot ascertain the attitude of W.B. Ross. Lovett is of the opinion that he is very anxious to clean up and get what cash he can. In that event I would be quite satisfied to have him do so; but if he stands in the same position to our interest that he used to occupy *before the dividing line was drawn between Halifax and Montreal,* I owe it to him to retain my close association with him. I think you will understand what I mean, and I will expect to hear from you fully. I would prefer that you would not dictate any answer to the stenographer.[24] (Emphasis in the original)

After a few days in Halifax, Killam concluded that W.B. Ross was still on Aitken's side, and Aitken permitted Ross to roll his RSC holdings into the Utilities Securities Company. Harris, meanwhile, was being more difficult than ever. He owed more than $17,000 to the RSC on his Porto Rico underwriting and was using every excuse imaginable in his refusals to come up with the cash.[25] The truth was that Harris was unable to pay at this time. He had overextended himself during the panic of the previous October, when he had used funds that were due on his underwriting to purchase 1,600 Scotia common stock at bargain prices in order to gain additional control over the enterprise of which he was president. At the time, Aitken had been so infuriated that he had threatened to sue Harris on his underwriting agreement, and he had no intention of letting him off the hook at this point.[26] Although 1 March was the date set for Farrell's purchase of the RSC, Aitken refused to allow the transfer until Harris had settled his account. Harris, for his part, had no intention of immediately paying off his debts by selling stock at fire-sale prices, particularly if he could annoy Aitken by delaying matters.[27] Left in the lurch, Farrell threatened to withdraw from the purchase agreement.[28] To break the deadlock, George Stairs used his influence at the Union Bank of Halifax to secure a loan on Harris's behalf so that Harris could pay off his debt to the RSC. Stairs wanted to put an end to the whole affair. He had become impatient with Harris's attitude.[29] Thus, one month past the original deadline, Harris at last turned over the money and the RSC name was handed over to Farrell.[30] Then the unexpected struck.

On 1 April, George Stairs and W.B. Ross were finalizing the accounts on the RSC liquidation,[31] and in the late afternoon Stairs stopped for a moment to chat with his nephew Gilbert Stairs. All of a sudden, Stairs's voice became low and his speech slower, and he fell forward out of his chair onto his desk – struck dead by a heart attack. Stairs was only fifty-two years old.[32] Like his brother John F. Stairs, he may have inherited a weak heart, but the stress caused by the battle that had led to the RSC's liquidation and sale could not have helped his condition, and it may even have contributed to his early death.

Aitken stopped briefly in his hectic schedule to pay his respects to George Stairs, but he was little disturbed by the event compared with his distress at John F. Stairs's death three and a half years earlier. He remarked to one associate, 'It is sad indeed that his lifetime is now over, but there is nothing ... to do but go on.'[33] Others were more upset. Almon Lovett, who was in England on vacation when he received the news, wrote to Aitken saying that he 'was very much shocked and grieved' to receive the telegram informing him of Stairs's heart attack. 'With his death,' Lovett wrote, 'it seems that a large part of the vigour of business life in Halifax will go by the board.' As far as Aitken was concerned, it had gone by the board the day John F. Stairs had died. Nonetheless, he could agree with Lovett's sentiment that, 'as to the future,' they could not expect to 'look for very much assistance from East.'[34] Aitken's final connection to Halifax was now irrevocably severed.

The sale of the RSC had been a strenuous affair involving so much bitterness that George Stairs's fatal heart attack seemed a fitting if tragic finale. It almost turned out to be the end for the Royal Securities Corporation as well. Aitken may have been slightly suspicious of Farrell at the time of the sale, but he could not have predicted what was to follow.

Within five months, Gerald Farrell drove his securities company into the ground. Aitken lost $5,000 on the deal, money he had lent Farrell to purchase a small part of the RSC's new $50,000 share capital. Others lost substantially more, especially the new investors whom Farrell had brought into the company. The largest included William Mackenzie and Donald Mann, of Canadian Northern Railway fame, and Nathaniel Curry, the president of the Rhodes Curry rolling stock manufacturing company of Amherst, Nova Scotia.[35]

Aitken's first impression of Farrell had turned out to be correct. Farrell was a good sales manager but a terrible spendthrift. He spent his first two months running the RSC from London, England, on the pretence of getting new business, while in fact he was enjoying the extravagance of high-society living. By September, the firm's expenses so exceeded its revenues that even Farrell realized he was finished.[36] In a final pathetic gesture, he assigned to Aitken his carriage and harness in partial settlement of his debt.[37]

When they recovered from their initial shock, Farrell's creditors and shareholders realized that they were stuck. Since the RSC owned virtually nothing in terms of assets, liquidation would not solve anything. At this point, Aitken stepped in. After convincing his fellow Montreal Trust board members to acquire control of the RSC, he offered to repurchase the RSC charter and settle Farrell's debts. Having few other options, the RSC's creditors and shareholders quickly agreed, and Montreal Trust purchased 75 per cent of the RSC stock.[38]

Extending Control by Stacking Ownership

At the price of some five months' worth of damage to the RSC's good name, Aitken had achieved his objective of directly linking both companies and controlling them from Montreal, even if Montreal Trust was now the holding company for Royal Securities rather than the reverse as he had originally intended. Nonetheless, Aitken was now finally free to manage both firms in a consistent and mutually supportive manner without interference from Halifax, especially from 'that podgy gentleman' Robert E. Harris.[39]

Aitken purchased the remaining 25 per cent of the RSC's stock so that he could personally select shareholders who would be most useful to him in future financing. Among the first to join was Edward Clouston, Aitken's closest ally in the Montreal business establishment. In addition to his position as general manager and vice-president of the Bank of Montreal, Clouston was vice-president of the Royal Trust Company and president of the Montreal Rolling Mills, and he held directorships on eight other corporate boards.[40] One month after Aitken repurchased control of the RSC, Clouston was created a baronet in recognition of his contribution to Canadian business and society. Everyone assumed that Sir Edward would succeed Sir George A. Drummond as president of the Bank of Montreal when eventually he retired after many years as general manager.[41] While Clouston's $35,000-a-year salary from the Bank of Montreal was considerable for the time, it was his extensive business interests outside the bank that had made him a millionaire.[42] His decision to purchase shares in Aitken's RSC was only natural given his appetite for profitable business ventures and his confidence in Aitken. In fact, Sir Edward was to receive much more of a return on his investment than he bargained for during the next two years, not all of it desirable.

Aitken also invited Charles Cahan and Almon Lovett to purchase shares in the RSC. Since both now had their own law firms in Montreal, they expected to benefit from handling the legal work Aitken generated in promoting and floating companies. Of the two, Cahan was closest to Aitken.[43] Cahan had just lost a bitter dispute with Dr Pearson and his Toronto allies, Zebulon Lash and E.R. Wood, over Mexican Light and Power's relationship with a second Pearson utility in Mexico, and he was eager to rebuild his position in Montreal using Aitken's enterprises as his foundation.[44] He possessed a useful combination of legal, financial, and managerial skills, and was welcomed with open arms by Aitken, who used Cahan in virtually every financial deal from this point on, until their acrimonious split two years later.[45]

In the first major company promotion of 1909, a hydroelectric proposition in the Vancouver area, Cahan joined Aitken, as did Lovett and Clouston. Capitalized at $5 million, the new Western Canada Power Company issued $2.5 million of bonds underwritten by the RSC as well as by the 'Bank of Montreal interests acting through Sir Edward Clouston,' as Aitken phrased it. All four men received a generous common stock payment for their promoting and underwriting activities.[46] Cahan was appointed president of the new enterprise, and the board of directors was made up of new RSC shareholders. While Clouston himself remained off the Western Canada Power board, his executive assistant Arthur Doble joined the board, along with the bank's Vancouver manager. The Bank of Montreal's connection to the project was further accentuated by Doble's appointment as Western Canada Power's secretary-treasurer.[47]

Now that Aitken was back in control of the RSC, he could have disbanded the Utilities Securities Company and the Bond and Share Com-

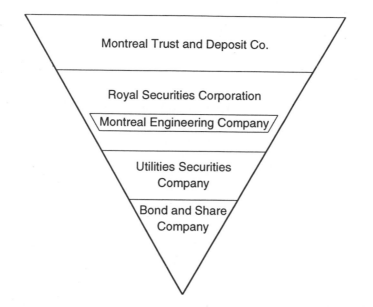

FIGURE 7.1 Aitken's inverted pyramid of ownership and control, October 1908 to July 1909

pany. But he did not do so. Instead, he created an inverted pyramidal structure with Montreal Trust at the top, the RSC in the middle, and the Utilities Securities Company and Bond and Share Company at the base, as illustrated in figure 7.1. Despite the fact that Aitken reserved Montreal Trust stock only for investors who were capable of bringing new business to the company, the trust company's shares were the most widely held. Consequently, its operations were open to greater public scrutiny than the RSC's. This is represented in figure 7.1 by the broader space occupied by Montreal Trust compared with the RSC.[48]

Montreal Engineering was a wholly owned subsidiary of the RSC with no connection to the other companies except through the RSC. Its role was to construct and supervise the utility projects conceived and then marketed by the RSC. The engineering company held shares in the utility companies but was not a utility holding company per se. To complete the holding company structure, the RSC took over Aitken's personal holdings in the Utilities Securities Company, which made up 62 per cent of the total, as well as the holdings of Will Ross, Almon Lovett, and Fred Teele, who took RSC shares in exchange. The Utilities Securities Company then bought almost all the shares in the Bond and Share Company.[49] By this device, Aitken managed to increase his personal control without spending an extra cent of his own money. At the same time, he had four corporate vehicles at his disposal, each with a different set of attributes.

While Montreal Trust had more financial resources at its disposal and a greater potential to garner cash by attracting public deposits, its shareholding structure required Aitken to hold regular meetings and be attentive to the needs of his fellow shareholders and directors and to the laws governing trustees and trust companies.[50] Aitken had much more control over the RSC, but he did have to keep his largest shareholders informed of what was going on. More importantly, the RSC was a complex enough organization that Aitken could not have complete control, and considerable managerial authority gradually came to reside in the office managers, especially Blake Burrill, Arthur Nesbitt, and Walton Killam. By contrast, Aitken had almost complete control over the Utilities Securities and Bond and Share companies, both of which were exempt from virtually any form of public scrutiny. Their lack of public persona was also their weakness in the sense that only a group of insiders would be prepared to enter into agreements with such shadowy entities, and certainly no bank would lend money to such institutions.

The result of this inverted pyramid was simple. Aitken's control increased as he descended the pyramid. Through his ownership stake in Montreal Trust, as well as through his position as managing director, he commanded Montreal Trust, but he had to be vigilant to keep control and careful not to annoy fellow shareholders and directors. With the RSC, because of Montreal Trust's majority ownership of it, as well as Aitken's personal block of shares and his position as president and general manager, he had far more effective control. By hand-picking shareholders for both companies, he could minimize any potential threat to his control, especially in the case of Montreal Trust. It was also convenient to have alternatives. Sir Edward Clouston, for example, was prevented from becoming a Montreal Trust shareholder because of his position in Royal Trust, but no *direct* conflict of interest arose out of his holdings in the RSC.

Finally, because of the RSC's majority stake in the Utilities Securities Company and because of the latter's majority ownership of the Bond and Share Company, Aitken dominated both companies as firmly as if he held all the shares in his own name. His complete authority with respect to both these companies was questioned on only one occasion. In the autumn of 1909, Aitken asked Almon Lovett to draft some new by-laws for the Utilities Securities Company giving Aitken the *express* right, as managing director, to exercise all the powers of the board of directors. Lovett suggested, 'as a friend,' that Aitken might be creating a legal problem for himself in the future. In particular, he warned Aitken that 'any shareholder who was dissatisfied might suggest that you had used this Corporation not in the interests of its shareholders, but in your own interests, putting this Company in a position where it would take the burden in matters which turned out unprofitable and you taking for yourself the things that are profitable.' To avoid this problem, Lovett suggested that Aitken appoint as general manager a trusted associate who would always act under Aitken's directions. Lovett then observed that lawyers 'often get anything but thanks for these friendly suggestions' and said that he was prepared to take the risk because 'I think it is my duty, both as your legal adviser and your friend.'[51]

Aitken swiftly rejected Lovett's suggestions. He wanted the by-law drafted and the resolutions passed by both the directors and shareholders of the Utilities Securities Company without further debate or discussion. Lovett's reply was conciliatory, even servile:

So far as I am concerned, I will agree and vote that you should exercise all the powers of the Board, and, if you like, that you should never refer to the board or submit anything to the Board, but that the affairs of the Company should in every respect be left entirely and solely in your hands, and, if you desire, I will join you in purchasing the shares of any and every shareholder who does not wish to have the Company managed on these lines; or, if you prefer, I will agree that the Company should be wound up and the assets distributed or to any other thing that you may wish to do in reference to the matter.[52]

The Impossible Boss

Even after regaining possession of the Royal Securities' charter, Aitken spent less time at the corporation's new head office at 179 St James Street than at Place d'Armes, where he ran the Montreal Trust Company.[53] Most of 1908 had been devoted to extending Montreal Trust's banking and bond business, in the hope that this would considerably enhance the firm's profitability. In fact, the 1908 financial statements disclosed that Montreal Trust had made a return of 11.7 per cent on its capital, a significant improvement over 1907, and that its accumulated profit stood at $76,000, compared with $3,000 in 1906.

How did Aitken achieve such results, not only with Montreal Trust but with all the ventures with which he was connected? His own ability, often translated into organizational changes and greater efficiency, explains some of his success, but his achievements also rested on his ability to attract extremely talented individuals as associates and employees. This was a product of his electric personality and enthusiasm, characteristics that were particularly appealing to like-minded young men. The fact that individuals such as Arthur Nesbitt, Walton Killam, and Ward Pitfield (who joined the RSC in 1914) became the dominant financiers in Canada during the interwar years, and that their firms became the chief invest-ment banks in the country in the twentieth century, speaks for itself.[54]

The flip side of Aitken's personal magnetism and his ability to spot tal-ent was his single-mindedness. Once they were recruited, all these men quickly discovered that their performance, no matter how good, could never meet Aitken's exacting and at times unrealistic standards. His man-agement style was one of continual confrontation and reappraisal, in which he incessantly nagged and criticized his employees. Moreover, like many self-made men, he had great difficulty in delegating responsibility, and he too often interfered with the decisions made by his managers.

Montreal Trust provides an instructive example. Despite the company's superb record, Aitken constantly complained that its performance was poor. Everyone from the general manager, V.J. Hughes, to the heads of the various departments came in for vigorous criticism on even the most minute aspects of their management. In his broader assaults on Montreal Trust's management, Aitken used words such as 'disgraceful' to describe the company's monthly earnings reports, and in letter after letter to Hughes and other officers he claimed to be 'ashamed' of the firm – at a time when the trust company was experiencing record earnings.[55] As the Montreal manager of Royal Securities a few years later, Arthur Doble summed it up well when he told Aitken that if severe criticism was to have a positive 'disciplinary effect,' it had to be justified. Moreover, while it might be 'inevitable' that Aitken would judge men by his own talents, he would 'never get a staff to measure up' to himself. 'You may not believe it,' Doble said, 'but you have a number of men of more than average abil-ity, and of quite unusual loyalty, willing to give you the best that is in them. If you look for more than this I do not know where your require-ments can be supplied.'[56]

Aitken did look for more, and the result was predictable. He lost some of his best people. Blake Burrill was the first to go. As manager of the RSC's head office, he came into his share of criticism. He had to run the office in Aitken's absence for weeks at a time, carefully supervising salesmen, monitoring brokers and underwriters, and watching the RSC's cash flow like a hawk while collecting instalments from recalcitrant underwriters, including the senior directors of the RSC. Burrill received little praise for his efforts, but he performed his tasks with great efficiency and was widely respected in the investment community in Halifax.[57]

After Aitken moved to Montreal, Burrill found himself increasingly caught in the dispute between Aitken and Harris. He remained loyal to Aitken but questioned whether Aitken had reserved a place for him from his new base of operations in Montreal. As a consequence, he began to devote more time to buying and selling securities on his own account, and although the Halifax office did not seem to suffer much in consequence, Aitken took great offence at this change.[58] Aitken complained to Horace Porter in Saint John that he thought Burrill's salary of $3,500 was too high given his outside trading activities. The information travelled back to Burrill, who then wrote to Aitken saying, 'I am grieved to learn that you would make any reference to such a matter to a man occupying a subordinate position to myself,' and he hinted that he might be better off working on his own.[59] Despite his desire to keep Burrill, Aitken did nothing to smooth his feathers after this incident, and he certainly did not apologize for his tactless remark. When Burrill announced that he was leaving to set up his own firm in Yarmouth, Aitken coolly replied, 'I note that you propose to leave us, and deeply as I regret your decision, it is not entirely unexpected. While you have done great work, and while we have profited from your efforts, nevertheless your probable withdrawal from the Corporation has been a constant source of apprehension to me.'[60] Aitken then peevishly wrote to Nesbitt, observing, 'Two years ago I thought B.G. Burrill indispensable to the Corporation. Today I find his going out will result in the saving of $3,500 salary.'[61]

Nesbitt was the next to go, leaving the following autumn to set up his own investment bank.[62] He had been Aitken's golden boy, personally selected over Gerald Farrell to manage the all-important Montreal office of the RSC. After Burrill, Nesbitt was the second RSC employee whom Aitken had wanted on the corporation's board of directors.[63] But Nesbitt, too, had been the recipient of some of Aitken's strongest criticism. Unlike Burrill, he had actually deserved some of Aitken's censure. In early 1907, for example, he had decided to buy some common stock on margin to see if he could make some quick money. He bought up a block of Lake Superior Corporation in the expectation that the stock would recover from its low of $15 and climb back to its previous high of $25. Unfortunately for Nesbitt, his 'Soo' common dropped steadily during the following months, hitting $4 a share by autumn and forcing him to cover the losses on his margin account.[64] Not having the money on hand, he borrowed a few thousand dollars from the RSC corporate account with the intention of returning it within a few days. He then took out a personal loan from the Metropolitan Bank to purchase more stock on margin in a futile effort to recoup his loss. As market conditions continued to deteriorate during 1907, Nesbitt was soon short again on his margin account, and he borrowed more money from the RSC.

When Nesbitt finally realized that he had lost control, he went to Aitken and admitted what he had done. Aitken then agreed to lend Nesbitt $2,000 to take care of his debts, but on the understanding that he would give an accounting of his indebtedness and 'never go into the market again.'[65] During the next few months, however, share prices continued to fall and Nesbitt found himself having to top up his margin account with his broker while trying to repay bank loans. When Aitken discovered that Nesbitt had made further unauthorized withdrawals from the RSC, totalling $9,000, plus some suspicious withdrawals for travelling expenses, he hit the roof. He wrote to Nesbitt, who was then in England selling securities, and demanded that he produce a complete and final accounting of his indebtedness. 'It would be impossible,' Aitken noted, 'for you to spend more money than you earned, were it not for your unfortunate speculation in stock.'[66] In a later letter, he continued to upbraid Nesbitt:

I am very much worried about the way in which the situation has developed. I do not know where you are going to. I would not hesitate to stand back of you for one moment if you would just make one clear cleanup. Show me exactly where you stand. Get with my consent and with the consent of the Board of Directors the necessary funds to carry you through, and we will be satisfied. But I had supposed you to be cleaned up a half dozen times, and each succeeding month I find your account a little bit higher than the month before. If you keep on long enough you will absorb all of our capital. The whole system which we are endeavoring to build is being shattered and destroyed by the manner in which you are drawing on the Corporation.[67]

Instead of dealing with the main problem, Nesbitt reacted angrily to Aitken's assertion that he was using travel expense money for other purposes, and he threatened to leave the RSC if Aitken could no longer trust him with RSC funds.[68] Aitken held his ground arguing, 'There is a right way for me to act as the Managing Director for the Shareholders of the Royal Securities Corporation and there is a wrong way.' The real question, Aitken stated, 'was whether you have treated the Corporation and me ... properly,' and he added, 'If you will look back upon the times when you withdrew money from the Corporation, you will remember what your own conscience told you at such times.'[69] Nesbitt finally surrendered. He gave a complete accounting of all his debts and asked to be forgiven. Stating that the matter was now 'permanently closed' as far as he was concerned, Aitken took over all Nesbitt's debts for the time being.[70]

Nesbitt then returned from Britain and set up Montreal Trust's new bond department; but unfortunately for him, the next few months were difficult ones for bond sellers. Unable to get bank loans and squeamish after the market break of 1907, investors were still holding on to their cash. Aitken blamed Nesbitt and sent letter after letter complaining about his poor performance, until Nesbitt had had enough:

From the way you are criticising this Department it seems to me that you evidently are not satisfied with the way I am carrying on the business ... If you think you can get someone else who will take more interest in securing business and work harder ... I am prepared to resign. I have been putting forth my best efforts on behalf of the Company, not only as regards the selling of bonds, but endeavoring to secure other business at the same time, consequently I do not consider that this criticism which has been going on for some time is justified.[71]

Aitken's reply was uncompromising:

You are not giving as great efforts to your business to-day as you were two years ago. I must insist upon criticizing your business ... If you expect me to remain quiet until such time as the Montreal Trust Company is doing the best bond business at least in Montreal you are very much mistaken. We have got the money, position and board of directors. We have got to do the business.[72]

The truth was that bonds were almost impossible to sell in the immediate aftermath of the Panic of 1907. Since Aitken's attacks appeared groundless, Nesbitt must have felt that he was being punished for his earlier transgressions. In the circumstances, it seemed best to strike out on his own, which he did in the autumn of 1908.[73]

Walton Killam also left Aitken, at least temporarily. After he had finished acting as Aitken's agent in the liquidation of the RSC during the spring of 1908, Killam went to Quebec City to sell bonds on behalf of Montreal Trust.[74] Aitken made him an offer; if Killam could sell $50,000 of bonds, he could establish a branch of Montreal Trust at Quebec that would operate under his own management.[75] Although Killam was a superb salesman, even he could not sell bonds in the prevailing market conditions; so since Aitken would not let him open the Montreal Trust branch, he decided to stay in Quebec and establish his own bond house. When he told Aitken of his plan, Aitken's response betrayed his desire to keep the young man:

You would be crazy to start a securities corporation. You don't need capital, and you are getting along first rate. For Heaven sake make your money for yourself, and not for other people. You cannot own any stock in a securities company because you have not got money to pay for it. Take the advice of a man who has been through the mill, and leave securities companies alone. You know perfectly well that I owned such interests in the Royal Securities that I could afford to work for that Company, but no man can afford to work for other people when he is not given money in the first instance. Why don't you accumulate a credit at the Montreal Trust office, and work with that Company as your financial support? You are getting foolish.[76]

Unlike the way John F. Stairs had generously assisted Aitken, however, Aitken did not buy Killam a substantial share in Montreal Trust, though admittedly this would have been a more difficult proposition considering that the company had ten times the capitalization of the RSC. As a consequence, Killam set up his own company in Quebec.[77] He was hardly being foolish. Months later, at Aitken's request, Killam returned to the RSC on his own terms. He established a new branch in Quebec City for Aitken's revitalized RSC in early 1909. Later that year, he went overseas to London to monitor the RSC's security flotations, and by the end of 1910 he was managing the RSC's new office in London. Eventually, Killam became the top man in the organization. His survival was due to his independence and his remarkable ability not to take Aitken's criticism or actions personally. It must also be said, though, that he became Aitken's successor as president and chief shareholder of the RSC partly because his two more qualified rivals for the position, Blake Burrill and Arthur Nesbitt, were no longer with the RSC.

Preparing for a Bull Market

Despite the time Aitken devoted to Montreal Trust, he continued to think of the Royal Securities Corporation as his paramount interest. As 1909 and the bull market began, he grew increasingly bored with the trust

company's operations and began to concentrate on the business of promoting companies. After all, the business of a trust company, even when
stretched to taking deposits and lending money, was rather mechanical
and boring compared with investment banking. Aitken toyed with the
idea of selling out all his interests in Canada and using his money to buy
a bank or trust company in New York, where share prices were still
depressed as a consequence of the financial panic.[78] He felt he had
reached the limits of what was possible with trust companies in Canada.
The chartered banks would let him move only so far into a general banking business before retaliating, perhaps by attacking Montreal Trust for
exceeding the 'legally' proscribed functions of a trust company by receiving deposits making advances, or underwriting and selling securities.[79]

In January 1909 Edson Pease, the vice-president and general manager
of the Royal Bank of Canada, offered Aitken $135 a share to purchase
control of Montreal Trust. Aitken was tempted but advised his board to
decline the offer, explaining that he could work out a more advantageous
arrangement.[80] He preferred the idea of forming an alliance with a
smaller chartered bank, since that would allow him to continue to dominate Montreal Trust and eventually to exercise hegemony over the bank
itself. At that point, he would change the ownership structure so that the
RSC would be placed at the top of a new inverted pyramid.[81]

Complicating matters was the desire of two new associates in England,
Ion Hamilton Benn and Andrew Bonar Law, to form a transatlantic
investment bank with him. Following up on Nesbitt's trips, Aitken had
spent from October to December 1908 in Britain, his first experience of
the Old World, in an effort to unload securities that were still not selling
in Canada. At this time, Montreal Trust was acting as one of the underwriters for the Canada Iron Corporation's security flotation in England,
and Aitken was supervising the flotation to protect the trust company's
investment.[82] Ion Hamilton Benn, a City financier, had recently visited
Canada and had been impressed with the country's industrial potential.[83]
Benn had just incorporated Western Canada Trust, an investment bank
specializing in new Canadian issues, and this was his first Canadian flotation. Contrary to Aitken's expectations – he was dubious about industrials
and had not been reassured by the amateurish format of Benn's original
prospectus – the issue turned out to be a success.[84]

Through Benn and a letter of introduction, Aitken met Bonar Law,
another financier, who was also a Conservative MP.[85] Born in New Brunswick and, like Aitken, the son of a Scottish Presbyterian minister, Bonar
Law had moved to Glasgow when he was twelve years old. By 1908 he had

become one of the leading lights in the Unionist Party, Joseph Chamberlain's imperialist and anti–Irish Home Rule wing of the British Conservative Party.[86] After selling Law securities, Aitken discussed the possibility that Law and Benn might take a more direct interest in either Montreal Trust or the RSC. Both men were evidently impressed with Aitken, for when he returned to Canada he received the following letter from Benn:

I have had some discussions with Mr. Bonar Law lately. He is very much interested in the Montreal Trust, and he would like to be in with you and me, but he thinks that the General Election is so imminent that it would be impossible for him to join the Board. You know he is sure to get one of the important posts in the next Ministry, and Ministers in England are not allowed to hold any directorships. He wishes, however, to take a substantial interest in the Company, and both he and I would like to have a share with you in the Royal Securities Company on the lines that you discussed with me in December, – that is to say, we would like to be in your inner circle.[87]

Aitken's main objective was to set up a transatlantic investment bank with a strong presence in the City. He was prepared to use banks, trust companies, or whatever institutions he needed to accomplish his purpose, but he also intended that the RSC, and thus himself, would dominate the enterprise. He had not worked so assiduously to rid himself of Robert E. Harris and the Scotia group in order to be controlled by wealthy City men such as Benn and Law. But he needed their influence as well as their knowledge of the British market, and he therefore gave them the impression that he would eventually join forces by selling them shares in some of his companies.

Benn, on the other hand, wanted a partnership arrangement with Aitken, and he went so far as to suggest an immediate winding up of Western Canada Trust. In its place, Benn and Aitken would establish a London branch of Montreal Trust. This suggestion was predicated on the Montreal Trust and Deposit Company's forging a powerful link with a Canadian chartered bank and, to suit Benn's sense of decorum, changing its name to the Montreal Trust Company. For his part, Benn would recruit Law and other wealthy financiers to double Montreal Trust's capital.[88] Since Montreal Trust's capital had been doubled just months before to $1 million, this meant a financial institution with $2 million of share capital to draw upon.[89]

Aitken shortened the trust company's name but stalled on the rest of the proposal.[90] Linking up with a chartered bank was problematic. The

Royal Bank was simply too powerful a partner to allow Aitken control in any merger, so he cast around for a smaller bank. He returned to Montagu Allan and the Merchants Bank of Canada but soon found that Allan was considering a merger with another chartered bank that would swamp Aitken's rather small Montreal Trust Company.[91] Aitken's second difficulty was with Ion Hamilton Benn's insularity. Refusing to see some of the advantages in certain North American innovations, Benn remained wedded to the English way of doing business, which precluded advertising or dealing with other houses that were in any way competitors on other issues. Aitken had no intention of entering into an equal partnership with Benn, but to keep Benn temporarily satisfied he agreed to buy part ownership in Western Canada Trust. With Benn assuming that a merger of their interests was about to be consummated, Aitken sent Walton Killam to London so that Benn's Western Canada Trust men could learn North American ways. At the same time, Killam was instructed to learn as much as possible about the City and its curious practices.[92]

With his British connection in place, Aitken felt that he was ready to take advantage of the great bull market in industrial securities. As 1909 began, a small handful of Canadian manufacturing companies had found investors eager to snap up their bonds and preference shares. Canadians were feeling confident about their country, their industries, and their future and were beginning to buy every decent bond and stock in sight after the money famine of 1907–8. By mid-February, both the bond department of Montreal Trust and Aitken's recently salvaged Royal Securities Corporation had run out of securities to sell.[93] Aitken, now 'hard pressed for new issues,' had to return to the business of manufacturing new securities.[94]

By April, mergers with enormous capitalizations – for instance, National Breweries, with an issued capital of $7 million, and Amalgamated Asbestos, with its issued capital of $18 million – were cobbled together with an eye to exploiting this new interest in industrial securities. In addition, larger issues such as Montreal Cotton, National Drug and Chemical, and the Lake Superior Corporation were sold in the City, and everyone recognized that the British market was where the real action lay.[95]

The financial barons of Toronto and Montreal enthusiastically supported the idea of raising money for Canadian industry in Britain; they were helped immensely by a small group of City brokers and bankers who were bullish on Canadian investments. Even Governor General Earl Grey helped boom Canadian securities, proclaiming to his son-in-law (a City banker who had invested heavily in safer Canadian municipal and railway bonds) that the 'time had come when British Capital should be attracted to Canadian industries.'[96] But Sir Edward Clouston, speaking in his role as the dominion's most important banker, warned the financiers of Toronto and Montreal against spoiling this great opportunity by sending the riskier grades of investments to England.[97] Meanwhile, he worked behind the scenes with Aitken, helping him assemble and then sell the securities of industrial mergers to British investors.

8

Manufacturing the Canada Cement Company

Between the idea
And the reality
Between the motion
And the act
Falls the Shadow

T.S. Eliot, 'The Hollow Men'

The year 1909 marked the beginning of a bull market that was to sweep the country and produce the first great merger wave in Canadian history. During the next four years, the country saw almost two hundred old firms disappear into fifty multifirm consolidations. In 1909 alone, more than $100 million of securities of Canadian manufacturing companies were issued, many to British investors.[1] The frenzy continued through 1910, 1911, and 1912, slowing with the sharp recession of 1913, and finally dying with the outbreak of the First World War. As outlined in the new statistical series presented in the appendix, not until the speculative bubble of the second half of the 1920s did Canadians again see anything like it.

Unlike the wave of the 1920s, which struck all the major industrial nations at the same time, the first Canadian merger wave came one full decade after similar waves in the United States, Britain, and Germany, in large part because a substantial market for industrial securities did not emerge in Canada until after the turn of the century.[2] The notion that a well-developed market for industrial securities is a prerequisite for any sustained merger wave was first advanced during the early 1950s by economist George Stigler and business historians Thomas Navin and Marian

Sears.[3] Their evidence was restricted to the evolution of the American market for industrial securities and the central role played by the Great Merger Wave between 1898 and 1902, but the argument is applicable to other advanced industrial countries, including Canada. The common element is that the bonds and shares of domestic manufacturing companies became an accepted form of investment only after the successive entrenchment of government, municipal, railway, bank, and public utility securities.

Industrial bonds and preference shares at this infant stage had a reputation akin to the modern junk bond, being both high risk and potentially high yield relative to more established securities. Attracted to the newly consolidated enterprises because of their size and presumed stability and, in some cases, monopoly power, many American, British, and German investors bought industrial securities for the first time during the merger waves at the turn of the century. Until industrial securities proved themselves over the next two decades, however, a higher interest or dividend rate had to be offered investors to offset the higher risk identified with these early junk bonds.

The market for Canadian industrial securities did not evolve as quickly as the American, British, and German markets for two main reasons. On the supply side, until the early 1900s the capital requirements of the vast majority of Canadian manufacturing companies were easily satisfied through retained earnings, family savings, and bank advances. When external finance beyond bank loans was required, these firms issued securities in their local communities – securities that were rarely traded and therefore were not listed on public stock exchanges.[4] On the demand side, the pool of capital available in Canada was so shallow as to necessitate the creation of an external market for Canadian industrial securities.[5] Canada's close political and economic relationship with Britain provided it with a privileged entrée to the international capital market centred in the City of London. However, since British investors were interested in purchasing only the securities of the larger Canadian industrials, preferably those that appeared to have some monopoly power, this encouraged the merger of regional firms into national consolidations that had the desired size and market power.[6]

A developed market for industrial securities, combined with high and rising security prices (a bull market), was certainly a precondition for the first Canadian merger wave, but it was not a sufficient reason in itself. After all, financiers could not have convinced industrialists to sell their assets unless the industrialists also had a strong incentive to alter the status quo. In many industries, the most immediate impetus to change was the sudden decline in prices caused by overproduction. Technological innovation in high-throughput production processes provided the long-term stimulus, but the industrial recession of 1908, which came in the wake of the Panic of 1907, was the more immediate spur. Survival could no longer be guaranteed by price fixing through cartels of independent producers. Now, tight combinations – amalgamations that produced a single unified enterprise, often with enough market power to impose prices at least temporarily – provided some respite from the crush of competition. Since they were unable to trust one another after years of rivalry and since they were unskilled in the ways of high finance, these owners generally turned to merger promoters to assemble and then market the consolidation of their firms.

The Rise of the Merger Promoter

The first merger wave had a profound impact not only on the structure of Canadian business but on the average Canadian's view of the men at the economic helm, and in particular that exotic subspecies, the company promoter and high financier. By collapsing almost twenty existing companies into three enormous enterprises – the Canada Cement Company, the Canadian Car and Foundry Company, and the Steel Company of Canada – Max Aitken was immediately recognized and quickly vilified as the leading merger promoter and financier of the era.

As can be seen in table 8.1, Aitken was not alone in the business of merger promotion between 1909 and 1913. The new business attracted some of the country's most ambitious financiers. Some, like Garnet P. Grant of the Dominion Bond Company, are no longer remembered, because their financial empires crashed during the 1913 recession. Others, like Arthur Nesbitt, cut their teeth during the merger wave and went on to become leading promoters during the speculative merger bubble of the late 1920s.[7] These promoters generally did more than issue, underwrite, advertise, and market securities; they were directly involved in the formation of new merger enterprises. These more entrepreneurial activities included conceiving merger opportunities, negotiating and purchasing options on existing companies, incorporating new enterprises, deciding on the amount and type of securities and their distribution, and seeking out prospective new management. These varied activities can be classified into three distinct phases of merger promotion: discovery, assembly, and selling.

TABLE 8.1 Largest consolidations during the first Canadian merger wave, 1909–13

Merger	Date	Head office	Firms absorbed	Total capital ($000)	Amount issued ($000)	Locus of issue	Principal promoters	Lead financial institution
National Breweries, Ltd	4/09	Montreal	14	12,500	7,029	CAN	C.R. Hosmer	none
Amalgamated Asbestos	4/09	Montreal	5	25,000	17,500	US/BRIT	E.B. Greenshields and C.J. McCuaig	McCuaig Bros. & Co.
Black Lake Asbestos	8/09	Montreal	4	5,500	5,000	CAN	C.J. McCuaig and R. Forget	McCuaig Bros. & Co.
F.N. Burt Co. Ltd	8/09	Toronto	4	16,500	1,500	CAN	A.E. Ames and R. Forget	A.E. Ames & Co.
Canada Cement Company	9/09	Montreal	12	38,000	29,000	CAN/BRIT	W.M. Aitken	Royal Securities
Carriage Factories, Ltd	10/09	Montreal	4	5,000	2,700	CAN	G.P. Grant and W.M. Weir	none
Canadian Consolidated Felts, Ltd	10/09	Montreal	3	2,500	2,500	CAN	D.L. McGibbon	none
Canadian Car and Foundry, Ltd	10/09	Montreal	3	16,500	12,000	BRIT/CAN	W.M. Aitken	Royal Securities
Dominion Steel Corporation, Ltd	10/09	Sydney, NS	2	52,500	none	–	E.R. Wood and W.M. Aitken	Dominion Securities
Canada Bolt and Nut Co.	2/10	Toronto	4	3,500	2,450	CAN	L. Harris	none
Robin, Jones & Whitman	2/10	Halifax	3	3,750	3,358	CAN	–	–
Dominion Canners, Ltd	2/10	Hamilton	15	12,500	5,198	CAN/BRIT	G.P. Grant and C. Meredith	Dominion Bond
Canadian Cereal and Milling Co., Ltd	4/10	Toronto	8	5,000	3,250	CAN	A.J. Nesbitt	Investment Trust
Maple Leaf Milling Co.	4/10	Toronto	2	5,000	5,000	CAN	C. Mulock	Guarantee Trust
Canadian Cottons, Ltd	5/10	Montreal	3	19,000	1,800	BRIT	–	–
Steel Company of Canada	6/10	Hamilton	5	35,000	25,496	BRIT	W.M. Aitken	Royal Securities
Canada Machinery Corporation, Ltd	7/10	Galt, Ont.	5	4,000	1,962	CAN	G.P. Grant	Dominion Bond
Steel & Radiation, Ltd	10/10	Toronto	2	6,500	1,649	CAN	H. Pellatt	Pellatt & Pellatt
Canadian North Pacific Fisheries, Ltd	10/10	Toronto	4	5,947	5,947	BRIT	W. Mackenzie and D. Mann	–
Riordan Pulp and Paper Co., Ltd	12/10	Montreal	2	8,500	7,000	–	–	–
Canadian Steel Foundries, Ltd	2/11	Montreal	2	10,000	8,050	BRIT	A.J. Nesbitt	Investment Trust
Standard Chemical Iron & Lumber Co. of Canada	3/11	Montreal	2	7,000	5,686	BRIT	H. Pellatt	Pellatt & Pellatt
Canadian Coal and Coke	3/11	Toronto	4	18,751	18,751	CAN	H.A. Lovett and C.H. Cahan	Montreal-London Securities

TABLE 8.1 (*Concluded*)

Merger	Date	Head office	Firms absorbed	Total capital ($000)	Amount issued ($000)	Locus of issue	Principal promoters	Lead financial institution
Belding Paul and Corticelli Silk Co.	4/11	Montreal	4	26,000	2,350	CAN/BRIT	C. Meredith and G.P. Grant	C. Meredith & Co./ Dominion Bond
International Milling Company of Canada, Ltd	4/11	-	3	5,000	3,779	CAN	A.J. Nesbitt	Investment Trust
Steel and Radiation, Ltd	5/11	Toronto	2	6,500	2,222	CAN	H. Pellatt	Pellatt & Pellatt
Sherwin-Williams Company of Canada, Ltd	6/11	Montreal	3	12,000	9,450	CAN	J.W. McConnell and C.H. Cahan	Montreal-London Securities/Johnston, McConnell and Allison
Canada Carbide Company	7/11	Montreal	3	4,150	2,230	CAN	-	-
Canada Bread Co., Ltd	8/11	Toronto	5	5,000	5,000	CAN	C. Mulock	Guarantee Trust
Canadian Jewellers, Ltd	8/11	Montreal	4	5,000	5,000	CAN	J.A. MacKay	MacKay & Co.
Mathews Laing, Ltd	10/11	Toronto	3	7,000	4,700	CAN	-	-
Canadian Pacific Lumber Co., Ltd	12/11	Vancouver	5	5,000	3,750	BRIT	none	-
Canada Foundries and Forgings, Ltd	2/12	Brockville	3	4,750	1,987	CAN	C. Meredith	C. Meredith & Co.
Canadian Soaps, Ltd	5/12	-	2	2,000	1,325	CAN	G.P. Grant	Dominion Bond
Tuckett Tobacco Company	6/12	Hamilton	3	2,000	4,500	CAN	-	-
Spanish River Pulp and Paper Co., Ltd	8/12	Toronto	2	11,000	9,250	BRIT	E.M. Edgar	Sperling & Co.
British Columbia Breweries Ltd	10/12	Vancouver	4	10,000	5,750	BRIT	-	-
Smart-Woods, Ltd	12/12	Montreal	2	5,000	2,500	CAN	-	-
Dominion Manufacturers, Ltd	3/13	Montreal	8	3,550	3,500	CAN	C.B. Gordon	-
Dominion Glass Co., Ltd	5/13	Montreal	4	11,000	8,850	-	-	-
Provincial Paper Mills	5/13	Toronto	2	5,000	5,000	-	-	-
Ontario Steel Products Co., Ltd	6/13	-	4	2,100	2,100	-	-	-

Source: Gregory P. Marchildon, 'Promotion, Finance and Mergers in Canadian Manufacturing Industry, 1885–1918' (PhD diss., London School of Economics, 1990), 262–72, and "Hands across the Water": Canadian Industrial Financiers in the City of London, 1905–20,' *Business History* 34, no. 3 (July 1992), 94–5; *Annual Financial Review* (Canadian), 9–15 (1909–13); *Canadian Journal of Commerce*, 1909–13; *Monetary Times*, 1909–13; *Monetary Times Annual Review* 50 (1913); 76–87

The discovery of the merger opportunity meant deciding on an industry in which a merger made economic sense, not because the promoter wanted to improve the efficiency of the industry for its own sake but because his profit came largely in the form of bonus common stock, which could only gain value if the enterprise performed profitably over the medium to long term. The promoter therefore had to have imagination and enough knowledge of both the industry and the individual firms in order to make a solidly based gamble on the likely impact of a given consolidation.

The assembling of the merger involved convincing the chief shareholders of the merits of consolidation to the point that they were willing to sell the promoter a controlling interest in their firm. In practice, the promoter negotiated an option – a contractual right to purchase a company at a fixed price within a definite time in exchange for an agreed sum of money, which would be forfeited if the promoter did not complete the purchase by the expiry date. The promoter tried to obtain the firm at the lowest possible price, preferably in the common stock of the new company, of which the promoter would have a large supply; senior securities (preferred shares and bonds) would also do, but cash buy-outs were to be avoided, the promoter being security rich but cash poor. To gain support for the merger, the promoter could also give extra common stock to strategically placed shareholders, officers, and directors, and perhaps offer positions on the new company's board or executive. In some cases, the promoter might even select the senior management for the new enterprise in order to improve the consolidation's chances of success. Once a majority of options were signed, the promoter would incorporate a company to which he would assign all his options; he would then issue the company's securities, in return for which he would receive all the common stock of the company and most (if not all) of the senior securities. These bonds and shares would be used to buy the properties entering the merger. Common stock alone would be used to pay off underwriters and bait investors. Any stock remaining would constitute the promoter's profit.

The third phase was the marketing of the merger in terms of floating the senior securities of the company. To accomplish this, the promoter needed to exploit the reputation of those whom he chose to adorn the merger's board of directors, as well as the individuals and institutions financially backing the merger. During the Laurier boom, the promoter enticed the 'right' people on both sides of the Atlantic through common stock payments so that both the Canadian and the British flotations could take place simultaneously without slippage on either side. Since any fall in the price of the merger's securities could damage investor confidence, promoters had to be ready to purchase large quantities of stock in the open market in order to stiffen its price while the flotation was occurring.

Most of the individuals listed in table 8.1 were full-fledged promoters in the sense that they were involved in some way in all three phases of promoting. Aitken's abilities stand out in terms of the first phase; he was unsurpassed in dreaming up merger possibilities in industries that could benefit most from reorganization and the introduction of more modern management and plant. Invariably, he chose the growth industries of the Laurier boom – those directly connected to the enormous investment in building and transportation infrastructure – and from an economic viewpoint, Canada Cement, Canadian Car and Foundry, and Stelco were solid bets from the beginning. Aitken's record in terms of assembling and selling mergers was more mixed. While he masterfully assembled and sold the Canadian Car and Stelco consolidations, he was beset by difficulties in his first industrial merger – problems that continued to plague him for years after the Canada Cement merger.

All the significant gilded age promoters were backed up by substantial financial organizations as well as by more informal but nevertheless crucial networks of financial colleagues, on which they could depend in any new merger venture. In Canada, the preferred financial intermediaries were bond houses, but trust companies and brokerage firms were also used; in practice, all tended to resemble in function wholesale bond houses like the RSC and the Dominion Securities Corporation. Garnet P. Grant, for example, soon formed the Dominion Bond Company of Montreal specifically to back his promotional activities.[8] By 1911 he had set up a Dominion Bond office in London, a must for the more aggressive Canadian merger financiers, given the quantity of securities issued on the British market.[9]

Shortly after leaving Aitken, Arthur Nesbitt convinced a number of other financiers to contribute capital to his Investment Trust Company, setting himself up as general manager. Relying heavily on the British market as an outlet for his securities, Nesbitt had set up a London office for Investment Trust in 1910 to help him promote the Canadian Cereal & Milling, Canadian Steel Foundries, and International Milling Company of Canada mergers the following year.[10] In late 1911 Nesbitt resigned as general manager of Investment Trust and formed Nesbitt, Thompson Company, which although not a major player during the gilded age, became one of the most active promotional firms during the merger wave of the late 1920s.[11]

The institutional nucleus of the merger promoter could also be a more traditional brokerage firm, as in the case of McCuaig Brothers & Co. The senior member of this Montreal firm, Clarence J. McCuaig, helped set off the merger wave in April 1909 with the Amalgamated Asbestos consolidation. The public portion of the bond issue was floated simultaneously in London, New York, Philadelphia, and Montreal. This was quickly followed by another asbestos merger promoted by McCuaig and associates in September 1909. McCuaig worked in conjunction with a clique of Montreal lawyers and financiers, including the Greenshields family and one of the most well-connected French-Canadian financiers of the day, Rodolphe Forget, who gave McCuaig privileged access to the French and Belgian capital markets. Despite these advantages, Amalgamated Asbestos turned out to be one of the biggest flops of the merger movement. The promoters took stockwatering to new heights in an industry that was experiencing precious little technological change. In addition to $8,250,000 in par value common stock, the promoters distributed $1,750,000 preference shares as a sweetener to brokers and investors to purchase $7,500,000 of bonds.[12]

Less indulgent in stockwatering, two Toronto stockbrokers, Cawthra Mulock and Henry Pellatt, had more success as merger promoters. Both stayed closer to home, raising little capital outside the market they knew best, and both used brokerage firms as their institutional base, though Mulock did set up the Guaranty Trust Company in June 1910 in order to give him access to additional funds.[13] Mulock and Pellatt never attempted the enormous consolidations tackled by Max Aitken and Garnet P. Grant, but neither financier had to endure the press attacks faced by Aitken, and both survived the recession of 1913, unlike Grant.

With few exceptions (Henry Pellatt being one), the business of merger promoting was a young man's game, and almost all of Aitken's fellow promoters were in their twenties. Like Aitken, they were extremely ambitious, willing to take on the enormous risk necessary to make extraordinary profits. The 1913 recession was to ravage their ranks. Garnet P. Grant saw his heavy investments in Spanish River Pulp and Paper and similar companies lose their value almost overnight, and the Dominion Bond Company, which had grown more than any other securities firm during the merger wave, was out of business within months. Clarence J. McCuaig was already having many problems with his asbestos merger when the 1913 downturn finished off what was left of the company's residual value. J.W. McConnell and his newly formed securities corporation in Montreal, with which he had intended to finance many more mergers, fell victim to a sinking market for his securities in both Britain and Canada, and was also out of business by the end of the year. On the other hand, Aitken's consolidations, including the infamous Canada Cement Company, survived the 1913 recession with flying colours, and consequently so did the Royal Securities Corporation.

Reconstructing the Canada Cement Merger

Aitken received more attention than any other Canadian promoter of the Laurier boom mainly because his Canada Cement merger became a *cause célèbre*. The company's enormous capitalization – including $13.5 million of common stock 'water' – and its presumed monopoly position in the Canadian economy intrigued and provoked the public and press from · the very beginning. In the past, Aitken had always played down his role in financial operations in order to avoid public attention. Now, he could not escape scrutiny as the newly proclaimed 'financial wizard' of St James Street. From the beginning, his celebrity was to be accompanied by notoriety.

On the announcement of the Canada Cement merger, the Halifax *Herald* noted that while Aitken had always shunned 'publicity of any kind,' he was now being 'fairly showered by congratulations by leading banks and capitalists.'[14] In January 1910, two months after the flotation of Canada Cement, the *Busy Man's Magazine* (soon to be renamed *Maclean's*) ran a feature article on Aitken entitled 'A Young Canadian with a Genius for Organization.' In it, he was described as a financial Napoleon, a man who commanded success. 'He is courageous, confident, insistent, and yet a man of impulse,' announced the article; he never attacks anything in a 'half-hearted way,' and when he begins something 'he leaves not a single stone of detail unturned to make the expected success a reality.' In addition to possessing *sang-froid,* Aitken was said to have 'a happy faculty of inspiring confidence that at once carries him half way to victory and which has been a prime factor in placing a score of financial triumphs to his credit.'[15]

Such reports were more than offset by the free trade and populist press, in which he was portrayed as the ultimate manipulator, a high financier who stripped the assets of perfectly good firms and then created monopolies from their carcasses. Since Aitken burdened these mergers with mounds of worthless stock, they could only meet their interest and dividend obligations by gouging the Canadian consumer. This perception became *de rigueur* when one of Canada's most respected citizens, Sir

Sandford Fleming, called for a public investigation into Aitken's promotion of Canada Cement and accused Aitken of stealing millions of dollars from the company's treasury. The charges were taken seriously. Fleming was, after all, the president and chief shareholder of two of the firms entering the merger and was honorary president of the merger company itself; and in his prime, as the engineering genius behind the Canadian Pacific Railway (CPR) and the inventor of standard time, he had been one of the most celebrated Canadians of his day.[16] Sir Sandford's attack was picked up by every newspaper in the country at the same time as Prime Minister Laurier and his fellow Liberals were attempting to convince an edgy electorate of the benefits that would flow from a free trade agreement with the United States. In this highly charged political atmosphere, the Canada Cement affair illustrated for many the evil results springing from Canada's tariff-protected industry and its financial allies.

Aitken expected to be attacked on the political front, as indeed he was. What he did not anticipate was the antagonism that his rapidly gained wealth had engendered among his business associates – the fate of the parvenu everywhere. Even before Sir Sandford Fleming launched his campaign against him, Aitken had begun to suffer from his own success. In 1910 he formally applied for membership in the Mount Royal Club of Montreal, the most prestigious business club in the country, and although he was supported by some very prominent members, including William Molson Macpherson, who exercised 'what influence he could,' he was rejected – 'pilled,' in club parlance. The following day Macpherson wrote to Aitken bemoaning the result: 'Your financial career has been so prominent and so successful that I presume you have in some way created a feeling of jealousy, which is the only reason I can imagine for their strange actions.' These animosities were kept alive for decades in Montreal. During the interwar years, for instance, Killam was rejected by the members of the same club largely because of his earlier relationship with Aitken.[17]

None of this could have been anticipated in April 1909 when Aitken first met with Joe Irvin, the managing director of Western Canada Cement and International Portland, the two portland cement companies affiliated with Sir Sandford Fleming.[18] Western Canada Cement was facing bankruptcy, and Irvin and Fleming expected the merger to pull the company out of its difficulties. Aitken agreed to manage the merger syndicate, but he soon forced Irvin and Fleming into an agreement by which they would have four months to reduce Western Canada Cement's indebtedness or face the prospect of being excluded from the merger.

Unable to get the required percentage of bondholders to accept a discounting in the value of their securities, Fleming attempted to use his position as honorary president of Canada Cement to pressure his fellow directors into accepting Western Canada Cement on more generous terms. They refused, and Western Canada Cement was forced into bankruptcy – with its assets soon picked up at bargain prices by the merger company – leaving Fleming and Irvin holding the company's unsecured debts.

What actually happened remains murky, with little agreement even on the most basic facts: the initial negotiations and the incorporation and flotation of the Canada Cement merger; the demands in the House of Commons in 1911 for a formal investigation of the company's promotion; and the subsequent lawsuit launched by the Bank of Montreal against Irvin and Sandford Fleming. The two most substantive biographies of Beaverbrook have presented entirely different views of the Canada Cement affair. A.J.P. Taylor in his sympathetic biography uncritically accepts Aitken's version of the events.[19] In an appendix devoted to the affair, Anne Chisholm and Michael Davie present a lopsided case against Aitken, relying mainly on Joe Irvin's very different version.[20] At best, both accounts are incomplete, a natural enough outcome for biographies concentrating on Aitken's career in Britain rather than Canada; the Canada Cement affair may be a tasty titbit, but it is no more than an hors-d'oeuvre to the main course of Beaverbrook's political and personal escapades in his adopted country. At worst, both accounts are unreliable.

The following description and analysis of the Canada Cement merger is based primarily on the correspondence and other documentation generated by the events themselves, including letters, telegrams, and memoranda circulated among the members of the promotional syndicate and others involved in the merger, as well as the minutes, agreements, and correspondence of the provisional and permanent directors and officers of the Canada Cement Company.[21] This is the best information available, given the inability of the various protagonists in the Canada Cement affair to alter the archival record to suit their biased and polarized view of events *ex post facto*.[22] Less accurate sources, including financial press reports, and more contentious sources, such as the evidence produced after the Bank of Montreal launched its lawsuit against Joseph Irvin and Sir Sandford Fleming in December 1911, are relied upon only if they are consistent with the correspondence and other documentation produced at the time of the merger itself. This reconstruction involved poring over a mountain of documents and correspondence, from which emerged an intricate piece of skulduggery that had begun long before Aitken ever met Joe Irvin or conceived the idea of the Canada Cement merger.

Irvin, Fleming, and the Western Canada Cement & Coal Company

The Western Canada Cement & Coal Company was the brainchild of Joe Irvin. Born in Illinois in 1862, Irvin had participated in the wildcat promotion of portland cement companies in the United States at the end of the nineteenth century. He was a close associate of William F. Cowham, the brilliant construction and engineering consultant who promoted and built ultramodern, high-throughput portland cement factories on contract for industrialists. After constructing an impressive series of plants in the United States, Cowham and Irvin invaded Canada in 1902, offering the 'Cowham system' to Canadian manufacturers. Since few were immediately willing to risk hundreds of thousands of dollars, Cowham and Irvin set up a show-piece cement mill at Hull, Quebec, called the International Portland Cement Company.[23]

Once on stream, the new plant made believers out of sceptics, and Cowham and Irvin were able to recoup their investment by selling most of their shares to British and Canadian investors, including Sir Sandford Fleming, who became president after investing a considerable sum of money in the company. While Cowham continued his promoting and building in the United States, Irvin remained as general manager of International Portland. His real ambition was to keep building plants in Canada on the Cowham system, using other people's money. In particular, he wanted to establish a mill in western Alberta (the mill that became known as the Western Canada Cement & Coal Company).[24]

The higher-quality and scientifically proportioned product called portland cement – the name used to separate it from lower-quality 'natural' cement – was the building material of choice during the second industrial revolution because of its strength, durability, and low price.[25] By the turn of the century, Americans such as Cowham were in the vanguard of the technological revolution sweeping the industry. International Portland's plant was among the first in Canada to manufacture cement from limestone, a rock that was plentiful, rather than from shell marl, a much rarer material. Although it was more economical to quarry and grind limestone than it was to dredge and drain marl from old lake beds, expensive and sophisticated equipment was required to quarry, crush, and grind the rock.[26]

Irvin did not have the capital to build a second cement plant, nor was he yet well enough known in Canada to raise the money himself, so he did everything possible to convince Sandford Fleming of the merits of establishing a cement company in western Canada. By then close to eighty years of age, Fleming spent most of his time at his stately home in Ottawa enjoying the fruits of his various investments (including a CPR directorship) and his presidency of International Portland.[27] An ardent imperialist, he spent far more time ruminating over imperial transatlantic cable schemes than worrying about business, and he was less than keen when Irvin first attempted to interest him in the Western Canada Cement scheme.

Irvin decided to set up the skeleton of the company without Fleming's help, using some of his own money – and begging and borrowing from other investors – for the down payments on the tracts of coal and limestone lands in the beautiful Kananaskis Valley, approximately 60 miles from Calgary on the CPR mainline to Banff. For the plant, Irvin selected the site where the Stoney Creek flows into the Bow River, and he named the town he proposed to build around the plant Exshaw, after one of his investors. He then went back to Fleming, claiming that the whole enterprise would fail unless he could enlist Sir Sandford's help and reputation to raise the $1 million still needed for the cement mill itself. In addition to needing money and a 'name' to gild the new board of directors, Irvin wanted Fleming because of his CPR connection. From the beginning, Irvin envisaged that the CPR would be Western Canada Cement's main customer as it continued to construct branch lines throughout western Canada. As well, Fleming might be able to convince the CPR to lower its transportation rates, since whatever cement was left over would have to be shipped to foreign customers from the CPR's railhead in Vancouver.[28]

Never a modest man, Fleming succumbed to Irvin's flattery, for Irvin had put the request in the larger context of Sir Sandford's historic role in developing the West. Irvin promised that the new company would do at least as well as International Portland. Pushing aside his doubts, Fleming invested $500,000 of share capital in Western Canada Cement & Coal; and because he had taken an overdraft from the Bank of Montreal, he gave the bank a personal guarantee for $100,000. To protect his family's investment, Fleming sent his son Hugh to work with Joe Irvin on the construction of the mill. Hugh was made secretary-treasurer and used his position to watch and to report to his father in Ottawa on all expenditures.[29]

Irvin then went to England to convince the group of investors holding International Portland bonds to purchase £225,000 (roughly $1.1 million) worth of bonds. The prospectus indicated that every cent invested would go into the new plant, with $500,000 earmarked for machinery alone. Very happy with their return on International Portland, the British investors snapped up Irvin's new bonds. When Irvin returned to Canada, however, Hugh Fleming discovered that the company was short of $500,000 that it required for construction. Irvin had taken exactly that amount as a personal profit for promoting the venture. Sir Sandford was quickly apprised of the disturbing fact by his distraught son.[30] Irvin had shamelessly used Sir Sandford's reputation and name to get investors to subscribe to a company that now faced an enormous and perhaps fatal shortage of cash. Fleming had, of course, expected Irvin to be compensated, but only after the cement mill had come on stream. 'I do not,' he complained to Irvin, 'and never did object to the promoter being handsomely rewarded but in my judgment actual payment of the reward to him should follow the erection of the works, and should not have been the very first payment made out of a fund raised specially for the erection' of the plant.[31]

The Flemings had committed too much to the project to let it collapse, however. So both Sir Sandford and Hugh concealed Irvin's 'theft' from existing and prospective investors, and helped Irvin float a second £85,000 bond issue in England, worth roughly $415,000, to make up for most of the loss. Sir Sandford felt trapped. He needed Irvin – to run the Hull plant and oversee the construction of the new Exshaw plant – more than Irvin needed him. Even if he had had the time and money to hire a manager to replace Irvin, he could hardly have afforded the bad publicity that would have come with a high-profile firing; blowing the whistle would have only served to scare off investors and would have done irreparable harm to the share value of both enterprises.

As for Irvin, he no doubt felt that he deserved every penny of the $500,000. There had never been a fixed agreement with the Flemings on his compensation, and he had taken all the risk in the initial stage of the Western Canada Cement promotion. Since he was (assuredly, in his own view) the best cement company manager and construction consultant in the country, he considered that he deserved to be well rewarded for his valuable services; besides, the Flemings and the British investors would get their money back – with interest. Irvin assumed, of course, that the demand for portland cement in Canada would continue to grow at an exponential rate, and certainly that appeared to be the case when he first promoted Western Canada Cement in 1905.

New reinforced concrete bridges, factories, office buildings, and 'unsightly' new skyscrapers were rising like mushrooms in and around Canadian cities.[32] But unfortunately for Western Canada Cement, Irvin was not the only 'cement man' in Canada who was trying to take advantage of this great opportunity. Portland cement mills began to spring up throughout the country – there were even spillover branch plants entering Canada from the United States at the very time that Irvin was peddling his Western Canada Cement bonds in London. One brand-new competitor in particular was to become a major irritant. A central Canadian cement man by the name of John Kilbourn erected an ultra modern plant of his own near Calgary under the name of the Alberta Portland Cement Company.[33] Kilbourn's plant was soon producing cement, and with the bulk purchases of his first major customer, the CPR, Kilbourn was able to recoup some of his initial outlay.

Irvin and Fleming had no such luck. The shortage of money created bottlenecks in construction. After not receiving payment for months, suppliers stopped sending materials, and a dispute over payment to the firm that was contracted to do the structural steelwork for the plant caused further delays. Added to this were cost overruns, unusually intemperate weather conditions, labour shortages, and an insufficient supply of CPR railcars to transport construction materials, with the result that the mill was not ready to go into production even by the spring of 1907. Everything that could go wrong had gone wrong, and Fleming in particular was becoming increasingly desperate.[34]

Sir Sandford began to sell off a large quantity of his CPR stock to cover some of his losses, and he borrowed a further $80,000 from the Bank of Montreal as a bridge loan to hold him until the Western Canada Cement Company began producing and selling cement; both his son and Irvin assured him that the plant would start operating and making money the following year.[35] In the spring of 1908, three years after they had begun its construction, Western Canada Cement's mill finally came on stream, but the ill-fated enterprise was about to face even more bad luck; just when Western Canada's logo made its appearance, the Canadian market was being glutted by cement.[36]

The speculative bubble in North American cement production had burst under the weight of the industrial recession following the Panic of 1907. With construction slowing even while new plants came into operation, cement prices tumbled; domestic production exceeded consumption by almost 25 per cent at the end of 1908.[37] By this time, there were twenty-one cement plants in the country, many under single ownership and control, and although some were older, inefficient operations, all contributed to the cement glut. The *Monetary Times* estimated that the capacity of these twenty-one plants – 5 million barrels of portland cement – was at least double domestic consumption in 1908.[38] The glut was exacerbated by the fact that the more modern cement operators, including Irvin and Kilbourn, had to run their plants at full capacity in an effort to keep unit costs of production as low as possible. Relying on accumulated profit from previous years and selling at record low prices, Irvin's Hull plant scraped through the 1908 industrial downturn. Although it netted a profit of only $168,000, damaged as it was by sales that had dropped by 14 per cent, International Portland survived the crisis.[39]

In contrast, Western Canada Cement was unable to pay interest on its debentures* at the end of the first operating year in 1908.[40] During the summer and autumn, the CPR was hit with a crippling strike and was unable to supply freight cars to transport cement from Exshaw or to provide coal to keep the cement plant's furnaces operating. Sir Sandford was staring bankruptcy in the face, and he began to pull out all the stops to save his company. First, he approached the Canadian Pacific Railway, which was awaiting payment of a number of freight bills for transporting Western Canada's barrels of cement. He had been the company's engineer in chief during the 1870s and had been on the board until the year before, when he had had to sell off much of his stock. Given his past services, he felt that he was entitled to a little special consideration from the CPR.

He begged the CPR's president, Sir Thomas Shaughnessy, to give his company a break, arguing that his cement company would face disaster unless the CPR forgave part of its debt and reduced its future freight rates. In Fleming's words, Western Canada Cement could not 'exist without a certain amount of reasonable and friendly co-operation of the CPR. The two are partners not in law but in fact.' He readily admitted that he could not 'sell a bbl. of cement without paying the CPR,' while the CPR could, if it so chose, 'put obstacles in the way of the cement company finding a market and saving the means of keeping the machinery going.'[41]

In November 1908, Fleming wrote to Sir Edward Clouston seeking some forbearance from the Bank of Montreal because of its close connection with the CPR. Claiming that his cement company had become a

---

*In British and Canadian usage, a type of bond generally secured by a mortgage on the property. To be distinguished from the American use of the term, meaning an unsecured bond.

TABLE 8.2 Portland cement production, imports and price, Canada, 1896–1914

Year	Production (tons)	Imports (tons)	Price per barrel (= 350 lbs)
1896	13,718	35,772	
1897	20,959	36,903	
1898	28,540	53,653	
1899	44,690	65,021	
1900	51,122	65,068	$1.92
1901	55,487	80,622	1.78
1902	104,056	98,581	1.73
1903	109,856	115,843	1.84
1904	159,315	123,819	1.41
1905	235,650	211,420	1.42
1906	370,964	142,429	1.48
1907	426,464	117,710	1.54
1908	466,432	82,084	1.39
1909	711,860	24,884	1.31
1910	831,958	61,129	1.34
1911	996,275	115,835	1.34
1912	1,248,247	251,022	1.28
1913	1,515,314	44,466	1.28
1914	1,255,203	17,154	1.23

Source: D.H. Stonehouse, Cement in Canada (Ottawa 1973), 7; calculated price data from A. Ernest Epp, 'Cooperation among Capitalists: The Canadian Merger Movement, 1909–13' (PhD diss., Johns Hopkins University 1973), 459, 462

victim of the 'great Railway strike' that year, he explained that he did not want to state this publicly, since 'the Railway management is really entitled to the thanks of the community over the strikers, a victory which will long have a beneficial influence in the public interest.' Nonetheless, the strike had ground the operations of the Exshaw plant to a halt, and he felt that he deserved some restitution for not kicking up a fuss at the time. Western Canada Cement planned to start manufacturing again after Christmas, he said, and to continue steadily throughout 1909, but he needed 'a little assistance' from the bank 'to tide over the present difficulty.'[42]

Since Western Canada Cement was equipped with the most modern kilns and equipment in North America, Fleming and Irvin were convinced that the plant just needed some running capital for a couple of years and it would become a money maker. The problem was what to do in the meantime while the CPR, the Bank of Montreal, and various other creditors were nipping at their heels. Technically, Western Canada Cement was already bankrupt, but too large an investment had been made to allow it to go under. In addition, Fleming and Irvin feared that during the liquidation proceedings the English bondholders might discover that $500,000 cash had been taken out of the company for 'promotional expenses,' contradicting the original prospectus, in which case they might face lawsuits from dozens of irate British investors.

In early March 1909 the Flemings and Irvin made a proposal to the company's bondholders, who had not yet received any return on their investment and were threatening to sue the company for payment. They suggested that if the bondholders would agree to a reorganization of the company's capital (thus reducing their claims), Western Canada Cement would rapidly become a paying proposition. Unfortunately, the English bondholders, who would be bearing the brunt of this debt reduction scheme, rejected the plan.[43] Irvin and the Flemings then asked their investors to consider the possibility of consolidating the Hull plant with the Exshaw plant, and perhaps one or two other modern plants, into one large company that would have the financial resources necessary to cover Western Canada Cement's debt load.[44] Frank Dunsford, the leading British bondholder and a director on Western Canada Cement's board, convinced his fellow investors to give the idea a chance, since it seemed the best way of preserving the full value of their investment. He sailed to Canada and, along with Irvin and Hugh Fleming, went to Sir Edward Clouston's office in Montreal to obtain yet another 'temporary' loan for Western Canada Cement to tide it over while the merger was being organized.[45]

After Irvin had outlined the rescue plan, Clouston asked him if he had already organized a merger syndicate. Irvin had in fact reviewed the plan with Rodolphe Forget, the Montreal stockbroker and financier, and Grant Morden, a local company promoter. Clouston was concerned about the enormous securities issue – about $15 million – that was being contemplated by the group, and he asked Irvin to bring in another promoter, Max Aitken, whom he described as a tremendously capable financier. Irvin agreed to see Aitken, whereupon Clouston agreed to advance Western Canada Cement a further $115,000, for which personal guarantees from Irvin and the Flemings were extracted.[46] The very next day, Irvin invited Aitken to his suite at the Windsor Hotel, where the two men were locked in discussion until the early hours of the morning reviewing the merger plan.[47] Aitken suggested that the consolidation should include a few more companies in order to solve the industry's overcapacity problem. By the time he left, however, he was sufficiently attracted to the proposal to pay his $200 fee to enter the syndicate.

The Negotiations Begin

From April to June 1909, Aitken stayed in the background. He explained various negotiating strategies so that Irvin could obtain options at the lowest price possible.[48] Discussions were opened with two American-owned operations – the Lehigh Portland Cement Company of Belleville, Ontario, and the Vulcan Portland Cement Company of Montreal – branch plants that had aggressively cut prices since beginning production in Canada.[49] In New York City, Irvin met with R.W. Kelly, the chief representative of the Vulcan firm. Kelly was 'decidedly in favour of the cement merger,' but he was apprehensive about the merger syndicate's financial backing. Since Irvin and Aitken wanted to purchase Vulcan's Montreal property with securities rather than cash, Kelly wanted to be certain that the syndicate had the requisite financial strength to execute a large flotation. The American owners of the Lehigh plant expressed the same reservation.[50]

When Irvin returned to Canada, he met with W.D. Matthews in Toronto. Matthews and his business partner E.B. Osler were the dominant shareholders in the Canadian Portland Cement Company. Through their ownership and control of the Dominion Bank as well as numerous other financial and industrial companies, Matthews and Osler were among the most powerful businessmen in Canada, and Irvin worked assiduously to convince them of the merits of a merger.[51] Canadian Portland ran two plants, a modern limestone (or 'rock') mill at Port Colborne on the north shore of Lake Erie, and an older marl plant at Marlbank, approximately 40 miles northeast of Belleville.[52]

Matthews told Irvin that the Marlbank plant would have to be part of any deal involving the more sought-after Port Colborne plant, and he insisted that both he and Osler receive a private payment in common stock in return for convincing the smaller shareholders to go along with the merger.[53] Matthews also wanted assurances that the merger syndicate was financially powerful enough to float such a large company. More problematic, Matthews said that he and Osler would only submit the proposal to their board if all the rock plants in the country were going into the consolidation.[54]

Irvin had better luck in Ottawa, where he immediately received an option from J.W. McNab, the president and managing director of the Belleville Portland Cement Company. In production since 1903, the Belleville plant had been among the first rock mills in the country, along with International Portland, but McNab was now facing competition from Lehigh Portland Cement's plant nearby. He and his fellow shareholders were anxious to sell, and at a very reasonable price.[55]

Naturally, Irvin had little difficulty securing options on his own companies. Western Canada Cement immediately gave an option for a value equal to what the company would have been worth if Irvin had not earlier helped himself to $500,000. Similarly, International Portland Cement's directors wasted little time in accepting Irvin's generous offer of $200 cash for each share. This high price reflected in part the upward drift of the company's shares from $135 in March, when rumours of a merger were first leaked to the press.[56] Most surprising of all, Irvin received a third option on a company that was not yet even in existence. That March, when Clouston had given his blessing to the merger, Irvin had brought together some new investors for what would become known as the Eastern Canada Portland Cement Company and, with their money, had begun to construct a cement mill near Quebec City. Of course, his intention was to do only the foundation work and then sell at an inflated price to the merger that he was instrumental in putting together. To the delight of his investors, he took out an option on Eastern Canada Portland's undeveloped properties, again at an inflated price.

With his four options in hand, Irvin went back to Aitken and suggested that they go ahead with the merger on the assumption that when the other companies found out, they would be eager to join.[57] Aitken looked at the options and realized that Irvin was trying to pull the wool over his eyes; the whole scheme was little more than a clumsy effort to enrich Irvin and his fellow shareholders at the expense of later creditors and investors. This was in fact a type of Ponzi scheme, in which the original investors sell out to a larger circle of suckers, who then preside over a house of cards that is destined to collapse. Of course, Irvin's intention was that Aitken would be the biggest sucker of all.

Aitken decided to play along with Irvin while quietly outflanking him through a new scheme that was designed to make suckers of Irvin and his associates. The trick was to make Irvin believe that nothing was afoot, and his secret weapon was his close relationship with Clouston and, by extension, the Bank of Montreal. Aitken did not reject Irvin's options directly but said that they would need further options to make the merger viable. As the productive capacity of the four plants constituted less than 50 per cent of total manufacturing capacity, the new merger would be unable to impose price discipline in the country and would not therefore be seen by the other owners as a credible alternative to the status quo. Moreover, given the cement glut, the merger had to be marketed to potential investors as a 'trust' capable of exercising some monopolistic power. The answer would be to get all the modern rock mills under the merger tent; price discipline would follow, and investors would automatically be lured to the new securities.

Innocent of Aitken's design, Irvin was happy enough to reopen negotiations with the American owners as well as with Matthews and Osler, but he baulked when Aitken insisted that he get an option on the Calgary and Montreal mills owned by John Kilbourn.[58] Kilbourn also owned two antiquated marl plants in Ontario, one at Shallow Lake near Owen Sound, the other at Lakefield, just north of Peterborough. Despite their age, they remained large producers, and Aitken suggested that they be included in the merger for good measure.[59] Irvin, however, felt that Kilbourn's Alberta Portland Cement had stripped away business that should have gone to Western Canada Cement and that his older plants were worth little more than the value of the land they stood on.[60]

Aitken used Irvin's antipathy to the Kilbourn interests as an excuse to play a more direct role in the negotiations. He invited all the major Canadian cement manufacturers, including Kilbourn, to a general meeting at a Montreal hotel in June 1909. After an open presentation designed to convince everyone of the merits of consolidating, Aitken discussed in separate and private meetings the terms at which each would 'come into the merger.' Since most of his guests were enthusiastic about the prospect of the merger's putting an end to the cement glut and declining prices, the individual meetings went well. Immediately after the owners left the hotel, however, Irvin refused to follow up the Kilbourn negotiations, and this prompted John Kilbourn to appeal directly to Aitken to take over the negotiations or leave Irvin's companies out of the negotiations entirely. In Kilbourn's opinion, it was unconscionable that Irvin could be constructing a new plant even as he was negotiating a merger intended to limit production.[61]

The Bank of Montreal Connection

Aitken had long ago concluded that Joe Irvin would have to be removed from any decision making in the merger. In addition to antagonizing Kilbourn, Irvin could prevent the existing syndicate from lowering the price on his properties. After much thought, Aitken decided to use the shell he had created the year before – the Bond and Share Company – to obtain control over the merger. He was able to placate Irvin by guaranteeing that he and the other members of the original promotional syndicate would continue to receive their agreed-upon share of the promoters' stock profit.[62] However, since Bond and Share's promotional profit would have to come out of common stock, Aitken would have to inflate Canada Cement's issue of common stock.

To give himself added leverage in negotiating the options, Aitken wanted the Bank of Montreal to be the merger's official banker and listed on the prospectus as such, a tricky business given Clouston's concern about being caught out in a conflict of interest. Aitken also asked for $1 million as a bridge loan for the Canada Cement issue. But Clouston baulked. He was worried about the sheer size of the flotation, involving as it did an issue of $30 million par value worth of securities, and the potential risk to the bank if the merger was unsuccessful. After all, he was only too aware of the original motive behind the merger – the indebtedness of the Western Canada Cement and Coal Company. Although it might be hidden from prospective investors in the merger, this level of debt could only serve to weaken the new consolidation. On the other hand, Clouston felt that the Bank of Montreal might never get all its money back from Western Canada Cement without the merger.

In the end, Clouston decided to lend Aitken the money, but on terms that significantly reduced the bank's risk. In return for 'purchasing' $1 million of the cement consolidation's bond issue at 90 per cent of par, the RSC (not the merger syndicate) would be contractually obligated to repurchase the bonds at 95 plus 6 per cent interest four months later. This meant that the Bank of Montreal would exact the equivalent of a 23 per cent commission on what was in effect a loan, even while carrying the bonds as security. Aitken considered that Clouston was asking too much, but he knew that the Bank of Montreal's support – whatever the cost – would convince all the cement manufacturers of the merger's viability; hence, he kept his opinion to himself and struck the Faustian bargain with Clouston.[63]

While Clouston may have been unwilling to put his bank at risk, he personally wanted to benefit from the merger, so he took a large slice of the bond underwriting – almost $700,000 worth – in his own name. Moreover, under his influence, his two closest associates in the bank, his executive assistant Arthur R. Doble and his superintendent of the Maritime branches William E. Stavert, signed up for a total of $400,000 of the merger's underwriting.[64] As members of the bond underwriting syndicate, Clouston, Doble, and Stavert were to be paid a 50 per cent common stock bonus for guaranteeing the sale of the issue. Of the total $2 million par value of common stock ultimately distributed to the six-member bond underwriting syndicate, Clouston received $333,000, while Doble and Stavert were each given $100,000. These figures may be compared with the $500,000 allotted to E.R. Wood and the Dominion Securities Corporation, the $500,000 to Rodolphe Forget, and the $467,000 given to Aitken himself.[65]

In other words, three Bank of Montreal officers, all in their private capacity, had agreed to guarantee the sale of more than one-quarter of Canada Cement's bond issue. Although the bank itself was not an underwriter, Clouston, Doble, and Stavert had been welcomed as underwriters (and promoters) by Aitken and Irvin precisely because they were identified with the bank. At the very least, all three were using their positions at the Bank of Montreal in order to reap a personal profit. Clouston in particular was in a powerful position as both chief executive officer and vice-president of the bank.

Irvin later claimed that Clouston had been paid $1 million in common stock by Aitken as a promotional profit for giving his bank's support to the merger. While there is no direct evidence of this, all the circumstances suggest that Clouston was likely paid a substantial sum for his efforts. Moreover, given their enormous stake in the cement merger, it was natural for Clouston, Doble, and Stavert to want some say in the affairs of the promotional syndicate, and Aitken and Irvin encouraged their participation since it affirmed the Bank of Montreal's support for the merger.[66] Aitken and Irvin tried to hide the identities of Doble and Stavert (and thus their connection to the Bank of Montreal, as well as Stavert's connection to C. Meredith & Co.) by having Aitken act as trustee on their behalf in the merger syndicate.

Clouston's own role was ostensibly limited to authorizing the 'loan' to the Royal Securities Corporation and underwriting in his personal capacity. Nonetheless, by virtue of his existing holdings in the RSC, Clouston owned a piece of the Bond and Share Company and therefore would automatically share in all the profits taken by it as the promoting company, a fact that Aitken and Clouston conveniently hid from Irvin and the other members of the cement syndicate – and that Clouston also hid from his fellow officers and directors at the Bank of Montreal.[67]

All this evidence suggests that three Bank of Montreal officers were connected, both directly and indirectly, to the inner circle promoting the

Canada Cement merger. First, Clouston's executive assistant as well as his Maritime superintendent were members of the promotional syndicate and benefited directly from the consolidation. Secondly, all three had a circuitous but nonetheless solid connection to the promoting company. Finally – and this is the most damning piece of evidence – each entered into a separate (and secret) agreement in which he agreed to transfer his common stock underwriting profits to the RSC at $15.50 per share in return for stock in the RSC. Since the RSC was the majority holder of Bond and Share stock, this meant that all three men had a large stake in the successful outcome of the merger.[68]

Aitken designed the financing so that the Bond and Share Company would receive a total of $4 million par value common stock from the merger company in return for its promotional work – in effect, adding $4 million of additional water to the company's capital. This amounted to more than 30 per cent of the total of $13.5 million in common stock issued by the cement company.[69] This may be compared with the $2.5 million divided up among the members of the original promotional syndicate, the $3.75 million distributed to the underwriters, and the $3.25 million distributed to the old cement companies and their owners and directors.

Aitken and his Bank of Montreal associates also benefited from some of the $2.5 million of common stock earmarked for the original promotional syndicate. Aitken, Irvin, and Forget, the three most important syndicate members, were entitled to $400,000 each. George Smithers (as the syndicate secretary) and Charles Cahan took a further $200,000 each. This left $900,000, of which $200,000 was held by Aitken in trust for Stavert and Doble (known as trustees no. 1 and no. 2 in the written promoters' agreement); a further $200,000 was held by Rodolphe Forget in trust for Morden; and the final $500,000 was held by Aitken in trust in two equal lots for two individuals or institutions, mysteriously recorded as trustee no. 3 and trustee no. 4.[70]

The identities of trustees nos. 3 and 4 were never revealed, but it is quite possible that the beneficiaries were in fact the Bank of Montreal and Clouston, as later alleged by Irvin and vigorously denied by both the bank and Clouston.[71] It is highly likely that at least one of the trustees was Clouston. Certainly, it is curious that while Aitken subsequently went to great lengths to argue against Irvin's assertions concerning Clouston and the Bank of Montreal being members of the promotional syndicate, he consistently refused to reveal the identity of trustees nos. 3 and 4 in subsequent correspondence with the RSC and his own lawyers.[72]

Even if Clouston and the Bank of Montreal were not trustees nos. 3 and 4, Clouston was nonetheless a member of Aitken's inner circle in the cement merger by virtue of his participation in the bond underwriting and – most important of all – by virtue of his holdings in the RSC and the corporation's ownership of the Bond and Share Company. Clouston may have been investing as a private individual, but his participation (to say nothing of the participation of Stavert and Doble) was desired by Aitken and Irvin precisely because of his position as general manager and vice-president of the Bank of Montreal. Had Clouston been acting in his official capacity, he would have been in a direct conflict of interest because of the Bank of Montreal's creditor relationship with Western Canada Cement. To be precise, the best solution for the Bank of Montreal would have been for Western Canada Cement to be supported in a consolidation of stronger companies irrespective of the long-term impact this would have on the merger company, whereas Clouston's personal interest dictated a Canada Cement Company made stronger by not taking on Western Canada Cement's enormous debt load.[73]

Pressure at the Eleventh Hour

As the first step in exerting his personal control over the merger, Aitken required that all of Joe Irvin's options would have to be transferred into the name of the Bond and Share Company. The second step was to take out a new corporate charter that would supersede that taken out by the original promoters (in which Aitken was merely one of eight incorporators, most of whom had been selected by Irvin).[74] Taking out a new charter in the name of the Canada Cement Company on 20 August 1909, Aitken justified the change on the grounds that the original charter had contemplated fewer companies than those now joining the consolidation. He then added eight additional subscribers to the Canada Cement Company, including Fred Clarke of Montreal Engineering and Victor Drury, his wife's brother and an employee of the RSC.[75] Naturally, these new subscribers would, under Aitken's influence, accept the Irvin-Fleming properties only at the lower option prices negotiated in the name of the Bond and Share Company.[76]

The third step in taking control was to have Charles Cahan added to the promotional syndicate and to have him draft and negotiate the options for the Bond and Share Company. Irvin did not know Cahan, but he reluctantly agreed, hoping to keep the favour of both Aitken and Sir Edward Clouston, a concern uppermost in his mind now that Western

Canada Cement owed $300,000 to the bank.[77] In redoing the options, Cahan and Aitken played a good-cop–bad-cop routine. Aitken presented the positive aspects of the merger to the owners, describing the benefits that would flow from consolidation and the money that could be made from the flotation now that the Bank of Montreal was backing it. Cahan would then do the nasty work, invariably offering the owners less for their properties than the figures initially considered by Irvin or Aitken. When the owners baulked, Cahan threatened to leave their plants out of the merger.[78]

Moreover, the option agreements, which had been made on the basis of the existing accounting data on assets and earnings, were subject to revision based on independent appraisals of plant and equipment and on audits of earnings. Since the appraisals and audits were expected to take from two to three months, the option contracts stipulated that Canada Cement had either sixty or ninety days in which to exercise the options.[79] However, Aitken had no intention of waiting this long before conducting the first share flotation. Both the Canadian and British markets were ready for a big Canadian industrial flotation, and Aitken wanted to move as fast as possible before both markets became jammed with securities emanating from the many other mergers that were being negotiated by Canadian promoters. He depended on pressure from Cahan to get the options in as quickly as possible.[80]

The good-cop–bad-cop strategy worked. In two frantic weeks of arduous negotiations, Cahan obtained less expensive options from every one of the companies Aitken wanted in the merger.[81] The high point came during the first week of September 1909, when Cahan and Aitken refused to offer International Portland Cement's shareholders any cash on the new option agreement – cash which Aitken now realized he would need to purchase the Kilbourn and Osler-Matthews companies in addition to the American plants.[82] Irvin was furious. In place of the original offer of $200 cash per share, Aitken was offering $175, and this only if International Portland Cement's shareholders accepted Canada Cement preferred shares in place of cash.[83] Aitken also told Irvin that he would have to reduce the price for Eastern Portland Cement's plant near Quebec City. Ominously, Aitken then began to talk about the Exshaw plant's debt load in front of Irvin.[84]

Irvin immediately went to the Bank of Montreal's head office in an effort to enlist Sir Edward Clouston's support against Aitken, but the general manager had left for western Canada on business and was not expected back until mid-September. In his absence, Clouston had asked

William E. Stavert to take care of Canada Cement matters.[85] When Irvin told Stavert what Aitken had done, Stavert asked Aitken to meet with him and Irvin. Aitken did so but stood his ground; either Irvin accepted his terms or he would have to risk his companies being left out of the merger completely. Stavert then took on the role of good cop by suggesting that if Aitken was not willing to take Western Canada Cement at Irvin's old price, he should at least offer a reasonable compromise. In response, Aitken made his final offer. If Irvin and his fellow International Portland Cement shareholders would accept $175 instead of $200 per share, and this in exchange for Canada Cement preferred shares rather than cash, and if Irvin would accept considerably less for his own profit for promoting Eastern Canada Cement, and if Western Canada Cement's debt load was reduced by February 1910, then Bond and Share would accept options on all three properties.[86]

Irvin had to confer with the Flemings before making any final decision, but Aitken sent Arthur Doble to see Irvin to convince him that all the other companies also had been forced to accept securities in place of cash for their properties.[87] With Western Canada Cement teetering on the edge of bankruptcy – a fact well understood by Aitken and the Bank of Montreal but not by the owners of the other companies entering the merger – Aitken had Irvin and Fleming over a barrel, and they reluctantly agreed to his terms. But when Irvin and Fleming presented the Bond and Share option to their fellow International Portland Cement directors, the other directors insisted that Aitken attend an emergency board meeting and explain himself. Aitken rented a private railway car for the train journey from Montreal to Ottawa and brought along Arthur Doble to represent the Bank of Montreal in Clouston's absence.

In International Portland's boardroom, Aitken faced a predictably hostile audience. Bombarded with questions, he refused to disclose what he had paid for the other properties entering the merger. He told the directors that he had no intention of bargaining; they either had to accept his price or risk remaining outside the merger. Sir Sandford Fleming had already softened up his fellow directors to the offer, and he now began to cajole them into accepting, which they did when they realized that Aitken had no intention of backing down. But since the new deal involved taking a direct interest in the new consolidation in lieu of cash, they demanded some assurance from Aitken that the flotation would be a success. In particular, some directors wanted to know the extent to which the Bank of Montreal was backing the new merger. Aitken looked at Doble, and Doble dutifully confirmed that the Bank of Montreal supported the venture.[88]

Despite its lack of specificity, Doble's statement was enough to get most of the directors to give the option on Aitken's terms to the Bond and Share Company on 6 September. Three days later, Bond and Share obtained a considerably lower-priced option on Irvin's Quebec property, as well as an option on Western Canada Cement, on the condition that Irvin and Fleming would reorganize the company's capital in order to reduce its debt load within five months.

The next day, 10 September, Aitken transferred to the Canada Cement Company all his rights and responsibilities under these option agreements, as well as the options obtained by Cahan from the nine other cement companies. In return, Bond and Share received $13,500,000 par value of Canada Cement's common stock, $10,500,000 par value of preference stock, and $1,348,000 worth of bonds – the remaining $3,652,000 in bonds being sold to Bond and Share at 10 cents less than par. Out of these securities, it was understood that Bond and Share (i.e., Aitken) had to pay for all the properties entering the merger, all the administrative costs of promoting and negotiating, and all the costs involved in leading and protecting the new security issues.[89]

Finally, there was the matter of the Western Canada Cement & Coal Company. Aitken personally negotiated the terms of its entry into Canada Cement. Before entering the consolidation, Western Canada Cement would have to create a new issue of 5 per cent first mortgage debentures, which would be exchanged at par for the old 7 per cent first and second mortgage debenture issues. Only then would Canada Cement purchase the Exshaw company's debentures, and then at a discount of 92.5 up to a maximum expenditure of $925,000. Along with the debentures, one-half of Western Canada's stock would have to be transferred free of charge to Canada Cement. Any liabilities above $925,000 were to be assumed by the remaining shareholders. In other words, a company originally costing its bond investors roughly $2.5 million would be bought four years later at just under $1 million, and large shareholders such as Sir Sandford Fleming would see their modest gains from the debenture sale more than swamped by the outstanding debts of the company.[90]

Fleming had to swallow very hard to accept the deal, but it seemed the only way to cut a much larger potential loss. Aitken tried to add some sugar to the bitter medicine by telling the Flemings and Joe Irvin that all the other cement company owners had, in the end, accepted substantially less for their holdings than originally negotiated in the spring and summer. He would not, however, tell them exactly what he had paid for the other properties. In fact, the other owners had accepted rather marginal deductions compared with the Fleming-Irvin interests, which were, in effect, being forced to pay the freight for the merger.

The War Begins

Even if it was not on the terms that they would have preferred, Sir Sandford Fleming and Joe Irvin were relieved to see the Canada Cement merger consummated. Aitken immediately offered Sir Sandford the office of honorary president of Canada Cement, and Irvin a seat on the board of directors. Both accepted, unconcerned by the fact that the Western Canada Cement option was contingent and that the company was not yet part of the merger. Aitken drew the noose tighter by having Charles Cahan appointed as provisional president of Canada Cement.[91]

After the merger, Aitken and Cahan had to obtain appraisals for all the properties; the Bond & Share agreements had clearly stipulated that the original option prices would be modified on the basis of the results.[92] These adjustments would ultimately generate months of conflict between Canada Cement and the cement companies that had entered the merger, but Aitken tried to minimize problems with the Fleming and Irvin companies at this point.[93] Relations were so good in fact that Irvin generously assisted Aitken by providing detailed suggestions on the organization of Canada Cement's new departments.[94] At the same time, Aitken helped Irvin and Hugh Fleming obtain further bank loans so that they could keep the Exshaw plant running while they attempted to convince the English bondholders to reduce the company's capitalization before the 9 February deadline.[95]

On 28 December, Sir Sandford Fleming and Joe Irvin held a meeting in Ottawa with the representatives of the English bondholders in which they proposed that the interest on both of Western Canada Cement's bond issues be reduced from 7 to 5 per cent. They asked that a further issue of bonds be authorized to pay off the company's liabilities and provide some working capital. The proviso was that this new issue, designated as 'prior lien bonds,' would be secured by a mortgage 'constituting a first charge' on the cement company's assets.[96] In other words, under the terms of the proposed reorganization, the existing English bondholders' security would be downgraded relative to investors in the new bond issue. The bondholders rejected the proposal, arguing that it was unfair that they should bear the burden of reducing Western Canada's debt load when shareholders like Fleming and Irvin would ultimately benefit the most from Western Canada Cement's purchase by the merger company.

After all, as bondholders they had a greater claim to assets than the shareholders did.

By December, Western Canada Cement had run out of operating funds, and the Exshaw plant was about to be shut down. Desperate, Hugh Fleming asked Canada Cement Company for a loan, but Almon Lovett, whom Aitken had appointed counsel for the company, refused to advance any funds until the reorganization had been successfully completed, for he knew full well that Fleming would not be able to deliver.[97] By this time, information about the prices paid by the Bond and Share Company for the cement firms entering the merger was beginning to leak out. Irvin and Fleming finally realized that Aitken had underpaid them for their properties. It was also clear that they had been lied to about the very nature of the payments – many firms had in fact received large cash settlements. Moreover, the amount paid by Aitken for all the properties should have left more than enough securities to pay the original asking price for the Exshaw property. In their view, Aitken had kept the purchase price money originally earmarked for Exshaw as his own profit, and he could be dragooned into turning it over if Irvin and Fleming raised the matter directly with his fellow Canada Cement directors.[98]

The controversy opened with Fleming alleging that Aitken had misappropriated Canada Cement securities that had been designated for acquiring the properties of companies entering the merger, and he demanded to see all the documentation concerning the original promotion of the company.[99] On 17 February 1910, at the next Canada Cement board meeting, Irvin made a motion, seconded by Fleming, to have a four-member committee struck to investigate Fleming's allegations and see whether a settlement could be worked out. To pacify Fleming and thereby prevent the matter from becoming public, Canada Cement agreed to strike a committee made up of four directors, one of whom, Senator Robert McKay, had a seat on the CPR board and was well known to Fleming.[100]

Fleming exerted supplemental pressure on Aitken by writing letters to various Canada Cement directors. On 5 March 1910 the vice-president received a letter in which Fleming alleged that the Bond and Share Company had received some $27.2 million par value of Canada Cement securities, while the actual amount paid by Aitken for the various properties was only $14.6 million. On 10 March, at the board meeting preceding the first annual shareholders' meeting, Fleming objected to the adoption of the balance sheet on the ground that the first line on the assets side, which stated that the entry of $27 million was for the cost of the properties entering the merger, was highly misleading. Fleming reminded his directors that Aitken had actually paid far less for these properties than this figure suggested. The directorate understood, however, that the 'cost of properties' figure had been used to offset liabilities of $29 million in issued securities; since the accounting convention of the day was to record the par value rather than the market value of securities, liabilities were overstated by a substantial margin, necessitating an equally exaggerated entry under assets. For this reason, the directors rejected Sir Sandford's argument and approved the balance sheet at the general meeting.[101]

On 24 March, the directors' committee wrote to Fleming stating that it had found that the company's promotion had 'been legally and properly carried out.'[102] That same day, Aitken tried to settle the dispute before it got out of hand by writing to Frank Dunsford, who was once again in Canada on behalf of the English bondholders. He said that if Dunsford and his English bondholders would cooperate in financially reorganizing Western Canada Cement, he himself would either provide the company with $50,000 in new capital or personally cover a portion, up to $50,000, of the money that Western Canada Cement's directors owed to the Bank of Montreal, which had been secured through personal guarantees; and to demonstrate its desire to settle the Exshaw problem, the Canada Cement board would re-elect Sir Sandford Fleming as honorary president and would give the executive committee of the board – made up of George E. Drummond, C.C. Ballantyne (vice-president), and F.P. Jones (general manager) – the authority to negotiate an agreement to take over the Western Canada Cement property 'on terms fair to the Canada Cement Company.'[103] As part of the deal, Aitken required that Sir Sandford Fleming should state in writing that he had properly and lawfully organized and capitalized the Canada Cement Company.[104]

Anxious to settle on behalf of the Western Canada Cement bondholders, Dunsford put pressure on Fleming to write the necessary letter. Fleming finally relented, but he addressed the letter to Dunsford and Irvin rather than to Aitken and the Canada Cement board. The wording was careful, even crafty:

I daresay you know that at my instigation some of my co-directors of the Canada Cement Company, recently held an investigation, taking legal council [sic], and they express themselves satisfied that everything has been legally and properly carried out, in respect to the organization of the Company.

In securing an investigation, I feel that I have accomplished my purpose, and with unanimity on the part of the four gentlemen making it, it remains for me to accept their decision as over-ruling. The responsibility must rest with them.[105]

Dunsford immediately handed over Fleming's letter to Aitken in the hope that it would meet Aitken's requirement. Aitken rejected the letter but – still wanting the matter resolved – stated that his offer would stand so long as there was no further 'attempt on the part of Sir Sandford Fleming to attack the organization and capitalization of the Canada Cement Company, Limited, by bringing legal proceedings or notifying the company of his intention so to do, or by public criticism or by circularizing the shareholders of the company.'[106] The Bank of Montreal became a party to the agreement by undertaking not to enforce its claims as a secured creditor against Western Canada Cement, and the agreement was signed on 4 April 1910.[107]

Joe Irvin, Hugh Fleming, and Frank Dunsford all intended to live by the terms of the agreement; but Sir Sandford, who was increasingly succumbing to dementia under the pressure, could not be controlled. Without a pause, he stubbornly continued his campaign to embarrass Canada Cement into accepting Western Canada Cement on easier terms. Aitken immediately retaliated by calling on his secret weapon – Sir Edward Clouston. The Bank of Montreal called in its loans, forcing Western Canada Cement into receivership. As trustee for the debenture holders, the Royal Trust Company (of which Clouston was vice-president!) appointed a new manager to operate the plant for the benefit of the creditors, the single largest of which was the Bank of Montreal itself.[108]

When Sir Sandford discovered what Clouston had done, he exploded. Buttonholing Canada Cement board members, he demanded access to all the documents relevant to Aitken's handling of the Canada Cement merger. He grabbed old friends connected to the Bank of Montreal and the CPR and told them how he had been defrauded by Aitken and mistreated by Clouston. Since more than $12 million of the securities of the Canada Cement Company had been overissued to the Bond and Share Company, he should receive restitution for his losses, he maintained. And if he did not, he would take legal action against Bond and Share, embarrassing everyone – his fellow Canada Cement board members, Clouston, and the Bank of Montreal as well as Aitken – in the process.[109]

The pressure was so intense that Almon Lovett, still acting as Canada Cement's chief counsel, suggested that Fleming be allowed to review all the promotion documents in order to calm him down, and on 27 June he met with Fleming and Fleming's Ottawa lawyer, John F. Orde. Together they reviewed all the contracts under which the Bond and Share Company had acquired the companies transferred to Canada Cement, as well as the important 10 September 1909 contract between Bond and Share and Canada Cement. In the end, Orde found himself agreeing with Lovett; Aitken had done nothing wrong. Fleming, of course, was not prepared to accept this verdict; while Aitken had perhaps avoided doing anything that could be used against him legally, he had purposely lured Fleming and his associates into a trap which had resulted in the receivership of Western Canada Cement. Unlike his reaction when he had been taken advantage of by Irvin, this time Fleming would blow his whistle long and hard.[110]

Meanwhile, Royal Trust began proceedings in the Supreme Court of Alberta so that it would be allowed to sell Western Canada Cement's properties by the beginning of 1911. Naturally, Clouston retained Aitken's old friend R.B. Bennett, who in any case had been on retainer for years by both the CPR and the Bank of Montreal.[111] Bennett and Aitken came up with a plan on how to repurchase Western Canada Cement at the lowest possible price. Bennett would let the company go into liquidation, and Aitken would arrange to send Bennett the money required to purchase the property at foreclosure, whereupon Bennett would resell it to Canada Cement at a small profit. The debenture liabilities would be taken care of through the sale of the fixed assets (land and plant), but the sale of liquid assets would leave shareholders such as Fleming – according to Bennett's calculations – about $100,000 short on what they owed the Bank of Montreal. Of course, Sir Sandford and Hugh Fleming, along with Joe Irvin, had given personal guarantees, and the Bank could recover these funds directly.[112]

Sir Sandford Fleming could not possibly have been paranoid enough to realize the full extent of the conspiracy working against him. Working closely with Bennett, Frank Jones, and Sir Edward Clouston, Aitken had every possible thread running through his own hands. Moreover, he began to work actively with the Bank of Montreal in London. Together, they convinced Western Canada's English bondholders to demand that the company be liquidated so that they could recover at least a portion of their debts.[113]

Meanwhile Aitken, who had gone over to London, worked hard to prevent Fleming from reorganizing Western Canada Cement before the liquidation.[114] He opened negotiations directly with Frank Dunsford and his English bondholders on behalf of Canada Cement, offering to exchange Canada Cement bonds for Western Canada bonds at a discounted price of 85 per cent for the first mortgage bonds and 77 per cent for the second mortgage bonds.[115] Meanwhile, Fleming was asking the bondholders to allow him and Irvin to reorganize the company (still largely at the bondholders's expense) and run it as a rival to the cement merger.[116] Fleming's proposal was rejected outright by the bondholders, all of whom preferred the Canada Cement offer.[117]

As a consequence, the Exshaw plant was formally transferred by the sheriff to the Canada Cement Company in February 1911.[118] The sale had left Sir Sandford Fleming and Joe Irvin out in the cold. In their personal capacities, they had been among the largest unsecured debtors of Western Canada Cement, and their claims were wiped out through the bankruptcy sale.[119] Fleming estimated Western Canada Cement's unsecured debts at $690,000, of which he and his family were owed the lion's share – hence, he was determined to avenge himself on all those who he believed had forced his cement company into bankruptcy, principally Aitken, but also Canada Cement and the Bank of Montreal. In a letter addressed to W.C. Edwards, Cahan's permanent successor as president of Canada Cement, Fleming resigned his position as honorary president of the merger company and sent a printed circular containing his allegations to all the directors of the merger company.[120] Since Aitken was the most vulnerable villain of the piece, Fleming targeted him (and his Bond and Share Company), shrewdly avoiding any direct attack on Canada Cement and the Bank of Montreal. Nonetheless, the cement company and Clouston had already begun to feel the sting of Fleming's assault. Both Aitken and Clouston were to pay heavily for ignoring the Roman dictum that defeated enemies must be offered a golden bridge over which to retreat.

Clouston's Resignation

In 1910 Sir Edward Clouston was at the very peak of his career. Following the death in February of Bank of Montreal president Sir George A. Drummond, everyone outside the bank (and perhaps almost everyone inside) automatically assumed that the sixty-one-year-old banker who had been general manager since 1890 would succeed Drummond. Instead, the board deliberated for more than five months and then selected Richard B. Angus as the new president. Angus had a closer relationship with the CPR than with the Bank of Montreal, so the choice seemed peculiar to most outside observers.

Angus was surprised by the action of his fellow board members, for he considered himself unqualified for the position. Only after pressure had been placed on him by Sir Thomas Shaughnessy, who also was a director on both boards, did he agree, but on condition that he could step aside as soon as a 'younger and better qualified man can be found.'[121] Clouston was both younger and eminently more qualified than Angus, so it was 'only natural that considerable conjecture should have arisen' about why Clouston had been passed over. In his history of the Bank of Montreal, Merrill Denison speculated that Clouston was not prepared to accept the reduction in salary that went with the presidency, given that the two positions could not be held simultaneously according to bank custom – an unconvincing rationalisation considering the unimportance of Clouston's salary to his overall wealth.[122]

A better explanation is that by the time Sir George A. Drummond died, some members of the bank's board had become aware of Clouston's involvement with Aitken and realized the extent to which Western Canada Cement's exclusion from the merger had put at risk the loans the bank had made to the company. No doubt, Fleming had used his influence with some of the bank's board members – perhaps Shaughnessy, Angus, or E.B. Osler, all of whom were also long-standing members of the CPR board – to complain about the involvement of certain high officials of the bank in Aitken's cement merger syndicate. Clouston had put his own interests before those of the bank and, as a consequence, would not be given the one position for which he had been patiently waiting all his adult life.

At the same time, the Bank of Montreal had much to lose by publicizing the real reason behind the decision, and it tried to dampen speculation by referring to Clouston's 'poor health.' When Clouston formally resigned from his position as general manager in November the following year, he received the equivalent of one year's severance pay and was allowed to continue living in the general manager's house for another year, at the end of which he would be given the option of purchasing it for $100,000, less furniture. In lieu of any future claim on the bank's pension fund, Clouston was to continue to receive $15,000 a year, on condition that he 'not enter the service of any Bank or financial concern without the approval of the Bank.'[123]

Clouston's resignation was announced at the Bank of Montreal's annual shareholders' meeting on 4 December 1911. From the floor came a carefully prepared resolution. Charles Cahan expressed the shareholders' 'high appreciation of the invaluable services which Sir Edward Clouston, Bart., has rendered for over twenty years as chief executive officer of the Bank, and their sincere regrets that he has, owing to his length of services and present state of health, now decided to retire from that office.' The resolution was carried unanimously.[124]

Some of the press's surprise over Clouston's resignation was alleviated by references to rumours of his declining health. Much was made of the fact that he would be continuing in the office of vice-president. Nonetheless, it was difficult to avoid the main point – Clouston's career as the country's most powerful banker was over, and some of the newspaper reports quite properly carried the tone of an obituary. London's *Daily Telegraph*, for example, summed up his long career by stating that he had 'occupied a commanding position in Canadian banking circles, dominating the leading financial institution of the Dominion.'[125]

Repeating the conventional wisdom, the *Telegraph* also said that Clouston was a 'man cautious in his transactions.' It is very unlikely that Vincent Meredith, Clouston's replacement as general manager, shared this view, but it was hardly in the bank's interests for him to contradict it. If Clouston and fellow Bank of Montreal officers were to be exposed as company promoters and 'stock market operators,' the bank's reputation as a pillar of stability and financial conservatism would undoubtedly suffer.

Within a few months of Clouston's resignation, Doble and Stavert also left the bank. Doble joined the RSC to become its new Canadian general manager, a position he retained until 1914, when Aitken and Killam ruthlessly forced him out. Stavert joined a new investment bank, Corporation Agencies, which had just been set up by Cahan and Lovett.[126]

Aitken's Profit

Were Sir Sandford Fleming's allegations concerning Aitken's excessive profit even close to the truth? The short answer is no. Not only was Fleming inaccurate, but there is a high probability that he purposely misled the public in this respect. Based on the contract between Canada Cement and the Bond and Share Company, Aitken received $13,182,680 market value of securities. He paid out a total of $10,633,261 for eleven of the twelve properties (excluding Western Canada Cement) that entered the merger. He also distributed a cash value of $1,634,400 in common stock to other promoters and underwriters for their services. This left him with a gross cash profit of $915,419. When other expenses, including legal bills, advertising, appraisal, and audit fees are subtracted, Aitken was left with a net profit of $825,019, of which perhaps $600,000 would have gone into his own pocket as the majority shareholder in the Bond and Share Company.

TABLE 8.3 Calculation of Aitken's profit in promoting the Canada Cement merger

Form of payment	Amount received by Aitken		Amount paid out by Aitken	
	Par value	Cash value	Par value	Cash value
Ordinary shares	$13,498,400	$2,699,680[a]		
c/o properties			$2,155,850	$ 431,170[a]
c/o services			8,172,000	1,634,400[a]
Preference shares	10,500,000	9,135,000[b]		
c/o properties			2,129,300	1,852,491[b]
c/o services			0	0
Bonds	1,348,000	1,348,000		
c/o properties			1,348,000	0
c/o services			0	0
Cash	0	0		
c/o properties				7,011,600
c/o services				90,000
	$25,346,400	$13,182,680	$13,805,150	$12,357,261
Net profit cash value		$825,419		

Source: Archives of Ontario, Fleming Papers, MU 1051, env. 49, printed letter with enclosures, Fleming to W.C. Edwards, president of Canada Cement, 13 Feb. 1911; Beaverbrook Papers, House of Lords Record Office, G/3/9, memorandum dated 27 Sept. 1909, letter, Cahan to Aitken, 22 Jan. 1910

[a] Canada Cement common stock was assigned a market value of $20 based on 1910 Montreal Stock Exchange prices, which ranged from a low of $15 to a high of $25 after listing on 21 March 1910 (*Annual Financial Review* [Canadian], 11 [Apr. 1911], 153).

[b] Canada Cement preference stock was assigned a value of $87, which is the selling price of $93 per share minus the 25 per cent common stock bonus (or the $6.25 cash rebate at the option of buyer) (Guildhall Library Manuscripts, 18,000/146B/830, information in application for listing of preference shares on the London Stock Exchange).

The calculation of net profit in table 8.3 is very close to Aitken's rough estimate at the time, a profit he considered more than justified: 'My own profit on the transaction amounted to 6000 shares, and the profit of my company amounted to 20,000 shares. For these two commissions, our joint and several liabilities amounted to $9,000,000. Assuming the stock was worth $20 a share, the commission to us was less than $600,000 for a liability of $9,000,000. I do not think any Bank would undertake the liability for less commission.'[127] But was his profit excessive in more objective terms? Most Canadians at the time thought so. The first question is whether the merger added enough value to the industry and consumers to justify any profit at all. As explained in greater depth in chapter 10, to the extent that Canada Cement created a short-lived monopoly capable of setting higher prices, the merger had a negative impact. But to the extent that the merger rationalized and modernized the Canadian industry in the long run, it had a positive impact on the economy. In both cases, the new consolidation made money, and by conceiving, assembling, and marketing Canada Cement, Aitken had a right under the raw logic of capitalism to take a cut. How much is another question. The evidentiary problem here is one of calculating risk in an environment of tremendous uncertainty. In fact, Aitken's $600,000 was an entrepreneurial profit, entirely different from a commission paid on a relatively routine loan or even securities issue. There was nothing routine – and much that was perilous and uncertain – about consolidating twelve companies into one enormous industrial concern.

That said, $600,000 was an enormous amount of money for the time. To put such an amount into perspective, if we can assume that the average net income for a western wheat farmer during this same year was less than $1,000, then Max Aitken made more than six hundred times the income of a person who faced great hardship and many uncontrollable risks. It is little wonder that many people at the time (and since) have considered this degree of profit taking unconscionable.

9

Merger Promoter Extraordinaire

Mergers are falling upon the investor in Canada as thick as autumn leaves.

'Monetary Times,' 18 September 1909

I believe in 'consolidations.' They are more efficient. They give better service to the consumer. In a large country such as Canada, they reduce the distribution costs. They are good for the consumer.

Sir Maxwell Aitken, interview, 'Maclean's,' September 1911

Although Aitken may eventually have made up to $600,000 out of Canada Cement, much had gone wrong. Some problems were unavoidable in a consolidation involving so many conflicting interests, but others were unquestionably caused by Aitken's headlong rush to get the securities floated before many of the details – including terms of entry, audits, and appraisals – had been completed. This produced bad press and bitter disputes between Aitken and the owners. Lessons were learned, however, and Aitken's two subsequent mergers in the rolling stock and steel industries were smooth affairs compared with the Canada Cement fiasco.

Towards the end of October 1909, just weeks after the Canada Cement flotation, Aitken surprised the business community and financial press with a consolidation of the three largest railway car manufacturers in the country. This time, he was better prepared: a more informative prospectus kicked off his publicity campaign, and more competent agents sponsored the issue in Britain. Immediately afterwards, he began work on a major steel consolidation which, as he originally conceived it, was so large that it had to be developed in stages. His ultimate goal was to consolidate the steel industry of Nova Scotia with the largest primary and secondary manufacturers of central Canada. The first stage, the Dominion Coal and Dominion Iron and Steel merger, was completed by the end of 1909, but the consolidation's president, J.H. Plummer, showed no interest in Aitken's larger project and began to fight his steel merger. The second stage, the takeover of Nova Scotia Steel, had to be aborted in the face of Robert E. Harris's implacable opposition. As a consequence, Aitken was forced to abandon his grand scheme and leave the Nova Scotian companies behind, and to concentrate on a less ambitious consolidation – that of a small primary producer in Ontario with some secondary steel producers in southern Ontario and Montreal. Although this was a small affair relative to his earlier ambitions for the industry, the Steel Company of Canada (Stelco) merger turned out to be perhaps his greatest success.

In July 1910 Aitken followed his security issues to London, where he decided to reside on a permanent basis. The profits from his industrial mergers permitted him and his family to live in regal splendour in England and allowed him to secure a position in the British Conservative Party. By December, one month after establishing the Royal Securities Corporation in the City of London, Aitken had a seat in the British House of Commons and a respectable position among his new City associates. Just six dizzying years after John F. Stairs's passing, Aitken had turned his mentor's small Maritime bond house into a transatlantic investment bank and was operating in the very centre of the British Empire and world finance. Stairs would have been astonished.

The Canadian Car & Foundry Merger

Railway building epitomized the boom mentality of the Laurier years and was at the very heart of the country's rapid economic growth.[1] Immigrant settlers and goods from the industrial east filled long lines of cars rolling westward in the spring, while wheat rolled eastward in the autumn.[2] With the CPR building spur lines throughout the prairies and British Columbia, and with the Canadian Northern Railway and Grand Trunk Railway constructing their own transcontinental systems after 1900, the business of manufacturing rails and rolling stock was booming.[3]

Steel was the backbone of industrialization during the Laurier boom, and the rapidly expanding network of steel rail provided a convenient market for Canada's primary steel producers. Steel was not just used to

TABLE 9.1 Railway and rolling stock expansion, 1896–1914

Year	First track railway (miles)	Steel rails produced (short tons)	Freight cars in service (number)	Passenger cars in service (number)
1896	16,387	672		
1897	16,687	560		
1898	16,870	672		
1899	17,359	935		
1900	17,824	784		
1901	18,294	998		
1902	18,868	38,024		
1903	19,078	1,392		
1904	19,611	40,506		
1905	20,601	200,351	87,574	3,130
1906	21,518	350,422		
1907	22,446	348,836	107,407	3,642
1908	22,967	300,935	115,709	4,026
1909	24,004	386,210	117,779	4,192
1910	24,730	410,441	119,713	4,320
1911	25,400	403,813	127,518	4,513
1912	26,840	474,751	140,918	4,946
1913	29,304	567,514	182,221	5,696
1914	30,795	428,225	204,190	6,002

Source: M.C. Urquhart and K.A.H. Buckley, eds., *Historical Statistics of Canada* (Cambridge 1965), series Q283, Q286, S24, S78, and S85. Rolling stock figures for 1905 are from A. Ernest Epp, 'Cooperation among Capitalists: The Canadian Merger Movement, 1909–13' (PhD diss., Johns Hopkins University 1973), 534.

make rails to carry trains. It was needed to manufacture the wire fences, implements, and machines used by western farmers.[4] The numerous finished-steel manufacturers of southern Ontario and Montreal grew so rapidly during these years that mergers and new security issues became the norm rather than the exception.[5]

Naturally, the rolling stock industry grew exponentially during the Laurier years. The railways were buying everything produced by the few car works in the country, for instance, the Crossen Car Company and Preston Car & Coach in Ontario and the Silliker and Rhodes Curry companies of Amherst, Nova Scotia. These firms together could not keep up with demand, and larger operations were quickly established. In 1904 a group of American investors set up a car-manufacturing works in Montreal, the Canada Car Company, at the same time as the CPR's Angus car-manufacturing works came into operation. Two years later, the Dominion Car and Foundry Company began operating a factory in Montreal that specialized in steel railcar production.[6]

Despite these new plants, the demand for railcars, particularly immigrant passenger cars and the new steel refrigerator and coal cars, was running ahead of the country's productive capacity.[7] Aitken had been trying to get into the industry since 1905, when he had made a proposal to Nathaniel Curry, president and chief shareholder of Rhodes Curry, the largest of the older car firms.[8] Aitken's plan was to increase Rhodes Curry's capitalization and use the capital raised from a new issue to expand the Amherst facilities and increase output from fifteen to twenty freight cars per day. As part of the deal, Aitken offered to purchase an option on Curry's share of the new issue, about $1,050,000, so that Curry could retire a millionaire. Curry wanted a little more time to make a final decision but told Aitken to begin the preliminary work.[9]

Aitken was in the process of arranging the financing through Clouston at the Bank of Montreal when Curry had second thoughts about leaving the business to which he had dedicated most of his life.[10] Although disappointed, Aitken decided that he could wait for Curry to change his mind.[11] In the meantime, he kept himself busy with a promotional scheme for a new rolling stock company in Toronto, which took months of discussion but never materialized.[12]

Patience has its rewards. It took another three years, but not only did Aitken get his chance to issue new securities on behalf of Rhodes Curry, but he was also able to reorganize most of the Canadian rolling stock industry. In the summer of 1909, Rhodes Curry bought out the Malleable Iron Company of Amherst; Curry had at last decided to expand the company's car-making capacity. Remembering the earlier plan, he asked Aitken to make another proposal.[13] Aitken suggested that a total capitalization of $3 million ($500,000 more than the 1906 plan) was justified and in fact was conservative, given Rhodes Curry's earning record, a judgment shared by the financial press.[14] They would sell $2 million of preference shares to the general public; $800,000 par value of common stock would be designated as profit for promoters and underwriters, and a further $200,000 would be earmarked as a bonus to investors. Curry liked the plan, and this time he had no second thoughts. Clouston and his Maritime branch supervisor William E. Stavert were also in favour of the deal. Working through the bank's affiliated brokerage house in Montreal, C. Meredith & Co., of which Stavert was vice-president, they agreed to help the RSC underwrite the issue.[15]

In July 1909 the RSC successfully floated the new Rhodes Curry Company. Catching the first updraught of the Canadian investors' new interest in industrial securities, the timing of the issue could not have been better.[16] Then, in October, as the securities were waiting to be listed on the Montreal Stock Exchange, a separate car reorganization presented Aitken with an unforeseen opportunity.[17] Aitken discovered that the Canada Car and the Dominion Car and Foundry companies of Montreal were attempting to consolidate. Approaching both firms, he persuaded them that Rhodes Curry should be a party to the merger. By including the Amherst manufacturer, the proposed consolidation's manufacturing capacity would dwarf all the remaining rolling stock-firms.[18] Aitken concluded the deal within two weeks, and the merger was announced publicly the last week of October. Events had moved so fast and Aitken had been so successful in preventing leaks to the press that the merger turned out to be one of the great surprises of the merger movement.[19]

Since all three companies accepted securities in the new firm in lieu of cash for their holdings, they had a major stake in the long-term profitability of the consolidated company. They insisted on a conservative capitalization; only $3.5 million of common stock was distributed to the syndicates for promoting and underwriting $8.5 million of Canadian Car's senior securities. Brokers, investors, and the financial press were enthusiastic about the issue, in part because of the limited amount of 'water' that had been added, and Aitken had no difficulty selling the issue.[20]

Still trying to finish marketing his cement issue in Canada at the end of October 1909, Aitken decided that he would first float $3 million of car preference stock on the British market. This time he hired Ion Hamilton Benn and his Western Canada Trust to lead the issue in the City, on the understanding.that it would be widely underwritten – thereby distributing common stock profits among a large number of brokers, who in turn would advise their many clients to purchase Canadian Car shares.[21]

The issue was a conspicuous success, despite the fact that the shares were not accompanied by a 25 per cent stock bonus as in the Canada Cement flotation.[22] This time, however, Aitken had obtained appraisals and audits *before* the flotation, and his prospectus contained much more complete information concerning the assets and earnings of the old companies. This not only gave investors greater confidence but allowed Aitken to make applications for stock exchange listings shortly after the flotations – a far cry from the Canada Cement situation, in which investors had received little information and had then complained that stock exchange listing was taking inordinately long.[23] The following February,

Aitken was able to float $3 million of Canadian Car bonds in Britain, the United States, and Canada at 2.5 per cent above par value, the price advancing to $106 per share by the end of the first week.[24]

As the first president of Canadian Car, Nathaniel Curry presided over one of the largest industrial concerns in the country.[25] He had promptly moved his family from tiny Amherst to the bright lights of Montreal, where almost overnight he took his place among the great central-Canadian industrialists by virtue of the size and importance of his new firm. Within months, he was elected vice-president of the Canadian Manufacturers' Association, and his vigorous role on the antireciprocity side in the 1911 election was to be applauded by his new associates as doing God's work itself.[26]

Aitken benefited at least as much from the merger as Curry did. In terms of its conception, assembly, and financing, Canadian Car and Foundry had been a remarkable success, and Aitken was beginning to be regarded as the ablest merger promoter in the country.[27] At the very least, he now had the requisite connections and reputation to take on what he thought would be the Canadian equivalent of the 'deal of the century,' the Wall Street phrase used to describe J.P. Morgan's United States Steel consolidation.[28]

The Canadian Steel Monopoly

Between 1901 and 1911, primary steel production in Canada increased thirtyfold, from 29,000 tons to 882,000 tons. During this time, Nova Scotia Steel and Coal extended its existing operations, while new firms such as Dominion Iron and Steel, Hamilton Steel and Iron, and the Lake Superior Corporation (Algoma) began to produce steel ingots, rails, blooms, and other basic shapes in ever larger quantities.[29] Aitken wanted to reshape these companies into a Canadian version of Morgan's U.S. Steel – in his opinion, the wave of the future. It was not simply that the U.S. Steel merger had created $1.5 billion in securities (although this no doubt had its appeal); it was also the fact that the company seemed to define technological and organizational modernity. Enormous plants ensured production economies of scale; downstream integration into finished steel products provided a steady market for ingot production; and upstream integration into coal and iron ore guaranteed an uninterrupted supply of raw materials.[30]

With U.S. Steel actively searching for a branch-plant operation in Canada, Aitken felt that he had only a limited time in which to create a

Canadian steel corporation capable of competing against U.S. Steel by adopting its organizational form and methods.[31] As far as the Canadian companies were concerned, the timing also seemed right. They were apprehensive about the much-discussed possibility that the federal government would soon be removing steel bounties. Most of the Canadian companies had become highly dependent on these annual government handouts, and they were actively looking for new ways to keep profits up without the help of subsidies.[32]

Opportunity knocked almost immediately after the Canadian Car and Foundry flotation when Aitken was asked to join a syndicate headed by E.R. Wood with the purpose of merging Dominion Iron and Steel (DISCO) with Dominion Coal. For years the two companies had been locked in a bitter dispute over the terms of a coal delivery contract. Both company presidents, J.H. Plummer of DISCO and James Ross of Dominion Coal, used the courts rather than compromise in order to settle what had become an intensely personal struggle. The contest was finally decided in February 1909 when Canada's highest court of appeal, the Judicial Committee of the Privy Council in London, decided in favour of Plummer and DISCO's interpretation of the contract.[33]

Defeated, James Ross soon lost the desire to continue acting as president and decided to sell his considerable stake in Dominion Coal. This allowed for the consolidation of the two Dominion companies, which might have occurred years before had it not been for the personal conflict between Ross and Plummer.[34] Aitken joined E.R. Wood and Sir Henry Pellatt, a Toronto financier and a close associate of Wood's. Together, they purchased from James Ross $5 million of Dominion Coal stock at $95 per share, paying one-quarter cash, the balance plus interest to be paid over the next thirty months. They then invited all the remaining shareholders who wanted to sell on the same terms as Ross to deposit their shares with the Royal Trust Company. Although the various steps in the merger (including the incorporation of a holding company eventually known as the Dominion Steel Corporation) would drag on into the next year, the absorption of Dominion Coal into DISCO was largely completed by the end of December 1909.[35]

Over the years, Aitken had gradually become more favourably disposed to DISCO as he had watched the company emerge from the hole of debt into which its original promoter, Henry Whitney, had sunk it. Whitney's replacement, J.H. Plummer, was turning the company's fortunes around, partly through his careful selection of general managers; first, he had hired Scotia's founder, Graham Fraser, on a two-year contract beginning in 1904, and at the end of Fraser's term he had appointed Frank P. Jones, a plant and sales manager who had previous experience at DISCO, Scotia, and Canadian General Electric.[36] During the steel-coal negotiations, Aitken was so impressed by Jones that he decided to hire him as Canada Cement's new general manager.[37]

Although Jones was not a cement man, he had a track record in managing large enterprises that was superior to that of any of the cement plant manufacturers.[38] Always ready for new challenges, he welcomed Aitken's advances. Thus, on 11 November 1909, in the midst of the steel-coal merger, Plummer discovered that his general manager was leaving DISCO for Canada Cement for the princely salary of $30,000 a year.[39] To sweeten the deal, Aitken had also given Jones approximately 600 common shares, worth almost one-half of his annual salary at the time.[40]

Plummer must have been angry that Aitken had taken Jones away from DISCO at such a critical time, but he chose not to complain publicly. On the other hand, James Ross, eager to take any opportunity to thumb his nose at Plummer and DISCO, issued a press release crafted by Charles Cahan of all people. While denying that he had had anything to do with Jones's resignation, Ross 'expressed his very high opinion' of Jones and said that Canada Cement ought to be congratulated for securing the services of this 'very efficient and successful Manager.'[41]

From this point forward, Aitken's relations with Plummer were difficult. Not only would he be unable to convince Plummer of the merits of joining his Canadian Steel Corporation, but he was incapable of stopping Plummer from launching a publicity campaign against the proposed merger. Aitken had paid a high price in blood for Frank Jones, but he gained not only a superb big-business manager but someone who understood the steel industry better than anyone else in the country. As a consequence, Jones was to act as Aitken's chief 'technical' adviser as he attempted to assemble the various firms that would make up his new Canadian steel consolidation. Aitken's ultimate success in the Stelco merger owed much to Frank Jones.

The Scotia Steel Raid

While the steel-coal negotiations were taking place, speculation was fuelled by dozens of newspapers reports, some planted by the protagonists. The Montreal *Daily Witness*, for instance, reported that 'E.R. Wood and his associates [in the steel-coal syndicate] had made an offer to the

Nova Scotia Steel & Coal Company to come into' their 'proposed Canadian steel corporation.' The offer had been rebuffed, the report said, because Scotia was already 'self-sustaining, having both its coal and iron-ore deposits,' and therefore did not need to merge with any other firm. Moreover, the company was stronger than ever, and 'in the opinion of many of the shareholders' it was 'in the interests of the Company to allow President Robert E. Harris and Manager Thomas Cantley to work out' Scotia's future without interference from central-Canadian financiers.[42] The raid on Scotia Steel had begun.

For months, Harris and Cantley had been fretting about Scotia's vulnerability to a takeover.[43] They were particularly concerned about Aitken, who for months had been openly criticizing Harris's financial management of Scotia. Harris had introduced a controversial bill to the Nova Scotia legislature allowing Scotia to repurchase the 7 per cent preference share issue at a fixed price of $120 per share and to issue in its place 5 per cent bonds. This would have raised more capital for Scotia at the same cost, because of the lower rate of return, but it was precisely this lower rate of return that bothered professional investors.[44] When Harris discovered that Aitken was one of the bill's most vituperative opponents, he wrote to him directly, defending the action.[45]

Aitken's reply was uncompromising. He had found nothing in Harris's defence that suggested 'the slightest justification for this proceeding,' he said, and he assured Harris that the bill would continue to receive his 'open and hearty opposition.' Disputing the assumption 'that an act which enables two-thirds of a class who have paid less than 120 for their stock to compel the other third who have paid more than 120 to surrender at that figure is fair, either to the minority or the Company,' Aitken concluded:

Since you have written me on the subject, I take the opportunity of telling you that as a shareholder I believe your scheme for raising new moneys is not a wise one or in the interests of your Company. I am interested in the Company. My friends have bought its shares on my advice, and I have protected the market [in Scotia common] on the decline from 64 to 56 since your scheme was announced, to the extent of purchasing on my own account 958 shares.

It is possible you may be able to convince me that your scheme is in the interests of the Company, or it may be immaterial whether I am convinced or not since the majority governs, but in any case it is due to myself to let you know where I stand, so that we may eliminate the possibility of any personal animosity in doing everything we can to make our respective views effective.[46]

Aitken was being very disingenuous; the two men had been at war for years, and Aitken was certainly motivated by his animosity towards Harris, whom he had never forgiven for keeping him off the Scotia board. Moreover, toying with the idea of taking control of Scotia, Aitken and some of his central-Canadian associates, including Will Ross, Almon Lovett, E.B. Osler, J.W. McConnell, Rodolphe Forget, and J.N. Greenshields, had used the price decline to purchase more Scotia common. In their collective view, Scotia could only benefit from new management; Harris in particular appeared to be intent on driving the company into the ground, but Scotia's general manager Thomas Cantley was not much better.[47]

Aitken tried but failed to convince Ion Hamilton Benn to join his syndicate. Benn's reasoning – that 'too much appears to hang upon the value of the submarine areas' – was remarkably perceptive, and it spoke volumes about Scotia's predicament and Harris's desperate attempts to raise capital.[48] Benn was referring to Scotia's Wabana iron ore mines, located underwater off Bell Island in Conception Bay, Newfoundland. Scotia had first explored its submarine areas in 1904 and had begun production in 1908; by the following year, it was clear that all future ore would have to be mined underwater.[49]

Since the future viability of Scotia depended on the quality of this iron ore and also on the cost of extracting and transporting it (and for which only the roughest estimates existed), Aitken asked Frank Jones to gather all the intelligence possible on the submarine areas. Jones's initial report of November 1909 was disturbing. Scotia had just discovered that the ore deposits were much farther away from shore than had been expected. Consequently, Jones gave it as his opinion that the Wabana ore beds and thus Scotia Steel might no longer 'be commercially viable.'[50]

Aitken was wary of Scotia from this time on, for he realized that the company's problems were caused by more than Harris and Cantley's shortcomings and therefore could not be addressed simply by bringing in more competent management. At the same time, he was vindictive enough to carry on with the charade of the takeover in order to cause Harris as much discomfort as possible. So although he stopped buying Scotia shares on his own behalf, he let the other members of the syndicate continue their efforts with full vigour. From then on, Aitken allowed Rodolphe Forget to lead the takeover syndicate. Forget's appetite grew quickly. Using his extensive financial connections as well as his position as chairman of the Montreal Stock Exchange, he began to purchase Scotia shares on margin. Forget was being as incautious as Aitken had hoped he would be.

Towards the end of 1909, Harris realized that a takeover bid was under-way and he began to take defensive measures. He convinced his board to pass a 20 per cent stock bonus dividend to shareholders in order to secure their loyalty to the existing board and raise the cost of any poten-tial acquisition. Since Scotia had paid only 1.5 per cent on its common stock the previous year, the new dividend, which in effect added $1 mil-lion in 'water' to Scotia's existing $5 million common stock issue, was the subject of much commentary and speculation in the press.[51] The nor-mally sedate Canadian business community sensed the beginning of a showdown and relished the thought of watching the drama unfold.[52] Even the *Wall Street Journal* noticed these northern capers, reporting that the 'leading interests behind the Nova Scotia Steel & Coal Co. are opposed to the company being included in the merger that will be known as the Canadian Steel Corporation.'[53]

Meanwhile, the members of the takeover syndicate bought shares directly and also indirectly through friendly brokers, who agreed to hold them on margin. By January 1910, they felt that they had secured majority control, and Forget was boasting to the financial press that Scotia would soon be in different hands.[54] But the battle was far from over. Harris had his own syndicate of brokers, who also had been purchasing Scotia stock on margin, and he asked the steel company's Scottish investors to increase their holdings. Both Harris and Cantley tried to reassure inves-tors satisfied with Scotia's existing management that they would prevent the 'outsiders' from 'obtaining control, or dictating as to the composi-tion of the Board.' Cantley told one investor in Quebec: 'Yourself and other friends of Scotia can rest perfectly easy when the Annual Meeting takes place [on 30 March] the present Board will easily control the situa-tion, notwithstanding all the items that have appeared, or may appear, stating that Mr. Forget has secured control etc. etc. All this newspaper-advertising is part of the program of the stock exchange opera.'[55]

Privately, Cantley and Harris were far less sure of themselves. Three weeks before the meeting, they employed F.B. McCurdy, a prominent Halifax broker with little love for Aitken, to load the dice in their favour.[56] McCurdy arranged with various Montreal brokers (many of whom had little or no idea that they were holding Scotia common on behalf of a takeover syndicate) that he would borrow their stock on 30 March, returning it the next day with a half-point profit to the brokers. When the fateful day arrived, Harris had an extra 1,500 shares with which to do battle, and the Scotia raiders had 1,500 less than they thought.[57]

When the raiders, led by Forget, arrived in New Glasgow the day before the shareholders' meeting, Aitken was conspicuously absent. He had told his associates that other pressing business had arisen, and he watched the takeover attempt from afar. Although he had received advance intelligence that Forget and company might not gain control, he hoped they would have enough shares to remove Harris from the presidency and the board. It was just as well he did not attend, for he would have found the drama that unravelled less than gratifying.

The loss of 1,500 shares, through McCurdy's subterfuge, had defeated the raiders even before the meeting began at noon, and they knew it. That morning, Harris offered an olive branch to the raiders. Since Scotia had two vacancies on the board, he proposed that Forget's group select the nominees to fill these positions, as well as choosing a third nominee to replace an existing director. Forget refused – he wanted seven directors – and the defiant raiders filed into the only place suitable for such a large gathering of shareholders – the assembly hall of the New Glasgow YMCA.[58]

As president, Harris called the meeting to order, and after the minutes were read, Cantley took the floor to talk about the 'improved financial condition of the company' and its rosy prospects for the future. Harris then delivered the directors' report, emphasizing that the development of the 'submarine iron ore properties at Wabana' had lived up to Scotia's high expectations and that there was 'no longer any doubt as to the values of these areas.' Aitken knew better – as did Harris and Cantley – but Forget and the other raiders, as well as the shareholders enjoying the show, did not. Immediately after the report was adopted, Forget took the floor and nominated himself, J.N. Greenshields, J.W. McConnell, Almon Lovett, Will Ross, and Aitken among others to be the new members of the board; some old directors such as Thomas Cantley, Robert Jaffray, and Senator James D. McGregor were also included, but all the Halifax directors were excluded. Greenshields seconded the nomination. At this point, Senator McGregor jumped to his feet to renominate all the existing board members, including the Halifax members, as well as two individuals who were friendly to Harris, to fill the vacancies.[59]

Tallying the votes took up the rest of the day, during which Harris constructed elaborate legal arguments to explain why his telegraphic proxies should be accepted by the board, which he still controlled, and why the proxies supporting the takeover syndicate should be rejected. He selected three scrutineers, headed by F.B. McCurdy. While the votes and proxies were being counted, the takeover syndicate gave the board and the audience its reasons for dissatisfaction with Scotia. Forget admitted his predicament right at the beginning: 'Up to last night, I had control of this Company, but enough shares were borrowed over night to defeat me.' Is this fair? Forget demanded to know. And is it fair that a group that owns almost one-half of the voting shares should be kept from adequate representation on the board? In explaining why he was dissatisfied with the management, he argued that Scotia was 'going too slowly,' that it was 'behind the pace of modern times.' Greenshields followed the French Canadian's emotional appeal with a warning about the financial consequences of such Maritime stubbornness: 'With forty-eight or forty-nine per cent of the votes of this Company we should have more representation than one director on the board. You may talk about the injustice of Montreal people coming here to try to gain control of this property. Where would you obtain your money but in Montreal and Toronto. They are the money centres of the Dominion. If you antagonize these money centres by declining to give them proper representation on the directorate, your action will react against you.'[60]

Playing to the crowd, Harris interrupted to say that it was not the usual practice in the Maritimes 'to elect a lot of stock brokers to control a Company of this nature.' Greenshields shot back, 'What about lawyers?' Harris said lawyers could and did do well in business, whereupon Forget remarked that 'he had heard of stock brokers who had done the same thing.' The two sides continued to trade insults until the evening, when they wrangled over Harris's ruling concerning the proxies, with Forget and Greenshields challenging Harris every step of the way. At 10:20 P.M. the scrutineers appeared with the final tally, and F.B. McCurdy read the results. The meeting ended in defeat, as Aitken had known it would.[61]

Harris assumed that Aitken was the mastermind behind the takeover attempt, and he gloated about having defeated him. Just days after the meeting, Harris wrote an account of the struggle, which was reprinted in the Halifax *Morning Chronicle* in three unsigned instalments. In it, he vented his spleen against Aitken in a satirical reconstruction of the Scotia raid.[62] Harris's first scene opens in Montreal a few days before the Scotia meeting, when the members of the takeover syndicate are drinking champagne in the Windsor Hotel. Aitken arrives in a hansom cab. He jumps out, flings the driver some Canada Cement stock as a tip, and bursts into the hotel. He is greeted by his partners in crime with shouts of 'Here's Max!' Champagne glasses are 'raised to acclaim the man who had engineered the great Scotia Coup, and who, with his friends, now waited merely to put the finishing touch on the Nova Scotia hayseeds.' When Max is asked why he is sore at the Halifax crowd, he replies,

Sore! Damn it, man, they were my friends! When I went down there a few years ago they couldn't have floated a cork on a bucket of lye. I did everything for them. They used to sit and let me talk about myself by the hour. Finally I had one or two good things and I let them in on them and started a Bank for them. And then after all that, after making them, I wanted them to let me take this Scotia and finance it so I could make a whacking big pile out of it. And what did the ungrateful beggars do! They refused. Said they had to look after the shareholders, or some rot like that.[63]

Whatever Aitken may have felt about Harris's gaining the upper hand, he wasted no further time with Scotia, whatever its nuisance value. Over the next months, Harris would have to repurchase a large number of overvalued Scotia shares, reducing his own net worth in the process. Aitken no doubt foresaw some of Harris's coming difficulties – hardly the full-blooded revenge he had been seeking – but it was time to return to more important matters: his Canadian steel consolidation, now minus Scotia.[64]

Negotiating the Steel Merger

Aitken's central-Canadian negotiations, like many of his past deals, had begun with Sir Edward Clouston. It was Clouston who had introduced him to William McMaster and the Montreal Rolling Mills Company, the largest and one of the most profitable semifinished steel producers in the country. Clouston happened to be president because of his bank's long-standing relationship with the Montreal steel manufacturer, but the real force behind the company was McMaster, the firm's largest shareholder and its managing director. An old man now, McMaster wanted to retire gracefully and comfortably from the business and was looking for a buyer. With Clouston's help he had recently tried to sell out to DISCO, but J.H. Plummer – still preoccupied with the steel-coal merger and busy looking for a new general manager to replace Frank Jones – was uninterested, despite the fact that Montreal Rolling Mills had always been DISCO's best customer, and despite the fact that both McMaster and Clouston sat on the board of DISCO.[65]

For months, McMaster and Clouston had also been talking to Hamilton Steel and Iron and another Hamilton company about a possible merger. But McMaster wanted out of the steel business both financially and managerially, and the Hamilton companies were not offering to pay cash. Fully aware of Aitken's plans for a Canadian steel corporation,

Clouston suggested to McMaster that the young promoter might be willing to buy him out. As a result, Aitken met with McMaster in early March 1910. Pointing out the quality of his operations and their earning power, McMaster said he wanted $4,200,000 for the Montreal Rolling Mills.[66]

Aitken's sleeping partner in the venture was Herbert Holt, now president of the Royal Bank of Canada. Holt had been one of the RSC's regular clients since the Camaguey Company promotion in Cuba. The previous summer, he had purchased Montreal Trust so that the Royal Bank would have a trust company alliance similar to those enjoyed by the Canadian Bank of Commerce and the Bank of Montreal. Holt had been so impressed with the way in which Aitken had reinvigorated Montreal Trust that he asked him to remain on the board and to continue in his position as vice-president after the sale. Although not easily impressed by most businessmen, Holt had been very impressed with Aitken's acumen, and when he discovered Aitken's plans for a Canadian steel corporation he immediately offered his support. Aitken was delighted. He saw his alliance with Holt as a splendid offset to what he viewed as his dangerous dependence on Clouston and the Bank of Montreal.[67]

Both Aitken and Frank Jones inspected the Montreal Rolling Mills' equipment and plant. Jones soon concluded that the properties might actually be worth more than McMaster's asking price.[68] A few days later, Aitken received a copy of an appraisal prepared by Price Waterhouse for McMaster, assessing the value of land, plant, equipment, and inventory at $4.1 million. Since liquid assets, such as accounts receivable and cash on hand, were not included, Aitken was convinced that Jones had been correct in his assessment.[69] Aitken told McMaster that if he could interest other companies in a consolidation, he would definitely pay what McMaster wanted for the Montreal Rolling Mills.[70] Having held the Hamilton men on a string for over a week while Aitken was inspecting the premises, McMaster finally cabled Charles Wilcox of Hamilton Steel and Iron to let him know that he was considering a cash offer for his business and hence would not be joining Wilcox's proposed merger.[71]

Aitken's next stop was the Dominion Wire Manufacturing Company of Montreal. William H. Farrell, brother of the future president of U.S. Steel, was the majority shareholder in Dominion Wire, and he ran the company as an affiliate of U.S. Steel.[72] Dominion Wire's chief attraction was this connection with U.S. Steel and consequently its monopoly on certain galvanized wire products made under licence or imported directly from U.S. Steel.[73] In fact, five months earlier, Farrell had been asked by Charles Wilcox whether he would consider joining Hamilton Steel and

Iron and Canada Screw in their proposed consolidation. Farrell had replied that he would only consider a cash sale, setting his price at $225 per share, or approximately $1,125,000 in total. But the Hamilton industrialists could not consider any outright acquisition until they had agreed on a merger among themselves.[74]

Farrell told Aitken that he was still interested in a cash buy-out; Aitken asked to see the company's balance sheets and profit and loss statements, while Frank Jones asked to inspect the plant. Farrell agreed, insisting, however, that they not divulge what they saw to anyone outside the purchasing syndicate. After they were done, Aitken said he might be willing to offer Farrell $1 million. Although this was less than his original asking price, Farrell said he would think about it.[75] Aitken then spoke with Thomas Drummond to see whether he would be willing to bring the Lake Superior Corporation (to be renamed Algoma Steel in 1912) into the merger discussions. Drummond was noncommittal, so Aitken decided to move on to the Hamilton manufacturers.[76] When he learned that they were in the midst of putting together their own merger, he asked whether they would consider delaying in view of the possibility of including the Montreal Rolling Mills along with one or two other companies. The Hamilton men agreed.

When Aitken returned to Montreal two weeks later with an option on the Montreal Rolling Mills, he began the steel merger negotiations at the Windsor Hotel. By this time, Drummond had decided that Algoma would not participate, but Aitken was now ready to proceed to the first stage without Drummond.[77] Charles Wilcox and Cyrus Birge, the president and chief shareholder of Canada Screw, were eager to hear Aitken's proposal.[78] They were joined by Lloyd Harris, who represented the Canada Bolt and Nut Company. A scion of the agricultural machinery family and a Liberal MP, Harris had just consolidated his own Brantford Screw Company with three small and rather antiquated Ontario steel finishers: Gananoque Bolt and Nut; Belleville Rolling Mills; and Toronto Bolt and Forge. Harris grandly called this ragtag collection the Canada Bolt and Nut Company, but he had delayed issuing new securities in the hope that he could sell or merge his new interests in a larger consolidation.[79] When Harris had first approached the Hamilton firms, he had found that they were uninterested in his properties, so he had threatened to issue $150,000 in securities and use the cash to build a new nail plant that would compete directly with Canada Screw. Wilcox and Birge quickly changed their tune and invited Harris to join their discussions with Aitken. McMaster, however, had been decidedly cool to the idea of Harris's obsolescent plants joining the consolidation, and he continued to question the value of Harris's properties during the Windsor Hotel meeting.[80] At this meeting, the various parties were not able to conclude a consolidation agreement, so Aitken decided that they should negotiate in a more secluded location where they would be without the distraction of other business or the press. The plan was to hold one marathon session in New York at the Waldorf-Astoria, allowing no one to leave until the deal was done or until it was clear that the parties could not agree.[81] If the merger discussions turned out to be successful, Aitken would then negotiate the Dominion Wire purchase with Farrell, who would be standing on deck at the U.S. Steel head office in New York.[82]

The industrialists and promoters who met together at the Waldorf-Astoria in early April were intent on putting together the merger.[83] In fact, some matters had been settled before the meeting started. The merger was to be called the Canadian Steel Corporation, as Aitken wanted. Charles Wilcox would be the president of the consolidation and Robert Hobson, his general manager, would perform the same role in the new company. Cyrus Birge, ready for retirement, would be the inactive vice-president. Almost everyone around the table would be made a director. They would also be given first crack at underwriting the merger's securities, an attractive aspect of the deal in the eyes of the promoters and the more financially savvy of the industrialists. Really, the only outstanding question was the price that would be placed on their respective properties.

The two main groups at the meeting were the Hamilton Steel and Iron representatives on one side and the Montreal Rolling Mills group on the other. Accompanying Wilcox and Hobson were W.D. Matthews and E.B. Osler, two of the company's most influential shareholders. Although both had participated in the Canada Cement merger and had supported Aitken in his public arguments with Robert E. Harris over Scotia, neither trusted him very much. They were disappointed with the final price they had received on their cement properties, and they had blown a lot of money for nothing in the attempted Scotia takeover. Although they were not averse to entering another deal with Aitken, they were determined to watch his every move.[84]

On the Montreal Rolling Mills side of the table, Aitken was flanked by Frank Jones and Herbert Holt. Jones was acting as Aitken's technical adviser, and his job was to prevent Wilcox and Hobson from buffaloing the Montreal crowd on the value of the steel properties.[85] Holt was the money man, taciturn and wily, making sure that Matthews and Osler would not get the better end of any financial deal. Having taken considerable risk in the Montreal Rolling Mills purchase, Holt now wanted to enjoy an even more considerable profit. Aitken naturally felt the same way.[86]

All agreed to take the merger's senior securities in repayment for their net assets, fixed and liquid, and common stock for their earning power and goodwill, but the negotiations over the exact amounts took days.[87] In the end, the sticking point turned out to be not the value of Canada Bolt and Nut as anticipated, but the price tag for Montreal Rolling Mills. The Ontario men would agree to pay only $4 million in senior securities for the Montreal properties. Backed up by Jones's advice and the Price Waterhouse appraisal, Aitken and Holt wanted closer to $5 million. Some of the Ontario men, particularly Matthews and Osler, felt that Aitken had paid too much for the property. After all, $5 million was almost as much money as the Hamilton people wanted for their steelmaking plant, which they considered the foundation stone of the consolidation.[88]

Finally Aitken suggested a compromise that seemed to satisfy everyone around the table. The Canadian American Appraisal Company would estimate the value of the fixed assets, and Price Waterhouse would do an updated appraisal on all other assets. If their joint valuations of net assets amounted to less than $4 million, Aitken and his Montreal associates would pay any deficiency so calculated to the merger; if their valuations came in at more than $4 million, the Ontario men would owe the Montrealers the difference.

Thus, on 9 April 1910, less than two weeks after the Scotia debacle, the merger agreement was signed and deposited in the safety deposit vault of the Waldorf-Astoria.[89] Acting on behalf of the syndicate, Aitken then paid Farrell $1,000 for an option to purchase Dominion Wire for $1 million within forty-five days.[90] The whole merger agreement was now predicated on Aitken's raising the necessary money to buy Montreal Rolling Mills within the same time period.[91]

The Million-Dollar Flip

As Sir Edward Clouston was president of the Montreal Rolling Mills as well as a major shareholder in the RSC, he was the first person whom Aitken thought to ask for a loan. Clouston, however, was just then the subject of much discussion by various Bank of Montreal board members who were trying to fathom his connection to the Canada Cement merger. The bank had been without a president since Sir George A. Drummond's death in February, and Clouston was being blocked from ascending to the presidency until the matter could be cleared up to everyone's satisfaction. This was the wrong time for him to be party to an Aitken-inspired transaction financed by the Bank of Montreal and involving the purchase of the assets of a separate company of which he was president.[92]

The Royal Bank was also out of the question. Holt had already extended himself in the deal. So Aitken decided to look outside Canada. Leaving behind both New York and the intense negotiations at the Waldorf-Astoria, Aitken sailed to England with his wife.[93] Within days of his arrival in London, he managed to put together the syndicate for the Canadian Steel Corporation's British issue. As part of the deal, one of the underwriters, the prominent merchant bank of Lazard Bros. & Co., purchased a large block of RSC stock at a premium of $300 per share.[94] Writing to Holt from the elegant Savoy Hotel on the Strand, Aitken explained that he had also secured the money necessary to exercise the option on the Montreal Rolling Mills, having obtained a loan from Parrs Bank, a long-established English bank. In Aitken's view, this removed the Bank of Montreal connection, 'at the same time relieving Sir Edward Clouston from the question of dealing with a loss to us of sufficient money to purchase the Company of which he is now President.'[95]

Aitken sailed back to Canada on 7 May 1910, the day after King Edward VII's death.[96] On his arrival, he exercised his option to purchase the Montreal Rolling Mills and soon held a directors' meeting to erase the last traces of Clouston's connection with the transaction by having him resign as both director and president. Holt, Aitken, and their appointees then became directors, and Holt was voted in as the new president.[97]

A few days before the 30 May deadline, Aitken had tried to convince DISCO president J.H. Plummer that the new consolidation would pose no threat to him. Plummer had refused to participate in the negotiations from the beginning, but his anger over losing his most valuable customer, the Montreal Rolling Mills, so soon after Frank Jones's defection to Canada Cement made him a dangerous opponent. Plummer also feared that the inclusion of Dominion Wire in the merger might give Aitken's Canadian Steel Corporation monopoly control over U.S. Steel's wire exports to Canada. Aitken tried to conciliate Plummer through private negotiations, but without success.[98] When the merger was announced in the press, Plummer told the *Montreal Herald* that he 'did not regard the merger of the smaller Canadian company' as one that would allow 'Canadian interests to compete with U.S. Steel.' In fact, 'he very strongly objected to a merger' of his companies with the so-called Canadian Steel Corporation.[99]

The dispute acquired a petty dimension when Aitken took out a federal corporate charter in the name of the Steel Corporation and Plummer threatened legal action. Plummer had previously taken out a Nova Scotia charter in the same name for his DISCO and Dominion Coal merger, and he now made it clear that he would contest Aitken's effort to use the name, arguing that the smaller merger could not presume to be *the* Canadian Steel Corporation.[100] Although Aitken had received federal letters patent in the name of the Canadian Steel Corporation on 8 June, he decided it would be best to avoid potential litigation with Plummer, and two weeks later he applied to have the name changed to the Steel Corporation of Canada – Stelco for short.[101] As Aitken was anxious to get the prospectus prepared for Stelco's $4.5 million bond issue, a tactical retreat seemed advisable in the circumstances.[102]

The only other outstanding matter was the adjustment required for the Montreal Rolling Mills. The two appraisals, when they finally arrived, did not surprise Aitken. He had trusted Frank Jones's ability to assess the value of steel properties, and Jones had been unerring from the beginning. Montreal Rolling Mills' total net asset value was $4,901,491. Now the merger syndicate owed Aitken and his Montreal associates just under $1 million.[103] In accordance with the terms of the Waldorf-Astoria agreement, the money was transferred to the Montreal Rolling Mills, and Aitken and Holt both reimbursed themselves by declaring a bonus dividend of 80 per cent on their stock in the company before it was formally transferred to Stelco.[104]

There was considerable grumbling among the Ontario manufacturers about the results, but the position of Aitken and his Montreal associates was unassailable. After carefully combing through the appraisals, it was clear to the Ontarions that Aitken's party was entitled to the money – even though Matthews, Osler, and one or two others could not get over feeling that they had been tricked into accepting Aitken's compromise during the Waldorf-Astoria negotiations and that Aitken had somehow known from the beginning that the appraisals would come in close to $1 million high.[105]

Naturally, Aitken, Holt, and Jones were delighted with the outcome. Since Aitken owned the largest interest in the Montreal Rolling Mills, he gained the most from the sale of the property to the steel syndicate. He had made at least as much money from flipping the Montreal company to the steel syndicate as he had from the whole cement merger, plagued as it had been with so many problems. Let Matthews and Osler complain all they wanted, the deal had been a fair one under rules which they had all agreed to months before.

More than satisfied with the justice of the bargain, Aitken once again did not offer any opportunity for his opponents to save face, much less share in his windfall profit. His relentlessness was beginning to make him new enemies at every turn, and similar business struggles had grown more frequent and more intense. Cursed with a thin skin, he suffered miserably from these disagreements. He affected a tough exterior – and in fact showed little mercy for the suffering or losses of his associates – but these feuds were rapidly eliminating the joy he had previously derived from being a financier and deal maker. More disturbing, he was beginning to have misunderstandings and disagreements with old friends, the most notable being Charles Cahan, who felt that he was owed considerably more for his services in the Canada Cement merger than he had been paid.[106]

Aitken was desperate to spend some time away from the recent scenes of battle in order to lick his wounds and recoup his strength. Friends noticed his new weariness. Just before Christmas 1909, R.B. Bennett had advised Aitken to cut back on work: 'You cannot stand all this strain forever & you must husband your energies for use in the years that are to come.'[107] Aitken agreed; it was time for a change.

Plunging into London Society and Politics

On 19 July 1910, Aitken set off with Gladys 'in a car as big as a house' for Saratoga, New York. There they met with William Price. Although the conversation involved a large issue of securities on behalf of Price's pulp and paper company, this was not the main purpose of their journey; Aitken and Gladys were on their way to New York to catch a steamer to England, where they planned to vacation for a couple of months.[108]

On arriving in London, they took a flat in Cavendish Square. Bored with sightseeing within days, Aitken began to help Ion Hamilton Benn and his syndicate sell the Stelco stock issue.[109] Benn introduced Aitken to some of his City friends, the most notable being Edward Goulding who, like Benn himself, was a great supporter of Joseph Chamberlain's combination of imperialism and tariff reform. Goulding had organized Chamberlain's 1903 campaign for tariff reform and he helped found the Tariff Reform League. As one of the most important operators in the Conservative Party, Goulding became Aitken's first point of entry into British high society and politics.[110]

A wealthy forty-eight-year-old bachelor, Goulding had a large house on the Thames in Berkshire, where he regularly held weekend parties for some of the more interesting men and women of his set. A few weeks after he arrived in England, Aitken became a habitué of these gatherings, which included not only Conservative MPs such as Benn, Bonar Law, Sir Edward Carson (leader of the Ulster Unionists), and F.E. Smith (later Lord Birkenhead), but also opinion leaders such as the editors of the *Observer*, the *Daily Express*, the *St. James Gazette*, and the *Morning Post*. This was heady company, but Aitken does not seem to have been in the least intimidated; perhaps it helped that he was richer than all the people he met, despite their conspicuously self-indulgent and luxurious lifestyles. At his first weekend party, Aitken proclaimed during lunch that he would soon be joining Benn, Carson, and Smith in Parliament.[111]

At the time, this would not have seemed an absurd sentiment. The Parliament at Westminster was considered the mother of all parliaments within the empire. Every British citizen, wherever born, had the right to stand for election, and Aitken would hardly be the first colonial to enter the Commons chamber. Moreover, in an era without passports, even those who were technically not citizens of the empire could and did enter Westminster on occasion. As for Aitken's background, this was a time when City financiers of middle-class background were often to be found running for Parliament, either in the Unionist wing of the Conservative Party or for Lloyd George's Liberal Party.[112]

An election having unexpectedly been thrust upon the country, Goulding had already broached the idea of Aitken's running on behalf of the Conservative Party. Aitken was no doubt flattered, but he was not entirely fooled by the gesture. He wrote to Bennett: 'I believe I am being selected on my merits or supposed merits. They say money does not count but I am sometimes suspicious.'[113] He had every reason to be sceptical. He had just begun to explore the power of money through the dispensing of lavish gifts, and he did not find it lacking. Goulding was the first recipient. Having just discovered that the Rolls-Royce motor car firm was up for sale, Aitken used some of his Canadian profits to buy a controlling share of the company; and since the investment was more of a whim than real business, he put Goulding on the board to represent his interests. Goulding (later Lord Wargrave) was to remain chairman of Rolls-Royce and grateful to Aitken until his death in 1936.[114]

Although Aitken was soon to enter British politics, he spent most of his time in London on RSC business. The Stelco flotation proceeded smoothly, with the bonds selling at ten cents above par.[115] Moreover, Aitken had learned enough about City practices that he personally put together the underwriting syndicate for the Price Brothers flotation.[116]

The issue was so attractive to investors that Aitken was able to close down the subscription one day ahead of schedule; even by then, the issue had already been more than 25 per cent oversubscribed.[117]

Earlier that autumn, in preparation for the Price Brothers flotation, Aitken had opened a Royal Securities office at 75 Lombard Street in the heart of the City.[118] He now presided over a transatlantic investment bank that had two de facto head offices, one in the industrial and financial capital of Canada, the other in the financial centre of the world. The securities from his issues were distributed through branches in Halifax, Saint John, Quebec City, and, most recently, Toronto.[119] In less than seven years since John F. Stairs's death, Aitken had not only proved himself a worthy successor to his mentor, but he was recognized by many as the most capable and daring financier in Canada. He could have kept going forward. Instead, he decided to prove himself in a very different career and – despite his beliefs about imperial unity – in a very different country.

In October 1910, Goulding had come up with a vacant seat for Aitken in North Cumberland in the Lake District.[120] Aitken went north to investigate but declined the honour when he discovered the extent to which the scenic constituency was a Liberal, or radical, stronghold. He wanted a safer and more urban seat.[121] One month later, Aitken had a second chance. Bonar Law had decided to give up his safe seat in Dulwich, south of London, in favour of a more difficult seat. As one of the best-known MPs in the Conservative Party, Law wanted to use his strength to defeat the Liberal candidate in a previously free trade constituency, giving the safer seat to a less recognized candidate. Aitken suggested himself for the latter but was turned by the Conservative central office. Meanwhile Law, having first chosen Ashton-under-Lyne, a textile town six miles from Manchester, changed his mind and selected an even more difficult seat, North West Manchester. This left a vacancy, so Law asked the Conservative chairman to consider Aitken, describing him as 'a young Canadian, not much over 30, who without any outside help has made a large fortune.' Law pointed out that although Aitken was a political novice, he was 'a keen imperialist' with 'a distinct personality,' who he believed 'would be attractive in any constituency.'[122]

Since the party was not able to find a local citizen of Lancashire to run, it bowed to Law's request and offered Aitken the nomination. Aitken baulked at first. Ashton-under-Lyne was well known as free trade country and he was afraid of losing the election. He realized, however, that he was unlikely to be offered any safer seat, and after obtaining promises from some of the party's leading figures, including Edward Goulding and

F.E. Smith, that they would give speeches on his behalf, he finally accepted. Goulding also asked Rudyard Kipling, who had agreed to make one speech for the Conservative Party, to give it in Ashton-under-Lyne.

Once committed, Aitken put all his organizational abilities into an effective urban barnstorming campaign, which resembled an American far more than a British election. He asked Gladys to help organize the campaign as well as address various groups, since his own speech-making ability was wretched. Predictably, his campaign propaganda took considerable liberty with the truth. The local Conservative newspaper described him as having studied 'law with governor Tweedy' of New Brunswick, later occupying 'a prominent position' in the provincial government. Aitken tried to play down his past as a financier and merger promoter and to pass himself off as an industrialist – a more solid type of 'commercial man' who would be likely to appeal to voters in the heart of England's traditional textile industry. The Liberal opposition, on the other hand, described Aitken as a 'devious financier' and 'ruthless millionaire speculator' who had cornered the market in cotton and wheat, raising prices and creating unemployment in Lancashire. Aitken retorted that he had 'never bought or sold a bale of cotton or a bushel of wheat' and had 'never carried on any speculative transaction' or 'any speculative enterprise.'[123]

While it is easy to mock Aitken's statement on the grounds of commonly accepted definitions of speculation, the interesting fact is that Aitken did not regard himself as a speculator.[124] Apart from his early adventures in Scotia and some utility ventures, he had rarely been a 'plunger,' charging in and out of securities in the hope of short-term gain. He preferred to see himself as an investment banker who invested over the long term in operations which he created, reorganized, or consolidated. When his clients asked for market tips, he invariably told them that he personally held every stock, sometimes for years, until he was able to sell out at better prices. He would add that, naturally, this plan could be followed with safety only if the stocks were not carried on margin.[125]

He even regarded the RSC's retail operation through this prism, as he patiently explained to his errant lawyer brother, Traven Aitken, who had just wasted a year attempting to get rich by speculating in gold properties – against Aitken's advice. Aitken wrote: 'You understand my position is that I am looking for an investment of capital. You will appreciate that I would be wholly dependent upon the capacity and experience of the practical men I might be associated with. I always sell out my investments in the shape of bonds and stocks, and it is absolutely necessary to the continuance of my business that the interest on bonds and dividends on stocks sold by me should be assured beyond doubt.'[126]

Aitken easily survived being called a speculative financier during the campaign, but he had more difficulty with being stigmatized as a pushy colonial, especially as he was running against a local man. His 'twangy' Canadian accent was ridiculed, and the Liberal newspapers suggested that he return to Canada where he belonged, whereupon the Conservative organs exhorted the men of Lancashire (women, of course, were still prohibited from voting) to 'vote for Aitken on polling day,' for 'he's the man and he's come to stay.'[127]

Using his Canadian origins to best advantage, Aitken dedicated almost all his campaign speeches to the British Empire and the need for protectionist tariff reform (in order to prevent Britain's further economic decline) by binding vigorous colonies such as Canada closer to the imperium. Breaking away from his written text in one particularly poor speech, Aitken emotionally blurted out, 'If I could make you men of Ashton realize what this Empire of ours means, there would not be one Radical left in the place.' On 2 December 1910, Aitken fittingly ended his campaign with a torch-lit procession led by young men from the Junior Imperialist League. The results the next day gave him a narrow victory. He had won by a 196-vote margin. His victory speech amounted to one sentence: 'I am now a Lancashire man, a Lancashire man from Canada.'[128]

Like most of Aitken's business triumphs, this political victory was followed by his nervous collapse into sickness and by allegations of irregularities and sharp practice. Aitken successfully defended the charges, and he went on vacation to the Continent with Gladys in order to recuperate from the stress of the campaign. When he returned to London in early February 1911, he entered the House of Commons as a novice opposition MP, restricting his few questions to matters he knew best, such as trade and finance.[129] Almost from the beginning, though, his attention was diverted by events in Canada, where a political storm was brewing. In a few weeks Aitken was to find himself at the very centre of the maelstrom.

10

Combines, Canada Cement, and the Reciprocity Election

There are two sides to the trust question – the inside and the outside. Nobody on the inside of a trust was ever known to object to it, and nobody on the outside was ever known to do anything else.

'Grain Growers' Guide,' 1910[1]

And there is the essence of the whole of this measure. It is not aimed against combinations as such, but against the abuse of their power by combination.

Minister of Labour Mackenzie King, during second reading of his
Combines Investigation Act, 1910[2]

The amount of ability which enables a man to cut a very respectable figure in a Cabinet is extraordinarily low, compared with that demanded in the world of industry and finance.

Beaverbrook editorial, 'Sunday Express,' 27 February 1921

The Ashton freeholders who elected Aitken to the House of Commons on 3 December 1910 must have found it difficult to understand his preoccupation with the British Empire. Most Britons took the empire for granted, occasionally debating its value to Britain itself but generally assuming its inevitability and permanence. Few had challenged this conventional view until Joseph Chamberlain launched his tariff reform campaign in 1903. Yet even a man as forceful and charismatic as Chamberlain

Preparing to Save Canada

Anti-reciprocity forces saving Canada, 1911. *Source: Grain Growers' Guide*, 23 Aug. 1911, 4

had been unable to convince even a large minority that his project for a modern imperial federation was worth pursuing.[3] Now, seven years later, a Canadian had arrived in Britain repeating Chamberlain's message with a new sense of urgency. Without revitalizing the empire, Aitken had told the Ashton crowds, both Britain and Canada would be lost. He believed every word of it.

Months before his arrival in London, Aitken had been fighting tooth and nail against what he regarded as Canada's 'continental drift' away from Britain. This drift took two forms. The first was Prime Minister Laurier's insistence on creating Canada's own 'tin-pot navy' rather than directly contributing to the empire's naval defences at a time when Germany was building a modern fleet and challenging Britain's long-held naval supremacy. The second was Canada's improving relationship with the United States and Laurier's decision to use this opportunity to lower tariffs between the two countries. In Aitken's mind, both policies were intended to strengthen continentalism at the expense of empire and would eventually lead to the separation of Canada from the mother country and ultimately to its absorption by the United States.

Aitken well understood the economic merits of the continentalist argument. He greatly respected the burgeoning business civilization that had evolved in the United States, and he was a keen observer and admirer of American financial methods and industrial organization. Because of the seemingly limitless opportunities available there to those with his cast of mind, he had been tempted more than once to move to the United States. Not only did he always decide against such a move, but when any of his acquaintances announced that they were leaving, Aitken bemoaned their departure as an occasion of profound regret. In 1905, when telling an associate that he was sorry to hear he was moving to Duluth, Minnesota, he said, 'I hoped that you would stay in Canadian territory. I am sorry to hear of any of my friends going to the United States.'[4] A year later, he wrote to another acquaintance who was leaving: 'I believe the great weakness of our country is due to the inducements the United States offers to men of your calibre.'[5]

In Aitken's view, Laurier's policies emphasized Canada's weakness rather than building on its strength – its position within the British Empire. Aitken's main weapon in his personal struggle against the Laurier government's emerging continentalism was the press. Years later, he would boldly proclaim that he ran the *Daily Express* solely for the purpose of propaganda.[6] This sentiment perhaps more closely fitted the *Canadian Century*, an intellectual weekly started by Aitken at the end of 1909 with the express purpose of fighting against what he saw as encroaching Americanism. Unlike his later English newspapers, such as the *Express* and the *Daily Standard*, the *Canadian Century* haemorrhaged money from day one and was useful only as an instrument of propaganda.[7] After his election to Parliament at Westminster, Aitken fought Laurier's free trade agreement with the United States through a string of antireciprocity articles in the *Century*, and the magazine became one of the major antireciprocity organs during the election campaign.

When it was clear that an election would be held on the issue, Aitken decided to return to Canada to assist directly in the Conservative campaign, but he changed his mind when he became the centre of attention in a press campaign directed by Sir Sandford Fleming. Aitken's struggle with Fleming was to continue after the defeat of Laurier and reciprocity in September 1911, and he continued to suffer opprobrium as the chief rascal of Canadian finance.[8] For those who had battled for years against the 'eastern monopolies' only to see themselves defeated by big business in the 1911 election, Aitken symbolized the robber-baron capitalism that thrived under the protectionist tariff system.

The Opposition to Monopoly

For more than two decades the Canadian public had been unhappy about the uncompetitive practices of a business community that regularly suppressed market forces by fixing prices.[9] Their political representatives, many of whom were lawyers and businessmen accustomed to restraints on competition, thought differently. The only politicians who opposed anti-competitive behaviour on principle were a small number of ideological free traders within the Liberal Party. Since they regarded the competitive gale winds of free trade as the only long-term solution to price fixing, they considered antitrust legislation a rather ineffective and short-term weapon against cartels. Despite this, they were willing to initiate and support antitrust measures at various times, given the opposition within their own party to dismantling the National Policy of tariff protection.

Passed in 1889, the first antitrust legislation came on the crest of public pressure led by farm organizations after a parliamentary investigation of cartels – called the Committee on Alleged Combinations – had revealed pervasive price-fixing practices at every level of the Canadian economy.[10] Appended to the Criminal Code but lacking the necessary administrative machinery for enforcement, the new anticombines law was laughable in its ineffectiveness.[11] The first prosecution of a price-fixing 'combine'* failed miserably in 1897.[12] Since Wilfrid Laurier's Liberals had just been elected by a constituency that demanded government action against the combines, the Tariff Act was amended in 1897 to permit the removal of tariff protection for any industry engaging in cartel activity. At the time, free traders believed that this measure would be a far more effective weapon against collusive agreements than the main anticombines law. So did the newspaper owners making up the Canadian Press Association, who used the new legislation to put an end to the newsprint manufacturers' cartel. Although the press association ultimately won its case and duties on some types of paper were reduced by 40 per cent, the costs incurred in the process were so prohibitive that this anticombines provision was never again used.[13]

Nonetheless, the perception of pervasive anticompetitive behaviour, sustained by weak laws, must be balanced against the less publicized fail-

---

*Defined as any firm or association of firms that engage in price fixing. This term was used more commonly in Canada than the word 'trust,' with the result that antitrust law became known in Canada as anticombines law.

ure of industry associations to enforce price and quantity agreements.[14] New cartel arrangements were constantly being set up because they were continually falling apart. When opportunity knocked, cartel members bolted from agreements, cut their prices, and supplied their customers. Imposing prices that ignored the law of supply and demand meant that producers and suppliers had a strong incentive to dump their surplus inventory at cut-rate prices. Owners tried to conceal these breaches of trust from their fellow cartel members, but sooner or later they were bound to be discovered.

As students of classical political economy, the free traders within the Liberal Party were convinced of the harmful impact of combines on the body politic. However, their remedy of freer trade was not possible in the late nineteenth century because the United States, Canada's largest trading partner, was wedded to a protectionist policy, as it had been ever since the Civil War.[15] The Dingley Tariff of 1897 raised trade barriers even higher. Thrown on the defensive, the Laurier government responded by increasing tariffs on American products while granting a preference to British goods. Since both countries adhered to high tariffs, Canadian producers, as well as Americans who set up plants in Canada, were shielded from export competition from the United States. For some goods, this protective tariff translated into higher prices. It also meant that consumers in western Canada could not benefit from the lower prices of goods manufactured in the American Midwest.[16]

In one respect, Prime Minister Laurier was very fortunate. The prosperity of the economic boom that followed his 1896 election victory calmed the agitation against the combines enough to allow his government to concentrate on other matters for the next dozen years. Industrial expansion in the East and the settlement of the West absorbed the energies of the country. But with growth and prosperity came an increasing amount of dissatisfaction in the newly settled areas. By the time Saskatchewan and Alberta were created provinces in 1905, the farmers of the West had already organized grain growers' associations in order to change the way in which grain was purchased, stored, and handled by the grain dealers, the elevator companies, and the railways. But as the first decade of the new century wore on, prices began to climb and a new danger now faced the farmers.[17] Although inflation was a common enough feature in all countries experiencing prosperity at the time, the grain growers – who were now mechanizing their farms – blamed eastern finance, industrial combines, and the tariff for their higher input costs.[18] The merger wave in general, and the Canada Cement monopoly in particular, seemed to be directly responsible for price increases, reawakening the old agitation against the combines.

Canada Cement and the Minister of Combines

When floating Canada Cement's first issue, Aitken had known instinctively that the sheer size of the company would open him up to public attack.[19] This was, after all, the single largest merger ever attempted in the country. The subscription list for shares in Canada Cement had hardly closed when the assault began. The *Grain Growers' Guide*, the journal of the organized western farmers, claimed that the Canada Cement combine had, almost overnight, increased the price of cement in western Canada by forty cents, a real jolt to the many farmers who used concrete as a base for their new houses, barns, and machinery sheds. 'The consumer hardly knows,' the *Guide* complained, whether to continue cement work 'under the present hold-up conditions.'[20]

By November 1909 the allegations had moved from the free trade press to the floor of the House of Commons, where opposition politicians, especially the western members, seized the opportunity to embarrass the Laurier government while ingratiating themselves with their constituents. The Conservative MP for Selkirk asked whether the government was aware that the 'price of cement to the consumer' had been 'very much increased' as a result of the Canada Cement merger. 'Is it the intention of the government,' he asked, 'to take action to protect the public' against this consolidation? William Fielding, who had given up the premiership of Nova Scotia to become Laurier's minister of finance, invited those harmed by the Canada Cement merger to use the existing anticombines measures in the Criminal Code and the Tariff Act – hardly a satisfying reply given the proven ineffectiveness of these provisions.[21]

Aitken did not fear prosecution, but he knew that negative publicity would dampen investment demand for Canada Cement shares. He could expect some negative coverage in the agrarian and free trade press, but when, shortly afterwards, disapproving comments started to appear in the business press, he had good cause to worry.[22] The *Monetary Times* complained that Aitken's prospectus did not reveal the prices paid for the cement companies and thus did not give 'the investor an opportunity to judge intelligently of the investment merits of the proposition.'[23] Since it also pointed out that Canada Cement's capitalization was far in excess of the aggregate capital of the twelve companies entering the merger, the *Monetary Times* was seriously undermining Aitken's efforts to sell securities. In an attempt to stem the damage, Aitken called up the editorial office and gave an interview. Without disclosing the purchase price of the companies, he said that the major benefit flowing from the consolidation would be to lower the costs of manufacturing and delivering cement throughout the dominion. His argument would have been more persuasive if he had explained how much each cement company cost, but this would have told Sir Sandford Fleming and Joe Irvin precisely how badly they had been treated by Aitken in the deal.[24]

In newspapers that printed his point of view without alteration, Aitken argued that the rationalization of the newer plants would *eventually* lead to lower cement prices for the consumer.[25] Meanwhile, he wrote to the owners or editors of newspapers that had reported high cement prices, rejecting some of the more exaggerated charges against Canada Cement while defending the firm's new pricing policy. Some regions of the country were paying more for cement, he suggested, because the company was now adding the cost of transporting cement from its plant to these markets; but the regional variations would diminish over time as Canada Cement erected new plants to serve the more remote areas of the country.[26] He argued that in all cases the company was charging only a very small percentage above its cost of production.[27]

Behind the scenes, however, Aitken had personally put together a price-fixing agreement that bound all the cement companies entering the merger even before Canada Cement was floated. Prices were stiffened in central Canada and increased in certain parts of western Canada. The areas farthest from a producing plant experienced the largest increases.[28] A centre such as Winnipeg, which was hundreds of miles from Canada Cement's Alberta or Ontario mills, saw retail cement prices rise from $1.78 per barrel to $2.18. Comparatively, there was a 15¢ rise in Montreal, and a 40¢ hike in Toronto, where cement respectively cost $1.25 and $1.20 a barrel in the months preceding the merger.[29] Prices might (and in fact soon did) decrease, as Aitken had predicted, but the merger had unquestionably enabled the manufacturers to raise prices in the short term.[30]

Higher prices encouraged further press attacks. Charles Cahan used his newspaper skills and contacts to help Aitken devise a thoroughgoing strategy to deal with the press in the months following the merger, but their efforts were totally ineffective in reversing the tide of negative coverage. When the London *Times* wrote asking Aitken for information about the Canada Cement merger, since he knew 'more about it than any other person,' his irritation was palpable:

If you want a defence of the consolidation of Cement Companies, I will be very glad to write you a defence providing you agree to publish it as I have written it, or not publish it at all.

On the other hand, if you want a condemnation of the Canada Cement Company, I would be pleased to refer you to some of my esteemed friends who are so anxious to protect the long-suffering consumers.[31]

To make matters worse, rumours were circulating that the Laurier government was about to introduce new and effective antitrust legislation designed to prevent mergers like that of Canada Cement. At the time, Aitken had only just floated Canada Car and Foundry and was attempting to put together the Canadian Steel Corporation. His associates in these ventures had been concerned for some time about his increasing visibility because of Canada Cement. Earlier they had asked him to discontinue some of his less important merger projects because these might 'result in considerable outcry,' thereby interfering with the merger promotions that really counted.[32] Now, in response to the possibility of a new trust-busting law, they asked him to keep as low a public profile as possible.[33]

The rumours turned out to be partly correct. On 18 January 1910, in order to defuse the growing controversy over trusts, Laurier's young minister of labour, William Lyon Mackenzie King, introduced a bill to investigate 'combines, monopolies, trusts and mergers which may enhance prices or restrict competition to the detriment of consumers.'[34] Known as the Combines Investigation Act, the new law seemed tailor-made to fit the Canada Cement case, and at first the *Grain Growers' Guide* endorsed the legislation as providing some needed relief from the combines.[35] One western MP spoke for many in the prairies when he said that Laurier's Liberals had 'never done a single act to protect the farmers of the west from being eaten up body and soul by these combines, their farms mortgaged, their children half-naked,' but 'at last, this gracious government, and its Minister of Labour' had 'awakened from their Rip Van Winkle sleep' and 'proposed to do something.'[36]

Mackenzie King was to disappoint them, however. Having familiarized himself with the organization and operation of modern industrial enterprises while studying and working in the United States years before, King admired big business, which he viewed as a natural and progressive development.[37] He believed that this was the 'age of organization' and 'world-wide competition' and that 'any industry or any nation which wishes to hold its own in the field of competition must do much in the way of perfecting organization.' By improving production, highly organized industry would 'lead to greater efficiency and economies of one kind and another' and would therefore 'benefit the consuming public.'[38]

American antitrust law was wrong-headed, in King's opinion, because it penalized enterprises that expanded as a consequence of their superior organization. Rather than indiscriminately attacking all large organizations, his legislation would separate good monopolies from bad monopolies through investigation and publicization. A complaint alleging an abuse of monopoly power laid by at least six persons would be followed by a judicial review. If *prima facie* grounds existed for the allegation, then a board of inquiry would be appointed to investigate and report. By not providing any administrative machinery, however, Mackenzie King ensured that the costs of the complex procedure rested on the applicants. The procedure might indeed safeguard companies against frivolous complaints, as King desired, but the cost and complexity would also serve to deter most complainants with real grievances.[39]

One week after introducing the bill, Mackenzie King was forced to reply in the House of Commons to allegations that the Canada Cement Company was artificially inflating the price of cement. King admitted that he had received numerous complaints about Canada Cement but said he felt that it was too early to take a position on the issue.[40] Ten weeks later, on second reading of his anticombines bill, King finally took a stand. Canada Cement, he had concluded, was a good monopoly; through its large-scale organization and the geographical distribution of its plants, it was able to manufacture its product at the lowest cost possible.[41] Reaction in the Commons was swift. King was told that he had missed the point; in fact, Canada Cement was using its monopoly power arbitrarily to raise prices. When one MP alleged that cement was costing 25 per cent more in Ottawa than it had the year before because of Canada Cement, King admitted that he had received this complaint but said he had also received information from elsewhere that no price increases had occurred. 'In speaking with some gentlemen associated with this merger,' he explained, they felt that they 'were being much misrepresented in the popular opinion,' since 'no unfair profits were being charged.'[42]

While explaining his convoluted legislation for four full hours, King endured taunts from members of the opposition, who dubbed him Minister of Combines. The Ontario industrialist and Conservative MP John Currie claimed that the bill was 'class legislation' aimed unfairly against the business community and that it 'had been brought into the House by the Minister of Labour ... largely for the purpose of meeting the reflex echo of a tremendous muck-raking campaign that [had] been carried on in the United States against the so-called trusts and combines.'[43] The Americans were to blame, according to Currie, who pointed out that the Lehigh plant at Belleville had forced Canadian cement prices below the cost of production in an attempt to drive the Canadian companies into a 'great big cement trust' in the United States.[44] Other MPs said that the new law did not go far enough and suggested that it would prove even less efficacious than the anti-cartel law it was superseding.[45]

Anti-Tariff Agitation Builds

The Laurier government was unconcerned about Conservative criticism of the Combines Investigation Act. The law had been passed as an expedient measure to keep a lid on the government's populist supporters in the prairie West, who were putting increasing pressure on the government to do something about the consolidation wave. Behind this critique was the belief that the existing system of tariff protection was the single reason why monopolies could thrive in Canada, but Laurier's Liberals hoped that the new law would keep the populists at bay until tariffs could be lowered. However, the new law did little to quell western discontent. Everyone – from the farmers in the West to the merger promoters in the East – soon realized that the legislation was too cumbersome and expensive to be used in practice.[46]

Western Liberals, some of whom feared the emergence of a farmers' party or a third party committed to free trade that would undercut their base in the prairies, urged Laurier to travel to their constituencies in order to rally support. Not having visited the West since his days in opposition, the prime minister agreed to make a three-month tour.[47] Laurier's western tour was soon being trumpeted in the agrarian and free trade press. In May 1910 the *Grain Growers' Guide* addressed a letter to each of the twenty-seven members of the House of Commons from the prairie provinces, informing them that the grain growers' associations as well as other farm organizations had arranged to state their views to the prime minister at all his stops.[48] In some doggerel especially prepared for the occasion, the *Grain Growers' Guide* proclaimed Laurier's coming to the West:

To softly smooth the farmer man
    and gently pat his hand;
To garner if only he can,
    the tillers of the land.[49]

When his train arrived in Manitoba, Laurier was met by hundreds of farmers, petitions in hand. The farmers insisted that the government's selective tariff reductions did not go far enough, and they argued passionately for the complete abolition of the protective tariff. They pointed out that the recent rapid rise in the cost of living was due to the high prices charged by tariff-protected Canadian manufacturers and that the most recent price increases were a direct consequence of the mergers sweeping Canadian industry.[50] Similar petitions and complaints greeted Laurier at every stop.

Rebuttals from central Canada were fired back at the grain growers. The Canadian Manufacturers' Association (CMA) disputed the claim that its members were somehow responsible for the recent increases in the cost of living.[51] Nevertheless, it was concerned about the political impact of the allegations, and it devoted more space than ever in its house monthly, *Industrial Canada*, to defending protectionism – a favoured topic even in calmer times. The CMA branded the *Grain Growers' Guide* a misinformed and subversive organ because of its position on free trade.[52] Eastern businessmen in general had little patience or sympathy for the western farmers' arguments. The Toronto meat-packing magnate Joseph Flavelle argued that the farmers were being diverted 'from enterprise' and were looking 'for returns through agitation.'[53]

Aitken was busy pounding the same line through his own publication. After the Canada Cement and Canadian Car and Foundry mergers in the autumn of 1909, he had established the glossy and rather highbrow weekly magazine, the *Canadian Century*.[54] Hiring A.E. Dean as both editor and general manager, and the well-known journalist Edward Farrer to head up the Ottawa department, Aitken had rented space in the same building in which the Royal Securities Corporation's Montreal office had first been located and in which the Montreal Engineering Company was still lodged, at 179 St James Street. Costing five cents per copy and printed in an ultramodern format, the *Canadian Century* was launched on 8 January 1910 by an announcement reminiscent of Aitken's old Newcastle weekly: 'It is the mission of THE CANADIAN CENTURY to succeed where others have failed and then speed onward and outward.' Its goal was to become 'Canada's National Magazine' and its purpose, 'which we shall preach from our pulpit, weekly' was the 'Canadian shop for the Canadian workman' and 'the Canadian market for the Canadian manufacturer.'[55]

The *Century* began with a series of antireciprocity pieces penned by George Foster, a front-bench opposition member who had been the last Conservative finance minister before the long Laurier reign began. Like

Aitken, Foster was a transplanted New Brunswicker living in central Canada. He was actively involved in several businesses and was at home in Aitken's circle.[56] To add variety to its official line, the *Century* included an article examining the merits of Laurier's naval policy and another representing the views of Olivar Asselin, the French-Canadian nationalist.[57] Nonetheless, the *Century* clearly supported the British Empire over continentalism, protectionism over free trade, and British-Canadian nationalism over the home-grown and isolationist varieties prevalent in French-speaking Quebec and western Canada. Some of Aitken's business associates, for instance, Thomas J. Drummond, were asked to contribute articles. Almost all of Aitken's financial associates advertised in the new magazine, and although lengthy political editorials on reciprocity and the empire dominated, the journal was liberally sprinkled with articles on security investing with titles such as 'Public Utility Bonds,' 'The Price of Bonds: Factors That Determine the Figures,' and 'Investing Your Savings.'[58] As a political magazine aimed at the younger businessmen who were beginning to control economic life in central Canada, the *Canadian Century* was a world removed from the grain fields of western Canada.

The polarization between the farmers of the West and the financiers and industrialists of the East was brought home to all Canadians during the farmers' siege of Ottawa in December 1910. Taking a special CPR 'delegate' train, eight hundred representatives of farm organizations, the majority from the West, arrived in Ottawa to press home the arguments made during Laurier's western tour. They were joined on the train by members of the Canadian and American press, as well as by eight Conservative MPs who were trying to embarrass the Laurier government.[59] On 15 December they all met in the Grand Opera House to pass a series of resolutions denouncing protectionism.[60] By supper time, all the resolutions had been prepared for presentation to the government, and the farm representatives convened for an evening of more informal meetings, largely with journalists who had come to cover the story. Next morning the delegates assembled in front of the opera house 'and marched four abreast up Parliament Hill' and into the House of Commons. Since the chamber was not large enough to hold the eight hundred farmers, some spread out into the galleries.[61]

At this point, the prime minister walked into the House and took his place surrounded by his cabinet, including Mackenzie King, and for the rest of the day he was subjected to the farmers' resolutions and speeches. The *Canadian Century* sniffed that the farmers 'did not beseech, they demanded,' and that whether or not these radical farmers truly represented the West, they 'exhibited Western selfishness, anyway.'[62] The *Century* went on to observe: 'The Delegation misrepresented itself. It was ill for men who boasted that their united money-worth was thirty millions, accumulated in from ten to fifteen years, to cry poverty and attempt to show faces ground by [tariff] taxation and corporate plundering. History affords but one parallel – the extraordinary Chevalier de Casanova, slashing his best embroidered dress to play the part of a pauper in a masquerade.'[63]

Laurier could not have agreed more. When at the end of the day he rose to speak in response to the farmers, he noted simply that although the delegation purportedly represented the 'agricultural interests of the whole of Canada,' it was the Western spirit,' informed by 'far more radical ideas,' that had dominated the speeches and resolutions.[64] In private, he told one of his back-bench MPs that the resolutions were 'so exaggerated' that 'they would rather defeat themselves.'[65] Nonetheless, he recognized the danger of ignoring the tariff demands of this new and apparently powerful political force, a movement that could no longer be controlled by his party.

Predictably, the farmers had trotted out the cement trust as their chief exhibit of corporate buccaneering, and they demanded that the tariff on cement be removed or reduced. Henry Horton Miller, a Liberal backbencher, pleaded with Laurier not to succumb to the pressure to reduce the tariff on cement, since this would 'ruin and shut down all the cement plants' in his constituency in western Ontario.[66] On the question of cement prices, he explained:

Two or three years ago the price of cement was so low in Canada that most of the factories were operated at a loss. After the merger was effected the prices were raised but not unreasonably and not more than to allow a reasonable profit. While the prices have been raised, cement is yet sold at *very much* lower figures than prevailed before we manufactured our own cement in Canada. Prices were lowered toward the latter part of last summer [1910], and are now lower than the prices fixed after the forming of the merger. There is yet a strong competition between the merger and the many non-merger companies, and this competition will ensure continuance of reasonable prices to the consumer.[67]

Laurier admitted that the matter was 'not free from some danger,' and he asked Miller to 'gauge public sentiment very closely' in his 'section of the community.'[68]

The Laurier-Taft Deal

Ironically, during the farmer's siege of Ottawa, the Laurier government had been hard at work secretly negotiating a comprehensive bilateral reduction of tariffs with the United States. Relations between the two countries had improved dramatically during the previous months after being difficult for many years. With thorny disputes over fisheries and boundaries finally out of the way by the spring of 1909, only trade irritants were left unresolved. Then, in the spring of 1910, a new American flexibility led to the quick resolution of potential problems created by the Payne-Aldrich tariff, with an agreement to have a reciprocal reduction of tariff duties on some natural products.[69] By autumn, President William Howard Taft was plumping for a full-fledged free trade agreement.

Although Laurier was delighted with this fundamental change in American attitude, he had to dampen Taft's enthusiasm. Discussions on free trade, he said, would have to be restricted to natural products – foodstuffs and raw materials. The Americans agreed, and the first conference was held in Ottawa on 5 November 1910.[70] Laurier's political rationale was simple. He could assuage populist agrarian discontent both by obtaining a tariff-free market in the United States for Canadian foodstuffs and by reducing the tariff on American-made agricultural machinery and cement.[71] At the same time, he would keep the business community happy by maintaining the high tariff wall on all other manufactured goods.

Caught off guard by Laurier's political coup, Robert Borden and the Conservative opposition floundered, doing little to censure the proposed reciprocity agreement.[72] Instead, they chose to assail the government for doing nothing about the excesses of the merger movement. Borden argued that two types of merger were injuring Canadians: those that excluded competition and raised prices and those that were grossly over-capitalized.[73] Another opposition member suggested that securities legislation be drafted to prevent the abuses of merger promoters.[74]

Western Conservatives, pushed by their farm constituencies, went even further. Arthur Meighen, representing the seat of Portage la Prairie, Manitoba, demanded an investigation into all the trusts in the country. 'If not checked,' Meighen asserted, 'the power of these corporations could become [even] more autocratic and despotic.'[75] Forced to break from the Conservative Party line by his prairie constituents, Meighen applauded the Laurier Liberals for reducing the tariff on agricultural machinery and cement, and even suggested that they should have gone further to help out the farmers.[76] At the same time, demands were being made in the House of Commons for a royal commission to investigate the connection between mergers and inflation, and to inquire into the damage caused by high-risk methods of flotation – as exemplified by Canada Cement.[77]

By this time, Laurier had had his fill of the western element's complaints. It was one thing to fight Conservative opportunists in House who pretended to defend the farmers of the nation, but it was quite another to be constantly under attack from these same farmers, most of whom knew that the Conservatives would never reduce even one tariff. On receiving a letter from a Manitoba farmer who complained yet again of the Canada Cement merger, Laurier responded by sending him a copy of the Combines Investigation Act, pointedly asking the man why he he – along with others who had apparently suffered so much from the cement combine – had not taken advantage of the remedial legislation.[78]

The political fireworks set off by Canada Cement and the merger movement were feeding the populist critique of high finance as practised during the gilded age. Stockwatering became the central issue of the controversy. Before the gilded age, ordinary shares had represented a firm's real assets and past earning power. Worth a par value of $100 when first issued, each common share had fluctuated in value according to the growth or decline of the firm. During the gilded age, the function of common stock changed. Bonds and preference stock were issued in place of common stock, which was now reserved for the promoter's profit – a bonus whose value was based on intangibles such as goodwill and future earning power. The merger movement made the practice widespread. Even some businessmen were concerned about the shift. The old and venerable president of the Lake of the Woods Milling Company, Robert Meighen, argued that stock should never be issued on the basis of goodwill or future earning power, and he wanted a bill introduced in Parliament that would make stockwatering a crime punishable by imprisonment.[79]

Aitken admitted that the capitalization of the Canada Cement Company could only be justified on the grounds that the common stock issue had 'discounted Canada's future growth and development.'[80] He put it even more bluntly in a personal letter to Robert Borden many months later: 'Either the system of bonus stocks is good or bad. It has been generally practised, and it is countenanced by the Companies Act.'[81] Most people outside the corporate business community assumed that it was bad. In an article entitled 'Over Capitalization and the Tariff,' the pro–free trade *Toronto Sun* argued that common stock was a tax on the future earnings of a company, and that it could be recouped only by charging consumers higher prices. Genuine investors were also being taxed by stockwatering, argued the *Sun*, since future earnings that should have been earmarked for reinvestment – bond interest and dividends on preference stock – went instead into the pockets of promoters in the form of dividends paid on the par value of common stock.[82]

This debate was not resolved until the interwar years, which saw the introduction of non-par shares and the discontinuation of the use of common stock as promoters' profit.[83] In the meantime, all the company promoters and financiers of the gilded age were vulnerable to attack for playing the game by the rules of the day – and none more so than Aitken, whose fight with Sir Sandford Fleming was becoming increasingly public.

1911: Election Campaign of the Century

By March 1911, Robert Borden had regained his political footing. Resistance to the reciprocity agreement within the Laurier government (especially the revolt of prominent Liberal MPs such as Clifford Sifton and Lloyd Harris), as well as significant business opposition, had convinced Borden that he should force an election on the issue.[84] Many of Aitken's closest associates – Sir William Van Horne, Charles Cahan, and Nathaniel Curry, to name only a few – were leading the business campaign against reciprocity.[85]

Although Aitken was in England, he contributed to the fight against reciprocity through the *Canadian Century*, which dropped all pretence of objectivity and railed against the proposed agreement, vilifying it as continentalism run rampant.[86] He also skirmished with Earl Grey, the governor general of Canada. Of a classical liberal bent, Grey supported Laurier and the proposed reciprocity agreement to the point that he tried his best to convince one renegade Canadian Liberal MP to return to the fold. When Aitken discovered what Grey had done, he told his Canadian friends that he would publicly expose Grey's actions in the British House of Commons. Grey knew full well that as a governor general, it had been inappropriate to involve himself in partisan political issues, so when he was told of Aitken's plan he immediately sent an aide to explain to the renegade MP that his earlier visit 'had been misunderstood.'[87] He would not forgive Aitken for forcing this humiliation upon him.

Aitken desperately wanted to jump into the fray by becoming a candidate and organizer for the Conservative Party. On 4 March he told a Conservative member of the Canadian parliament that he would gladly join the campaign if he thought his 'connection with the mergers and trusts would not interfere' with his party: 'I would resign from the Parliament here and go to Northumberland, N.B., as an Imperial Preference anti-American agreement candidate.'[88] In fact, Borden was encouraging Aitken to leave his seat in Britain in order to help the Conservative campaign, particularly in New Brunswick, where Douglas Hazen's Conservative government was refusing to extend much aid to the federal Conservatives because of the popularity of reciprocity in the province. Borden thought he could invigorate the New Brunswick campaign by having Aitken run in Northumberland, a strong Liberal constituency with Newcastle and Chatham at its centre, and on 5 April he wrote to Aitken asking him to return and help defeat Laurier.[89] 'I realize,' Borden stated, 'that you owe a duty to your constituents in Great Britain: but you owe a closer duty to Canada at this juncture. We want you here in the forefront of the firing line where you will be fighting not only for Canada but for the whole Empire.'[90]

With Borden behind him, Aitken knew that the nomination would be thrown his way, and he sent $10,000 to be spread around as patronage in the constituency to prepare for his return.[91] However, he continued to be nagged by the fear that the press would use his candidature as an invitation for fresh attacks on him as a promoter, and a few days later he suggested to Borden that he might not be able to get his British colleagues' consent to leave Westminster. Borden wrote back on 1 May, saying that it might well be 'fatal' if Aitken was prevented from fighting alongside him in 'the impending struggle': 'That conflict will assuredly determine whether Canada's future path must lie within or without the Empire. Any public man in Great Britain whose vision extends beyond the three mile limit must realize this truth from which several deductions might be made. One only I desire to emphasize – that it is the plain duty of the Unionist party to release you from any obligation which would prevent you from joining us at the first signal.'[92]

Encouraged by Borden's entreaties, Aitken began negotiating with Conservatives in Canada to be, in effect, the party's boss in the Maritime provinces and a cabinet minister in the next government.[93] He invited Borden to stay with him in London during the coronation of George V – no doubt to discuss his position in the upcoming campaign – but at the last minute Borden decided to absent himself from the coronation in order to prepare for the coming election.[94] To help make up his mind, therefore, Aitken decided to go to Canada to investigate the situation personally that May.[95]

At the same time as Aitken was planning his return to Canada, Sir Sandford Fleming was making one last, desperate attempt to avenge himself on Aitken, Canada Cement, and the Bank of Montreal. On 5 April, shortly after his resignation as honorary president of Canada Cement, Fleming sent his pamphlet of allegations to Laurier and requested a meeting with the prime minister.[96] His covering letter said that he had, under legal advice, 'omitted the name of the person who has pocketed so many millions wrongfully (viz. William Maxwell Aitken),' and he made it clear that Aitken would be the main topic of conversation.[97] During their meeting, Fleming tried to convince Laurier that Aitken had perpetrated a heinous fraud. Laurier had some difficulty figuring out Fleming's charges, but he finally told Fleming that some public inquiry might be useful – without specifying the type of inquiry or when it might be held.[98]

Fleming waited for five weeks. When no action was forthcoming, he took matters into his own hands. In an attempt to reduce its debt-servicing charges, Canada Cement was just then sponsoring a private member's bill in Parliament to replace its 7 per cent preference stock with a 5 per cent debenture (bond) series – basically the same type of exchange that Aitken had objected to so strenuously in the case of Scotia Steel two years before. Fleming laid his allegations of fraud before the parliamentary committee responsible for private members' bills and called for a public inquiry into what he saw as the fraudulent organization of the cement merger.[99]

When the chairman of the committee publicly read Fleming's letter of protest on 11 May, he caused a sensation.[100] The press immediately took up the issue, and editorials began to appear throughout the country, viciously attacking Canada Cement and especially Aitken, for his role as the merger's promoter. The Toronto *Globe* asserted that Canadians in all parts of the nation were up in arms against the Canada Cement merger and that the feelings of the people warranted 'drastic action by the Government.'[101] The government responded to the outcry by announcing its intention to hold an inquiry.[102]

Aitken was caught off guard not only by Fleming's action but by the vehemence of the press campaign against him as Canada Cement's promoter. In Canada, the Liberal press drowned out the few favourable reviews of Canada Cement and Aitken. In Aitken's view, the *Montreal Herald* was the only newspaper in either Canada or Britain that had the courage to defend his actions.[103] Worse was yet to come. Aitken's generous donations to the Conservative cause in Britain as well as his support of Unionist leader Bonar Law resulted in his receiving a knighthood just when the uproar over Canada Cement was reaching a climax. He was informed of the decision on 20 April (in the coronation honours list), but it was not conferred until June – just in time to add fuel to an already fierce fire in Canada.

'Why has a gentleman who has contributed to do public evil, and never done anything else of note except get rich out of the evil, been selected for honour at the hands of the crown?' asked the *Ottawa Journal*. And why should 'an archmergerer, a wholesale stock waterer' be created a knight, screamed the *Montreal Witness*, when 'there are thousands of people in Canada who have done more to deserve such an honour?'[104] Governor General Earl Grey stoked the fire purposely by sending word back to Whitehall that Aitken's name on the coronation honours list was evoking 'a howl of indignation and disgust throughout the Dominion.'[105]

These and similar sentiments were soon copied from the wire services and reprinted by the Liberal press at Ashton-under-Lyne and in Britain more generally.[106] Over and over again, the Canadian newspaper accounts were repeated in Britain. Helplessly, Aitken watched his reputation being destroyed before his eyes.[107] His political friends and foes began to wonder aloud about the brash Canadian in their midst. When Winston Churchill (who was still a Liberal at the time but had become friends with Aitken despite their political differences) suggested Aitken for a position on the Imperial Trade Commission, Prime Minister Asquith replied, 'Aitken is quite impossible. I take it that his Canadian record is of the shadiest.'[108]

Unlike most of his new English acquaintances and friends, Edward Goulding did not assume the worst about Aitken, and he sent him a letter of reassurance in the midst of the storm. Aitken gratefully responded, revealing that the publicity following Fleming's charges had cut him to the quick:

I am so pleased to get your letter ... It came at a time when I was feeling rather blue and cheered me up very much indeed.

I am under very heavy fire, and must forgo everything for the moment, so that I can keep a good return fire going. The Canadian public is laughing at the attacks being made on me, but the radical [Liberal] press are making the most of it .... Please do not say anything to any person, and particularly don't let anybody know I am taking the slightest notice of it, because I must keep an undisturbed exterior.[109]

Certainly, Aitken's first impulse was to strike back. He wrote to his Canadian associates threatening to 'institute suits all round' and bring every fact out into the open.[110] His friends appealed to him not to take any notice of the attacks, arguing that the onslaught would last only a few days and would not hurt him politically. The government, they said, was using the prospect of an investigation merely as a bluff to keep Aitken out of Canada in the coming election. Laurier could not afford an investigation because there were some influential Liberals associated with Canada Cement.[111] The latter contention might have been correct, but the prediction that the attacks would not harm Aitken and would soon disappear without a trace were spectacularly wrong. Although Borden and Bennett continued to encourage him to return and beat the Liberals in the Northumberland constituency, Aitken now refused, realizing that his reputation as a dishonest promoter would mean certain defeat at the polls.[112]

Frank Jones and his Canada Cement directors became increasingly worried about the possibility of an investigation into Canada Cement as the political campaign intensified, and they used Aitken's decision to remain in Britain as the basis of a deal.[113] The interlocutor was the editorial writer for the *Montreal Herald*, the one person who had publicly defended Aitken's promotion of Canada Cement. He was to go to Ottawa and assure Laurier and his cabinet that Aitken would agree not to return to Canada 'to take charge of New Brunswick and Nova Scotia on behalf of the Conservative party' in the coming election if no investigation was ordered into the Canada Cement affair. Borden and his fellow Conservative MPs now realized that Aitken was a political liability. At the same time, some of Laurier's MPs had participated in the cement merger from the beginning, and the prime minister hardly knew where an investigation might end.[114]

The deal was readily accepted by both sides. Aitken removed his name for the nomination, though he provided 'the entire election expenses' for the new Conservative candidate in Northumberland and donated money to other Conservative candidates, including R.B. Bennett. He also threw more money than ever into the *Canadian Century*, which became an increasingly shrill pro–British Empire and antireciprocity mouthpiece.[115] This was not lost on the reciprocity forces, who attacked Aitken for using the profits of his ill-gotten merger to support the Conservative election machine.

The campaign that summer was perhaps the most emotional and divisive in Canadian history; the only comparable campaign came more than seventy-five years later and involved much the same issue – the long-

The cement monopoly profit grinder, 1911. *Source: Grain Growers' Guide*, 26 July 1911, 4

standing Canadian fear of integration with the United States. Anti-Americanism was the one constant theme. Aitken's friends and business associates were among the most militant and effective antireciprocity campaigners. Sir William Van Horne, temporarily forgetting that he was American by birth, went around giving anti-American speeches in which he asked his audiences whether Canadians should 'play gosling to the American fox.'[116]

In Quebec, Charles Cahan masterminded a machiavellian alliance with Henri Bourassa's nationalists to break Laurier's hold in the province. He was helped immensely by French-Canadian Conservatives, or *Bleus*, such as Rodolphe Forget. Holding the seat of Charlevoix since 1904, Forget had been too concerned with high finance to be an effective opposition politician, but he helped Cahan cement the anti-Laurier coalition of Bourassa nationalists, many of whom had been Liberals, with his old *Bleu* friends. The alliance they forged proved to be the single most important factor in bringing down the Liberal dynasty that October, and Forget was duly knighted for his efforts.[117]

As vice-president of the Canadian Manufacturers' Association, Nathaniel Curry led the antireciprocity charge on behalf of big business. The CMA believed that this election would seal the fate of the country; either Canada would become a nation in which the protective tariff continued to encourage rapid industrialization or it would be a nation flooded by cheaper American goods, and Canadians would once again be reduced to being hewers of wood and drawers of water. As a consequence of this platform, Curry had little difficulty in collecting donations for the Conservative war chest, and his efforts were rewarded with a Senate appointment.[118]

Carefully spreading around Aitken's money, R.B. Bennett ran a strong campaign in Calgary. Although free trade was the dominant sentiment in Alberta, Bennett did not mince his words about the tariff. He was for it, and he fully intended to convince everyone of its merits, including every farmer and rancher. This was impossible, of course, but Bennett convinced enough city voters, and he became the only Conservative to win a seat in free trade Alberta. Meanwhile, on Aitken's advice, Rudyard Kipling submitted an open letter to the *Montreal Star* suggesting that reciprocity for Canada really meant reciprocity with the much higher murder rate in the United States. The letter appeared at the very height of the campaign, and it struck like a thunderbolt. For months afterwards, Aitken delighted in telling Kipling how the Liberals had 'gone mad' over his reference 'to the high murder rate on the American side.'[119] On election day, it was Kipling who wrote the famous words, 'It is her own soul that Canada risks today.'[120]

On 21 September 1911, after fifteen years in office, the Liberals were defeated. Although they kept virtually every seat in Alberta and Saskatchewan, where populist free trade sentiment was strongest, they lost ground in Manitoba and the Maritime provinces, were devastated in Ontario, and suffered the humiliation of splitting Quebec with the Conservatives. Laurier managed to keep his seat, but many in his cabinet went down to defeat, including his favourite, Mackenzie King. An era had come to an end.

Before Robert Borden even had a chance to move into the prime minister's official residence at 24 Sussex Drive, he was assailed by Sir Sandford Fleming with an eight-page letter setting out the Canada Cement affair.[121] This was eventually followed by a twenty-two-page printed circular of relevant correspondence and documents.[122] Replying some three weeks later, Borden did the typical political bob and weave. His government, he said, might consider a permanent tariff commission, which could look into firms such as Canada Cement if they raised prices too much; he might even consider some legislation to deal with the problem of overcapitalization; but as for Fleming's allegations of fraud, 'they would not properly form the subject of investigation by Royal Commission,' since the courts offered Fleming a more appropriate avenue of redress.[123] Of course, given his association with Aitken, Cahan, and Bennett, all of whom had done more than their bit to help his Conservatives win the election, Borden had no intention of doing anything to harm their interests. Nor, in the end, did he enact legislation to deal with price fixing or overcapitalization. Big business, particularly the members of the CMA, had supported and financed Borden throughout the election.

Canada Cement soon recovered from the bad publicity generated during the election campaign. Aitken's reputation did not. Bad as the rumours and gossip based on the newspaper reports had been in England, the effects had been far worse in Canada, so Aitken decided to settle with his family at Cherkley Court in Surrey, south of London. He returned to Canada with Edward Goulding for a short congratulatory visit with Borden after the election, but he realized that his future now lay permanently in England.[124]

Fleming v. Aitken: The Final Act

Immediately after Sir Edward Clouston's resignation in November 1911, the Bank of Montreal sued Sir Sandford Fleming and Joe Irvin on their personal guarantees to the bank. In retaliation, and perhaps in an attempt to blackmail Aitken into 'inducing the Bank of Montreal to withdraw its claim,' the Fleming forces again attempted to use Parliament as a platform for a public assault on Aitken and Canada Cement.[125] R.B. Bennett, now in Ottawa as an MP, kept a close eye on Fleming on behalf of Aitken. The Fleming crowd knew that Bennett was in cahoots with Aitken, and tried (but failed) to have him 'pilled' at the Rideau Club when he applied for membership. As Bennett explained to Aitken in November 1911, he would take care of the Fleming problem: 'I am after them: they know it & I think I can without egotism say that when I finish with that old man & his crowd they will not be particularly anxious to indulge in further discussion.'[126]

Bennett had been busy collecting evidence on Irvin's original flotation of Western Canada Cement in 1905, and he had come to the conclusion that both Irvin and Sir Sandford had sold their British investors a fraudulent bill of goods when setting up the Western Canada Cement Company. Both men had known that the assets of the company had intentionally been overvalued for the purpose of the mortgage bonds and that their British investors would never be able to recoup anything close to the full extent of their investment in the company in the event of bankruptcy. Bennett suggested that he, rather than Aitken, should 'put the facts fully before the public.' As he explained to Aitken, 'It would come perhaps with more force from me than you.'[127] By early December 1911, Bennett considered that he had conclusive incriminating evidence against Fleming and his accomplices, but he now felt that he should use it only to silence Fleming if he misbehaved. Public interest in the cement affair was waning – 'dead,' according to Bennett – and more harm than good might be done by reopening it. Just the month before, he had discussed Fleming's lobbying efforts with Prime Minister Borden and had come to the conclusion that Borden, along with half of Ottawa, had already decided that the old man was certifiably mad. As he explained to Aitken, there could be no 'kinder method of disposing' of Fleming.[128]

By the time the Bank of Montreal lawsuit reached the examination for discovery stage in the autumn of 1912, Sir Sandford Fleming was truly senile and the potential threat of a parliamentary inquiry into Canada Cement had disappeared.[129] Nonetheless, the publicity from the lawsuit, once the trial started, threatened a wide circle of individuals and one institution in particular: the Bank of Montreal. The examinations were disturbing enough. At this stage, counsel for both sides were permitted a preliminary examination of the opposite parties, in the hope that the disclosure of facts and the production of key documents might result in a settlement before trial date.[130] The Bank of Montreal's counsel chose to examine Joe Irvin and Hugh Fleming – Sir Sandford no longer having the requisite mental capacity to give evidence under oath.

The first examination was held on 23 November 1912. By this time, Joe Irvin had moved back to the United States, where he had been promoting a cement company in Spokane, Washington.[131] He was more than a little annoyed that the Bank of Montreal was represented by John F. Orde, the lawyer who had represented Sir Sandford Fleming for many years. Irvin was not, however, about to concede anything in the lawsuit. He made it clear that the Bank of Montreal, acting through Clouston, Stavert, and Doble, had been Aitken's partners in the Canada Cement merger. Together, they had pushed him to the sidelines and engineered the rejection and ultimate collapse of the Western Canada Cement Company.[132]

Later that same day, ninety miles away in Montreal, Clouston went to the Royal Securities Corporation office on St James Street to see Arthur Doble, his old executive assistant, who had been managing the RSC's Canadian operations since leaving the Bank of Montreal. They spoke for some time. All of a sudden, Clouston collapsed and then died in the office. The obituaries mention his conferring with Doble at the time of the attack but do not report the subject of their conference.[133] Even though senility may have prevented Sir Sandford from enjoying his victory, he had finally collected his pound of flesh.[134]

Almost one year later, on 6 October 1913, Clouston's successor as general manager and vice-president of the Bank of Montreal, Vincent Meredith, was examined by counsel for the Flemings and Irvin. Meredith denied that Clouston, Doble, Stavert, or the Bank of Montreal had had any business relations with Aitken and the Bond and Share Company.[135] But two days later, Hugh Fleming, in his examination, repeated Irvin's claim that the Bank of Montreal, through its senior officers, had been behind the merger and the collapse of Western Canada Cement.[136]

Some fourteen months before Clouston died, Sir Sandford Fleming and his son Hugh, along with Joe Irvin, had uncovered the role that the Bank of Montreal's top officers had played in the liquidation of Western Canada Cement. In their collective opinion, it was 'outrageous an institution with the reputation of the Bank of Montreal going into such a deal – so that some of the officials can make a large amount of money.' Immediately afterwards, Frank Dunsford lobbied the top officials of the Bank of

Montreal in London, while the Flemings and Joe Irvin did their part in Canada.[137] Their campaign must have made Clouston's final months a living hell, and Vincent Meredith and other Bank of Montreal executives no doubt had to do everything in their power to prevent a major scandal. Meredith, who in a few years would be made the bank's president, was even prepared to lie under oath to protect his institution's hallowed reputation.

After Clouston's death, Joe Irvin was examined a second time by the Bank of Montreal's lawyer. Now all hell threatened to break loose, because Irvin alleged that he and Aitken had offered, and Clouston had accepted on behalf of the 'Bank of Montreal syndicate,' a $1 million common stock payment conditional on the bank's supporting the merger. Asked why he had not presented this very material evidence earlier, Irvin claimed that he had been too embarrassed to disclose the arrangement before Clouston's death.[138]

The trial in the Ontario Superior Court in Toronto was set for 17 November 1913. Aitken had carefully prepared his evidence and sent it to his Canadian lawyer, A.M. Stewart. He said that he was not at all afraid to give a complete account of what had transpired. As Stewart explained to him, however, there were other factors involved: 'If you were put into the box by us as a witness, the other side could go a long way on cross-examination and might be allowed to ask as to the distribution of [common] stock. As I understand the situation, your answer would not hurt you, but would hurt others you wish to protect. I do not think that, even if you were here, we would put you in the box.'[139]

Aitken knew very well what impact his testimony would have on the reputations of Doble, Stavert, and the Bank of Montreal (and also on that of the late Sir Edward Clouston), but he was using the threat of appearing in court to pressure the bank into settling its suit with Sir Sandford Fleming and Joe Irvin. He personally had no more stomach for scandal and was even willing to pay if the suit could be dropped. As a consequence, the lawsuit was settled eleven days before trial. Without any substantive defence to the action, Irvin and the Flemings agreed to pay $75,000 of the $110,000 they owed the Bank of Montreal. Unknown to the defendants, however, the remaining loss was split between Aitken and the Bank of Montreal.[140]

Six days after the settlement, Doble wrote to tell Aitken that the Canada Cement Company, through Frank Jones, had offered to pay Aitken's legal expenses. Doble believed that the company would be willing to do even more, for Jones was prepared to 'do whatever' Aitken asked of him.

After all, as Doble explained, 'the Cement Company got a bargain in the Exshaw plant at the cost of a great deal of worry and unpleasantness for every one else concerned.'[141] In fact, the Canada Cement Company was the only entity that benefited from the whole sordid affair. Aitken had outsmarted Joe Irvin and the Flemings and made some quick money in the process, but in the end he paid dearly for doing so. Sir Edward Clouston spent his final years in private humiliation. Arthur Doble and William Stavert were forced to give up promising executive careers with the Bank of Montreal. And Sir Sandford Fleming lost a sizable chunk of his family's fortune and then damaged his considerable reputation as he single-mindedly pursued Aitken, Canada Cement, and the Bank of Montreal in an effort to recoup his loss.

Running Royal Securities from Britian

Despite the Canada Cement affair and its consequences, Aitken continued to do business in Canada, often working with R.B. Bennett. In 1910, for example, he and Bennett, along with Clouston and Cahan, had set up the Calgary Power Company, which delivered hydroelectric power to the rapidly growing city of Calgary, a venture that kept Bennett busy for years. Two years later, they promoted an enormous merger in the grain-handling and -shipping business. The Alberta Pacific Grain Company was a consolidation of eighty grain elevators belonging to two separate firms, and a grain terminal operation in Vancouver belonging to a third company. The purpose of the venture was to concentrate the westbound grain business in Calgary and to increase the number of elevators needed for an expanded westbound grain commerce, which would shortly be made possible by the opening of the Panama Canal. Then there was the infamous Venezuela Ore Company, a speculative (and ultimately disastrous) mining venture, which had brought together Aitken, Bennett, Clouston, and Frank Jones.[142]

Meanwhile, Aitken's political and business interests in Britain were steadily increasing, and they began to sap the energy he needed to run the RSC and its affiliated enterprises. It was only a matter of time before he realized that he was doing the corporation more harm than good by attempting to manage it from his base in London. This was most evident in terms of Montreal Engineering and the Caribbean utility enterprises. By the summer of 1912, at the same time as he was promoting the Alberta Pacific Grain Company merger, he had in fact lost control of his West Indian utilities, as well as some of his key associates.

Months before, the head office of Porto Rico Railways had been moved to Toronto and had come under the sway of Will Ross, A.E. Ames, and D.E. Thomson. Although Aitken had become president of Porto Rico Railways on the resignation of W.B. Ross in 1911, he was merely a figurehead.[143] The corporation's financial decisions were made by Fred Clarke, who had left Montreal Engineering for Toronto, and all operational decisions were made by Fred Teele, who was now running the company in Puerto Rico without any links to the old St James Street organization.[144] By 1913, Porto Rico's directors, tactfully explaining that Aitken's residence in England deprived them of his 'counsel and experience' at their board meetings, attempted to remove him by shunting him into the newly created office of honorary president. The meaning was not lost on Aitken, who had done the same to Sir Sandford Fleming.

Aitken fought the resignation for months. Then, realizing the futility of the struggle, he submitted to the inevitable by making way for D.E. Thomson to become president in 1914.[145] When Aitken resigned from the board itself in 1916, he expressed his 'appreciation of the kindness' shown by his fellow directors 'in retaining me on the Board long after my use to the Company had ceased to exist'; he apologized for his previous intransigence, admitting, 'My long and intimate connection with the Company made it difficult for me to sever my connection at the time when perhaps I ought to have done so.'[146] Clarke wrote a personal letter in reply, saying that the years during which Aitken had 'actively supervised the affairs of this Company' were 'the very pleasantest,' and thanking him for all the opportunities he had been given when Montreal Engineering was first established.[147]

At the same time as Porto Rico Railways' head office was moving to Toronto, the head offices of the Demerara Electric and Camaguey companies were moving to Halifax. (Aitken had never succeeded in moving Trinidad Electric from Halifax to Montreal.) Since Aitken was no longer in Canada to supervise affairs, the Halifax shareholders and directors (especially W.B. Ross, R.E. Harris, F.H. Oxley, and T.G. McMullen) began to take a more active role in financing and operating the utilities.[148] They were aided in their efforts by the sudden weakening of Montreal Engineering.

During the summer of 1911, Carl Giles had left the presidency of the Montreal Engineering Company to join Charles Cahan and Almon Lovett in their new combination appraisal company and investment bank, Corporation Agencies. By this time, there was little new construction work to keep Montreal Engineering busy, and Giles's replacement had found so little to do that he left within eight months.[149] By 1913 Aitken was considering winding up Montreal Engineering, but he chose to keep it going in the hope that he might be able to reinvigorate the Canadian operations at some future time.

The RSC received relatively more attention from Aitken during these years, for it was a necessary component of his investment banking operation in Britain. In 1912 Aitken temporarily named Arthur Doble, who was then manager of the Montreal head office, as president of the RSC. In reality, Aitken, with Killam's assistance, continued to run the operation from his London base, and by early 1914 he was again listed as president on the RSC's letterhead.[150] The RSC not only survived the stock market plunge of 1913 but passed a dividend of 17 per cent to its small circle of shareholders. With so many securities companies going under, Aitken told Doble that he was 'very glad to see the spirit that dominates the organization in Montreal.' He felt grateful that they had 'not plunged into deep waters at any rate.' In fact, the RSC was so well off that Aitken said they were 'entitled to congratulate' themselves.[151]

Despite this success, Aitken considered that his Canadian operation – particularly the Montreal head office – had become too complacent. He decided to send Killam to Canada to shake up Doble and his employees, from Halifax to Toronto. Killam was given the authority to use any means available, including the services of Ward Pitfield, a new and aggressive employee from Saint John whom Aitken had just acquired from another securities company.[152] Soon after their arrival, Killam and Pitfield set to work. Doble was incredulous. He wrote to Aitken demanding to know whether Killam's actions had his blessing, for in his opinion the results were entirely destructive: 'All discipline, all feelings of respect and loyalty have disappeared. Everybody is wondering where the lightning is going to strike next and the place is being run like a pawn shop instead of like a respectable financial Institution. If we are going to continue in business surely it is necessary to carry some kind of an organization during bad times. After all our past successes I do not see why we should not keep up some degree of appearance and preserve our self respect.'[153]

Needless to say, Aitken saw no merit in keeping up appearances in business. Perhaps some degree of appearance and self-respect was of benefit in politics, but the purpose of business was to make profit, and it was profit – not appearance or respectability – that was the measure of success in business. With Aitken's approval, the wrecking ball continued to swing until the end of the year, when Doble finally left, to be replaced by Killam with Pitfield acting as his second-in-command.

At the same time, Aitken resurrected the Montreal Engineering Company by rehiring Carl Giles. Giles's first task was to set up a rescue plan for Camaguey and Demerara, both of which were languishing. He did so, but on condition that their head offices be moved back to Montreal. There was some resistance, but the utilities needed the money and Montreal Engineering was soon coordinating and monitoring the utility companies from St James Street.[154]

With the British Empire's declaration of war on 4 August 1914, the nature of Aitken's business world changed fundamentally. Almost from the beginning, the First World War promised enormous profits to North American businesses such as Canadian Car, Stelco, and Canada Cement if they were willing to diversify into armaments manufacturing. Financiers, and investment banks such as J.P. Morgan & Co. were to find profit in the large security issues needed to raise the cash used to manufacture or purchase war materiel. Aitken could easily have moved into the business of war finance. Instead, he chose to play a direct role in the war effort, one that could rehabilitate his now tarnished reputation. To do this, he would have to find an occupation more honourable and respectable than that of war profiteer.[155]

He used his friends back in Canada to help him secure just the right position. Aitken wanted to act as the liaison between the Canadian government and the Canadian troops in the field who were fighting under British command, reporting back to Ottawa on the war's progress from the Canadian perspective. R.B. Bennett in particular pushed hard. Prime Minister Robert Borden finally obliged, a reward for past favours. Thus, on 16 January 1915, Aitken was appointed eyewitness for the Canadian Expeditionary Force, which was currently in England but would soon be fighting in the trenches of France; he was also to be chief of records, in charge of the information flow from the front back to Canada.

The titles may have been obscure, but as in the case of his knighthood, the appointment elicited a howl of indignation. In an article that was promptly copied in the Montreal *Gazette*, the *Manchester Guardian* demanded to know why Aitken had obtained the appointment; it contended that there were many others better qualified to fill the position.[156] The reaction again astounded Aitken. He had turned over the presidency of the Royal Securities Corporation to Walton Killam in order to devote himself full-time to his new occupation. Although he kept majority control – this was not sold to Killam for another four years – he would never again take an active interest in managing the RSC.[157]

The public reaction to his appointment did not stop him from immediately throwing himself into his new job, using a part of his own fortune to help set up operations in London. In the end, he did manage to rehabilitate his reputation to some extent, and he left a lasting legacy to the efforts of Canada's fighting forces – not too shabby an achievement for a man whose major preoccupation had previously been profit.[158]

This job, together with his subsequent cabinet appointment as Britain's minister of information, was to keep Aitken away from business for years. When he emerged from the First World War as Baron Beaverbrook, Aitken's life had moved far from investment banking and the securities business. And when he returned to the business world, it was in the guise of a newspaper proprietor rather than an investment banker. It was up to Walton Killam to continue Aitken's most important legacy to Canada – the Royal Securities Corporation. Killam did so until 1954, a fellow Maritimer who, ironically enough, became the epitome of the St James Street financier. But it was Lord Beaverbrook in his many roles – financial wizard, newspaper baron, philanderer, and political intriguer – not Killam, who continued to hold the world's attention until his death in 1964.

11

Conclusion: From Profits to Politics

The rise of the great trusts, the obvious and glaring fact of the money power, the shameless luxury of the rich, the crude, uncultivated and boorish mob of vulgar men and overdressed women that masqueraded as high society – the substitution, shall we say, of the saloon for the salon – all this seemed to many an honest observer of humble place as but the handwriting on the wall that foretold the coming doom.

Stephen Leacock, 1917[1]

I laid the keel, you built the ship and brought her to still waters.

Aitken, writing to Ross McMaster, chairman of Stelco, 1959[2]

Although there is no evidence that they ever met, Stephen Leacock probably had Max Aitken in mind when he railed against the 'age of plutocracy' that had enveloped his English-Canadian world in Montreal in the years immediately preceding the First World War. In his *Arcadian Adventures with the Idle Rich*, Leacock reserved a special place for the Wizard of Finance, and although his portrait little resembles Aitken, Leacock had clearly made up his mind that high financiers were a parasitic class infecting the rest of the population with their amoral greed for profit and their disdain for knowledge unconnected with money making.[3]

Leacock's view would have been very common at the time, and it remains the standard perception even today. Yet it is peculiar that this view is often held by those who, like Leacock, agree with the basic premise that profit making is acceptable for most people in a capitalist society, but who have reservations about its legitimacy as applied to some people – in particular, high financiers. There appear to be two assumptions underlying this view: first, that financiers do not produce anything of substantive value; second, that they take far more profit than their services could possibly warrant.

Since they do not produce anything tangible, financiers seem to be mere middlemen, taking an unearned cut on the cash they somehow redirect to those who require it to produce real goods and services. Even people who depend on the capital raised by financiers sometimes hold them in contempt. As Fred Hartley, the chairman of Unocal, once said of Michael Milken, 'He doesn't invent anything, doesn't create anything. He just takes money from party A and gives it to party C, and he's in the middle as party B, getting a fee for having arranged the transaction.'[4] And the fee often seems far out of proportion to the modest service rendered by these financial middlemen. In 1986, for example, Milken reported an income of $718 million, the highest ever reported by an individual in a single year.

In his time, Aitken and his fellow Laurier boom financiers faced similar attitudes. Promoting, underwriting, and floating new securities appeared to many unfamiliar with the financial world to be a sure thing, with little downside risk. It is little wonder, then, that the prairie farmers, who regularly complained about the ill-gotten profits of the financial, transportation, and grain-handling middlemen, were particularly hostile to high financiers and found in Aitken – an 'archmergerer' and 'wholesale stock waterer' – all the attributes they held in contempt.

The preceding chapters have attempted to illustrate the inherent riskiness as well as the creativity encompassed by high finance. Investment banking lies at the very heart of modern capitalism and has been an essential part of the process of economic growth since the onset of the managerial and organizational revolution which Alfred Chandler called the second industrial revolution. To be sure, high financiers have played a hydra-headed role during the past century. While they have often added value to the enterprises they helped fund or create, they have also acted in such a way as to reduce the value of certain enterprises, and because of their immense power they have done damage to their country's economy in the process. The American case of hostile takeovers during the 1980s, in which assets were systematically stripped from previously healthy companies, provides the most graphic example of the potential negative impact of high finance. The dilemma is that in both positive and negative cases, the high financier can make a large profit, at least in the short term. This factor was mitigated somewhat during Max Aitken's day by the fact that almost all profit came in the form of bonus common stock which, almost by definition, is a profit based on the long-term performance of the enterprise in question.

In other respects as well, Aitken's career as a Canadian high financier elucidates the dual and almost contradictory nature of investment banking at a time when rules against self-dealing and insider trading did not exist. Unquestionably, Aitken regularly used and abused information in order to attain his ends. At the end of the day, however, he added more value than he took away from the enterprises he created and funded, even if he also created more debt for the firms entering the consolidations in the short term.[5]

Aitken's mergers were not mere financial creations intended solely as vehicles to issue securities, though they invariably performed this role very well. His security flotations were not mere Ponzi schemes intended to enrich insiders before their value collapsed to zero. And unlike the infamous British promoters E.T. Hooley and Horatio Bottomley (who sold securities they did not own or printed more shares than were authorized in official prospectuses), Aitken did not swindle prospective investors.[6] In other words, although he often resorted to deception and puffery to reap the largest possible profit in every transaction, his actions were never criminally fraudulent.

From Imitator to Innovator

Max Aitken followed a similar pattern throughout his career as a financier. He generally moved into new fields as an imitator, but within a short time, often less than a year, he would begin to see a novel way of organizing his activities to make them more effective and to generate higher profits. The transition from imitator to innovator came quite naturally to Aitken but often caused discomfort within the established Canadian business community; and, not surprisingly, his approach attracted some people but repelled others.

As John F. Stairs's executive assistant, one of Aitken's first jobs was to raise capital for the Trinidad Electric Company. By the time he was refurbishing the Demerara Electric Company and setting up his ventures in Cuba and Puerto Rico, Aitken was merely following a course already set by Canadian utility entrepreneurs in Latin America and the Caribbean. His operations proved successful because of his ability to keep costs down: first, by relying on more detailed accounting, designed to pinpoint all operational costs; second, by searching for alternative low-cost suppliers of tramway and power plant equipment; and third, by carefully monitoring construction costs.

His dissatisfaction with existing suppliers and construction companies led to the establishment of the Montreal Engineering Company and the in-house provision of accounting, engineering, and construction services for all RSC utilities. Montreal Engineering was the first of its type in Canada, and as a repository of information on the utility business, it allowed Aitken to circumvent the traditional weaknesses of small utility operations that were far removed from their head office. A truly innovative organizational response, Montreal Engineering was to play a very significant role in both North and Latin America for decades to come.[7]

When Aitken first moved into the trust company business, he again followed the lead of those already in the business. At first, his Commercial Trust Company in Halifax was hardly distinguishable from the trust companies with which it was competing. But by the time he moved to Montreal and took over the Montreal Trust and Deposit Company, he had begun to experiment with advancing call loans, receiving interest-bearing deposits, offering real estate services, and running a bond department, the first trust company to do so, at least simultaneously, in Canada. And Aitken's repurchase of Royal Securities through Montreal Trust in the autumn of 1908 proved of benefit to both institutions. The RSC was the source of new corporate trusteeships and transfer agencies for Montreal Trust, while the trust company provided much-needed liquidity for the RSC when money was tight in the months preceding the Panic of 1907.

In the securities business, too, Aitken was initially a follower rather than a leader. The RSC was not the first securities corporation in Canada. That honour went to Dominion Securities, which had been created two years earlier. Moreover, even though Aitken in his old age routinely took credit for giving birth to the Royal Securities Corporation, the RSC had actually been founded by John F. Stairs. Without doubt, however, Aitken took Stairs's basic idea and shaped it into a successful regional bond house and, in less than five years, into an international investment bank. As he was really only interested in selling the securities in which the RSC had a direct stake, Aitken concentrated on the wholesaling rather than retailing side of the business – which generally meant conceiving, assembling, and then marketing consolidations of existing companies such as Porto Rico Railways and Canada Cement, injecting new life into moribund firms such as Montreal Trust, and finally creating new entities such as Montreal Engineering.

Regardless of whether any given firm had been reorganized, consolidated, or created by Aitken, the RSC acted as his personal investment bank in underwriting and marketing its securities. The bonds and shares of other entities were sold by the RSC, but only reluctantly in an effort to satisfy the portfolio requirements of the RSC's increasingly diverse clientele. It was indicative of the difference between the two that while Dominion Securities regularly advertised the high quality of its bonds, whatever their source, the RSC promoted its close relationship with the enterprises that created the securities it sold. Because of this connection, the RSC's business was necessarily high risk and high yield compared with such firms as Dominion Securities. As an entrepreneurial investment bank taking a 10 per cent stock bonus off the top as remuneration for its promoting services, a further sizable stock bonus for its underwriting services, and a cash spread for marketing securities, the RSC could and did make a great deal of money – probably significantly more than Dominion Securities.

Industrial merger promoting, in particular, was profitable. Aitken's forte was in conceiving mergers that made sense from an economic and organizational standpoint. He was hard nosed in assembling these same mergers; he kept the prices of the firms entering the consolidation low and, in the process, incurred the wrath of the owners, who later felt that they had been outfoxed. In some cases, such as the Stelco merger, this was of little consequence; but in others, where he resorted to subterfuge and deception, as in the Canada Cement affair, the ensuing struggle almost destroyed both Aitken and the RSC. In most cases, Aitken sold his creations, reorganizations, and mergers with great skill to underwriters, brokers, and the investing public. The most vivid example of his ability in this respect was his marketing of Porto Rico securities before, during, and after the Panic of 1907.

High-risk investment banks by definition are capable of losing a great deal of money. Under Aitken's direction, the closest the RSC came to disaster, aside from the Panic of 1907, was the People's Bank fiasco in 1905; but if Sir Sandford Fleming had forced Aitken to pay what he had originally demanded for the Exshaw property, the Canada Cement merger might have produced a ruinous loss rather than a large profit, destroying Aitken's reputation as a wunderkid financier. He survived the 1913 recession in large part because the RSC had not invested heavily in pulp and paper companies. One of the most attractive sectors during the Laurier boom, pulp and paper was also the most hard hit sector during the 1913 recession, causing the demise of Garnet P. Grant and his Dominion Bond Company among others. The instability of this industry also did grave damage to Walton Killam's RSC, when one of his pulp and paper mergers turned into disaster with the market collapse and recession of 1921. The loss pushed Killam into reinvigorating and expanding Montreal Engineering, as well as creating a new utility holding company – International Power. Its success soon restored the RSC's reputation as the most entrepreneurial and profitable investment bank in the country.[8]

The Measure of the Man

Aitken was luckier than Killam partly because of his timing. He had not yet entered the business of industrial merger promoting when the gale winds of 1907 threatened enterprises that were dependent on enormous amounts of borrowed capital. His handling of the smaller Porto Rico Railways flotations at this time suggests that he might have had the skill to survive a much larger flotation in similar circumstances, but he was undoubtedly lucky that his debt load was still relatively limited. If the market had collapsed in the midst of the Canada Cement or Stelco flotations, Aitken would have been in a very different position. By the time the 1913 recession came, he had already completed all his major mergers, and he was to sell the RSC to Killam three years before the recession of 1921.

Aside from the question of the business cycle, Aitken was very much a product of the Laurier boom. He took every advantage of the prosperity that it produced, but had he been faced by years of recessionary belt-tightening instead of hothouse growth, he might have done very poorly in life. From the gilded age on, Aitken's personality was permanently linked to economic prosperity – he could see no reason for any other material state. In the end, the inflationary optimism of the boom years so pervaded his outlook that it became the leitmotif of his later life. For example, he regularly championed deficit spending, high wages, and increased consumer spending as a solution to Britain's interwar depression – not at all the conservative nostrum expected from a reactionary newspaper baron. He was an easy-money Keynesian before Keynes had even written the *General Theory*.[9]

It could be said that if a Max Aitken had not existed, the Laurier boom would have had to create him. In fact, this period did produce financiers very much like him. Many of the best shared Aitken's expansive entrepreneurial vision, but only a select few combined it with the organizational ability necessary to turn stockwatering into viable industrial undertakings. Profit was the product of Aitken's success, and he became richer through mergers than any of his fellow promoters, despite the fact that he moved to England after the first year of the merger wave. Since his real goal in life was adventure, profit led quite naturally to politics, mainly of the backroom variety, in both Britain and Canada.

In this new arena, Aitken was very clearly a product of his times, and he remained a prisoner to the political ideals of his Canadian youth for the rest of his life. The reason for his allegiance to the British Empire is not difficult to fathom. All those who influenced him during his formative years – his father, his teachers at Harkins Academy in Newcastle, his friend R.B. Bennett, his mentor John F. Stairs – were committed and impassioned imperialists. Moreover, such ideals made business sense during the Laurier boom. Huge capital flows from Britain after the turn of the century actually reinforced the links between the mother country and Canada. Aitken and his fellow financiers looked to the City of London as a permanent source of capital. Like most of his generation of English-speaking businessmen, Aitken wanted to encourage this British connection. His motives were therefore both pecuniary and ideological, and it would be impossible to determine which played the decisive role. Some found this fusion of self-interest and high principle disturbing, and one of Aitken's contemporary critics argued that 'people like him' were turning an 'altruistic ideal' into a 'mere medium for the social advancement of financial buccaneers.'[10]

Aitken's optimism about Canada and the British connection, as well as his fears about the United States, came to the fore during his 1910 election campaign in Britain and the 1911 reciprocity election in Canada. While his money and his magazine propaganda helped fuel the polarization in Canada during the reciprocity election, his career as a financier and merger promoter made him an easy mark. Both sides desperately sought out fears with which the general voter could easily identify. Aitken and his fellow Conservatives pointed to the threat the American republic posed to British-Canadian culture and institutions, and to the British Empire itself. The Liberals and their agrarian and free trade friends targeted the tariff, monopolies, and business morality; on all three counts, the Canada Cement affair was one of the principle exhibits in this political trial as the newspapers feasted on Sir Sandford Fleming's printed circulars and public statements. As the mastermind behind the cement merger, Aitken was a crook in the eyes of many Canadians; and in the view of the British public, which was just then becoming acquainted with Aitken, he was an adventurer with a dark past.[11]

Aitken's institutional legacy stands in stark contrast to the general view of Aitken as criminal. The Royal Securities Corporation, so much a product of his ambitions, became the most dynamic investment bank in the country during the Laurier boom, and would remain a distinctive feature of the country's financial landscape until its acquisition by Merrill Lynch in 1969. Quite apart from its organizational progeny (Montreal Engineering, for instance), the corporation was a training camp for Canadian high financiers in the twentieth century. Its graduates included Arthur Nesbitt of Nesbitt, Thompson & Co., Ward Pitfield, later of Pitfield McKay & Co., and, of course, Walton Killam, the pre-eminent money man of St James Street until his retirement in the early 1950s.

As the inheritor of Aitken's mantle, it was only fitting that Killam would continue his mentor's experimentation with industrial financing and utility venture capital companies. The creation of the International Power Company in 1925 took Aitken's ideas and organizations one step further in a direction that a future generation of Canadian capitalists would travel after the Second World War. Killam also became an extraordinarily wealthy man, and when he died in 1955 the taxes on his estate were large enough to bankroll the Canada Council.

As for the three great industrial mergers that were formed in less than twelve months by Aitken, two were eventually purchased as going concerns by foreign multinationals. One of the three still survives in its original corporate form, and today Stelco is the largest steel company in the country. All were created by an admittedly voracious appetite for profit and power, but all were also the gift of invention and improvisation in its most spirited form.

The First Canadian Merger Wave in International Perspective

Merger waves, defined as sustained periods of rapid external corporate growth, first appeared in some parts of the industrialized world at the end of the nineteenth century. They were a product of the abrupt technological, organizational, and financial upheaval then taking place, a process often referred to as the second industrial revolution. High-throughput technology required larger plants and multilayered administrative units – needs that could be rapidly satisfied through consolidation. The high fixed costs imposed by innovative technologies produced a new demand for security financing. Promoters and financiers were encouraged to cobble together firms large enough to be recognized as 'national enterprises' in order to capture the attention of potential investors. The consequent distribution of securities among hundreds, even thousands, of individuals accelerated the trend towards the separation of ownership from management.

The American Experience

Some scholars have concluded that the merger waves accelerated the development of the modern industrial economy. According to Ralph Nelson, mergers were a 'basic force' in moulding the industrial structure of twentieth-century America. Nelson generated a series of merger statistics for American companies, specifically to analyse the impact of the turn-of-the-century spurt of consolidations, the so-called Great Merger Wave, on the existing structure of the corporate economy of the United States. Nelson concluded that the Great Merger Wave was the turning point in the evolution of the American economy. It transformed 'many industries, formerly characterized by many small and medium-sized firms, into those in which one or a few very large enterprises occupied leading positions' and laid 'the foundations for the industrial structure that has characterized most of American industry' ever since.[1]

On the other hand, Alfred Chandler has singled out managerial organization and vertical integration rather than mergers as the operative factor in this transformation of the American economy. The inference is that mergers played a relatively neutral role in the emergence of the American corporate economy. Most mergers involved horizontal integration, but those that survived were found to have adopted a strategy of vertical integration after their brief burst of external growth. Backward integration to secure inputs, and forward integration into distribution and marketing, were more often achieved through more gradual, internal expansion. Consequently, according to Chandler, the Great Merger Wave was not the causal watershed in American business that Nelson depicted.[2]

Certainly, most of the mergers involved mainly horizontal rather than vertical integration.[3] Nevertheless, varying degrees of vertical integration were soon achieved even though many consolidations were in the beginning predominately horizontal in character. The reasons for this evolution are not difficult to fathom. The unprecedented size and scale of the new enterprises necessitated such profound organizational and technological changes that they were quickly pushed into a strategy of vertical integration in order to survive. Moreover, this aspect of mergers was often predicted by the organizers themselves.[4]

Firms that remained strictly horizontal consolidations were quickly smothered by new competitors, but the majority of mergers evolved into successful enterprises which then shaped the modern American corporate landscape. In Nelson's survey of the one hundred largest American corporations of 1955, sixty-three had gone through 'important mergers' at some time in their history. Of these, thirty-eight had their major merger before 1916, and twenty of the thirty-eight could be traced directly back to the Great Merger Wave of 1898–1902. Virtually two-thirds of the one hundred largest corporations of 1955 had at some point gone through an 'important merger' (defined by Nelson as a merger that propels a company into a leading position in the industry).[5]

In both the United States and Canada, the great multifirm consolidations of the gilded age were a response to the demands of investors for the securities of large manufacturing enterprises, particularly those perceived to be capable of wielding market power. Promoters catapulted a proposition into a shape that was acceptable to investors by melding together several similar enterprises, none of which were individually of interest to these same investors. The chain of causation ran from technology to organization to finance, with mergers to a lesser or greater degree being symptomatic of all three elements but with multifirm consolidations being most closely related to the factor of financial change.

The British and German Experiences

Because of the wealth of American merger statistics, gathered mainly in response to antitrust laws, conclusions 'about mergers and structural change have tended, *faute de mieux*, to be derived from the American experience.'[6] The poor quality and inconsistent nature of empirical data on merger activity in other advanced industrial nations had previously precluded fruitful comparisons with the American experience. However, recent empirical studies on early merger activity in Britain and Germany now permit some point of comparison.

Leslie Hannah has generated a relatively comprehensive series of merger statistics for Britain during the gilded age.[7] The results indicate a close correspondence with the American evidence. Britain experienced a dramatic increase in merger activity at the end of the nineteenth century, the peak years being 1898–1902. Most of these mergers were multifirm consolidations. This burst of activity corresponded with higher than average stock prices. There was one crucial difference, however. Whereas the Great Merger Wave in the United States resulted in a fundamental change in the nation's industrial structure, the majority of British mergers served to preserve the status quo. Multifirm British consolidations resembled the cartel associations from which they had evolved rather than the centrally directed, multidivisional industrial enterprises that were emerging from the American merger wave. It was not until the interwar period, particularly the merger wave of 1925–29, that the modern industrial enterprise became entrenched in Britain.[8] Using the one hundred largest British companies of 1948 as his yardstick, Hannah found that the majority of the most important mergers in British manufacturing industry occurred after the First World War. Of the fifty-one companies for which a major merger could be clearly identified, nineteen were concentrated in the decade of the 1920s.[9]

Richard Tilly's study of industrial mergers in Germany during the gilded age provides a third data set, even though his small-scale sampling technique limits comparisons to Britain and America. We now know, for example, that the timing of merger activity in the three most important industrial nations was almost identical. The impact of mergers in the German case was very similar to the American, although fewer German companies were propelled into 'commanding market positions' through merger.[10] This market position was available to German firms – and to British and Canadian firms too, for that matter – through cartels, an activity penalized in the United States by a vigorous antitrust policy; certainly, cartel behaviour was more prevalent in all three countries than in the United States after the passage of the Sherman antitrust act in 1890.[11]

Nonetheless, German cartels differed significantly from the British or Canadian variety in that their activities extended beyond price fixing into the shared control of resources and the establishment of selling agencies and head offices that coordinated the decision making of all the cartel members.[12] The end result was often the same kind of vertical integration and multidivisional organizational framework that was beginning to dominate the American corporate economy. Moreover, the combinations produced in the German cartel system were often tighter than the affiliations of British firms, which banded together within the legal framework of a corporation but continued to be a disparate collection of family firms without central authority and with little planning. Many multi-unit British consolidations (for example, the Calico Printers' Association and the Associated Portland Cement Manufacturers Company) initially, at least, did not put in place as effective managerial or organizational structures as their German, American, and Canadian counterparts.[13]

It may be significant that in Germany's leading industry, merger rather than cartel produced the winning combination of vertical integration, organizational structure, managerial hierarchy, technological innovation, and capital availability.[14] Mergers in Germany's heavy electrical engineering were, in Tilly's view, 'an important part of the recipe' for the success of that industry.[15] In fact, one-half of all German mergers were concentrated in the heavy industry group, a sector in which Germany was a world leader. Mergers therefore appear to have played more than a neutral role in Germany's industrial success. In Britain, on the other hand, mergers before 1914 had at best a neutral impact, and at worse a negative effect, on industrial structure.

Extrapolating from Tilly's sample, the German merger wave was smaller than the concurrent British and American waves, and the size of the average German merger was several times smaller than its American counterpart but was up to twice as large as its British counterpart. This comparison must, however, be heavily qualified by the incompatibility of Tilly's merger series with the American and British series. Since previously constructed merger series for Canada covering the gilded age are also incompatible with the Nelson and Hannah series, a new Canadian merger series was constructed in order to permit closer comparison.

The Limitations of Previous Canadian Studies

The first large-scale empirical study of Canadian merger activity was conducted by the Dominion Bureau of Statistics (DBS) in 1934–5, as part of the Royal Commission on Price Spreads.[16] To protect the confidentiality of the firms providing information to the DBS, the royal commission's report did not identify individual companies or indicate the types of firm that were included in the survey. However, the confidential background report used by the inquiry's commissioners disclosed the classes of industry included as well as the name of each firm.[17]

The DBS report provided both number and value data for mergers from 1900 until 1933; the annual number of mergers and of firm disappearances were tabulated, and for those before 1920 the value was based on issued capital, while after that date it was on net assets.[18] Although no calculation procedure was outlined in the DBS report, issued capital, appears to have included bonded debt in addition to equity capital, judging by the firm level information provided in the confidential report. Unfortunately, the calculation procedure for net asset value is not revealed in either the DBS report or the commission's confidential report.[19]

Naturally, the commission's industrial classification scheme differs in some respects from the Canadian standard industrial classification (SIC) scheme first introduced more than a decade later.[20] More significant in terms of this study, some of the DBS's classes of industry would not fall within the general category of manufacturing industry as defined in the 1948 SIC or more recent Canadian SICs.[21] These include some mining, quarrying, wholesale, and retail trade industries. Hence, the DBS series varies from the Nelson sample, which includes both manufacturing and mining industries, and the Hannah series, which is more narrowly restricted to manufacturing industry.[22]

J.C. Weldon reworked and extended the DBS series to 1948.[23] First published in 1966, Weldon's series, like the DBS sample, was limited to the mergers covered in the leading American and Canadian financial manuals and therefore excluded closely held companies as well as smaller, publicly owned companies. There are also some discrepancies in industry coverage, which produce differences in the number of mergers and firm disappearances between the DBS and the Weldon series. Weldon's definition of industry, while it excludes petroleum refining, includes public utilities (telephone, shipping lines, and light, water, and power companies) and trade and service companies such as movie theatres, food and clothing stores, and other retailers.

The DBS and Weldon series are further differentiated by the procedures used to estimate the value of mergers. Weldon uses 'gross assets (less depreciation) of the enterprises absorbed in the consolidations' but offers the reader little indication of the exact manner in which such asset figures were calculated. Where this could not be calculated, Weldon uses 'nominal weights.' Again, the formula or method used to calculate these weights is not disclosed, although this procedure was 'required for less than one-fifth of all mergers,' mainly concentrated in the early years.[24]

The DBS and Weldon series do not attempt to cover mergers before 1900. This is unfortunate, for that date represents the midpoint of the first large merger wave experienced in the United States and Britain and the beginning of the German merger wave. For the pre-1921 period, both the DBS and Weldon relied entirely on the statistics gathered by H.G. Stapells in his 1922 MA thesis.[25] Since Stapells relied mainly on the *Annual Financial Review*, a Canadian financial manual which only began to be published in 1900, all three series are limited to post-1900 data.[26] Given the fact that 1900 falls right in the middle of the first great merger waves in the United States, Great Britain, and Germany, any new Canadian series should provide data on the critical years preceding 1900.

The New Canadian Series

The sources from which the new series was constructed included public and private archives in Britain and Canada, financial manuals, government reports, industry histories, individual business histories, theses, and business periodicals. While this range of sources may appear much wider than those relied on by Nelson and Hannah to generate their series, in fact one Canadian source provided the bulk of data – the *Monetary Times*, the most broadly circulated business periodical of the age.

Nelson depended mainly on the *Commercial and Financial Chronicle*, a periodical aimed more at the professional investor than on the wider business audience targeted by the *Monetary Times*. Hannah relied on published business histories for the period 1880–1918, a source that would have produced few results in the Canadian context because of the paucity of such material.[27]

The sources determine the bias of each sample. Nelson's merger series is heavily weighted towards larger public companies with listings on the major stock exchanges. Given that only survivors commission business histories, Hannah's series is slanted towards the more successful firms but is less biased towards publicly quoted companies. The present series is biased towards the (larger) companies deemed newsworthy by the *Monetary Times*, but it may be more comprehensive than the Nelson series, which includes only publicly quoted (and therefore very large) companies.

The new merger index is restricted to Canadian manufacturing enterprises, as defined under the 1948 Canadian SIC, and therefore eliminates the public utility companies included in Weldon's sample. 'Canadian' is defined as companies incorporated under the federal or provincial laws of Canada *and* whose operations were conducted predominantly in Canada.[28] An exception was made only in the case of few 'free-standing' enterprises, which although organized in accordance with the laws of a jurisdiction other than Canada, had their administrative head offices and operations based entirely in Canada.[29] Merger activity involving Canadian firms, if it occurred outside Canada, was excluded. Acquisitions of Canadian enterprises in Canada by foreign firms were similarly excluded.

A minimum of four pieces of information had to be recovered for a merger to be included in the new series: (1) the corporate name of the new entity in a merger by consolidation or the name of the corporate acquirer in a merger by acquisition; (2) the number of firm disappearances in any single merger; (3) the calendar year in which the merger was completed; and (4) the specific manufacturing business of the merger company as defined under the 1948 SIC. Mergers missing any one of the four pieces of information were dropped from the sample since they lacked information essential for any useful comparison with the British and American merger series.

Mergers were defined to include both consolidations and acquisitions, hence the use of the phrases 'mergers by consolidation' and 'mergers by acquisition.' Acquisition involves the purchase of one or more firms by a company that retains its corporate identity. Consolidation implies the combining of two or more firms that submerge their identity into a new corporate entity.[30] The category of consolidation embraces the large number of multifirm amalgamations that were so typical of mergers during the gilded age in Canada, as well as in Britain and the United States. The definition of consolidation used in this study is identical to that used by Hannah, but it varies slightly from Nelson's definition of consolidation, which involves a fusion of a minimum of three firms.[31]

To assure equality of treatment between acquisitions and consolidations when counting mergers, one firm disappearance was subtracted from the total number of firm disappearances for each consolidation. There was generally little difficulty in discovering the number of firm disappearances as well as the names of the individual firms entering the mergers. In rare cases, however, the sources simply indicated that an unspecified number of firms had merged. In such cases, the following procedure, consistent with the approaches used by Nelson and Hannah, was adopted: one firm disappearance was assumed where words such as 'few' or 'some' were used to describe the number of companies involved in a merger; two firm disappearances were allocated where the words 'several,' 'a number,' and 'various' were used; three firm disappearances were assumed if the words 'many,' 'a large number,' or 'a lot' were used.

Efforts were made to date the mergers by month within every calendar year. The date of consummation was defined as the date of effective transfer of control. Where that information was not available, proxies such as the date of incorporation, corporate applications for changes in capitalization, date of issue of first prospectus, date of first flotation, or similar data were used. The most consistent source for dating was the *Monetary Times*, with which the following procedure was adopted: if the completion of the merger was announced after the tenth day of the month, that month was used as the effective date of the transfer of control; if before then, the preceding month was used.[32]

Merger Activity by Industry

As much information as possible was gathered on the business activities of the mergers in the new series. This was necessary in order to utilize the SIC system as the demarcation for inclusion in the series. The main difficulty lay in distinguishing between manufacturing industry and mining industry. While mining was excluded in the new series as well as in the Hannah series on Britain, Nelson included mining mergers in his series. Nonetheless, the three series are much more compatible than this might suggest. Nelson consolidated manufacturing and mining industries under one activity in the following manner: coke products (manufacturing) and bituminous coal (mining) under mining; granite product (manufacturing) and granite quarries (mining) as granite mining; cement manufacturing and cement quarrying as mining; lime manufacturing and lime quarrying as mining; talc refining (manufacturing) and talc mining as mining; iron and steel production and iron ore mining as manufacturing; and salt refining (manufacturing) and salt mining as manufacturing.[33] The Canadian series (consistent with the British series) classifies these 'difficult cases' as manufacturing if some secondary refining, processing, or manufacturing beyond the extraction stage is involved. Thus, many of the enterprises classified as mining by Nelson would come under the general manufacturing category in the Hannah sample and in the present series for Canada.[34]

In terms of the industries that experienced the most intense merger activity during the gilded age, the Canadian experience was remarkably similar to those in Britain and the United States.[35] Whether the number of mergers or firm disappearances is used to calculate merger activity by industry from 1885 until 1918, the most active areas were, in descending order of importance, food and beverage processing, iron and steel manufacturing, textile production, chemical products, nonmetallic mineral processing including cement production, transportation equipment (in particular railway rolling stock), and, finally, wood products, including pulp and paper manufacturing. During the height of the Laurier boom, the order of preference remained largely the same except for textile mergers, which were less numerous than in the 1880s and 1890s.

In terms of merger activity, the Canadian economy more closely fitted the pattern of the American rather than the British economy during the second industrial revolution. Both economies witnessed, for example, the largest amount of merger activity in the food-processing industry, while the British economy experienced relatively few consolidations in this industry. The reason likely can be found in the rapid adoption of refrigerated facilities or continuous-process machinery by North American meat, fish, and fruit and vegetable packers at a time when most British firms in the industry were beginning to lag behind technologically. American firms such as Swift and Armour pioneered integrated meat-packing operations using refrigeration, while Heinz, Borden, and Libby mastered the use of high-throughput continuous-process-canning assembly lines. The most prominent Canadian examples included the British Columbia Packers consolidation of 1902 and the Dominion Canners merger eight years later. Similarly, American and German industry had become technological leaders in the steel, chemical, and portland cement industries by the end of the nineteenth century, and Canadian companies quickly adopted the new methods, consolidating smaller firms into national companies capable of raising large amounts of capital through transatlantic share issues. In other words, the high-tech sectors of the second industrial revolution were also the locus of merger activity in Canada.

The Number of Canadian Mergers

Theoretically, the value, or 'volume,' of mergers and firm disappearances rather than the total number of mergers and firm disappearances in any given unit of time is a superior indicator of actual merger activity. Unfortunately, these are the most difficult data to obtain. In fact, in all the series discussed above, including the new Canadian series, value estimates could not be made for a significant percentage of mergers. Moreover, every one of these series used a different proxy to estimate the value of mergers and firm disappearances, thereby seriously limiting meaningful comparisons. As a consequence, the number of mergers and firm disappearances is at present a much safer basis of comparison than the corresponding value series.

The annual results of the new series in terms of the number of mergers and firm disappearances and the percentage of consolidations and acquisitions are summarized in table A.1. Measured in terms of both the number of mergers and the number of firm disappearances, the years 1909–13 constitute the most sustained period of merger activity during the gilded age. As illustrated in figures A.1 and A.2, this merger wave was preceded by smaller bursts of activity in 1889–93, 1899–1903, and 1905–7 and was followed by a larger merger wave in the second half of the 1920s. The first two subperiods are roughly coincident with increased merger activity in Britain and the United States, but these bursts, characterized by a tiny number of large consolidations, were substantially smaller in Canada. The Dominion Cotton Company merger of 1891 resulted in eight firm disappearances, while the British Columbia Packers consolidation of 1902 and the Canadian Canners merger of 1903 were responsible for forty-four and twenty-two firm disappearances, respectively. This pattern contrasts with the numerous British and American mergers during these years, and with the first Canadian merger wave of 1909–13 itself, when a significant number of multifirm consolidations were consummated with no single merger dominating in any one year.

By removing the largest merger (as measured by the number of firm disappearances) from every year, we can smooth out the series and reveal the underlying pattern, as illustrated in figure A.3. The three increases in merger activity before 1909 are now revealed as relatively small bursts, while the merger movement of 1909–13 retains the same contour and

TABLE A.1 Number of industrial mergers, consolidations, acquisitions, and firm
disappearances, 1885–1918

Year	Mergers	Consolidations	Acquisitions	Firm disappearances
1885	3	2	1	3
1886	0	0	0	0
1887	1	0	1	1
1888	1	1	0	1
1889	6	2	4	9
1890	3	2	1	14
1891	7	4	3	14
1892	6	4	2	10
1893	6	4	2	8
1894	0	0	0	0
1895	4	2	2	4
1896	0	0	0	0
1897	0	0	0	0
1898	2	1	1	6
1899	4	4	0	11
1900	7	3	4	10
1901	7	4	3	25
1902	3	2	1	51
1903	3	1	2	24
1904	4	1	3	5
1905	10	7	3	26
1906	8	5	3	14
1907	6	1	5	11
1908	3	3	0	7
1909	12	10	2	52
1910	22	20	2	69
1911	16	12	4	37
1912	13	8	5	21
1913	8	5	3	17
1914	1	0	1	2
1915	3	2	1	4
1916	1	0	1	1
1917	3	2	1	5
1918	1	1	0	3
Total	174	113	61	465

Source: Gregory P. Marchildon, 'Promotion, Finance and Mergers in Canadian Manufacturing Industry, 1885–1918' (PhD diss., London School of Economics, 1990), chap. 7

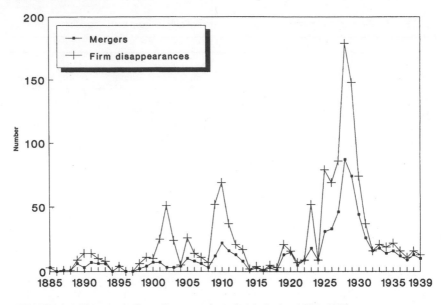

FIGURE A.1 Mergers in Canadian manufacturing industry, 1885–1939

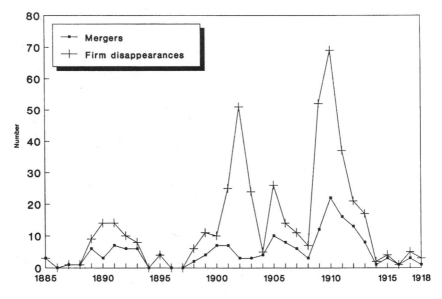

FIGURE A.2 Mergers in Canadian manufacturing industry, 1885–1918

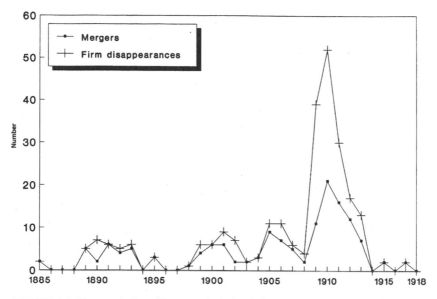

FIGURE A.3 Mergers in Canadian manufacturing industry, 1885–1918, smoothed data

intensity of the unadjusted series displayed in figure A.2. By revealing the relative absence of merger activity before 1909, figure A.3 better depicts the trend of Canadian merger activity between 1885 and 1918.

In absolute terms, the Canadian merger wave of 1909–13 was substantially smaller than the British and American waves at the turn of the century. Relative to its economic size, however, Canada's merger movement was quite remarkable in its intensity. Canada had a GNP approximately one-sixteenth and one-tenth the size of the respective GNPs of the United States and Britain as of 1900, and the country's per capita level of industrialization, as defined by manufacturing production, was between one-half and one-third of those of the same two nations in 1913.[36] Nonetheless, Canada experienced 196 firm disappearances during its merger wave (1909–13), relative to 775 and 2,653 firm disappearances, respectively, in Britain and the United States during their merger waves (1898–1902) – roughly one-quarter of the number in Britain and one-fourteenth of the number in the United States.[37]

Approximately 65 per cent of Canadian mergers over the period 1885–1918 took the form of consolidations rather than acquisitions, a trend that was particularly pronounced during the peak years of the merger movement from 1909 to 1913. Similar to the experience in the United

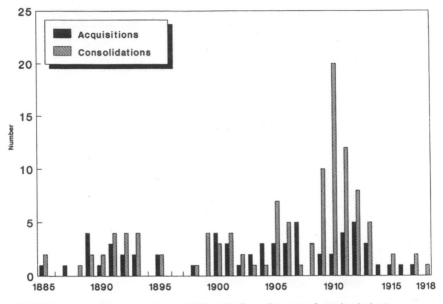

FIGURE A.4 Acquisitions and consolidations in Canadian manufacturing industry, 1885–1918

States and Britain, mergers by consolidation played a much more significant role than mergers by acquisition during the merger waves of the gilded age than they did in subsequent years. This is a reflection of the unique financial demands of the era as opposed to the technological or organizational rationale for such mergers. Figure A.4 contrasts the cyclical and relatively stable pattern of mergers by acquisition with the more unique configuration of consolidations clustered in the years 1909–13. As in Britain and the United States at the turn of the century, consolidations were the distinguishing characteristic of the first great Canadian merger movement. Multifirm consolidations dominated only the first major merger waves in these countries; subsequent merger waves, including those in the 1920s and 1960s, were dominated by acquisitions.

The Timing of the First Canadian Merger Wave

Perhaps the most difficult question to address is why the first merger wave in Canada did not appear until one decade after similar waves in Britain, Germany, and the United States. Earlier chapters have already discussed the connection between the introduction of higher-throughput manufacturing systems, overproduction, and consolidations aimed at better con-troll of an oversupplied market. Unfortunately, these factors, while very important preconditions, do not alone explain the precise timing of the Canadian merger wave. In fact, there is much evidence to suggest that financial conditions dictate the exact timing of merger movements, and preliminary econometric testing of Canadian data confirms the centrality of financial as opposed to industrial factors in triggering the first merger wave.[38]

That there is a robust correlation over time between sustained bull markets in industrial share prices and merger activity is a long-observed phenomenon in the advanced industrial countries. If a broad market in Canadian industrial securities had emerged in Canada by the turn of the century, it would be logical to infer that a sustained merger movement would have taken place. But unlike the situation in more industrialized countries such as Britain, Germany, and the United States, it would take another few years for this market to emerge. When the next bull market came – although not as sustained or vigorous as that which was experi-enced in the capital markets of London, Berlin, and New York from 1898 until 1901 – it was enough to set off a full-blown merger wave in Canada. When it struck, a new breed of young financiers, including Max Aitken, moved into the business of merger promoting in order to create millions of dollars of new securities.

Notes

Abbreviations

AFR	*Annual Financial Review* (Canadian)
AO	Archives of Ontario, Toronto
CAR	*Canadian Annual Review*
CDP	*The Canadian Directory of Parliament, 1867–1967* (Ottawa 1968)
CHA	Canadian Historical Association
CJC	*Canadian Journal of Commerce*
CMW	Henry J. Morgan, *Canadian Men and Women of the Time* (Toronto, 1st ed., 1898; 2nd ed., 1912)
DAL	Dalhousie University Archives, Halifax
DCB	*Dictionary of Canadian Biography*
DHC	*Debates of the House of Commons*, Government of Canada
DUR	Archives at the Department of Paleography and Diplomatic, University of Durham, Durham, England
GLSE	Guildhall Library Manuscripts, Records of the London Stock Exchange, City of London, England
HBK	Beaverbrook Papers at the House of Lords Record Office, London, England
LCA	Lafarge Canada, Inc., private archive, Montreal
LSE	London Stock Exchange
MSE	Montreal Stock Exchange
MT	*Monetary Times*
MTC	Montreal Trust [and Deposit] Company
NA	National Archives of Canada, Ottawa
NABK	Beaverbrook Papers at the National Archives of Canada, Ottawa
PANS	Public Archives of Nova Scotia, Halifax

RSC   Royal Securities Corporation
SRJ   *Street Railway Journal*
Stelco   Steel Company of Canada, private archive, Hamilton
TSE   Toronto Stock Exchange
UNBK   Beaverbrook Papers at the Harriet Irving Library of the University of
         New Brunswick, Fredericton
UNBEN R.B. Bennett Papers at the Harriet Irving Library of the University of
         New Brunswick, Fredericton

Preface

1 Sandra Gwyn, *Tapestry of War: A Private View of Canadians in the Great War* (Toronto 1992), 238.
2 R.V. Clemence and F.S. Doody, *The Schumpetarian System* (Cambridge, Mass., 1950). He in fact thought that corporate research and development activities would eventually eliminate the entrepreneurial function; see Joseph A. Schumpeter, *Capitalism, Socialism and Democracy*, 3rd ed. (New York 1950), chap. 12.
3 David S. Landes, 'Introduction: On Technology and Growth,' in Henry Rosovsky et al., eds., *Favorites of Fortune: Technology, Growth, and Economic Development since the Industrial Revolution* (Cambridge, Mass., 1992), 16.
4 William Lazonick, 'What Happened to the Theory of Economic Development?' in Rosovsky et al., eds., *Favorites of Fortune*, 273.
5 Connie Bruck, *The Predators' Ball* (New York 1991); Benjamin J. Stein, *A License to Steal: The Untold Story of Michael Milken and the Conspiracy to Bilk the Nation* (New York 1992); Jesse Kornbluth, *Highly Confident: The Crime and Punishment of Michael Milken* (New York 1992).
6 For more on this distinction, see Gregory P. Marchildon, 'British Investment Banking and Industrial Decline before the Great War: A Case Study of Capital Outflow to Canadian Industry,' *Business History* 33, no. 3 (July 1991), 74.

1: Max Aitken and the Nature of Finance Capitalism during the Laurier Boom

1 Rudolf Hilferding, *Finance Capital: A Study of the Latest Phase of Capitalist Development* (London 1981), 112; first English translation of original German publication (1910).
2 Quoted in 'Life Calls on "the Beaver": Top British Newsman Comes Back to Visit Old Home in Canada,' *Life*, 4 June 1951, 157.
3 Beaverbrook's partisan use of Britain's largest mass circulation paper, the *Daily Express*, angered his political and personal enemies, including the Brit-

ish prime minister Stanley Baldwin who said of Beaverbrook (and Rother-
mere) that he sought 'power without responsibility – the prerogative of the
harlot throughout the ages.' See Hugh Cudlipp, *The Prerogative of the Harlot:
Press Barons and Power* (London 1980).

4 Beaverbrook's early biographers concentrated on his careers as politician,
minister in both wartime governments, and newspaper proprietor. See F.A.
Mackenzie, *Beaverbrook: An Authentic Biography of the Right Hon. Lord Beaverbrook* (London 1931); Edgar Middleton, *Beaverbrook: The Statesman and the
Man* (London 1934); David Farrer, *The Sky's the Limit: The Story of Beaverbrook
at M.A.P.* (London 1943); Tom Driberg, *Beaverbrook: A Study in Power and Frustration* (London 1956); Peter Howard, *Beaverbrook: A Study of Max the Unknown*
(London 1964); Alan Wood, *The True History of Lord Beaverbrook* (London
1965); and Kenneth Young's biography of a friendship, *Churchill and Beaverbrook* (New York 1966). These are supplemented by some very personal
recollections: David Farrer, *G – for God Almighty: A Personal Memoir of Lord Beaverbrook* (New York 1969), and C.M. Vines, *A Little Nut-Brown Man: My Three
Years with Lord Beaverbrook* (London 1969).

5 A.J.P. Taylor, *Beaverbrook* (New York 1972), and Ann Chisholm and Michael
Davie, *Beaverbrook: A Life* (London 1992). See also Lord Beaverbrook, *Politicians and the Press* (London 1925), *Politicians and the War, 1914–1916* (1st ed.:
[2 vols.] 1928, 1932; rev. ed.: London 1960), *Men and Power, 1917–1918* (London 1956), and *The Decline and Fall of Lloyd George* (London 1963). For a critical view of Aitken's 'rewriting' of history, see John O. Stubbs, 'Beaverbrook as
Historian: "Politicians and the War, 1914–1916" Reconsidered,' *Albion* 14, no.
3–4 (Fall–Winter 1982), 235–53.

6 According to Christopher Armstrong and H.V. Nelles in *Southern Exposure:
Canadian Promoters in Latin America and the Caribbean, 1896–1930* (Toronto
1988), Aitken broke 'too flagrantly' the (already sufficiently loose) rules of
conduct of the Canadian financial community and was thus rejected (284):
'Aitken was thought by many business leaders ... to have misconducted himself over the steel and cement mergers in 1910, and he soon departed for
Britain' (350).

7 Opinion was divided about Fleming's reputation when in 1880, at the age of
fifty-three, he was fired as chief engineer of the Canadian Pacific Railway; see
Alan Wilson, 'Fleming and Tupper: The Fall of the Siamese Twins, 1880,' in
John S. Moir, ed., *Character and Circumstance* (Toronto 1970).

8 Gregory P. Marchildon, 'Promotion, Finance and Mergers in Canadian Manufacturing Industry, 1885–1918' (PhD diss., London School of Economics,
1990), chap. 4.

9 Aitken's first public defence of his actions in the Canada Cement merger

appeared in 1922 in a book dedicated to teaching young men how to succeed in business (Lord Beaverbrook, *Success* [Boston 1922], 69–70).

10 Lord Northcliffe, quoted in Taylor, *Beaverbrook*, 41.

11 A.J.P. Taylor, *Politicians, Socialism and Historians* (New York 1982), 28.

12 Taylor, *Beaverbrook*, xvii.

13 This was, for example, Michael Bliss's argument in his review of Taylor's book in *Acadiensis* 3, no. 1 (Autumn 1973), 109–13.

14 See J. Bradford De Long, 'Did J.P. Morgan's Men Add Value? An Economist's Perspective on Financial Capitalism,' in Peter Temin, ed., *Inside the Business Enterprise: Historical Perspectives on the Uses of Information* (Chicago 1991), and 'What Morgan Wrought,' *Wilson Quarterly* 16, no. 4 (Autumn 1992).

15 Thomas R. Navin and Marian V. Sears, 'A Study in Merger: Formation of the International Mercantile Marine Company,' *Business History Review* 28, no. 4 (Dec. 1954); Vincent P. Carosso, *The Morgans: Private International Bankers, 1854–1913* (Cambridge, Mass., 1987), 481–6.

16 See Roy C. Smith, 'After the Ball,' *Wilson Quarterly* 16, no. 4 (Autumn 1992), 16–43.

17 The companies that Milken financed, including Time Warner, MCI, McCaw Cellular, Tele-Communications, NewsCorp, Viacom, and Turner Broadcasting, are now worth far more than their market value at the time that Milken began to raise capital for them through junk bond financing; see table on Milken's companies in the *Wall Street Journal*, 2 Mar. 1993, 1. Milken started developing junk bond trading for Drexel Burnham in the early 1970s; he and others then used junk bonds to finance leveraged buyouts (LBOs) and hostile takeovers in the early 1980s; see Robert A. Taggart, Jr, 'The Growth of the 'Junk' Bond Market and Its Role in Financing Takeovers,' in Alan J. Auerbach, ed., *Mergers and Acquisitions* (Chicago 1988), 5–24.

18 Although now dated, chapter 1 of J. Peter Williamson's *Securities Regulation in Canada* (Toronto 1960) remains the foremost work on the evolution of Canadian securities law. Today, the Ontario Securities Act defines insiders as 'directors and senior officers of a company along with any person or company holding more than 10% of the voting shares of a company.' Insiders are required to file a report with the Ontario Securities Commission 'within ten days of the end of the month in which they become insiders, giving information on their holdings of securities; they are thereby put on notice that their buying and selling activities in these securities will be supervised (W.T. Hunter, *Canadian Financial Markets* [Peterborough, Ont., 1988], 190). At this time, requirements for listing on the Toronto and Montreal stock exchanges were minimal relative to the London and New York stock exchanges before the First World War (R.C. Michie, 'The Canadian Securities Market, 1850–

1914,' *Business History Review* 62, no. 1 [Spring 1988]). The Bond Dealers'
Association of Canada was not formed until 1916 (known as the Investment
Dealers Association of Canada after 1934), and the motive behind its creation
was not self-regulation but a response to the Canadian government's request
for a united effort in the financing of Canada's war effort (*The Canadian Securities Course* [Toronto, 1988], 237–8). Blue Sky laws were first passed in Manitoba (1912) and Saskatchewan (1914), jurisdictions where the grain growers
were most organized, but the merger promoters never set foot in those provinces (Williamson, *Securities Regulation in Canada,* 11–14). For the evolution of
disclosure requirements in terms of financial statements, especially prospectuses, see George J. Murphy, *The Evolution of Selected Annual Corporate Financial
Reporting Practices in Canada, 1900–1970* (New York 1988), chap. 2.

19 John D. Hicks, *The Populist Revolt: A History of the Farmers' Alliance and the Peo-
ple's Party* (Minneapolis 1931); Cedric B. Cowling, *Populists, Plungers, and Pro-
gressives: A Social History of Stock and Commodity Speculation, 1890–1936*
(Princeton 1965); Vincent P. Carosso, *Investment Banking in America: A History*
(Cambridge, Mass., 1970). This was also a common theme in the American
novels of the era, in particular Theodore Dreiser's *The Financier* (1912) and
The Titan (1914), which were based on the career of promoter Charles Tyson
Yerkes.

20 On the Pujo (Money Trust) investigation and its impact on J.P. Morgan, see
Vincent P. Carosso, *The Morgans: Private International Bankers, 1854–1913*
(Cambridge, Mass., 1987), chap. 18.

21 John A. Garraty, *The New Commonwealth, 1877–1890* (New York 1968), 1–4.

22 Solomos Solomou, *Phases of Economic Growth, 1850–1972* (Cambridge
1988).

23 Under the direction of Professor M.C. Urquhart, a team of seven scholars
spent a decade preparing a new set of national accounts covering the years
1870–1926. The results challenge the more gradualist interpretation of Cana-
dian growth during this era. See M.C. Urquhart, 'New Estimates of Gross
National Product, Canada, 1870–1926: Some Implications for Canadian
Development,' in S.L. Engerman and R.E. Gallman, eds., *Long-Term Factors in
Economic Growth* (Chicago 1986); Morris Altman, 'A Revision of Canadian
Economic Growth: 1870–1910 (a challenge to the gradualist interpretation),'
Canadian Journal of Economics 20, no. 1 (February 1987); and Kris Inwood and
Thanasis Stengos, 'Discontinuities in Canadian Economic Growth, 1870–
1985,' *Explorations in Economic History* 28, no. 3 (July 1991).

24 These estimates are based on Morris Altman's 'Revised Estimates of Real
Canadian GNP and Growth and Pre and Post World War Two Volatility of the
Canadian Business Cycle with Some Comparison to the American Record'

(unpublished working paper, Department of Economics, University of Saskatchewan, 1989), 45.

25 Wheat was definitely the leading sector in agriculture. Canada's exports of wheat increased from an average of 15.9 million bushels a year in the 1896–1900 period to 53.2 million bushels in the 1906–10 period; see Morris Altman, 'Revised Real Canadian GNP Estimates and Canadian Economic Growth, 1870–1926,' *Review of Income and Wealth* 38, no. 4 (Dec. 1992), 469.

26 M.C. Urquhart, 'Canadian Economic Growth 1870–1980,' discussion paper 734, Institute for Economic Research, Queen's University, 1988, 52.

27 Altman, 'Revised Estimates of Real Canadian GNP.'

28 Michael Edelstein, *Overseas Investment in the Age of High Imperialism: The United Kingdom, 1850–1914* (London 1982), 287. See also see Lance E. Davis and Robert A. Huttenback, 'The Export of British Finance, 1865–1914,' *Journal of Imperial and Commonwealth History* 13, no. 3 (May 1985).

29 For the British investor's view of Canada, see R.G. Moyles and Doug Owram, *Imperial Dreams and Colonial Realities: British Views of Canada, 1880–1914* (Toronto 1988), chap. 6.

30 Unfortunately, Canadian direct and portfolio investment statistics are not disaggregated until 1926; see F.H. Leacy, ed., *Historical Statistics of Canada* (Ottawa 1983), series G188–202. Total direct foreign investment did not exceed total portfolio foreign investment until 1952; see *Canada's International Investment Position: Historical Statistics, 1926–1992* (Ottawa 1993), 54.

31 See Gregory P. Marchildon, 'British Investment Banking and Industrial Decline before the Great War: A Case Study of Capital Outflow to Canadian Industry,' *Business History* 33, no. 3 (July 1991), and '"Hands across the Water": Canadian Industrial Financiers in the City of London, 1905–20,' *Business History* 34, no. 3 (July 1992).

32 On this theme, see Carl Berger, *The Sense of Power: Studies in the Ideas of Canadian Imperialism, 1867–1914* (Toronto 1970).

33 I am drawing on Chandler's concept of financial capitalism, which is surprisingly consistent with Rudolf Hilferding's Marxian concept of finance capitalism; see Alfred D. Chandler, Jr, *The Visible Hand: The Managerial Revolution in American Business* (Cambridge, Mass., 1977) and *Scale and Scope: The Dynamics of Industrial Capitalism* (Cambridge, Mass., 1990). See also Leslie Hannah, *The Rise of the Corporate Economy* (London 1983), and Alfred D. Chandler, Jr, and Herman Daems, eds., *Managerial Hierarchies: Comparative Perspectives on the Rise of the Modern Industrial Enterprise* (Cambridge, Mass., 1980).

34 The primary steel industry, for example, was not established in Canada until

the first decade of the twentieth century; see W.J.A. Donald, *The Canadian Iron and Steel Industry* (Boston 1915). For comparisons with Australia and Argentina, see W. Armstrong, 'Thinking about "Prime Movers": The Nature of Early Industrialization in Australia, Canada and Argentina, 1870 to 1930,' *Australian-Canadian Studies* 1 (Jan. 1983); D.C.M. Platt and Guido di Tella, eds., *Argentina, Australia and Canada: Studies in Comparative Development, 1870–1965* (New York 1985); and C.B. Schedvin, 'Staples and Regions of Pax Britannica,' *Economic History Review* 43, no. 4 (Nov. 1990).

35 Gerald Tulchinsky, *The River Barons: Montreal Businessmen and the Growth of Industry and Transportation, 1837–1853* (Toronto 1977); John McCallum, *Unequal Beginnings: Agriculture and Economic Development in Quebec and Ontario until 1870* (Toronto 1980); Paul Craven and Tom Traves, 'Canadian Railways as Manufacturers, 1850–1880,' in Douglas McCalla, ed., *Perspectives on Canadian Economic History* (Toronto 1987); and James M. Gilmour, *Spatial Evolution of Manufacturing: Southern Ontario, 1851–1891* (Toronto 1972).

36 Marchildon, 'Promotion, Finance and Mergers,' chap. 2.

37 Between 1782 and 1832, for example, the proportion of fixed capital to total assets ranged between approximately 9 and 33 per cent; see Sidney Pollard, 'Fixed Capital in the Industrial Revolution,' *Journal of Economic History* 24, no. 3 (Sept. 1964).

38 'Big' in this context is a relative term. The accumulated assets of the thirty largest nonfinancial enterprises in Canada in 1909 (with Canada Cement the eleventh largest and Canadian Car and Foundry the fifteenth) did not equal in aggregate the asset value of the United States Steel Corporation; see Graham D. Taylor and Peter A. Baskerville, *A Concise History of Business in Canada* (Toronto 1994), 311–12. See also Richard L. Nelson, *Merger Movements in American Industry, 1895–1956* (Princeton 1959); Naomi Lamoreaux, *The Great Merger Movement in American Business, 1895–1904* (Cambridge 1985); Leslie Hannah, 'Mergers in British Manufacturing Industry, 1880–1918,' *Oxford Economic Papers* 26, no. 1 (Mar. 1974); and Richard Tilly, 'Mergers, External Growth, and Finance in the Development of Large-Scale Enterprise in Germany, 1880–1913,' *Journal of Economic History* 42, no. 3 (Sept. 1982). For a comparative review, see Gregory P. Marchildon, ed., *Mergers and Acquisitions*, vol. 3 of the International Library of Critical Writings in Business History (Aldershot 1991), xi–xviii.

39 For very different analyses of competition in which entrepreneurship is central, see Israel M. Kirzner, *Competition and Entrepreneurship* (Chicago 1973), and Reuven Brenner, *Rivalry: In Business, Science, among Nations* (Cambridge 1987). See also Leslie Hannah, 'Entrepreneurs and the Social Sciences,' *Economica* 51, no. 3 (Aug. 1984).

40 Arthur H. Cole, quoted in Hugh G.J. Aitken, 'Entrepreneurial Research: The History of an Intellectual Revolution,' in Aitken's *Explorations in Enterprise* (Cambridge, Mass., 1967), 12.

41 John Maynard Keynes's view of the centrality of animal spirits in investment activity is most clearly revealed in his article 'The General Theory of Employment,' *Quarterly Journal of Economics* 51, no. 1 (Feb. 1937). See also Roger Koppl, 'Retrospectives: Animal Spirits,' *Journal of Economic Perspectives* 5, no. 2 (Summer 1991).

42 Beaverbrook Papers, House of Lords Record Office (HBK), A/171, S. Johnston to Aitken, 12 Nov. 1909.

43 For an introduction to the various approaches to the nature and functioning of profit in capitalist economies, see David Parker and Richard Stead, eds., *Profit and Enterprise: The Political Economy of Profit* (New York 1991).

44 Chisholm and Davie, *Beaverbrook*, 90.

2: Circuitous Road to Halifax, 1879–1904

1 Public Archives of Nova Scotia (PANS), Thomas Cantley Papers, MG1, vol. 170, Cantley to George Stout (Glasgow), 13 Apr. 1910.

2 Beaverbrook Papers, House of Lords Record Office (HBK), A/11, Aitken to M.S. Foley, 15 Apr. 1904.

3 A.J.P. Taylor, *Beaverbrook* (New York 1972), 5; Anne Chisholm and Michael Davie, *Beaverbrook: A Life* (London 1992), 19.

4 Lord Beaverbrook, *My Early Life* (Fredericton 1965), 19.

5 Former Old Manse Library (Newcastle), Harkins Academy teachers' reports, 1887–92, in which Aitken is continually referred to as Maxie.

6 Beaverbrook, *My Early Life*, 19.

7 Ibid., 35.

8 Former Old Manse Library, Harkins Academy teachers' reports, 1885–95. These reports were presented to Beaverbrook by the Hon. C.D. Taylor, New Brunswick's minister of education, in 1957. Aitken appears to have had a string of female teachers until the age of thirteen, when two male teachers, Philip Cox and Fred P. Yorston, taught him until he left school in 1895 at the age of sixteen.

9 Dr Yorston explained sixty years later: 'I had a bad habit of gritting my teeth when annoyed. He spotted this at once and would imitate the gesture every time I looked at him. At the time moustaches were just becoming fashionable and I was beginning to grow one. Every morning when I came into school and stood before my desk Max would promptly telegraph to the rest of the school how many more hairs I had grown during the night. He did this by sig-

nals on his fingers when he thought I was not looking his way' (Yorston, quoted in Chisholm and Davie, *Beaverbrook*, 24–5).

10 These are the recollections of Aitken's teachers Philip Cox and Dr Yorston, reproduced in Beaverbrook, *My Early Life*, 49–50.

11 Taylor, *Beaverbrook*, 9.

12 Mrs Charles Sargeant, quoted in Tom Driberg, *Beaverbrook: A Study in Power* (London 1964), 33.

13 Chisholm and Davie, *Beaverbrook*, 26–7.

14 Beaverbrook, *My Early Life*, 55–7.

15 Driberg, *Beaverbrook*, 37; Taylor, *Beaverbrook*, 9–10.

16 The *Union Advocate* was founded in 1867 by W.C. Anslow and his brother J.J. Anslow. The paper had no local competition until the *North Shore Leader* began printing in 1906; see Edith MacAllister, *Newcastle on the Miramichi: A Brief History* (Newcastle, NB 1974), 10.

17 Copies of the three sole issues of the *Leader* (dated 23 Nov., 30 Nov., and 9 Dec. 1893) were preserved by Earl Macdonald of Newcastle, who presented them to Lord Beaverbrook in 1947. They were then turned over to the library at the University of New Brunswick.

18 In the *Union Advocate* of 22 Nov. 1893, W.C. Anslow is listed as owner. There is a similarity of style between Anslow's weekly and the *Leader*. Aitken went so far as to reprint a couple of shorter items that had already appeared in the *Union Advocate*. See the *Leader*, 9 Dec. 1893: 'Owing to the large number of X'mas advertisements and the Supplement to the Advocate the publication of this paper will be discontinued for some time. W. Max Aitken, Manager.'

19 Quoted in Taylor, *Beaverbrook*, 9–10.

20 This encounter is described in Lord Beaverbrook, *Friends: Sixty Years of Intimate Personal Relations with Richard Bedford Bennett* (London 1959), 3–10.

21 R.B. Bennett's early life in New Brunswick is reviewed in Beaverbrook, *Friends*, 1–19, and James H. Gray, *R.B. Bennett: The Calgary Years* (Toronto 1991), 3–23.

22 Dr Yorston, quoted in Beaverbrook, *My Early Life*, 50.

23 The last teacher's report for Max at Harkins Academy is dated 9 July 1895 (former Old Manse Library, teachers' reports).

24 In some 1905 correspondence with a lawyer he had hired to represent him in his attempt to be admitted to the New Brunswick bar, Aitken was unclear whether he had been articling under Tweedie or Bennett (Beaverbrook Papers, National Archives of Canada [NABK], reel A1774, 1905 correspondence with R.A. Lawlor).

25 Beaverbrook, *Friends*, 14; Gray, *R.B. Bennett*, 22. In a letter to Aitken of 12 June 1941 (HBK, A/224), Bennett recollected how '45 years ago I was a candi-

date for the office of Alderman in the newly created "Town" of Chatham, NB
... I was supported by a youth of some – 17 – years who with his bicycle hurried
many to the polls and was a factor, a real factor, in my election.'

26 R.B. Bennett Papers, University of New Brunswick (UNBEN), reel 444, notice
in the *Chatham World*, 18 Jan. 1897. Lemuel John Tweedie first became a
member of the New Brunswick legislature in the 1870s. He eventually
became premier of New Brunswick (1900–7) and lieutenant-governor (1907–
12); see *Encyclopedia Canadiana*, rev. ed. (Toronto 1977), 10:162.

27 Years later, Tweedie complained of Max that 'after he had been in my office
for a month I was not sure whether he was working for me or I for him'
(quoted in Taylor, *Beaverbrook*, 11).

28 Beaverbrook, *Friends*, 16–17.

29 In his investigation to see whether Aitken had the requisite years of articling
to apply for the New Brunswick bar, R.A. Lawlor concluded that Aitken had
served two years with Tweedie. This would put his departure from Newcastle
sometime in the summer of 1897 (NABK, reel A1774, 1905 correspondence
between Aitken and Lawlor).

30 According to A.J.P. Taylor's second-hand source, Aitken failed the Latin portion of the Dalhousie entrance exam (*Beaverbrook*, 10). 'One of Aitken's contemporaries claimed in his later years that Aitken had come to Halifax in
order to attend Dalhousie University but he was doing "so much boozing"
and was so short of money that he had to leave' (PANS, G.M. Robinson to
Michael Wardell, 25 July 1960). I am indebted to Barry Cahill for providing
me with a photocopy of this letter.

31 This is Corbett's recollection of Aitken's reply, quoted in Alan Wood, *The
True History of Lord Beaverbrook* (London 1965), 17.

32 Wood, *Lord Beaverbrook*, 17.

33 Letter, Rev. William Aitken to R.B. Bennett, 6 Dec. 1897 (HBK, A/218),
reprinted in Beaverbrook, *My Early Life*, 88–9, an extract of which appears in
Beaverbrook, *Friends*, 15–6.

34 Ibid.

35 Beaverbrook, *My Early Life*, 91–3.

36 While trying to amass evidence that he had articled for four years, Aitken
wrote to Bennett saying: 'I do not know how I am going to make up four
years to present to the Barrister's Society, but am sure that I was some time in
Lougheed & Bennett's office in Calgary' (NABK, reel A1774, Aitken to Bennett, 29 May 1905). There is no record of Bennett's reply. There is no evidence to support Aitken's contention and he abandoned the application a
short time later, which suggests that Bennett refused to help him out in making up the four years.

37 Gray, *R.B. Bennett*, 45–6.

38 In a letter to Aitken twenty years later, Bennett looked on the bowling alley incident with more nostalgic eyes: 'Lougheed and I were looking out the window the other day and I pointed to the building across the street where some 20 years ago Max Aitken with McLean was the proud proprietor of a bowling alley: I ventured to think and say that in no country at any time had a man been produced who had been able in a score of years to rise to [your] place and power ... from such small beginnings' (HBK, A/224, Bennett to Aitken, 6 Dec. 1918).

39 Many years later, Bennett reminisced about 'the youth of 19 who "looked after" the halfbreed vote in the Hotel of "Irish" at the Elbow Bridge' (HBK, A/224, Bennett to Aitken, 12 June 1941).

40 Lord Beaverbrook, *Courage: The Story of Sir James Dunn* (London 1962), 28–9.

41 For Dunn's early life, see Beaverbrook, *Courage*, 25–39, and Duncan McDowall, *Steel at the Sault: Francis H. Clergue, Sir James Dunn, and the Algoma Steel Corporation, 1901–1956* (Toronto 1984), 97–101.

42 Dunn's words and their alleged impact on Aitken can be found in Beaverbrook, *Friends*, 22, and *My Early Life*, 98.

43 The Presbyterian Church played a role second only to the Church of England in propagandizing in favour of Canadian participation in the Boer War; see Carman Miller, 'A Preliminary Analysis of the Socio-economic Composition of Canada's South African War Contingents,' *Histoire sociale/Social History* 8, no. 2 (Nov. 1975), 224–7. For Maritime support, see Robert Page, *The Boer War and Canadian Imperialism* (Ottawa 1987), 11.

44 Beaverbrook, *My Early Life*, 103. A.J.P. Taylor speculates that Aitken's offer of enlistment may have been rejected on account of his already evident poor health (*Beaverbrook*, 13).

45 Glenbow Archives (Calgary), R.B. Bennett Papers, M126/2, Aitken to Bennett, 10 Nov. and [?] Nov. 1899. He worked for the Saint John branch of the Union Assurance Company of London, England.

46 Some evidence of Aitken's drinking comes from his boyhood friend Will Corbett, who remembered when Aitken returned to Newcastle from his adventures in western Canada. Corbett was visiting with Aitken when Aitken asked his mother if there was anything in the house for them to drink. 'Needless to say,' Corbett explained, 'we did not receive anything to drink' (Beaverbrook Papers, University of New Brunswick [UNBK], 71a/3, Will Corbett to Aitken, no date but likely sometime in 1956).

47 Beaverbrook, *My Early Life*, 104.

48 E.M. Archibald, 'Electric Railway System of Halifax, N.S.,' *Street Railway Journal (SRJ)*, 5 May 1900, 433–6; *Monetary Times (MT)*, 16 Nov. 1900, 621; *MT*,

8 Mar. 1901, 1176; and *Annual Financial Review* (*AFR*) 1 (July 1901), 182, 284. The role of B.F. Pearson and W.B. Ross in Dominion Coal and Dominion Iron and Steel is touched on in David Frank, 'The Cape Breton Coal Industry and the Rise and Fall of the British Empire Steel Corporation,' *Acadiensis* 7, no. 1 (Autumn 1977), 11–12, and Don Macgillivray, 'Henry Melville Whitney Comes to Cape Breton: The Saga of a Gilded Age Entrepreneur,' *Acadiensis* 9, no. 1 (Autumn 1979), 51–66.

49 See 'The New Railway, Light and Power Enterprise in Sao Paulo, Brazil,' *SRJ*, July 1899, 449–51; notes on Demerara Electric Company in *SRJ*, Dec. 1899, 75, and 13 Jan. 1900, iii; and 'The Electric Railways of Havana,' *SRJ*, 4 Aug. 1900, 724–31. Ross and Pearson were also the main promoters behind the Cape Breton Electric Tramway & Power Company (*SRJ*, 19 May 1900, vi). See also *Canadian Journal of Commerce* (*CJC*), 17 Nov. 1899, 1309.

50 Beaverbrook, *My Early Life*, 64; Chisholm and Davie, *Beaverbrook*, 35.

51 Beaverbrook, *My Early Life*, 114. Brazilian Traction is referred to in Aitken's autobiography (64) and in Chisholm and Davie, *Beaverbrook* (35), even though the company was not formed until 1911.

52 See entries for B.F. Pearson and W.B. Ross in Henry J. Morgan, *Canadian Men and Women of the Time*, 1st ed. (Toronto 1898; hereafter *CMW*1), 892, 975; and *The Canadian Directory of Parliament, 1867–1967* (Ottawa 1968; hereafter *CDP*), 510–11. B.F. Pearson's promoting career was summarized in the *Bluenose*, 27 Oct. 1900, 11, and on page 28 of the Album of the Nova Scotia Power Co., Ltd. (PANS, MG9, vol. 225).

53 Beaverbrook, *My Early Life*, 116.

54 PANS, H. Gerald Stairs, 'The Stairs of Halifax,' 135. I am indebted to Barry Cahill of PANS for making me aware of this manuscript family history with this most interesting anecdote.

55 Beaverbrook, *My Early Life*, 117.

56 Much of the biographical information concerning the Stairs family was culled from James D. Frost, 'The Business and Political Careers of John F. Stairs of Halifax' (BA honours essay, Dalhousie University, 1976), and J.B. Cahill's entry for John Fitzwilliam Stairs in the *Dictionary of Canadian Biography* (*DCB*), vol. 13.

57 T.W. Acheson, 'The National Policy and the Industrialization of the Maritimes, 1880–1910,' *Acadiensis* 1, no. 2 (Spring 1972), 19.

58 Frost, 'John F. Stairs', 56–8, 68, and Cahill, 'Stairs.' See also *MT*, 23 Jan. 1891, 897; *MT*, 4 Aug. 1893, 131; and *MT*, 7 Dec. 1900, 720.

59 PANS, Cantley Papers, MG1, vol. 168, file 10, John F. Stairs to T. Cantley, 30 May 1894; PANS, James M. Cameron Papers, vol. 3225, file 3, Graham Fraser (general manager of New Glasgow Iron, Coal and Railway Company

and the Nova Scotia Steel Company) to J.F. Stairs, 11 May 1894. See also L.D. McCann, 'The Mercantile-Industrial Transition in the Metal Towns of Pictou County, 1857–1931,' *Acadiensis* 10, no. 2 (Spring 1981).

60 *MT*, 9 Mar. 1906, 1200; Halifax *Herald*, 2 Apr. 1908, 1. George Stairs is first identified with the Dartmouth Ropeworks in the 1881–2 edition of *McAlpine's Halifax City Directory*, 277.

61 Halifax *Morning Herald*, 3 Nov. 1879, quoted in Frost, 'John F. Stairs,' 4.

62 *CDP*, 546; Cahill, 'Stairs.'

63 On patronage generally during this era, see Gordon T. Stewart, 'Political Patronage under Macdonald and Laurier, 1878–1911,' *American Review of Canadian Studies*, 10, no. 1 (Spring 1980).

64 See Ken Ramstead's discussion of Stairs in 'The "Eye-Witness": Lord Beaverbrook and "Canada in Flanders,"' *The Register* 5, no. 2 (1984), 299.

65 For how Canadians viewed imperial federation, see Carl Berger, *The Sense of Power: Studies in the Ideas of Canadian Imperialism, 1867–1914* (Toronto 1970); Robert J.D. Page, 'Canada and the Imperial Idea in the Boer War Years,' and Douglas Cole, 'Canada's "Nationalist" Imperialists,' *Journal of Canadian Studies* 5, no. 3 (Aug. 1970); and Terry Cook, 'George R. Parkin and the Concept of Britannic Idealism,' *Journal of Canadian Studies* 10, no. 3 (Aug. 1975).

66 Taylor, *Beaverbrook*, xiv and chaps. 11–13; Chisholm and Davie, *Beaverbrook*, 275–306; and Jerry M. Carlton, 'Beaverbrook's Split Imperial Personality: Canada, Britain, and the Empire Free Trade Movement of 1929–1931,' *Historian* 37, no. 1 (1974).

67 *CMW*1, 137, 442, and 2nd ed. (Toronto 1912; hereafter *CMW*2), 505.

68 *CMW*1, 181–2; *CDP*, 87; and *Encyclopedia Canadiana* 1:161.

69 W.D. March, 'Stewart, John James,' *DCB* 13:990–1; and Robert Craig Brown, *Robert Laird Borden: A Biography*, vol. 1, *1854–1914* (Toronto 1975), 29–30. As J.B. Cahill notes in his article on John Fitzwilliam Stairs (*DCB* 13:980), Stairs's 'reasons for standing down in favour of Borden are obscure.'

70 According to the *CJC*'s sketch of R.E. Harris (7 Feb. 1907, 260–1), Harris first articled under J.M Owens, KC, at Annapolis Royal and then moved to Halifax to continue his studies in the office of Thompson and Borden. On the advice of his brother, who was practising medicine in Yarmouth, Harris moved there to set up his own law firm. Early biographical details concerning R.E. Harris are drawn from entries in *CMW*1, 442, *CMW*2, 505, and *Encyclopedia Canadiana* 5:91.

71 Apparently, Harris was one of the youngest lawyer's ever appointed KC in Canada; see *Who's Who in Canada*, 1928–29 (Toronto 1929), 245.

72 PANS, Justice R.H. Graham portrait of Robert E. Harris, MG 100, vol. 161, no. 52.

73 *Who's Who in Canada, 1928–29*, 245.

74 The list of provisional directors of Eastern Trust, incorporated with a capital of $200,000, also included T.E. Kenny, Thomas Ritchie, J.C. Mackintosh, G.J. Troop, and J.W. Allison (*MT*, 7 Apr. 1893, 1188).

75 Gregory P. Marchildon, 'International Corporate Law from a Maritime Base: The Halifax Firm of Harris, Henry, and Cahan,' in Carol Wilton, ed., *Beyond the Law: Lawyers and Business in Canada, 1830 to 1930* (Toronto 1990). The firm eventually became known as Stewart, MacKeen & Covert, and most recently as Stewart McKelvey Stirling and Scales.

76 W.B. Ross was closely associated with W.S. Fielding and the Liberal Party until 1908, when he left the party over a dispute concerning a judicial appointment. In 1912 Ross was appointed to the Senate by Robert Borden, also a renegade Liberal, and in 1926 Ross became Conservative leader in the Senate, a position he held until his death on 10 January 1929 (*Halifax Chronicle*, 11 Jan. 1929, 1, 4).

77 Macgillivray, 'Henry Melville Whitney Comes to Cape Breton,' 55–6. See Colin D. Howell, 'W.S. Fielding and the Liberal Party in Nova Scotia, 1891–1896,' *Acadiensis* 3, no. 2 (Spring 1974), for general background on Fielding's provincial government.

78 McGillivray, 'Henry Melville Whitney Comes to Cape Breton,' 58–67.

79 HBK, A/20, Aitken to N.B. McKelvie of Hayden Stone & Co., 8 Mar. 1905.

80 As quoted on the Montreal Stock Exchange, Dominion Iron and Steel common shares dropped from a high of $72 in April 1902 to a low of $6.50 in October 1903, while Scotia declined from a high of $119 to a low of $68 at the same time (*AFR* 5 [July 1905], 142, 174). On Scotia's problems, see Kris Inwood, 'Local Control, Resources and the Nova Scotia Steel and Coal Company,' Canadian Historical Association (CHA), *Historical Papers* (1986), 254–82.

81 Representing the family's holdings, George Stairs was on the board of the Union Bank (*AFR* 3 [July 1903], 116).

82 These joint ventures included the Robb Engineering Co. and the Nova Scotia Shipping Co. (*MT*, 23 Nov. 1900, 652, and 3 Oct. 1902, 422).

83 *CMW* 2, 892, 975; *CDP*, 510; obituary of William B. Ross, Halifax *Morning Chronicle*, 11 Jan. 1929.

84 In 1903 B.F. Pearson sold his entire interest in Trinidad Electric to W.B. Ross and resigned as secretary and director (HBK, A/6, Aitken to Ross, 11 Dec. 1903; and *AFR* 4 [July 1904], 349).

85 The only government or municipal bond rate data extending back to the first decade of the twentieth century are Province of Ontario bond yields, which range from a low of 3.61 to a high of 3.79 from 1900 to 1906; see M.C. Urqu-

hart and K.A.H. Buckley, eds., *Historical Statistics of Canada* (Cambridge 1965), 275.

86 HBK, G/19/15, memorandum concerning the Trinidad Electric Co. Ltd, no date (but before the creation of the RSC), and RSC's Canadian bond prospectus for the Trinidad Electric Company, 1905; Christopher Armstrong and H.V. Nelles, *Southern Exposure: Canadian Promoters in Latin America and the Caribbean, 1896–1930* (Toronto 1988), 108.

87 In his old age, Aitken had convinced himself that the $10,000 fee he had received from the Union Bank of Halifax for acquiring the Commercial Bank of Windsor was his seed money for the Royal Securities Corporation (UNBK, 107/1c, Aitken to Alan Gordon [president, RSC], 9 Feb. 1964).

88 Beaverbrook, *My Early Life*, 117. The anecdotal version allegedly recounted by John F. Stairs's grandson and quoted in Chisholm and Davie, *Beaverbrook*, 36, is entertaining but probably not very reliable. Chisholm and Davie (39) also recount Aitken's subsequent unsuccessful attempt to purchase Alexander Gibson's lumber business.

89 Extract of letter from Rev. William Aitken to R.B. Bennett (HBK, A/218), quoted in Beaverbrook, *My Early Life*, 88–9.

90 Former Old Manse Library, Rev. William Aitken to Max Aitken, 19 Sept. 1902.

91 This discussion is based on chaps. 4, 8, 9, and 14 of E.P. Neufeld, *The Financial System of Canada: Its Growth and Development* (Toronto 1972).

92 *MT*, 3 Feb. 1905, 1022. A brief history of the origins of the Dominion Securities Corporation can be found in Michael Bliss, *A Canadian Millionaire: The Life and Business Times of Sir Joseph Flavelle, Bart., 1858–1939* (Toronto 1992), 69.

93 *Journals of the Nova Scotia House of Assembly* (Halifax 1904), app. 12, Provincial Secretary's Report for 1903, 56–9. See also PANS, RG73, vol. 18, registry of joint stock companies under Nova Scotia Companies Act, ledger for the RSC. The RSC may actually have started with a capital of less than $10,000. According to the first meeting of incorporation in the RSC minutes (in the possession of Merrill Lynch Canada Inc., Toronto), 26 May 1903, J.F. Stairs purchased twenty-nine shares for $2,900, while Harris, Cahan, and Aitken each purchased nineteen shares for a total of $5,700, and George Stairs purchased ten shares for $1,000. Aitken wrote the minutes and signed as 'secretary protem,' in other words as interim or temporary secretary.

94 HBK, A/3, Harris to Aitken, 27 May 1903, and A/107, Aitken to Killam, 25 Sept. 1908.

95 Inwood, 'Local Control,' 256–9. See also Marchildon, 'International Corporate Law,' 210–18, and 'John F. Stairs, Max Aitken and the Scotia Group:

Finance Capital and Industrial Decline in the Maritimes, 1890–1914,' in Kris Inwood, ed., *Farm, Factory and Fortune: New Studies in the Economic History of the Maritime Provinces* (Fredericton 1993).

96 HBK, A/3, June 1903 correspondence between Aitken and Hayden Stone & Co. of 87 Milk Street, Boston.

97 HBK, A/10, Aitken to Burnett & Co., 5 Aug. 1904; and Nova Scotia Steel and Coal 1904 annual report, *AFR* 5 (July 1905), 165.

98 The TSE high/low average for Scotia common in April 1904 was $77; in May, it had dropped to $74, and in June to about $72. MSE figures are roughly comparable. See *AFR* 5 (July 1905), 170.

99 HBK, A/16, Aitken to W.D. Ross, 5 Aug. 1904.

100 HBK, A/12, Aitken to R.E. Harris, 17 Sept. 1904.

101 See McDowall, *Steel at the Sault*, chaps. 2, 3.

102 Aitken recounted in *My Early Life* (135): 'We were together in the morning at the King Edward Hotel in Toronto. Mr. Stairs was negotiating for the sale of bonds in the Nova Scotia Steel and Coal Co. The blow fell before he had begun to carry out his task. During the month [actually 17 days] that elapsed between the first attack and his death I remained in constant attendance.'

103 The relationship between Massey and Scotia Steel went back to the 1880s; see PANS, Cantley Papers, MG1, vol. 168, file 5, Graham Fraser to Massey Manufacturing Co., 30 Sept. 1886, and A. Harris, Son & Co., to the Nova Scotia Steel Co., 4 Oct. 1886.

104 HBK, A/12, telegram, Aitken and W.D. Ross to G. Stairs, R.E. Harris, and other Scotia directors, 23 Sept. 1904.

105 HBK, A/12, telegram, R.E. Harris to Aitken (Metropolitan Bank, Toronto), 24 Sept. 1904.

106 HBK, A/12, Aitken to Jaffray, 31 Oct. 1904.

107 When Aitken wrote to John F. Stairs's grandson on 1 Sept. 1947 to comfort him on the death of his father, he stated: 'At any rate your father was spared the painful death which came to your grandfather through a weakness in his heart' (UNBK, 46a/1d, Aitken to J.F. Stairs).

108 Cahill, 'Stairs.'

3: Caribbean Adventurer

1 Three weeks after J.F. Stairs's funeral, a Montreal broker by the name of C. Simpson Garland said that he had 'heard several people in Toronto speak with admiration of the comfort and support you were to his family at the time' (Beaverbrook Papers, House of Lords Record Office [HBK], A/11, C. Simpson Garland to Aitken, 13 Oct. 1904.

2 Max chose 'What doth the Lord require of thee, but to do justly, and to love mercy, and to walk humbly with thy God'; see Ann Chisholm and Michael Davie, *Beaverbrook: A Life* (London 1992), 42. This epitaph is not, however, inscribed on John F. Stairs's gravestone in Halifax's Fairview Cemetery.

3 Lord Beaverbrook, *My Early Years* (Fredericton 1965), 136–7.

4 In one contemporary article featuring Aitken, most thought 'he was dead when Stairs died'; see James Grant, 'Sir Maxwell Aitken,' *Maclean's*, Sept. 1911, 148.

5 HBK, A/16, Aitken to W.D. Ross, 30 Sept. 1904.

6 HBK, A/27 Aitken to Ross, 4 July 1905, and A/32, Aitken to Dr M.A. Curry, 26 Nov. 1906, in which it is revealed that his Halifax physician believed his sickness 'was wholly brought about by overwork and hallucinations with possibly too great business strain' following John F. Stairs's death.

7 HBK, A/12, Aitken to Jaffray, 31 Oct. 1904.

8 John F. Stairs financially reorganized Robb Engineering in 1900 and joined the board. Two years later, Stairs and Aitken helped establish the Robb-Mumford company in Framingham, Mass. For their participation, Stairs received 125 shares while Aitken received 350 (out of a total of 1,475 shares) in Robb-Mumford (Dalhousie University Archives [DAL], Robb Engineering Company Papers, MS 4–14, miscellaneous papers box, historical employees file, J.A. Mumford and D.W. Robb to G.W. Cole, 17 Mar. 1903).

9 HBK, A/15, Aitken to J.C. Mackintosh, 19 Oct. 1904, and Aitken to D.W. Robb, 11 Nov. 1904; HBK, A/12, D.W. Robb to R.E. Harris, 4 Nov. 1904.

10 Aitken's views on Maritime industry are set out more fully in Gregory P. Marchildon, 'John F. Stairs, Max Aitken and the Scotia Group: Finance Capitalism and Industrial Decline in the Maritimes, 1890–1914,' in Kris Inwood, ed., *Farm, Factory and Fortune: New Studies in the Economic History of the Maritime Provinces* (Fredericton 1993).

11 HBK, A/14, W.B. Ross to Aitken, 10 Oct. 1904, and reply [no date]; HBK, A/10, and Aitken to F.C. Clarke, 21 Nov. 1904.

12 At Scotia's 1904–5 shareholders' meeting, J.C. Mackintosh asked whether 'any fresh securities would require to be marketed' to complete the works at Sydney Mines. Harris, as the new president of Scotia, replied that 'while it was rather difficult to tell exactly what amount would be necessary to complete the Sydney Mines plant, it was not proposed to make any fresh issue of securities in that connection'; see *Annual Financial Review* (*AFR*) 5 (July 1905), 166–7.

13 The Merchants' Bank of Halifax changed its name to the Royal Bank of Canada in January 1901. Although a Halifax group remained in control, the general manager, Edson L. Pease, was directing the Royal Bank from its

Montreal office by this time; see *Monetary Times* (*MT*), 4 Jan. 1901, 862, and 19 July 1901, 67; *AFR*, 1 (July 1901), 38, 50; and Duncan McDowall, *Quick to the Frontier: Canada's Royal Bank* (Toronto 1993), 74–5. In 1900 the Bank of Nova Scotia moved its general office to Toronto, and although its nominal head office remained in Halifax, the former became the effective centre of its operations; see James D. Frost, 'The "Nationalization" of the Bank of Nova Scotia, 1880–1910,' *Acadiensis* 12, no. 1 (Autumn 1982), 21; *MT*, 3 July 1903, 19.

14 The details of the near failure of the People's Bank because of fraudulent collateral and the subsequent cover-up by the bank's officials is recounted in Marchildon, 'Scotia Group,' 203–4.

15 The rate agreed was eleven shares of People's stock for each Bank of Montreal share (HBK, A/20, Aitken to Imperial Life Assurance, 16 May 1905).

16 HBK, G/1/1, Aitken to W.D. Ross, 14 March 1905.

17 HBK, A/20, Aitken to James A. Harding, 7 Oct. 1905, and A/28, Van Horne to Aitken, 22 Oct. 1905. See also *Street Railway Journal* (*SRJ*), 27 Oct. 1900, v–vi; 1 Dec. 1900, 1151; and 6 Apr. 1901, 419.

18 When the Mexican Light and Power Company was incorporated in 1902, for example, Clouston became a member of the board of directors, and his personal secretary from the Bank of Montreal, A.R. Doble (later, manager of the RSC), was appointed secretary. Clouston was joined on the Mexican board by George A. Drummond, a fellow director and soon to be president (1905–10) of the Bank of Montreal. See *AFR*, 3 (July 1903), 264; and Merrill Denison, *Canada's First Bank: A History of the Bank of Montreal* (Toronto 1967), vol. 2, app. B.

19 See Christopher Armstrong and H.V. Nelles, *Southern Exposure: Canadian Promoters in Latin America and the Caribbean, 1896–1930* (Toronto 1988) chap. 2, and Duncan McDowall, *The Light: Brazilian Traction, Light and Power Company Limited, 1899–1945* (Toronto 1988) chaps. 1–2. The Havana Traction Company promotion of 1899 included Van Horne, Cox, Mackenzie, and Nicholls among others (*Canadian Journal of Commerce* [*CJC*], 20 Oct. 1899, 1012). The Havana Street Railway company's main promoters were B.F. Pearson, W.B. Ross, and W.H. Covert (*MT*, 17 Mar. 1899, 1218). B.F. Pearson joined William Mackenzie in the São Paulo venture (*SRJ*, July 1899, 449–51).

20 Armstrong and Nelles, *Southern Exposure*, 38. Accompanied by W.B. Chapman and T.P. Brothers who represented the Montreal investors, Cahan's trip to Georgetown resulted in the creation of the Demerara Electric Company (1899) under the control of Van Horne (who became its first president) and his Montreal interests, although both B.F. Pearson and David MacKeen (the first general manager of the Halifax Electric Tramway Company) of Halifax

were prominent in the original Demerara group. Cahan's subsequent trip to Port of Spain resulted in the creation of the Trinidad Electric Company under the control of the Halifax promoters, including B.F. Pearson, W.B. Ross, and J.F. Stairs (*CJC*, 17 Nov. 1899, 1309; *CJC*, 29 Dec. 1899, 1780; *CJC*, 26 Jan. 1900, 280; *SRJ*, 13 Jan. 1900, iii; *SRJ*, 5 May 1900, 433–6; *SRJ*, 1 Dec. 1900, 1151; and Public Archives of Nova Scotia [PANS], MG9, vol. 225, album of the Nova Scotia Power Co., Ltd., 130).

21 Sometime between March and June 1901, Van Horne and his Montreal friends dropped out of the project, so the first board was an all-Halifax affair: J.F. Stairs, R.E. Harris, W.B. Ross, B.F. Pearson, W. Gordon-Gordon, and C. Archibald. There was no mention of Dr. Pearson after June 1901. See *SRJ*, 16 Mar. 1901, iv; 23 Mar. 1901, viii; 8 June 1901, viii; and 26 Sept. 1903, 621.

22 HBK, A/27, Aitken to W.D. Ross, 13 July 1905.

23 Armstrong and Nelles, *Southern Exposure* 85–8.

24 McDowall, *The Light* 66. Aitken's inability to set up the Hamilton-Galt interurban railway system in 1906 was a product of the power of two of Dr Pearson's most powerful associates, Fred Nichols and Alexander Mackenzie (HBK, A/42, Aitken to Gossler, 30 Mar. 1906, and Aitken is James W. Baillie, 31 Mar. 1906).

25 W.P. Plummer officially held himself out as a general export and commission agent and, on his letterhead, advertised that he was the principal agent for Trinidad Electric, Sao Paulo Tramway, Light & Power, and Rio de Janeiro Tramway, Light & Power (HBK, A/23, Plummer to Aitken, 29 Dec. 1905).

26 HBK, A/24, memorandum, Aitken to himself, 25 May 1905, and A/36, Aitken to 'The Matanzas Syndicate,' 20 Feb. 1906.

27 HBK, A/26, Aitken to W.D. Ross, 3 June 1905.

28 *CMW*2, 717; *The Canadian Directory of Parliament, 1867–1967* (Ottawa 1968, hereafter *CDP*), 423–4; HBK, A/27, A.K. Maclean to W.D. Ross, 30 Oct. 1905.

29 George E. Drummond, quoted in Harris to Aitken, 17 Aug. 1905 (HBK, A/20). George Drummond was in partnership with his younger brother, Thomas J. Drummond, and J.T. McCall under the firm name of D. McCall & Co., iron and steel merchants. The firm went on to establish the Canadian Iron Furnace Co., Ltd., the Montreal Pipe Foundry Co., the Canadian Iron & Foundry, Ltd., and the Londonderry Iron & Mining Co., Ltd (National Archives of Canada [NA], Drummond Family Papers, MG30/A88/1/1; *CMW*2, 345).

30 HBK, A/20, Aitken to James A. Harding, 7 Oct. 1905.

31 *SRJ*, 30 Nov. 1901, 16; McDowall, *The Light*, 61–5; Armstrong and Nelles, *Southern Exposure*, 43–4.

32 HBK, A/28, Aitken to Teele, 6 Dec. 1905.

33 Before joining Demerara in 1900, Bruce had been chief engineer of the Consolidated Traction Company of Pittsburgh (*SRJ*, 6 Apr. 1901, 419).

34 HBK, A/28, Aitken to Teele, 6 Dec. 1905, and A/29, and Bruce to Aitken, 2 Apr. 1906. H.B. Bruce was a partner in 'Rockwell & Bruce, Engineers and Constructors, New York City, Designers and constructors of complete electric plants and sub-stations, specialists in construction of high tension transmission and catenary suspension trolley lines and rail bonding.'

35 HBK, A/28, Aitken to Teele, 27 Dec. 1905.

36 HBK, A/28, Teele to Aitken, 14 Nov. 1905.

37 HBK, A/19, Aitken to A.R. Doble, 28 Oct. 1905.

38 HBK, A/20, Aitken to James A. Harding, 7 Oct. 1905.

39 HBK, A/28, Aitken to Van Horne, 16 Nov. 1905.

40 HBK, A/23, Aitken to W.P. Plummer, 6 Dec. 1905. According to McDowall (*The Light*, 64), Plummer was 'the linchpin' of the whole Pearson organization and was Dr Pearson's personal secretary during the 1890s.

41 HBK, A/38, Aitken to W.P. Plummer, 16 Jan. 1906.

42 HBK, A/33, Aitken to P.G. Gossler, vice-president of J.G. White & Co., New York, 11 Jan. 1906.

43 HBK, A/24, W.B. Ross to Aitken, 5 Dec. 1905, and A/20, and J.A. Harding to Aitken, 26 Dec. 1905. Given the very bigoted nature of Maclean's reports on most of the propositions, his perception of Venezuela in general could be considered generous: 'Everything that I have seen in Venezuela indicates progressiveness found only in Northern countries. While they have their revolutions, I imagine foreign capital is safe if it minds it's [*sic*] own business' (HBK, A/27, A.K. Maclean to W.D. Ross, 30 Oct. 1905).

44 HBK, A/28, Aitken to Teele, 6 Dec. 1905.

45 HBK, Aitken's 1905 correspondence with Teele and Van Horne (A/28), with A.O. Granger, Nathaniel Granger, and J.G. White & Co (A/20), with E.M. Cravath (A/18), and with W.P. Plummer (A/23).

46 HBK, A/32, Aitken (Montreal) to W.B. Ross (Halifax), 11 Jan. 1906.

47 HBK, A/32, Aitken to Cahan (Mexico City), 18 Jan. 1906.

48 The engagement was announced in the newspapers on 28 December 1905, and they were married one month later, although Max did not set the exact date for the wedding until the last minute. Nesbitt reveals that he only found out about the wedding because of a notice in the *Montreal Star* two evenings before. See HBK, A/17, Allen to Aitken, 28 Dec. 1905; A/38, Nesbitt to Aitken, 25 Jan. 1906; and A/33, S.A. Finley to Aitken, 30 Jan. 1906.

49 According to the Saint John *Globe*, 6 Jan. 1913, Charles Drury became a colonel in 1905, the year he was made commandant of the Maritime provinces, and in June the following year he became the first Canadian governor of the

military garrison at Halifax. When he died in 1913, he was a major general (Beaverbrook Papers, University of New Brunswick [UNBK], 71a/4).

50 See A.J.P. Taylor, *Beaverbrook* (New York 1972), 25, where he states that there is 'some evidence that the Drury family did not welcome the rough young adventurer at all warmly, until softened later by the flow of his bounty.' Taylor does not explain what this evidence is, and I could find none myself, but this seems a logical inference given the Drury family's circumstances, their position in Halifax society relative to Aitken's position, and the fact that Aitken hired Gladys's brother, Victor Montague Drury, in 1909, perhaps to curry favour with the family. By 1914, Victor was the manager of the RSC's Montreal office, and in 1919 he became the vice-president of the RSC. See *Encyclopedia Canadiana*, rev. ed. (Toronto 1977), 3:307.

51 The *Morning Chronicle*'s description, quoted in F.A. Mackenzie, *Beaverbrook: An Authentic Biography of the Right Hon. Lord Beaverbrook* (London 1931), 33–4

52 This was a passage in the original draft of Lord Beaverbrook's autobiography *My Early Life* but was later removed. See Taylor, *Beaverbrook*, 24–5.

53 According to the *Cuba Review* (Dec. 1905, 12), United Railways' 87 km journey from Havana to Matanzas was one of the most scenic in the country.

54 HBK, A/36, Aitken (Matanzas, Cuba) to 'The Matanzas Syndicate' (Halifax), 20 Feb. 1906.

55 The *SRJ* (Nov. 1898, 720) warned U.S. investors to refrain from moving to Cuba until the island's 'terribly unsanitary conditions' were 'thoroughly cleaned up' by the occupation authorities.

56 See chap. 3 of Louis A. Pérez, Jr, *Cuba under the Platt Amendment, 1902–1934* (Pittsburgh 1986).

57 Quoted in Louis A. Pérez, Jr, *Cuba and the United States: Ties of Singular Intimacy* (Athens, Ga. 1990), 118.

58 Quoted in Armstrong and Nelles, *Southern Exposure*, 276.

59 Florence J. Stoddard, 'The Canadian Invasion of Cuba,' *Busy Man's Magazine* [*Maclean's*], Feb. 1910, 33–9. See also early turn- of-the-century issues of the *SRJ* and the *Cuba Review*; and Armstrong and Nelles, *Southern Exposure*, 24, 36–40.

60 HBK, A/36, Aitken to 'The Matanzas Syndicate,' 20 Feb. 1906.

61 Ibid., and HBK, A/33, Aitken to P.G. Gossler, New York, 8 May 1906.

62 *Cuba Bulletin* [later *Cuba Review*], Jan. 1904, 6.

63 Contemporary population statistics on Camagüey vary considerably. The *Cuba Review* of Jan. 1908 (20–1), states 35,000, while that same magazine only eighteen months later (Aug. 1909, 16) gives an estimate of 60,000.

64 HBK, A/43, Teele to Aitken, 12 Apr. 1906.

65 HBK, A/41, W.D. Ross to Aitken, 13 Mar. 1906.

66 HBK, A/36, Aitken (Halifax) to C.E. Mackenzie, manager of the Royal Bank of Canada branch in Matanzas, 15 Mar. 1906, and A/34, Aitken to R.E. Harris, 2 Apr. 1906.

67 HBK, A/36, Aitken to C.E. Mackenzie, 15 Mar. 1906.

68 HBK, A/43, Aitken to Teele, 27 Apr. 1906.

69 HBK, A/33, Aitken to P.G. Gossler, 8 May 1906.

70 C. Lintern Sibley, 'Van Horne and His Cuban Railway,' *Canadian Magazine* 41, no. 5 (Sept. 1913), 444–51.

71 Incorporated in New Jersey with a share capital of $8 million, the Cuba Company directorate was made up almost entirely of Americans, including two generals who perhaps had participated in the occupation following the Spanish-American War (*SRJ*, 5 May 1900, 436).

72 *Cuba Review*, July 1905, 12.

73 By 1906, the Royal Bank of Canada, with its seven branches in Havana, Cardenas, Cienfuegos, Manzanillo, Santiago, Matanzas and Camagüey, was described by the *Cuba Review* (Sept. 1907, 26, and Nov. 1907, 19) as the 'single largest financial power' on the island.

74 HBK, A/36, Aitken to C.E. Mackenzie, 15 Mar. 1905.

75 Puerto Príncipe was the original name for the city of Camagüey, which was founded in 1514 as Santa Maria de Puerto Príncipe, at the site of present-day Nuevitas on Cuba's north coast. In 1528 the city was moved inland to the amerindian village of Camagüey.

76 HBK, A/34, Aitken to R.E. Harris, 26 Apr. 1906.

77 HBK, A/34, Aitken to Harris, 25 Apr. 1906.

78 HBK, A/43, Aitken to Teele, 12 Apr. 1906.

79 HBK, A/43, Teele (Trinidad) to Aitken (c/o Royal Bank of Canada, Havana), 12 Apr. 1906.

80 This was intended to be the holding company for the Camaguey Electric Company, the Camaguey Street Railway Company, and the Nova Scotia Land Company (HBK, A/29, Aitken to F.T. Burrill, 17 Oct. 1906).

81 HBK, A/43, Aitken to Teele, 27 Apr. 1906.

82 HBK, A/38, Nesbitt to Aitken, 2 June 1906; A/41, Aitken to W.D. Ross, 11 June 1906; and A/43, Aitken to Teele, 12 June 1906.

83 HBK, A/43, Aitken to Teele, 12 June 1906.

84 HBK, A/43, Teele to Aitken, 13 June 1906.

85 On the Canadian side of the story, see Stephen J. Randall, 'The Development of Canadian Business in Puerto Rico,' *Revista/Review Interamericana* 7 (1977), 5–20.

86 James L. Dietz, *Economic History of Puerto Rico: Institutional Change and Capitalist Development* (Princeton 1986) 85–92.

87 *SRJ,* Jan. 1899, 52.

88 In 1898, J.G. White & Co. bought the steam railway on the island. A few months later, the firm bought a seven-mile interurban railway connecting the capital, San Juan, with the prosperous suburb of Rio Piedras. At that time, the population of Rio Piedras was 12,000 while that of San Juan proper was estimated to be 30,000 (*SRJ,* Jan. 1899, 52).

89 HBK, A/41, Aitken to W.D. Ross, 22 June 1906.

90 *SRJ,* 30 Nov. 1901, 16.

91 HBK, A/41, Aitken to W.D. Ross, 22 June 1906.

92 HBK, A/41, W.D. Ross to Aitken, 1 Aug. 1906.

93 HBK, A/29, report to the RSC on the San Juan Light & Tramway Co., author unknown, describing inspection tour of July 1906 but dated 11 Sept. 1906.

94 *Porto Rico Review,* 13 Oct. 1906, 9, announced the negotiations between the 'Canadian capitalists' and J.G. White and Company.

95 Dietz, *Economic History of Puerto Rico,* 85.

4: Building the Royal Securities Corporation

1 Ranald C. Michie estimates that only 1.35 per cent of the Canadian population, a total of 114,125, invested in stocks and bonds by 1913. He speculates that the group was proportionally small because of the attractiveness of non-security investments such as mortgages. See 'The Canadian Securities Market, 1850–1914,' *Business History Review* 62, no. 1 (Spring 1988), 48.

2 Michael Edelstein, *Overseas Investment in the Age of High Imperialism: The United Kingdom, 1850–1914* (London 1982), 3. See the discussion in Gregory P. Marchildon, 'British Investment Banking and Industrial Decline before the Great War: A Case Study of Capital Outflow to Canadian Industry,' *Business History* 33, no. 3 (July 1991), 72–4.

3 Lance E. Davis and Robert A. Huttenback, 'The Export of British Finance, 1865–1914,' *Journal of Imperial and Commonwealth History* 13, no. 3 (May 1985).

4 Edelstein, *Overseas Investment,* 7.

5 For the Canadian financiers and firms involved in this transatlantic capital flow, see Gregory P. Marchildon, '"Hands across the Water": Canadian Industrial Financiers in the City of London, 1905–20,' *Business History* 34, no. 3 (July 1992), 69–79.

6 At least this is Aitken's recollection many years later; see Lord Beaverbrook, *My Early Life* (Fredericton 1965), 130.

7 Beaverbrook Papers, House of Lords Record Office (HBK), A/26, Aitken to W.D. Ross, 3 Jan. 1905.

8 Allan E. Marble, 'Farrell, Edward,' *Dictionary of Canadian Biography* (*DCB*), 13:334–5.

9 HBK, A/17, Aitken to B.G. Burrill, 5 Apr. 1905.

10 HBK, A/19, Farrell to Aitken, 7 Dec. 1905. Gerald Farrell was born into a well-off Halifax family; his father was a well-known physician and Liberal politician who had been defeated in the 1891 by J.F. Stairs (Marble, 'Farrell'). A superb athlete, Farrell had won the Maritime provinces' half-mile run in 1899 and was selected to represent Canada in international cricket. In his early twenties, Farrell went to South Africa in 1902, after which he toured great Britain as the vice-captain of the 'Canadian Rugby football fifteen.' See Henry J. Morgan, *Canadian Men and Women of the Time*, 2nd ed. (Toronto 1912; hereafter *CMW2*), 387.

11 HBK, A/26, Aitken to W.D. Ross, 3 Jan. 1905.

12 In the spring of 1904, for example, he was solicited by a prominent Montreal businessman about his interest in becoming the manager of a small chartered bank. Aitken politely declined the offer but asked to be kept in mind for the future. See HBK, A/11, M.S. Foley (editor and proprietor of the *CJC*, St James Street, Montreal) to Aitken, 12 Apr. 1904, and reply, 15 Apr. 1904.

13 Entries for William Donald Ross in *CMW2*, 975, and *Encyclopedia Canadiana*, rev. ed. (Toronto 1977), 88; Bank of Nova Scotia private archives, Metropolitan Bank of Toronto Records, finding aid and biographical sketch prepared by Hirem Kurtarici, Mar. 1993; and *Annual Financial Review* (*AFR*) 2, appendix (Jan. 1903), 48.

14 HBK, A/6, Aitken to W.D. Ross, 16 July 1903.

15 Edward Cronyn held Aemilius Jarvis & Co.'s single seat on the Toronto Stock Exchange (*AFR*, 5 [July 1905], 9).

16 HBK, A/16, Aitken to W.D. Ross, 17 Sept. 1904.

17 HBK, A/10, Cronyn and Aitken correspondence; 7 Oct., 14, 19 Nov. 1904, and 9 Dec. 1906; A/16, W.D. Ross and Aitken correspondence, 20 Sept. and 21 Nov. 1904.

18 HBK, A/13, Aitken to F.M. Manley of E.M. Gay & Co. (Montreal), 4 Oct. 1904, and Manley to Aitken, 21 Oct. 1904.

19 HBK, A/10, Aitken to Archibald P. Christmas, 24 Dec. 1904.

20 HBK, A/19, Farrell to Aitken and reply, 13 and 19 Dec. 1905; *Encyclopedia Canadiana* 7:265.

21 Beaverbrook, *My Early Life*, 128–9. This is substantially the same version Aitken wrote in 1941 when reconstructing the events that led to Nesbitt's hiring. See Beaverbrook Papers, University of New Brunswick (UNBK), 46a/1a, unedited and edited memoranda concerning Arthur Nesbitt's joining the RSC.

22 HBK, A/27, Aitken to Ross, 27 Dec. 1905. Nowhere in the RSC correspondence is there an indication that George Stairs, the titular president of the RSC, was involved in the decision to set up an office in Montreal.

23 Beaverbrook, *My Early Life*, 126. *The Canadian Encyclopedia*, 1st ed. (Edmonton 1985), 2:939.

24 HBK, A/17, Aitken to B.G. Burrill, 5 Apr. 1905.

25 HBK, A/33, Farrell to Aitken, 18 Jan. 1906.

26 HBK, A/30, Aitken to B.G. Burrill, 30 Jan. 1906.

27 HBK, A/35, Aitken to Killam, 9 Oct. 1906.

28 HBK, A/35, Killam to Aitken, 5 Oct. 1906.

29 Beaverbrook, *My Early Life*, 126.

30 HBK, A/34, Aitken to Harris, 25 Apr. 1906.

31 Except for W.D. Ross, all the members of the promotional syndicate were from Halifax. See HBK, A/30, Aitken to Botsford (RSC, Halifax), 15 June 1906.

32 HBK, A/34, Aitken to R.E. Harris, 25 and 26 Apr. 1906; and HBK, G/19/15, RSC prospectus for the Camaguey Company, Ltd, dated 27 Oct. 1911, Montreal. Van Horne asked to be released from his underwriting contract in June 1906, when he found that he had to raise a large sum of money in a short time for his own operations (HBK, A/34, Van Horne to Aitken, 15 June 1906.

33 HBK, A/43, Aitken to Teele, 27 Apr. 1906.

34 HBK, A/27, W.D. Ross to Aitken, 28 Aug. 1905.

35 HBK, A/20, Harris (Halifax) to Aitken (Manhattan Hotel, New York), 5 Feb. 1905.

36 HBK, A/34, Aitken to Harris, 1 Feb. 1906.

37 Public Archives of Nova Scotia (PANS), RG 73, vol. 18, Nova Scotia Companies Act ledger A, 22 Nov. 1905.

38 HBK, A/39, RSC to Aitken, 23 May 1906.

39 HBK, A/41, W.D. Ross to Aitken, 1 June 1906.

40 HBK, A/41, Aitken to W.D. Ross, 19 June 1906.

41 HBK, A/32, Aitken to Carter, 19 June 1906.

42 HBK, A/41, W.D. Ross to Aitken and reply, 1 and 19 June 1906.

43 HBK, A/41, Aitken to W.D. Ross, 19 June 1906.

44 By 1906, these included Blake Burrill, F.T. Burrill, Gerald Farrell, R. Carter, Walton Killam, and Arthur Nesbitt, in addition to three stenographers (one for each RSC office) and at least two full-time travelling salesmen in the Maritimes, Horace Porter and J.F. Hobkirk (HBK, A series, misc. correspondence for 1906).

45 HBK, A/32, Aitken to Carter, 3 Oct. 1906.

46 HBK, A/39, Aitken to Porter, 11 Oct. 1906.

47 HBK, A/38, Aitken to Nesbitt, 20 Aug. 1906.

48 HBK, A/38, Aitken to Nesbitt, 31 Aug. 1906.

49 HBK, A/34, Aitken and J.S. Harding, 21 and 23 Mar. 1906.

50 HBK, A/34, Aitken to Harding, 21 Mar. 1906.

51 In an undated letter to Aitken (HBK, A/62), Harding explained that 'the London investors jump at straws, for instance, the little trouble in Cuba last summer made it impossible to do anything with Camaguey or practically anything else in that Island.' Contrary to Harding's suggestion, the Cuban insurrection had caused widespread loss of life. Moreover, within weeks, the rebels were in control of the rural areas and all but three of the island's cities. See Louis A. Pérez, Jr, *Cuba under the Platt Amendment, 1902–1934* (Pittsburgh 1986), 94–5.

52 HBK, A/34, Harding to Aitken, 29 Sept. 1906.

53 HBK, A/34, W.M. MacLeod to Harding, 28 Sept. 1906.

54 HBK, A/34, Harding to Aitken, 29 Sept. 1906.

55 HBK, A/34, Harding to RSC (Halifax), 4 Oct. 1906.

56 HBK, A/35, Killam to Aitken, 26 Sept. 1906, and A/34, Aitken to Harding, 6 Oct. 1906.

57 HBK, A/19, Aitken to Allan A. Davidson (of Davidson & Aitken, Newcastle, NB), 27 June 1905.

58 HBK, A/27, Aitken to W.D. Ross, 4 July 1905.

59 HBK, A/32, Aitken to Dr M.A. Curry, 26 Nov. 1906.

60 HBK, A/33, Farrell to Aitken, 6 Oct. 1906.

61 HBK, A/34, Aitken to Harding, 6 Oct. 1906.

62 HBK, A/29, R.M. Aitken (of Kitcat, Mortimer & Aitken, 'Stock and Share Brokers,' Threadneedle Street, London, England) to Aitken, 25 Oct. 1906.

63 HBK, A/34, Harding to Aitken, 29 Dec. 1906, and A/62, statement of expenses prepared by Harding, 16 May 1907.

64 HBK, A/62, Aitken to Harding, 4 Feb. 1907.

65 HBK, A/48, Aitken to B.G. Burrill, 21 Feb. 1907: 'There will be a tremendously large issue of these [Porto Rico] securities; and ... the issue will undoubtedly be made in England.'

66 HBK, A/45, A.E. Ames (New York City) to Aitken, 26 Feb. 1907.

67 HBK, A/59, Aitken and E. Mackay Edgar, 6 and 18 May 1907.

68 HBK, A/70, Nesbitt to Aitken and reply, 17 and 21 May 1907.

69 HBK, A/70, Nesbitt to Aitken, 24 July 1907.

70 HBK, A/70, 1907 correspondence between Aitken and Nesbitt.

71 Marchildon, 'Hands across the Water.'

5: The Montreal Engineering Company

1 Christopher Armstrong and H.V. Nelles, *Southern Exposure: Canadian Promoters in Latin America and the Caribbean, 1896–1930* (Toronto 1988), 279.

2 These companies included Demerara Electric, Porto Rico Railways (by 1927), Venezuela Power Company, San Salvador Electric Light Company, and the Bolivian Power Company; see *Annual Financial Review (AFR)* 26 (July 1926), 467–8; and *AFR* 27 (July 1927), 520–1. See also Armstrong and Nelles, *Southern Exposure*, 251–2, and Douglas How, *Canada's Mystery Man of High Finance* (Hantsport, NS, 1986), 57–60. According to How, Killam sold the Camaguey Company at a 'substantial profit' to an unspecified American company.

3 Jack K. Sexton, *Monenco: The First 75 Years* (np 1982). This company history was written by Montreal Engineering's senior vice-president after his retirement, to commemorate the firm's 75th anniversary. Montreal Engineering is now known as Monenco AGRA Inc. and has its head office in Oakville, Ont.

4 See Mira Wilkins, 'Defining a Firm: History and Theory,' in Peter Hertner and Geoffrey Jones, eds., *Multinationals: Theory and History* (Aldershot 1986), and 'The Free-Standing Company, 1870–1914: An Important Type of British Foreign Direct Investment,' *Economic History Review* 41, no. 2 (May 1988).

5 S.J. Nicholas says this was originally Leslie Hannah's observation ('British Multinational Investment before 1939,' *Journal of European Economic History* 11, no. 2 [Winter 1982], 606).

6 Armstrong and Nelles, *Southern Exposure*, 282.

7 In *AFR*, 9 (April 1909), 472, 474, and 536, the address 179 St James Street, Montreal (the head office of the RSC), was also given as the head office address of Demerara Electric, Porto Rico Railways, and the Camaguey Company.

8 Wilkins, 'The Free-Standing Company,' 276.

9 D.G. Paterson, *British Direct Investment in Canada, 1890–1914: Estimates and Determinants* (Toronto 1976), 80–102.

10 On EBASCO, see Sidney Alexander Mitchell, *S.Z. Mitchell and the Electrical Industry* (New York 1960). On American public utility holding companies, see Arthur S. Dewing, *Corporation Finance*, rev. ed. (New York 1931), chap. 21, and William J. Hausman and John L. Neufeld, 'The Rise and Fall of Public Utility Holding Companies' (unpublished working paper, Department of Economics, College of William and Mary, February 1992).

11 Armstrong and Nelles, *Southern Exposure*, 279. See also Gregory P. Marchildon, 'A New View of Canadian Business History,' *Business History* 32, no. 3 (July 1990), 162–7, where this argument was first presented. And see Duncan McDowall, *The Light: Brazilian Traction, Light and Power Company Limited,*

1899–1945 (Toronto 1988), for a detailed discussion of the qualities of the managers and engineers of Brazilian Traction, the largest free-standing Canadian utility operation.

12 McDowall, *The Light*, 66.

13 W.P. Plummer's letterhead advertised that he was a general export and commission agent, and the principal agent for Sao Paulo Tramway, Light & Power, Rio de Janeiro Tramway, Light & Power, and Trinidad Electric, among others. See Beaverbrook Papers, House of Lords Record Office (HBK), A/23, letterhead, W.P. Plummer to Aitken, 29 Dec. 1905.

14 HBK, A/43, Aitken to Teele, 19 Oct. 1906.

15 HBK, A/43, Aitken to Teele, 7 Sept. and 19 Oct. 1906.

16 HBK, A/43, Aitken to Teele, 2 Oct. 1906.

17 HBK, A/32, Fred C. Clarke to Aitken, 29 Oct. 1906.

18 Col. Frederick H. Oxley was born on 18 July 1853 (*The Quarterly Militia List of the Dominion of Canada* [Ottawa 1907], 272).

19 HBK, A/63, Aitken to Harris, 8 Feb. 1907.

20 HBK, A/63, Harris to Aitken, 12 Feb. 1907.

21 HBK, A/16, Aitken to W.B. Ross, 4 Dec. 1904.

22 HBK, A/43, Aitken to Teele, 15 Oct. 1906.

23 HBK, A/53, Aitken to F.T. Burrill, 19 Mar. 1907.

24 HBK, A/63, Giles to Aitken, 30 Oct. 1907.

25 HBK, A/69, Teele to W.P. Plummer, 20 May 1907.

26 HBK, A/63, Aitken to Harris, 11 Oct. 1907.

27 HBK, A/63, Aitken to Harris (with copies to George Stairs and B.G. Burrill), 28 Oct. 1907.

28 HBK, A/79, Stairs to Aitken, 23 May and 15 Oct. 1907.

29 HBK, A/63, Aitken to Harris, 11 Oct. 1907.

30 HBK, A/63, Harris to Aitken, 14 Oct. 1907.

31 HBK, A/63, Aitken to Harris, 16 Oct. 1907.

32 HBK, A/66, Hon. David MacKeen (Halifax Electric Tramway) to Aitken, 15 Oct. 1907.

33 HBK, A/28, Aitken and Teele, 30 Oct. and 14 Nov. 1905. On 6 Dec. 1905, Aitken wrote to Teele: 'With reference to reports to Oxley. I would suggest that it would be in the best interests of the Holding Company [Dominion Trust] for you to pursue a medium course, neither optimistic or pessimistic until I write you that the time is opportune for assuming one attitude or the other.'

34 HBK, A/63, Aitken to Harris (with copies to George Stairs and B.G. Burrill), 28 Oct. 1907.

35 Clarke was henceforth listed as the secretary of the Demerara, Camaguey, and Porto Rico companies (*AFR*, 9 [April 1909], 472, 474, 536). He remained

secretary until 1912, when the head offices of Demerara and Camaguey were temporarily moved to Halifax and Porto Rico Railways shifted its head office to Toronto (HBK, misc. 1907 correspondence; HBK, G/19/15, the Camaguey Company's Montreal bond prospectus, 27 Oct. 1911, and Porto Rico Railways' London bond prospectus, 20 May 1912; and Beaverbrook Papers, National Archives of Canada [NABK], reel A1776, 1911 and 1912 correspondence between Fred Clarke and Aitken).

36 NABK, reel A1776, Oxley (secretary of Trinidad Electric) to Clarke (secretary of Montreal Engineering), 15 Nov. 1910, and Giles to Aitken, 7 Apr. 1914.

37 Incorporated as a federal company on 16 Sept. 1907 with an authorized capital of $100,000 and an issued capital of $50,000, Montreal Engineering was owned and controlled by Aitken: of the 500 original shares, Aitken held 250, the RSC held 245, and the remaining five shares were held by Giles, Clark, Killam, Nesbitt, and Traven Aitken. Giles was made president, Nesbitt, vice-president, and Clarke, secretary, a position he held until 1912 and then resumed from 1926 until 1946. See Sexton, *Monenco*, 12–17.

38 By 1911, Fred C. Clarke was still the secretary of the Camaguey Company; Harris was no longer on the board. The head office was nominally in Halifax, W.B. Ross remaining president, but since the secretary was in Montreal and the Montreal Engineering Company presumably continued servicing Camaguey, it appears that decision making was divided between Camagüey, Cuba, and Montreal (HBK, A/72, Aitken to W.B. Ross, 12 Nov. 1907; HBK, A/44, R.T.D. Aitken to Max Aitken, 18 and 21 Nov. 1907; and HBK, G/19/15, Camaguey Company's Montreal bond prospectus, 27 Oct. 1911).

39 HBK, A/44, R.T.D. Aitken to Aitken, 21 Nov. 1907 and 7 Dec. 1907.

40 A.J.P. Taylor, *Beaverbrook* (New York 1972), 86–100, 137–56; Anne Chisholm and Michael Davie, *Beaverbrook: A Life* (London 1992), 124–35. The fruits of Aitken's Canadian efforts were preserved in his two-volume *Canada in Flanders* (London 1916–17). For a commentary, see Ken Ramstead, 'The "Eye-Witness": Lord Beaverbrook and "Canada in Flanders,"' *Register* 5, no. 2 (1984): 295–314. His work as minister of information in 1918 is most vividly captured by one of his ex-employees in the ministry, Arnold Bennett, in his novel *Lord Raingo* (London 1926).

41 HBK, A/44, R.T.D. Aitken to Max Aitken, 21 Nov. 1907.

42 HBK, A/56, Aitken to Clarke, 9 Sept. 1907.

43 HBK, A/72, W.B. Ross to Trinidad Electric Company and Demerara Electric Company, October 1907.

44 HBK, A/72, W.B. Ross to Trinidad Electric Company.

45 Armstrong and Nelles, *Southern Exposure*, 251–3.

46 Dalhousie University Archives (DAL), index to pre-1900 registration books

for Dalhousie University; and Edith MacAllister, *Newcastle on the Miramichi: A Brief History* (Newcastle, NB 1974), 9. R.T.D. (Traven) Aitken graduated with a BA from Dalhousie University in 1895 and an LLB in 1897, after which he moved back to Newcastle to practise law, and within two years was the town clerk. At university, he was known for his 'dislike of labor' and mediocre marks, as well as his 'predilection for the weaker and fairer sex' (*Dalhousie Gazette*, 19 Oct. 1897, 29).

47 HBK, A/44, Aitken to R.T.D. Aitken, 28 Dec. 1907.

48 HBK, A/84, misc. 1908 correspondence; and *Street Railway Journal* (*SRJ*), 8 Aug. 1908, 456.

49 HBK, A/60, Aitken to Gray (Demerara Electric), 8 Nov. and 10 Dec. 1907; HBK, A/61, S.D. Harding (acting general manager, Trinidad Electric) to Aitken, 2 Dec. 1907, and A/56, and Clarke to Aitken, 14 Dec. 1907.

50 HBK, A/61, Aitken to S.D. Harding, 21 Dec. 1907.

51 British coal seemed less expensive than Nova Scotia coal and Aitken asked for quotations for coal shipments from Britain to Trinidad, British Guiana, Cuba, and Puerto Rico to be sent to the Montreal Engineering Company. See HBK, A/70, Aitken (Montreal) to Nesbitt (Savoy Hotel, London, England), 3 Dec. 1907.

52 HBK, A/96, Giles to Aitken, 3 April 1908.

53 HBK, A/41, Aitken to W.D. Ross, 22 June 1906.

54 HBK, A/73, Aitken to W.D. Ross, 19 Jan. 1907.

55 HBK, A/72, Aitken to W.B. Ross (Puerto Rico), 12 Apr. 1907.

56 Less than two months after the construction contract had been renegotiated, Aitken assailed J.G. White & Co. on the manner in which it 'has conducted its contracts in Porto Rico, which has not heretofore been to my liking, or to the liking of any of my associates' (HBK, A/82, Aitken to J.G. White & Co., 23 May 1907).

57 HBK, A/49, Aitken to B.G. Burrill, 2 May 1907, and A/56, F.C. Clarke to Aitken, 5 July 1907.

58 HBK, A/83, J.G. White to Aitken, 30 Aug. 1907.

59 HBK, A/57, Aitken to F. Kingsbury Curtis, 3 Sept. 1907.

60 HBK, A/83, Aitken to J.G. White, 3 Sept. 1907.

61 HBK, A/72, W.B. Ross to Aitken, 5 Sept. 1907.

62 HBK, A/46, Aitken to Ames, 18 Sept. 1907, and A/83, telegram, Lovett to Aitken, 21 Sept. 1907.

63 HBK, A/72, W.B. Ross to D.E. Thomson, 4 Nov. 1907.

64 HBK, A/99, Aitken to F.J. Hovey of Stone & Webster, Boston, 22 Jan. 1908.

65 HBK, A/60, Aitken and Giles, 11 and 15 Oct. 1907, and misc. letters, Oct.– Dec. 1907.

6: The Takeover and Transformation of Montreal Trust

1 *Annual Financial Review (AFR)*, 5 (July 1905), 404.
2 The fees charged for trust services can be deduced from the National Trust Company's schedule of negotiated prices: (1) trusteeship for bonds – between 35¢ and 50¢ per bond (whether bonds were $500 or $1,000) on a large issue; (2) transfer agencies – from $300 up, in accordance with the amount of capital and expected activity of shares; and (3) paying coupons – a minimum of $\frac{1}{8}$ per cent per security. See Beaverbrook Papers, House of Lords Record Office (HBK), A/35, Aitken to E.G. Kenny, 24 Dec. 1906.
3 HBK, A/21, Aitken to W.T. Mitchell, 3 Jan. 1905; and *Monetary Times (MT)*, 7 Apr. 1893, 1188.
4 HBK, A/1, Clarke to Aitken, 19 Sept. 1903.
5 *AFR*, 6 (July 1906), 436–45; HBK, A/23, Aitken to Plimsoll, 3 Jan. 1905, and A/50, B.G. Burrill to Aitken, 25 July 1907. In July 1907, B.F. Pearson informed Aitken that F.B. McCurdy, who in 1901 had established F.B. McCurdy & Co. (and was married to B.F. Pearson's daughter), had just purchased a controlling interest in Empire Trust in order to make a profit on the eventual consolidation of Eastern and Empire by a central-Canadian trust company. See also entries for Hon. Fleming Blanchard McCurdy in *1922 Who's Who in Canada*, 919, and *The Directory of Parliament, 1867–1967* (Ottawa 1968, hereafter *CDP*), 392.
6 HBK, A/20, letterhead, 13 Dec. 1905. During the negotiations between Aitken and Montreal Trust (A/78, Aitken and Wilson-Smith, 19–21 Feb. 1907), Aitken revealed that he owned 40 per cent of Commercial Trust's $55,000 share capital.
7 HBK, A/54, proofs of Commercial Trust's 1906 annual report.
8 HBK, A/78, Aitken to Wilson-Smith, 16 Feb. 1907.
9 HBK, A/24, Aitken to W.B. Ross, 29 Sept. 1905.
10 HBK, A/142, Aitken to Doble, 31 Dec. 1909; *MT*, 26 Dec. 1908, 1048, and 30 Jan. 1909, 1296.
11 HBK, A/54, E.G. Kenny to Aitken, 16 Aug. and 6 Oct. 1906; and A/35, Commercial Trust's 1906 annual report.
12 HBK, A/18, Aitken to Cahan, 9 Mar. 1905.
13 Lord Beaverbrook, *My Early Life* (Fredericton 1965), 142. Gregory P. Marchildon, 'John F. Stairs, Max Aitken and the Scotia Group: Finance Capitalism and Industrial Decline in the Maritimes, 1890–1914,' in Kris Inwood, ed., *Farm, Factory and Fortune: New Studies in the Economic History of the Maritime Provinces* (Fredericton 1993), 211–17.

14 HBK, A/41, Aitken to W.D. Ross, 11 June 1906, and A/35, and E.G. Kenny to Aitken, 6 Oct. 1906.
15 HBK, A/35, Commercial Trust Co. to Grier, 20 June 1906.
16 HBK, A/35, Aitken to Nesbitt, 20 June 1906.
17 David A. Sutherland, 'Kenny, Thomas Edward,' *Dictionary of Canadian Biography (DCB)*, 13:541–2; Duncan McDowall, *Quick to the Frontier: Canada's Royal Bank* (Toronto 1993), 31.
18 Edward G. Kenny's obituary, Halifax *Herald*, 11 Sept. 1911, 16, and Henry J. Morgan, *Canadian Men and Women of the Time*, 2nd ed. (Toronto 1912, hereafter *CMW2*), 606.
19 HBK, A/35, Aitken to Kenny, 6 July 1906.
20 HBK, A/35, Aitken to Kenny, 3 Oct. 1906 and 11 Jan. 1907.
21 HBK, A/35, Aitken to Kenny, 25 Oct. 1906, and A/64, Aitken to Kenny, 11 Jan. 1907. Aitken was referring to trust legislation as opposed to trust *company* legislation, of which there was none in Nova Scotia at this time.
22 HBK, A/35, Aitken to Kenny, 13 Oct. 1906; A/61, Aitken to Hobkirk, 30 Jan. 1907; and A/78, Aitken to Wilson-Smith, 16 Feb. 1907.
23 HBK, A/61, Aitken to Hobkirk, 30 Jan. 1907.
24 This conclusion is based on a review of Eastern Trust's financial statements as disclosed from 1904 to 1908 in the *AFR*. Under J.F. Stairs's earlier direction, however, Eastern Trust was less conservative, and it appears that he could not have floated Acadia Sugar's securities without Eastern Trust's assistance.
25 When Montreal Trust attempted to register in Nova Scotia under the province's Companies Act in 1908, Eastern Trust manager Henry Bertram Stairs (John F. Stairs's first cousin and Harris's former law partner) argued that Aitken's trust company 'was not an organization for the purpose of administering estates but for the purpose of conducting a promoting business.' Harris retaliated by opening an Eastern Trust office in Montreal and putting Henry Bertram Stairs in charge. See HBK, A/142, Aitken to Doble, 31 Dec. 1909; *MT*, 26 Dec. 1908, 1048; and *MT*, 30 Jan. 1909, 1296.
26 HBK, A/80, Aitken to C.A. Luhnow (editor and publisher of *Trust Companies Magazine* as well as a book entitled *The Modern Trust Company*), 3 Jan. 1907.
27 On the evolution of trust companies in the United States, see Larry Neal, 'Trust Companies and Financial Innovation, 1897–1914,' *Business History Review* 45, no. 1 (Spring 1971), and H. Peers Brewer, 'The Emergence of the Trust Company in New York City: 1870–1900,' *Papers of the Business History Conference* 3 (1974). For a contemporary Canadian account, see Ernest Heaton, *The Trust Company Idea and Its Development* (Toronto 1904).
28 Advertisement in preliminary section of the *AFR* 2 (July 1902). Only General

Trusts and National Trust advertised in the *AFR* at this time; neither referred to call loans or deposits.

29 HBK, A/54, proofs for Commercial Trust's 1906 annual report.

30 HBK, A/78, Aitken to Wilson-Smith, 16 Feb. 1907.

31 HBK, A/70, Nesbitt to Aitken, 14 Jan. 1907.

32 HBK, A/78, Aitken to Wilson-Smith, 16 Feb. 1907.

33 HBK, A/70, Nesbitt to Aitken, 14 Jan. 1907.

34 Heaton, *Trust Company Idea*, 44. E.P. Neufeld, *The Financial System of Canada: Its Growth and Development* (Toronto 1972), 295. Control of the trust companies was exercised through interlocking directorships rather than direct ownership.

35 HBK, A/78, Wilson-Smith to Aitken, 23 Feb. 1907, and Aitken to Kingsbury Curtis, 21 May 1907. Montreal Trust started life with paid-up capital of $60,000, which was later increased to $150,000. By January 1907, Montreal Trust had a capital of $500,000 relative to Commercial Trust's $55,000.

36 *Montreal Trust: The First 100 Years* (Montreal 1989), 2.

37 Ibid., 2–5, and Merrill Denison, *Canada's First Bank: A History of the Bank of Montreal* (Toronto 1967), 2:275, 306. On the corporate interlinkages, see Gilles Piédalue, 'Les groupes financiers au Canada, 1900–1930,' *Revue d'histoire de l'Amérique française* 30, no. 1 (June 1976).

38 HBK, A/78, Aitken to Wilson-Smith, 16 Apr. 1907; *CMW*1, 952; *CMW*2, 1040: *Montreal Trust*, 4–6.

39 HBK, A/78, Wilson-Smith to Aitken, 15 Feb. 1907.

40 HBK, A/78, Aitken to Wilson-Smith, 16 Feb. 1907.

41 HBK, A/64, Kenny to Aitken, 4 Feb. 1907.

42 HBK, A/78, Aitken to Wilson-Smith, 16 Feb. 1907.

43 HBK, A/78, Wilson-Smith to Aitken, 19 Feb. 1907.

44 *ARF*, 8 (Apr. 1908), 522.

45 HBK, A/78, Wilson-Smith to Aitken, 23 Feb. 1907, and Aitken to W.D Ross, 18 Feb. 1907.

46 HBK, A/78, Aitken to Wilson-Smith, 7 Mar. 1907.

47 HBK, A/78, Aitken to Wilson-Smith, 20 Feb. 1907 (1st letter).

48 HBK, A/78, Aitken to Wilson-Smith, 20 Feb. 1907 (2nd letter).

49 HBK, A/78, Wilson-Smith and Aitken, 19–21 Feb. 1907.

50 HBK, A/78, Aitken to Wilson-Smith, 1 and 9 Mar. 1907.

51 HBK, A/78, Aitken to Wilson-Smith, 7 Mar. 1907.

52 HBK, A/54, Aitken to Cahan, 9 May 1907.

53 HBK, A/47, Aitken to W.H. Bull, 22 Apr. 1907, and A/65, Aitken and Lovett correspondence, 13 Feb., 20 Mar., and 22 Apr. 1907.

54 Halifax *Herald*, 14 May 1907, 1. The most direct cause of this move, the take-

over of Montreal Trust, was not even mentioned in the article. It took another month before the merger was announced in the financial press (*MT*, 15 June 1907, 1977).

55 HBK, A/66, McCurdy to Aitken, 14 May 1907, and A/54, and Clarke to Aitken, 25 June 1907.

56 HBK, A/54, Collas to Aitken, 14 May 1907.

57 The move and its after-effects have been discussed in Gregory P. Marchildon, 'International Corporate Law from a Maritime Base: The Halifax Firm of Harris, Henry, and Cahan,' in Carol Wilton, ed., *Lawyers and Business in Canada, 1830 to 1930* (Toronto 1990), 216–17, and 'Scotia Group,' 214–15.

58 HBK, A/61, Van Horne to Aitken, 28 May 1907.

59 Wilson-Smith was not on the list of the forty-eight best-established businessmen (as measured by the number of directorships) in Canada at the time (Nathaniel S. Fineberg, 'The Canadian Financial Triangle,' *Moody's Magazine*, Nov. 1909, 374–81). Sir Hugh Andrew (Montagu) Allan was ranked eighteenth on Fineberg's list, while Cox and Clouston were ranked first and fourteenth, respectively.

60 HBK, A/54, Aitken to Cahan, 9 May 1907.

61 HBK, A/65, Aitken to Lovett, 20 Mar. and 22 Apr. 1907.

62 HBK, A/78, Aitken to Cahan, 13 Mar. 1907.

63 HBK, A/57, Aitken to Curtis, 21 May 1907.

64 Heaton, *Trust Company Idea*, 15–20. Neufeld, *Financial System of Canada*, 298.

65 HBK, A/78, memorandum dated February 1907, and A/57, Aitken to Kingsbury Curtis, 20 and 21 May 1907.

66 Montreal Trust Company (MTC), minutes enclosing annual reports, 30 Nov. 1908–9.

67 HBK, A/57, Aitken to Kingsbury Curtis, 21 May 1907.

68 HBK, A/91, Aitken to Thornton Davidson, 1 Sept. 1908.

69 HBK, A/54, Aitken to Cahan, 9 May 1907.

70 Neufeld, *Financial System of Canada*, 289.

71 The McTavish Royal Commission of 1906, set up to look into the Canadian life insurance industry, had just investigated the conflicts of interest and self-dealing involved in the Cox companies. See Ian M. Drummond, 'Canadian Life Insurance Companies and the Capital Market, 1890–1914,' *Canadian Journal of Economics and Political Science* 28, no. 2 (May 1962), 210–16. On the Cox group generally, see Michael Bliss, *A Canadian Millionaire: The Life and Business Times of Sir Joseph Flavelle, Bart., 1858–1939* (Toronto 1992), chaps. 1–4.

72 Denison, *Bank of Montreal*, 2:275.

73 HBK, A/108, Aitken to Lovett, 27 Apr. 1908.

74 HBK, A/41, Aitken to W.D. Ross, 19 June 1906; *AFR*, 8 (Apr. 1908, 62–121.

75 HBK, A/57, Aitken to Kingsbury Curtis, 21 May 1907; Neal, 'Trust Companies,' 37–45; and Heaton, *Trust Company Idea*, 9–14.

76 HBK, A/77, Aitken to T. Sherman, 11 June 1907.

77 HBK, A/78, Aitken to John M. Smith, 16 Aug. 1907.

78 HBK, A/58, Aitken to J.R. Douglas, 20 Mar. 1907.

79 HBK, A/49, B.G. Burrill to Aitken, 22 Apr. 1907.

80 HBK, A/72, Aitken to W.B. Ross, 11 June 1907.

81 HBK, A/66, Aitken to A.D. MacRae (Union Bank of Halifax), 8 May 1907.

82 HBK, A/49, Aitken to B.G. Burrill, 8 May 1907.

83 HBK, A/49, Burrill to Aitken, 15 May 1907.

84 HBK, A/50, Aitken to Burrill, 20 July 1907.

85 HBK, A/62, Aitken to Harding, 26 June 1907, and A/47, Aitken to Betancourt, 3 Sept. 1907. In a letter to Nesbitt (20 July 1907, HBK, A/70), Aitken stated, 'My advice and counsel to all the members of the Corporation is "sell."'

86 HBK, A/70, Nesbitt and Aitken correspondence, 1 Aug. 1907, and 2 Oct. 1907, and A/46, Ames to Aitken, 26 Aug. 1907.

87 HBK, A/31, Aitken to B.G. Burrill, 6 Sept. 1907.

88 Jon Moen and Ellis W. Tallman, 'The Bank Panic of 1907: The Role of Trust Companies,' *Journal of Economic History* 52, no. 3 (Sept. 1992). For various accounts of the 1907 panic in the United States, see Robert Sobel, *Panic on Wall Street* (New York 1988), chap. 9; Ron Chernow, *The House of Morgan* (New York 1990), chap. 7; and Vincent P. Carosso, *The Morgans: Private International Bankers, 1854–1913* (Cambridge, Mass., 1987), chap. 15.

89 HBK, A/57, telegrams, Curtis and Aitken, 22 Oct. 1907.

90 HBK, A/51, Aitken to Burrill, 24 Oct. 1907.

91 HBK, A/51, Aitken to the Trust Co. of America, 23 Oct. 1907.

92 HBK, A/51, Aitken to Burrill, 24 Oct. 1907.

93 A concise account as well as a convincing analysis of the 1907 financial panic in Canada is provided by George Rich, 'Canadian Banks, Gold, and the Crisis of 1907,' *Explorations in Economic History* 26, no. 1 (Apr. 1989).

94 The general decline of Canadian stock prices in October 1907 can be observed in the *AFR* 8 (Apr. 1908), 14–30. In terms of annual changes in real value-added, Canadian manufacturing increased 52 per cent in 1905, 40 per cent in 1906, and then decreased to 20 per cent in 1907, finally declining by 38 per cent in 1908; see Morris Altman, 'Revised Estimates of Real Canadian GNP and Growth and the Pre and Post World War Two Volatility of the Canadian Business Cycle with Some Comparison to the American Record' (unpublished paper, Department of Economics, University of Saskatchewan, 1989),

52–3, table 9. The Canadian money stock, which stood at $641 million in the first quarter of 1907, increased to $659 million and $660 million in the second and third quarters, dropped to $624 million in the fourth quarter, and then to $612 million in the first quarter of 1908: see Georg Rich, *The Cross of Gold: Money and the Canadian Business Cycle, 1867–1913* (Ottawa 1988), 241.

95 HBK, A/63, Aitken to Harris, 28 Oct. 1907.

96 A.J.P. Taylor, *Beaverbrook* (New York 1972), 248.

7: Hubris and the Young Financier

1 Beaverbrook Papers, House of Lords Record Office (HBK), A/79, George Stairs to Aitken, 23 May 1907.

2 HBK, A/70, Aitken to Nesbitt, 17 Dec. 1907.

3 Hughes, quoted in Anne Jardim, *The First Henry Ford: A Study in Personality and Business Leadership* (Cambridge, Mass., 1970), 236.

4 HBK, A/70, Aitken to Nesbitt, 31 Dec. 1907, A/116, Aitken to Nesbitt, 16 Jan. 1908, and A/108, Aitken to Lewis, 29 Jan. 1908.

5 Ranked forty-fourth in Fineberg's list of the top forty-eight Canadian businessmen (*Moody's Magazine*, Nov. 1909, 377), Robert Archer of Montreal's City & District Bank temporarily replaced Richard Wilson-Smith as a figurehead president, giving Aitken extra time to find a suitable candidate for the long term.

6 HBK, A/109, telegram, Aitken to W.B. McCurdy, 30 Jan. 1908.

7 Entries for George Edward Drummond and Thomas Joseph Drummond in Henry J. Morgan, *Canadian Men and Women of the Time*, 2nd ed. (Toronto 1912, hereafter *CMW2*), 345–6; and National Archives of Canada (NA), Drummond Family Papers, MG30/A88/1/1. On the Drummonds' involvement in the Lake Superior Corporation, see Duncan McDowall, *Steel at the Sault: Francis H. Clergue, Sir James Dunn, and the Algoma Steel Corporation, 1901–1956* (Toronto 1984), chap. 3.

8 HBK, A/57, Aitken to Curtis, 2 Dec. 1907.

9 HBK, A/108, Aitken to Lewis, 28 Apr. 1908.

10 HBK, A/51, Aitken to Burrill, 16 Oct. 1907.

11 The value of 20 per cent is the mean between the $130 per share offered by the Merchants Bank of Canada and the $135 offered by the Royal Bank of Canada in January of 1909 (HBK, A/133, Aitken to Benn, 12 and 23 Jan. 1909, and A/156, Aitken to Lewis, 7 July 1909).

12 HBK, A/79, George Stairs to Aitken, 23 May 1907.

13 On the struggle between Harris and Aitken, see Gregory P. Marchildon, 'International Corporate Law from a Maritime Base: The Halifax Firm of

Harris, Henry, and Cahan,' in Carol Wilton, ed., *Beyond the Law: Lawyers and Business in Canada, 1830 to 1930* (Toronto 1990), and 'John F. Stairs, Max Aitken and the Scotia Group: Finance Capitalism and Industrial Decline in the Maritimes, 1890–1914,' in Kris Inwood, *Farm, Factory and Fortune: New Studies in the Economic History of the Maritime Provinces* (Fredericton 1993).

14 HBK, A/79, Aitken to George Stairs, 31 Oct. 1907.

15 HBK, A/79, George Stairs and Aitken, 11 and 15 Nov. 1907.

16 HBK, A/63, Harris to Aitken, 5 Nov. 1907.

17 HBK, A/63, Aitken to Harris, 9 Nov. 1907.

18 HBK, A/51, Burrill to Aitken, 27 Oct. 1907.

19 HBK, A/105, Aitken to Killam, 11 Mar. 1908.

20 Aitken's concern over the office letters at this time presages his subsequent preoccupation with the control of correspondence, whether his own or others', including the personal papers of the British prime ministers Lloyd George and Bonar Law. See A.J.P. Taylor, *Beaverbrook* (New York 1972).

21 Shares in the Utilities Securities Company were initially distributed as follows: Aitken ($62,300); W.D. Ross ($17,100); H.A. Lovett ($12,000); Fred Teele ($7,300); A.D. Gurd ($1,000); F.C. Clarke ($100); C.C. Giles ($100); L.A. de Gruchy ($100). According to Aitken, transfers in stock took place from 'time to time,' but the 'holdings were not materially altered.' Gurd was a utility accountant who worked for a short time for Aitken; when he left, his shares were taken up by the RSC (HBK, G/3/7, Aitken to V.M. Drury, 1 Apr. 1912).

22 The Bond and Share Company appears to have been organized on 10 Mar. 1908, at which time 49 per cent of its share capital ($49,000) was purchased by the Utilities Securities Corporation. One year later, on 16 Mar. 1909, the Utilities Securities Corporation increased its holdings to 950 shares and, from that date until the Bond and Share Company's liquidation, was virtually the sole shareholder in the company. It is unknown whether Killam continued to be a shareholder, but Nesbitt no doubt had sold his interest months before, when he left Montreal Trust (HBK, G/3/7, Aitken to V.M. Drury, 1 Apr. 1912).

23 HBK, A/105–6, Aitken and Killam, Feb.–Apr. 1908.

24 HBK, A/105, Aitken to Killam, 9 Mar. 1908.

25 HBK, A/109, correspondence between Killam and Aitken, 25, 27 Feb. and 5, 9 Mar. 1908.

26 HBK, A/85, correspondence between Aitken and A.E. Ames, 17, 24, and 25 Jan. 1908.

27 HBK, A/105, Killam to Aitken, 25 and 27 Feb. 1907.

28 HBK, A/106, Aitken to Killam, 11 Mar. 1908, and A/94, telegram, Farrell to RSC board of directors, 12 Mar. 1908.

29 HBK, A/105–6, Killam to Aitken, 11 and 18 Mar. 1908.

30 HBK, A/106, Killam to Aitken, 18 Mar. 1908, and A/94, and undated letter from Farrell to Aitken near end of Mar. 1908.

31 HBK, A/109, McCurdy to Aitken, 1 April 1908.

32 Halifax *Herald*, 2 Apr. 1908, 1.

33 HBK, A/90, Aitken to George W. Foot, Dartmouth Manufacturing Co., 16 Apr. 1908.

34 HBK, A/108, Lovett to Aitken, 17 Apr. 1908.

35 HBK, A/94, Aitken to Farrell, 22 May 1908, Curry to Farrell, 9 Sept. 1908, and Farrell to Aitken, 23 Sept. 1908; A/111, Aitken to R.C. Matthews (manager of Farrell's new Toronto office), 7, 10, and 14 July and 21, 23 Sept. 1908. The 500 shares were divided as follows: Mackenzie and Mann (150 shares); W.J. Crossen (50 shares); W.D. Barclay (50 shares); J. & A. Scrimgeour (50 shares); and G.W. Farrell (50 shares). Clearly, Nathaniel Curry had sold out by September.

36 HBK, A/111, Aitken to R.C. Matthews, 7 and 10 July 1908.

37 Beaverbrook Papers, National Archives of Canada (NABK), reel A1741, Aitken to Hobkirk, 10 Oct. 1908. Farrell went on to get a job with another bond house, C. Meredith & Co. He quit soon afterwards to start his own brokerage house in Montreal. Then in 1917 he formed Farrell, Mather & Co. with Norman L.C. Mather (of Murray, Mather & Co.) and R.G. Muirhead (of G.W. Farrell & Co.), investment bankers, with a head office in Montreal and a branch office in Toronto. See *Annual Financial Review* (*AFR*) 17 (May 1917), xxix; and entry for Farrell in *CMW*2, 37.

38 MTC, minutes, 25 Sept. and 19 Oct. 1908. HBK, A/111, Aitken to Matthews, 22 Sept. 1908; and NABK reel A1741, Aitken to Hobkirk, 10 Oct. 1908.

39 Aitken's description, quoted in Taylor, *Beaverbrook*, 27.

40 Nathaniel S. Fineberg, 'The Canadian Financial Triangle,' *Moody's Magazine*, Nov. 1909, 377–81.

41 *Monetary Times* (*MT*), 14 Nov. 1908, 801. Merrill Denison, *Canada's First Bank: A History of the Bank of Montreal* (Toronto 1967), 2:299–30.

42 Clouston was identified by the *Montreal Star* as a millionaire in 1907 (*CMW*2, 241).

43 Aitken had expended a great deal of effort trying to get Lovett to leave Montreal in the spring of 1907. Lovett procrastinated until the end of the year, when he finally left Harris's law firm and took up permanent residence in Halifax (HBK, A/65, Aitken to Lovett, 13 Feb., 20 Mar. and 22 Apr. 1907). On Lovett's relationship with Cahan, see Gregory P. Marchildon, 'The Role of

Lawyers in Corporate Promotion and Management: A Canadian Case Study and Theoretical Speculations,' *Business and Economic History* 19 (1990), 193–8.

44 *MT*, 28 Nov. 1908, 882; *MT*, 16 Jan. 1909, 1187; and *MT*, 20 Feb. 1909, 1459. The dispute, as well as Sir Edward Clouston's position which was contrary to that of his bank's president, Sir George Drummond, and Charles Cahan, is explored in depth by Christopher Armstrong and H.V. Nelles, *Southern Exposure: Canadian Promoters in Latin America and the Caribbean, 1896–1930* (Toronto 1988), 99–104.

45 Cahan's relationship with Aitken is explored in Marchildon, 'International Corporate Law.'

46 HBK, A/140, Aitken to Cowans, 15 June 1909.

47 *MT*, 31 July 1909, 514.

48 Aitken rejected J.C. Mackintosh's request for shares in Montreal Trust on the grounds that despite the 'number of influential persons asking for this stock' it had to be reserved for 'those persons who will bring business to the Company' (HBK, A/153, Aitken to Hobkirk, 19 Jan. 1909).

49 HBK, G/3/7, Aitken to Drury, 1 Apr. 1912, and Aitken to Doble, 29 Jan. 1913.

50 When the Prudential Trust Company applied for wider powers (to receive deposits, to lend money on certain securities, and to do a general brokerage business) through a private member's bill in Parliament in 1909, the superintendent of insurance objected on the grounds that mixing trust funds with other funds 'might lead to improper speculation.' In his opinion, trust companies should not 'undertake transactions to or in excess of the functions of a trust company proper' (*MT*, 24 Apr. 1909, 1894).

51 HBK, A/156, Lovett (of Lovett and Surveyer, Barristers and Solicitors, 112 St James Street, Montreal) to Aitken, 5 Oct. 1909.

52 HBK, A/156, Lovett to Aitken, 7 Oct. 1909.

53 The RSC remained in that location until November 1909, when it moved into new offices just down the street in the London and Lancashire Building (*MT*, 20 Nov. 1909, 2142).

54 In 1914, Ward Pitfield quit the Eastern Securities Company to join the RSC, later leaving to establish Pitfield, McKay, Ross NABK, reel A1777, Doble to Aitken, 4 July 1914).

55 NABK, reel A1741, Aitken to Hughes, 6 and 7 July 1908.

56 NABK, reel A1777, Doble to Aitken, 6 Jan. 1914.

57 Arthur Nesbitt described him as a 'very strong man in the business' who was established and 'well thought of' in Nova Scotia (HBK, A/70, Nesbitt to Aitken, 25 Nov. 1907).

58 HBK, A/74, Aitken to W.D. Ross, 26 Dec. 1907.

59 HBK, A/50, Burrill to Aitken, 8 Aug. 1907.

60 HBK, A/52, Aitken to Burrill, with copies to Nesbitt and Stairs, 13 Nov. 1907.
61 HBK, A/70, Aitken to Nesbitt, 13 Nov. 1907.
62 His departure was noted in *MT*, 10 Oct. 1908, 597. His first firm was the Investment Trust Co., while Nesbitt, Thompson & Co. was founded in 1912; see Gregory P. Marchildon, '"Hands across the Water": Canadian Industrial Financiers in the City of London, 1905–20,' *Business History* 34, no. 3 (July 1992), 70.
63 HBK, A/51, Burrill to Aitken and reply, 14 and 28 Oct. 1907.
64 *AFR* 8 (Apr. 1908), 171. Highs and lows of Lake Superior common are as quoted on the Philadelphia Stock Exchange.
65 HBK, A/70, Nesbitt to Aitken, 3 May 1907.
66 HBK, A/70, Aitken to Nesbitt, 28 Oct. 1907.
67 HBK, A/70, Aitken to Nesbitt, 19 Nov. 1907.
68 HBK, A/70, Nesbitt to Aitken, 4 Dec. 1904.
69 HBK, A/70, Aitken to Nesbitt, 17 Dec. 1907.
70 HBK, A/116, Aitken to Nesbitt, 15 Jan. 1908.
71 HBK, A/116, Nesbitt to Aitken, 18 June 1908.
72 HBK, A/116, Aitken to Nesbitt, 24 June 1908.
73 *MT*, 10 Oct. 1908, 597. In 1947 Nesbitt and Aitken met for lunch in Montreal to talk about old times, but in a thank-you letter afterwards Nesbitt resorted to the formal 'My dear Lord Beaverbrook' (UNBK, 46a/1a, Nesbitt to Aitken, 10 Nov. 1947).
74 HBK, A/86, Aitken to Burrill, 27 Mar. 1908; MTC, minutes, 18 May 1908.
75 HBK, A/107, telegram, Aitken to Killam, 30 May 1908. Aitken had decided to open up a Quebec office by May 1908 (MTC, minutes, 18 May 1908).
76 HBK, A/107, Aitken to Killam (the Garrison Club, Quebec), 25 Sept. 1908.
77 The letterhead read simply I.W. Killam, Investment Securities, Quebec (HBK, A/107, Killam to Aitken, 16 Dec. 1908).
78 HBK, A/57, Curtis and Aitken, 25 Nov. and 21 Dec. 1907.
79 *MT*, 24 Apr. 1909, 1894.
80 HBK, A/133, Aitken to Benn, 12 and 23 Jan. 1909. In November 1908, Herbert Holt succeeded Thomas E. Kenny as president of the Royal Bank, and the general manager, E.L. Pease, became vice-president (*MT*, 7 Nov. 1908, 759, and *MT*, 21 Nov. 1908, 845).
81 During Aitken's 1908 negotiations with the Provincial Bank concerning a strategic alliance, it soon became clear that one condition of any 'merger' would be that Montreal Trust cease doing a general banking business (NABK, reel A1741, misc. 1908 correspondence between Aitken and Hughes).

82 HBK, A/90, George E. and Thomas J. Drummond to Aitken, 6 and 7 July 1908, and Aitken to T.J. Drummond, 21 Aug. 1908.

83 HBK, A/90, Aitken to T.J. Drummond, 21 Aug. 1908, and Aitken to Granger Farwell (Farwell Trust Co., Chicago), 24 Dec. 1908.

84 *MT*, 31 Oct. 1908, 722. The Canada Iron flotation is discussed in Marchildon, 'Hands across the Water,' 82–5.

85 Aitken received a letter of introduction to Bonar Law from Thomas Cantley, the general manager of Scotia (HBK, A/87, Cantley and Aitken correspondence, 20 Oct. and 5 Nov. 1908, and A/109, Aitken to McMaster, 17 Oct. 1908). Law had had a long relationship with Scotia during the 1890s as an iron merchant and broker in Glasgow.

86 The only biography of Law is Robert Blake, *The Unknown Prime Minister: The Life and Times of Andrew Bonar Law, 1858–1923* (London 1955). This book was apparently commissioned by Beaverbrook, but by the time Blake finished the project he had very mixed feelings about Beaverbrook, whom he described as being 'great fun to meet' but having an 'unscrupulous and sadistic streak'; see Lord Blake, 'Shrewd and Amusing Enemy of Humbug' (obituary of A.J.P. Taylor), *Independent*, 7 Sept. 1990.

87 HBK, A/133, Benn to Aitken, 9 Feb. 1909.

88 HBK, A/133, Aitken to Benn, 28 Jan. 1909.

89 MTC, minutes, 22 Dec. 1908 and 14 Jan. 1909.

90 MTC, minutes, 12 May 1909. See also *Statutes of the Province of Quebec* (Quebec 1909), 333, chap. 115, an act to amend the charter of the Montreal Trust and Deposit Company and change its name to the Montreal Trust Company, assented to 27 Apr. 1909.

91 HBK, A/156, Aitken and Lewis, 1 Feb. and 7 July 1909.

92 HBK, A/133, Aitken to Benn, 26 Apr. 1909.

93 RSC monthly sales during the first half of 1909 reflected the boom: Jan., $251,000; Feb., $307,000; Mar., $485,000; Apr., $716,000; May, $864,000; June, $985,000 (HBK, G/3, Killam to Cahan, 21 July 1909).

94 HBK, A/148, Aitken to Farwell, 15 Feb. 1909.

95 *MT*, 8 Jan. 1910, 223–5; *MT*, 3 Apr. 1909, 1774, *MT*, 10 Apr. 1907, 1815–16; and Marchildon, 'Hands across the Water,' 94. British investment in all new Canadian security issues (government and private) rose from £6.6 million in 1907 to £23.9 million in 1908, £24.1 million in 1909, and £33.8 million in 1910; see Matthew Simon, 'New British Investment in Canada, 1865–1914,' *Canadian Journal of Economics* 3, no. 2 (May 1970), 241.

96 University of Durham (DUR), Earl Grey (fourth earl) Papers, Grey to Arthur M. Grenfell (of the Canadian Agency), 2 Dec. 1908.

97 *MT*, 8 May 1909, 1992.

8: Manufacturing the Canada Cement Company

1 See appendix in Gregory P. Marchildon, '"Hands across the Water": Canadian Industrial Financiers in the City of London, 1905–20,' *Business History* 34 (July 1992), 94–5.

2 See Gregory P. Marchildon, 'Promotion, Finance and Mergers in Canadian Manufacturing Industry, 1885–1918' (PhD diss., London School of Economics, 1990), chaps. 1, 2, 8, and 9, where this hypothesis is more fully explored.

3 George Stigler, 'Monopoly and Oligopoly by Merger,' *American Economic Review* 40, no. 1 (May 1950), 23–34; Thomas R. Navin and Marian V. Sears, 'The Rise of a Market for Industrial Securities, 1887–1902,' *Business History Review* 24, no. 2 (June 1955), 105–38.

4 Marchildon, 'Promotion, Finance and Mergers,' 30–8.

5 Ranald C. Michie, 'The Canadian Securities Market, 1850–1914,' *Business History Review* 62, no. 1 (Spring 1988).

6 Britain was already a large investor in Canadian government bonds and railway securities. See Ian M. Drummond, 'Capital Markets in Australia and Canada, 1895–1914' (PhD diss., Yale University, 1959), some of which is reproduced in chap. 18 of Drummond's *Progress without Planning: The Economic History of Ontario from Confederation to the Second World War* (Toronto 1987).

7 For a lengthier discussion of these and other promoters, see Marchildon, 'Hands across the Water,' 69–79.

8 J.A. MacKay & Co. made the Carriage Factories issue, while C. Meredith & Co. underwrote the largest block of Dominion Canners' stock. C. Meredith & Co., and its principal Charles Meredith, appear to have taken care of much of the financial end of Grant's other mergers as well as the Tuckett Tobacco and Dominion Glass mergers.
    See *Monetary Times* (*MT*), 2 Oct. 1909, 1422, 29 Jan. 1910, 543; 19 Mar. 1910, 1254; 18 June 1910, 2514; 23 July 1910, 415, 22 Apr. 1911, 1625; and 25 Nov. 1911, 2245.

9 *MT*, 21 Oct. 1911, 1717.

10 *MT*, 29 Jan. 1910, 514;11 June 1910, 2432b; 11 Feb. 1911, 648; and 22 Apr. 1911, 1617.

11 *MT*, 10 Oct. 1908, 597; 15 July 1911, 321; 25 Nov. 1911, 2220; and 25 May 1912, 2143. Lafarge Canada Inc., Montreal (LCA), Canada Cement annual report, 1927.

12 *MT*, 10 Apr. 1909, 1816; 12 Feb. 1910, 716; 5 Mar. 1910, 1010; 15 Oct. 1910, 1643; and 4 Mar. 1911, 917, 932.

13 *MT*, 23 Apr. 1910, 1724, and 4 June 1910, 2332.

14 Clipping from October [no date] edition of Halifax *Herald* (Beaverbrook

Papers, House of Lords Record Office [HBK], A/137, attached to letter, McCurdy to Aitken, 21 Oct. 1909).

15 *Busy Man's Magazine* [*Maclean's*], Jan. 1910, 24–5. The article was actually written by W.R. McCurdy, Aitken's journalist friend from Halifax.

16 On the perception of Fleming as one of most gifted and charming Canadians of his day, see Sandra Gwyn, *The Private Capital: Ambition and Love in the Age of Macdonald and Laurier* (Toronto 1984), 122–3. See also Lorne Green, *Chief Engineer: The Life of Nation Builder – Sandford Fleming* (Toronto 1993).

17 HBK, A/157, Macpherson to Aitken, 3 Nov. 1909; and Douglas How, *Canada's Mystery Man of High Finance* (Hantsport, NS, 1986), 68–9.

18 HBK, G/3/6, examination for discovery of H.V. Meredith (Bank of Montreal lawsuit), 6 Oct. 1913 (hereafter referred to as Meredith exam), 19.

19 A.J.P. Taylor, *Beaverbrook* (New York 1972), 35–8, 64–5.

20 See Anne Chisholm and Michael Davie, *Beaverbrook: A Life* (London 1992), appendix on the Canada Cement Affair, 529–44.

21 There are three main sources for this information: the Beaverbrook Papers at the House of Lords Record Office in London, England (HBK); the Canada Cement minutes and other documentation held at the Lafarge Canada, Inc., private archive in Montreal (LCA); and the documents submitted for listing Canada Cement's shares on the London Stock Exchange, preserved in the Guildhall Library manuscripts in London, England (GLSE).

22 This does not alter the fact that some correspondence could have been – and likely was – destroyed by both sides in the conflict, leaving us with an incomplete picture of what transpired.

23 HBK, G/19/21, Drury to Aitken, 21 Dec. 1911. See also *MT*, 7 July 1905, 21; 3 Aug. 1906, 164; 11 Apr. 1908, 1735; and 21 Nov. 1909, 2115.

24 Robert W. Lesley, *History of the Portland Cement Industry in the United States* (Chicago 1924), 159–64. On the Cowham system, see Léon Dubois, *Foundations for the Future: The Lafarge Story* (Paris 1988), 149–53. See also National Archives of Canada (NA), Fleming Papers, MG29/B1/23/170, correspondence between Sandford Fleming and Irvin in 1905.

25 This technological revolution is the subject of Gregory P. Marchildon, 'Portland Cement: Product and Process Upheaval in Germany and the United States during the Second Industrial Revolution' (paper presented to the Society for the History of Technology Conference, October 1993).

26 Moreover, the supply of limestone rock was almost limitless, whereas marl deposits were scarce (*MT*, 25 Nov. 1911, 2214).

27 In early 1905, Sir Sandford Fleming was elected president of International Portland Cement. At that time he formally replaced William F. Cowham (erroneously identified in the *MT* as F.W. Cowan); see *MT*, 3 Feb. 1905, 1041–2, and 17 Feb. 1905, 1092. See also Henry J. Morgan, *Canadian Men and*

Women of the Time, 2nd ed. (Toronto 1912, hereafter *CMW*2), 568; *Souvenir of the History, Development and Future of Portland Cement* (Ottawa, 1909); and Dubois, *Foundations for the Future,* 150–1.

28 NA, Fleming Papers, MG29/B1/52/364, extract from Calgary *Daily Herald,* 10 May 1906, and Sandford Fleming to Sir Thomas Shaughnessy, no date.

29 NA, Fleming Papers, MG29/B1/23/170, Sandford Fleming to Irvin, 10 Nov. 1906.

30 NA, Fleming Papers, MG29/B1/15/105, Hugh Fleming to Sandford Fleming, 19 Sept. 1906; *MT,* 3 Aug. 1906, 164.

31 NA, Fleming Papers, MG29/B1/23/170, Sandford Fleming to Irvin, 10 Nov. 1906.

32 *MT,* 22 Sept. 1905, 387, referred to the first fifteen-storey Traders Bank concrete skyscraper in Toronto as 'unsightly.'

33 *MT,* 29 Sept. 1905, 448. Kilbourn also invested in the Vancouver Portland Cement Company established by R.P. Butchart, an old associate of his, near Victoria, which threatened Western Canada Cement's Pacific export business (*MT,* 1 Dec. 1905, 693).

34 NA, Fleming Papers, MG29/B1/15/105, Hugh Fleming to Sandford Fleming, 15 July 1906, Frederic Nicholls, general manager of Canada Foundry, to Hugh Fleming, 3 Sept. 1908, and printed circular sent to Western Canada Cement's share- and bondholders, 9 Oct. 1909.

35 NA, Fleming Papers, MG29/B1/3/17, Sandford Fleming's personal guarantee to repay $80,000 loan, dated 9 Apr. 1907.

36 Cement consumption in Canada increased from 116,000 tons in 1900 to 396,000 tons in 1905, to 487,000 tons in 1906, to 544,000 tons in 1907, and then stagnated at 549,000 tons in 1908; see D.H. Stonehouse, *Cement in Canada* (Ottawa 1973), 7, and *MT,* 21 Nov. 1909, 2115.

37 According to the preference share issue prospectus of the Canada Cement Co., Ltd, dated 14 Sept. 1909 at Montreal (HBK, G/19/15), the selling price of a barrel of cement had fallen by approximately 15 per cent from 1907 to 1908. In 1908 domestic production was 3.5 million barrels while consumption was less than 2.7 million barrels. A Canadian barrel of cement was equal to 350 pounds, or 157.5 kilograms. This information varies slightly from that in *MT,* 20 Feb. 1909, 1479, which states that consumption in 1908 was approximately 2.5 million barrels, of which 700,000 barrels were imported.

38 *MT,* 20 Feb. 1909, 1479.

39 *Annual Financial Review* (*AFR*) 8 (Apr. 1908), 167, and *AFR* 9 (Apr. 1909), 171.

40 HBK, G/3/6, Meredith exam, 12.

41 NA, Fleming Papers, MG29/B1/52/364, Sandford Fleming to Shaughnessy, no date (but shortly after spring 1908).

42 NA, Fleming Papers, MG29/B1/10/68, Sandford Fleming to Clouston, 2 Nov. 1908.

43 HBK, G/3/6, examination for discovery of Hugh Fleming (Bank of Montreal lawsuit), 8 Oct. 1913 (hereafter referred to as Fleming exam), 4.

44 *MT*, 10 Aug. 1906, 195. HBK, G/3/6, examination for discovery of J.S. Irvin in two parts (Bank of Montreal lawsuit), 23 Nov. 1912 (hereafter referred to as 1st Irvin exam) and 24 Oct. 1913 (hereafter, 2nd Irvin exam).

45 HBK, G/3/6, Meredith exam, 5.

46 The amounts covered by the personal guarantees is subject to dispute. Chisholm and Davie, *Beaverbrook*, assert that $110,000 was personally guaranteed. The personal guarantees signed by Sir Sandford Fleming, Hugh Fleming, S.H. Fleming, and J.S. Irvin were all dated 27 Mar. 1909, while one further guarantee from William Exshaw was signed on a later date. The loan was also secured under the Bank Act by a lien on Western Canada Cement's liquid assets (HBK, A/133, Aitken to Benn, 26 Apr. 1909, and HBK, G/3/6, Fleming exam, 4).

47 Three years after the events, Irvin claimed under oath that Sir Edward Clouston had *sent* Max Aitken to Irvin, whereas Aitken claimed at the time that Irvin had *invited* him to Irvin's Montreal hotel room to discuss the cement merger for the first time. Less than a year later, Irvin admitted (again under oath) that he had been concerned about the quality of the other men in his cement syndicate and felt it necessary to add Aitken to the syndicate (HBK, G/3/6, Irvin exams, and G/3/7, Aitken to Doble, 29 Jan. 1913).

48 HBK, A/138, telegram, Irvin to Forget, 31 May 1909, and Aitken to Irvin, 2 June 1909.

49 The Lehigh subsidiary, affiliated with the Lehigh Company of Allentown, Pennsylvania, had been incorporated under the Ontario Companies Act, whereas the Vulcan subsidiary, owned by the Vulcan Portland Cement Company of New York, had been incorporated under the Canadian Companies Act. The American plant in Belleville, which began operating in 1908, was one of the newest and best plants in the country. See LCA, memorandum of agreement between Canada Cement and the Bond and Share Company, 10 Sept. 1910, and the Narsted manuscript on the history of Canada Cement (hereafter referred to as Narsted), 96.

50 HBK, A/138, Irvin to Aitken, 5 June 1909.

51 According to Nathaniel S. Fineberg ('The Canadian Financial Triangle,' *Moody's Magazine*, Nov. 1909, 374–81), Matthews was the second most influential businessman in 1909 by virtue of his seventeen directorships on some of Canada's largest companies and his position as vice-president of Toronto's

Dominion Bank. Edmund B. Osler, president of the Dominion Bank, held a total of eleven directorships (*CMW*2, 743).

52 The Canadian Portland Cement Company was itself a 1900 merger, capitalized at $1.5 million, of the Rathbun Company's plant in Deseronto, Ont., the Beaver Portland Cement Company's plant in Marlbank, Ont., and the Canadian Portland Cement Company's two plants in Marlbank and Napanee Mills, Ont. Canadian Portland Cement's operations were soon rationalized and concentrated in Marlbank (LCA, Canadian Portland Cement Co., file of proceedings; and *Cement and Engineering News* 8 (May 1900), 72–3). Canadian Portland's plant at Marlbank is reputed to be the first (in 1891) to produce portland cement in Canada; see James A. Edie, 'Rathbun, 'Edward Wilkes,' *Dictionary of Canadian Biography* (*DCB*), 13:853–4.

53 HBK, A/138, Irvin to Aitken, 9 June 1909.

54 HBK, A/138, Irvin to Aitken, 6 July 1909.

55 HBK, A/138, Irvin to Aitken, 13, 17, and 19 June 1909, and A/139, McNab to Aitken, 11 Sept. 1909; *MT*, 22 Sept. 1903, 374; and LCA, Narsted, 96. The Belleville Company plant appears to have been significantly less productive than the Lehigh plant, judging by Canada Cement's subsequent individual plant earnings data, which reveal that Belleville made $5,865 while the Lehigh plant earned $435,226 in 1912 (HBK, G/3/7, Jones to Aitken, 12 Feb. 1913).

56 *AFR* 9 (Apr. 1909), 171. International Portland Cement had issued $1.25 million of shares; these were publicly listed on the Montreal Stock Exchange in June 1908 and began trading at a low of $116 and a high of $118. At the end of that fiscal year (30 Nov. 1908), International distributed a dividend of 10 per cent. By April 1909, the last month giving share price data in the *AFR*, International's stock was registering a low of $125 and a high of $136, with 145 sales in that same month. Rumours of consolidation continued to push up International's share price value through the spring and summer (*MT*, 7 Aug. 1909, 612).

57 HBK, A/32/Irvin, telegrams between J.S. Irvin and Aitken, 3 June 1909.

58 HBK, G/3/7, Aitken to Doble, 29 Jan. 1913; *MT*, 6 Oct. 1905, 448. Kilbourn's Montreal plant would become Canada Cement's flagship plant no. 1 (HBK, G/3/7, Jones to Aitken, 12 Feb. 1913). See also GLSE, 18000/153B/335, memorandum of agreement between Canada Cement and the Bond and Share Company, 10 Sept. 1909.

59 Kilbourn's Owen Sound Portland Cement Company was organized in 1888 with its plant located by a large marl deposit at Shallow Lake, about nine miles west of Owen Sound, Ont. The Lakefield company began constructing

a plant near the large marl deposits in the region in 1900. See *Cement and Engineering News*, Aug. 1898, 29, and Sept. 1900, 36.

60 HBK, G/3/6, Irvin exams.

61 HBK, A/139, Kilbourn to Aitken, 15 July 1909.

62 After 16 March 1909, 95 per cent of the 1,000 shares ($100,000) in the Bond and Share Company was owned by the Utilities Securities Company. When the Utilities Securities Company was formed on 2 March 1908, Aitken held 62 per cent of its $100,000 share capital. It appears that in early 1909 the RSC took over the individual holdings in the Utilities Securities Company, including Aitken's holdings; thus, Bond and Share was in fact both owned and controlled by the RSC and Aitken (HBK, G/3/7, Aitken to Drury, 1 Apr. 1912, and Aitken to Doble, 29 Jan. 1913).

63 HBK, G/3/7, Aitken to Doble, 29 Jan. 1913.

64 After the general manager and assistant general manager, the regional superintendents were the Bank of Montreal's top officers. Stavert was also vice-president of C. Meredith & Co., a bond house connected to the Bank of Montreal (HBK, G/3/6, Meredith exam, and A/148, C. Meredith & Co. 1909 letterhead).

65 HBK, G/3/7, memorandum accompanying Aitken's letter to Doble, 1 Apr. 1912. Stavert used his influence to procure business in the Maritime region, where Royal Trust did not have a branch (HBK, A/133, Aitken to Benn, 12 Jan. 1909).

66 HBK, G/3/6, Irvin exams.

67 H.V. Meredith, Clouston's assistant general manager and eventual successor as general manager and vice-president, claimed that he never suspected that Clouston was a shareholder in the Bond and Share Company or had any business connection with the RSC (HBK, G/3/6, Meredith exam, 6–10).

68 HBK, G/3/7, Aitken to Doble, 1 Apr. 1912 and 29 Jan. 1913. This was likely the result of Aitken's originally taking responsibility for $2 million (receiving $1 million common stock in consideration) and then distributing just over one-half to his associates at the bank.

69 HBK, G/3/9, memorandum dated 27 Sept. 1909 enclosed in letter from Cahan to Aitken, 22 Jan. 1910.

70 HBK, G/3/9, promoters' agreement of 31 Aug. 1909, as recorded in the memorandum of 27 Sept. 1909 enclosed in letter from Cahan to Aitken, 22 Jan. 1910 (hereafter referred to as promoter's agreement).

71 HBK, G/3/6, 2nd Irvin exam, 43–4.

72 HBK, G/3/7, Aitken's memorandum on Canada Cement affair, 1 Apr. 1912.

73 HBK, G/3/6, Fleming exam, 4.

74 HBK, G/3/9, Aitken to Cahan, 9 Aug. 1909, and G/3/7, Aitken to Doble,

29 Jan. 1913; HBK, A/156, Aitken to Lovett, 20 Aug. 1909; and LCA, Canada Cement minutes, 28 Aug. 1909. This early prospectus contemplated an issue of $25 million despite the fact that Canadian Consolidated Cement did not include the Kilbourn companies, and was heavily criticized in the *MT*, 6 Aug. 1909, 612, and the *Grain Growers' Guide*, 28 Aug. 1909, 10.

75 GLSE, 18000/132B/458, letters patent of Canada Cement accompanying bond listing, 16 Apr. 1910. LCA, Canada Cement minutes, 28 Aug. 1909; and HBK, G/3/10, Cahan to Aitken, 4 Nov. 1910.

76 LCA, Canada Cement minutes, 28 Aug. 1909. The first provisional meeting was held at Cahan's law office, at 35 Royal Insurance Building. The seven original subscribers to Canada Cement were Aitken, Irvin, Fleming, W.C. Edwards, J.R. Booth, Rodolphe Forget, and F.B. Dunsford, while the eight new subscribers aside from Clarke and Drury were Orick B. MacCallum, H.G. Boyle, Thomas Hood, K.M. Perry, S.B. Hammond, and C.A. Barnard (GLSE, 18000/132B/458, documents associated with Canada Cement bond listing, 16 Apr. 1910). Charles Cahan had come up with the scheme, claiming that it was the only way Aitken would be able to exert control over the company at the organizational stage.

77 Irvin's later evidence on this point is consistent with the correspondence at the time of Canada Cement's organization.

78 This is evident in the September and October correspondence, HBK, A/136–7. The arguments over the adjustments after the options were signed were equally bitter. Alfred Thorn, manager of the Canadian Lehigh plant telegraphed Aitken (9 Oct. 1909): 'It should not be expected that I am here to take abuse or to receive more ungentlemanly treatment from Mr. Cahan.'

79 HBK, A/136, misc. correspondence, and A/135, F.W. Cooper (Canadian Appraisal and Audit Company Limited) to Aitken, 31 Aug. 1909.

80 HBK, A/139, telegrams, Aitken to R.W. Kelly, 26 Aug. 1909.

81 Bond and Share obtained options on the Belleville Portland Cement Company (27 Aug.), the Kilbourn companies (30 Aug.), the International Portland Cement Company (6 Sept.), Lehigh Portland Cement (8 Sept.), and the Canadian Portland Cement Company (10 Sept.) (HBK, G/19/15, contracts listed in Canada Cement's preference share prospectus, Montreal, 14 Sept. 1909).

82 In the end, the Lehigh Company received $2.5 million in cash for its Belleville plant, and the Vulcan Company obtained $1.6 million cash for its Montreal plant, while the Kilbourn interests received $1.5 million and $1.4 million, respectively, in cash for their properties; see Archives of Ontario (AO), Sandford Fleming Papers, MU 1051, env. 49, page 6 of printed circular, Fleming to W.C. Edwards (president, Canada Cement), 13 Feb. 1911.

83 Decades later, Aitken claimed that the Canada Cement directors 'resolutely supported' his decision to accept only a lower price on the Exshaw property, an interpretation consistent with the evidence at the time (UNBK, 129/1b, Aitken to Wardell, 12 July 1956).

84 HBK, G/3/6, 1st Irvin exam, and A/140, Aitken to Cronyn, 16 Dec. 1909.

85 As H.V. Meredith pointed out in his examination for discovery, Clouston should have asked his assistant general manager rather than Stavert to take care of Bank of Montreal business during Clouston's absence. Clearly, Clouston's personal interest in the merger dictated that he select either Stavert or Doble, although they were expected to deal with Bank of Montreal business at the same time (HBK, G/3/6, Meredith exam, 19–20).

86 HBK, A/140, Aitken to Cronyn, 16 Dec. 1909; HBK, G/3/7, Aitken to Doble, 29 Jan. 1913, and Aitken's memorandum of 2 Apr. 1912 in response to Irvin's statement of claim.

87 NA, Fleming Papers, MG29/B1/170, Joe Irvin to Sir Sandford Fleming, 3 May 1911.

88 HBK, G/3/7, Aitken to Doble, 29 Jan. 1913.

89 LCA, memorandum of agreement between Canada Cement and the Bond and Share Company, 10 Sept. 1910, and letter [drafted by Cahan and F.P. Jones], H.L. Doble, secretary on behalf of Canada Cement, to Sir Sandford Fleming, 1 Feb. 1911, appended to Canada Cement minutes, 31 Jan. 1911.

90 NA, Fleming Papers, MG29/B1/15/105, printed circular sent to Western Canada Cement shareholders and debenture holders by Hugh Fleming, 9 Oct. 1909.

91 NA, Fleming Papers, MG29/B1/5/46, exchange of telegrams between Charles Cahan and Sir Sandford Fleming, Sept. and Oct. 1909.

92 LCA, Canada Cement minutes, 18 Oct. 1909.

93 HBK, A/137, Cahan to Aitken, 10 Oct. and 23 Nov. 1909; LCA, Canada Cement executive minutes, 13 Jan. and 10 May 1910.

94 HBK, A/138, Irvin to Aitken, 19 Oct. 1909.

95 HBK, H/85, Fleming to Aitken and reply, 1 and 3 Oct. 1909.

96 *MT*, 20 Nov. 1909, 2115.

97 Reference to letter from Hugh Fleming, secretary-treasurer of Western Canada Cement, to Cahan, provisional president of Canada Cement, 28 Dec. 1909 (LCA, Canada Cement executive minutes, 3 Jan. 1910).

98 NA, Fleming Papers, MG29/B1/15/105, Hugh Fleming to Sandford Fleming, Feb. 1910.

99 AO, Fleming Papers, MU 1051, env. 49, Fleming's letters, 11 and 15 Feb. 1910.

100 LCA, Canada Cement minutes, 17 Feb. 1910.

101 AO, Fleming Papers, MU 1051, env. 49, Sandford Fleming to C.C. Ballantyne, vice-president, Canada Cement, 11 Mar. 1910. Whether Fleming understood the problem is open to question given his age, but the fact that he had been involved in railway promotions decades before suggests that he did understand; see Alan Wilson, 'Fleming and Tupper: The Fall of the Siamese Twins, 1880,' in John S. Moir, ed., *Character and Circumstance: Essays in Honour of Donald Grant Creighton* (Toronto 1970).

102 HBK, H/85, Sandford Fleming to Dunsford, 2 Apr. 1910.

103 LCA, Canada Cement minutes, 29 Mar. 1910.

104 HBK, H/85, Aitken to Dunsford, 24 Mar. 1910.

105 HBK, H/85, Fleming to Dunsford, copy to Irvin, 2 Apr. 1910.

106 HBK, H/85, Aitken to Dunsford, 4 Apr. 1910.

107 LCA, Canada Cement minutes, 17 Feb. and 4 Mar. 1910 and 31 Jan. 1911; NA, Bank of Montreal Papers, MG28/2/2, reel M158, board minutes, 12 Apr. 1910 (the bank authorized the execution of the agreement between the bank, Western Canada Cement, and Canada Cement); and NA, Fleming papers, MG29/B1/3/17, Fleming to Bank of Montreal, London, England, 19 Apr. 1910.

108 NA, Fleming Papers, MG29/B1/54/379, notice from Sandford Fleming, Hugh Fleming, and Joe Irvin to Western Canada Cement's debenture holders, 17 May 1910.

109 On 10 May Fleming wrote to W.C. Edwards, president of Canada Cement, that 'possibly more than twelve million dollars of the Securities of the Canada Cement Company have been over-issued to the Bond and Share Company' (AO, Fleming Papers, MU 1051, env. 49).

110 LCA, Canada Cement minutes, 16 Aug. 1910.

111 Not long before, Bennett had purchased on Aitken's advice the Rocky Mountains Cement Company, with the intention of increasing its capacity and reselling it at a profit to the Canada Cement merger with Aitken's assistance (UNBEN, reel 470, Drury to Bennett, 19 May 1910).

112 As Aitken explained to Bennett (UNBEN, reel 470, 31 Aug. 1910), Canada Cement 'will regard our operations favorably, and of course we will work in harmony with them.'

113 LCA, Canada Cement minutes, 12 Oct. 1912; HBK, A/219, Bennett to Aitken, 13 Dec. 1910.

114 In early September, Western Canada Cement did ask for an extension of time for reorganization, but the Canada Cement executive board categorically refused (LCA, Canada Cement executive minutes, 9 Sept. 1910, and letter, H.L Doble, secretary on behalf of Canada Cement to Sandford Fleming, 1 Feb. 1911, appended to Canada Cement minutes, 31 Jan. 1911).

115 LCA, Canada Cement minutes, 2 Nov. 1910.

116 AO, Fleming Papers, MU 1051, env. 49, printed circular concerning proposal to Western Canada Cement's bondholders and the Exshaw Cement Company prospectus.

117 GLSE, 18000/153B/335, circular from bondholders' committee, Western Canada Cement, 1 Dec. 1910, included in Canada Cement's application to LSE for ordinary share quotation dated 24 May 1911.

118 *MT*, 11 Feb. 1911, 648.

119 AO, Fleming Papers, MU 1051, env. 49, Fleming to W.C. Edwards, president, Canada Cement, 5 Jan. 1911.

120 AO, Fleming Papers, MU 1051, env. 49.

121 NA, Fleming Papers, MG29/B1/2/11, Angus to Sandford Fleming, 29 July 1910.

122 Merrill Denison, *Canada's First Bank: A History of the Bank of Montreal* (Toronto 1967), 2:299.

123 NA, Bank of Montreal Papers, MG28/2/2, reel M158, board minutes, 28 Nov. 1911.

124 NA, Bank of Montreal Papers, MG28/2/2, reel M158, board minutes, 4 Dec. 1911.

125 McCord Museum (Montreal), Clouston papers, file A, newspaper clippings of November 1911.

126 HBK, G/3/6, Meredith exam, 8–9. By 1912 Stavert had moved on to become a corporate promoter and financier in his own right, and in 1913 he took over the ailing Spanish River Pulp and Paper from Garnet P. Grant when he and his Dominion Bond Company went bankrupt (NABK, reel A1777, Doble to Aitken, 15 June 1914).

127 Aitken to J.L. Stewart, 5 Dec. 1911, quoted in Chisholm and Davie, *Beaverbrook*, 538.

9: Merger Promoter Extraordinaire

1 At an annual growth rate of 12.4 per cent, transportation was the most rapidly growing sector of the Canadian economy between 1896 and 1913 (see table 1.2).

2 For the interconnection of the various factors – railway building, exhaustion of subhumid land in the United States, the technology of dry-farming techniques, and the rise in the price of wheat beginning in 1895 – inducing a flood of immigrants to the Canadian prairies during the Laurier boom, see K.H. Norrie, 'The Rate of Settlement of the Canadian Prairies, 1870–1911,' *Journal of Economic History* 35, no. 2 (June 1975). On the establishment and

growth of the western wheat economy during the Laurier boom, the best
work remains V.C. Fowke, *The National Policy and the Wheat Economy* (Toronto
1957).

3 On railway development generally, see John A. Eagle, *The Canadian Pacific
Railway and the Development of Western Canada* (Montreal 1989); G.R. Stevens,
Canadian National Railways (Toronto 1960); T.D. Regehr, *The Canadian Northern Railway: Pioneer Road of the Northern Prairies, 1895–1915* (Toronto 1976);
and A.W. Currie, *The Grand Trunk Railway of Canada* (Toronto 1957).

4 See Lyle Dick's article 'Estimates of Farm-Making Costs in Saskatchewan,
1882–1914,' *Prairie Forum* 6, no. 2 (1981), for an insightful examination of the
inputs needed by settlers and their costs in establishing a farm.

5 W.G. Phillips, *The Agricultural Implement Industry in Canada* (Toronto 1956),
chaps. 1–2. See also William Kilbourn, *The Elements Combined: A History of the
Steel Company of Canada* (Toronto 1960), chap. 4; Merrill Denison, *Harvest
Triumphant* (Toronto 1948), chaps. 9–10; and E.P. Neufeld, *A Global Corporation: A History of the International Development of Massey-Ferguson Limited* (Toronto 1969), chap. 1.

6 A. Ernest Epp, 'Cooperation among Capitalists: The Canadian Merger Movement' (PhD diss., Johns Hopkins University, 1973), 534; HBK, G/19/15,
Canadian Car and Foundry preference share prospectus, London, 4 Nov.
1909. Dominion Car and Foundry was the first company to construct steel
railway cars in Canada. In 1905 Rhodes Curry purchased a manufacturing
plant and property at Sydney, NS, in order to begin manufacturing pressed
steel cars, which were increasingly in demand by the railways. The project did
not survive because of the inability of the Dominion Iron and Steel Company
to roll suitable plates (*Monetary Times* [*MT*], 7 July 1905, 14, and 21 July 1905,
74).

7 *MT*, 23 Dec. 1904, 382, and 9 Feb. 1906, 1061. Epp, 'Cooperation among Capitalists,' 535–44.

8 A manufacturer of railway rolling stock, Rhodes Curry was first established
as a woodworking plant in 1877 in Amherst, NS, which then merged with
the New Brunswick Foundry, Rolling Mills and Car Works in 1893 (*MT*,
21 Apr. 1893, 1258, and T.W. Acheson, 'The National Policy and the
Industrialization of the Maritimes, 1880–1910,' *Acadiensis* 1, no. 2 [Spring
1972], 73).

9 *MT*, 3 July 1909, 136, and 14 Aug. 1909, 715.

10 Beaverbrook Papers, House of Lords Record Office (HBK), A/82, Aitken to
White, 1 Jan. 1907; A/33, Doble and Aitken correspondence, 26 and 29 Jan.
1906; A/32, Curry and Aitken correspondence, 25, 27, and 31 Jan. 1906; and
A/41, Aitken to W.D. Ross, 26 Apr. 1906. The original plan involved issuing

$1.25 million face value of bonds at a premium to raise $2 million's worth of new capital. A further $1.25 million common stock issue would be split between the Bank of Montreal and the RSC as remuneration for their respective services as guarantors, some shares of which were to be passed on to investors as bait for purchasing the bonds.

11 HBK, A/32, Aitken to Curry and reply, 27 and 31 Jan. 1906.

12 HBK, A/82, Aitken to J.G. White, 1 Jan. 1907. Aitken was well on his way to convincing J.G. White & Co. to take half the risk in the venture when the talks were derailed by attacks on J.G. White's handling of tramway construction in Puerto Rico.

13 *Nova Scotian and Weekly Chronicle*, 2 July 1909, 1. The Malleable Iron Company was a small Amherst manufacturer with only 80 employees, compared with the 1,200 workers employed by Rhodes Curry in 1907 (*MT*, 9 Nov. 1907, 747).

14 *MT*, 3 July 1909, 136.

15 HBK, A/175, Aitken to J.E. Wood, 29 June 1909, and A/169, Aitken to Stavert, 12 July 1909. C. Meredith & Co.'s 1909 letterhead (HBK, A/148) shows Charles Meredith as president, Stavert as vice-president, Gerald Farrell as secretary-treasurer, and one A.H.B. Mackenzie as manager.

16 *MT*, 5 June 1909, 2184.

17 Rhodes Curry preference shares were selling at a high of $88 and common shares were selling at up to $43 (*MT*, 14 Aug. 1909, 715). The death of Nelson A. Rhodes on 30 Sept. 1909 may have been connected to Curry's willingness to roll into the larger pan-Canadian merger; see Peter Latta, 'Rhodes, Nelson Admiral,' *Dictionary of Canadian Biography* (*DCB*), 13:865–66.

18 The consolidation would have a manufacturing capacity of 75 freight cars a day plus 160 passenger cars a day. Excluding the Angus car shops, Aitken estimated that all the other car companies together could produce only about 10 cars per day (HBK, G/19/15, Canadian Car and Foundry preference share prospectus, London, 4 Nov. 1909).

19 HBK, A/175, Aitken to J.E. Wood, 29 June and 25 Sept. 1909; A/169, Aitken to Stavert, 12 July 1909; A/173, Aitken to Williams, 9 Aug. 1909; A/174, E.R. Wood to H.S. Holt, 13 Oct. 1909; A/154, correspondence between Aitken and W.V. Kelley; and A/175, Aitken and Curry correspondence, 23 Oct. 1909.

20 *MT*, 5 Feb. 1910, 618, and 12 Feb. 1910, 716.

21 See Gregory P. Marchildon, 'British Investment Banking and Industrial Decline before the Great War: A Case Study of Capital Outflow to Canadian Industry,' *Business History* 33, no. 3 (July 1991), 86–8, where the Canadian Car preference share flotation is analysed in greater detail.

22 Or perhaps it succeeded because it did not offer bonus stock. According to the *MT* (24 Sept. 1910, 1335), British investors distrusted bonus common

stock because it was usually an indication of overcapitalization, thus it was 'a poor policy to bait the market with common stock' even if this was the established practice in North America.

23 *MT*, 18 Sept. 1909, 1209–11. HBK, G/19/15, Canadian Car and Foundry preference share prospectus, London, 4 Nov. 1909. On 2 Mar. 1910, preference shares were listed on the Montreal Stock Exchange; see *Annual Financial Review (AFR)* 11 (Apr. 1911), 147. Both preference and common shares were listed on the London Stock Exchange at approximately the same time; see Guildhall Library, London Stock Exchange records (GLSE), 18000/146B/870 and 18000/145B/759, applications to list Canadian Car and Foundry preference shares (25 Feb. 1910) and common shares (4 Mar. 1910). *MT* (25 Dec. 1909, 2626), comments on how audits were delaying the listing of Canada Cement shares.

24 $500,000 worth of bonds had been used to pay for the properties entering the merger (HBK, G/19/15, Canadian Car and Foundry bond prospectus, London, 1 Feb. 1910; *MT*, 5 Feb. 1910, 514, and 12 Feb. 1910, 716). On Canadian Car and Foundry flotation, see Marchildon, 'British Investment Banking,' 86–8.

25 Ranked by assets, Canadian Car was the fifteenth-largest nonfinancial corporation in 1909; if railways and utilities are excluded from the list, then it was the seventh-largest enterprise in the country (Graham D. Taylor and Peter A. Baskerville, *A Concise History of Business in Canada* [Toronto 1994], 312, table 15.1).

26 In recognition of his stature, Nathaniel Curry was elected vice-president of the Canadian Manufacturers' Association for the term 1910–11: (*Industrial Canada* 11 [Oct. 1910], 245).

27 W.R. McCurdy, 'A Young Canadian with a Genius for Organization,' *Busy Man's Magazine [Maclean's]*, Jan. 1910, 24–5; James Grant, 'Sir Maxwell Aitken: Character Sketch,' ibid., Sept. 1911, 147–53.

28 On the 'deal of the century,' see George David Smith and Richard Sylla, 'The Transformation of Financial Capitalism: An Essay on the History of American Capital Markets,' *Financial Market, Institutions and Instruments* 2 (1993), 2–5.

29 M.C. Urquhart and K. Buckley, eds., *Historical Statistics of Canada* (Cambridge 1965), 486. On Hamilton Steel and Iron, see William Kilbourn, *The Elements Combined*. On Scotia, see L.D. McCann, 'The Mercantile Industrial Transition in the Metal Towns of Pictou County, 1857–1931,' *Acadiensis* 10, no. 2 (Spring 1981); Kris Inwood, 'Local Control, Resources and the Nova Scotia Steel and Coal Company,' CHA, *Historical Papers* (1986). On DISCO, see David Frank, 'The Cape Breton Coal Industry and the Rise and Fall of the British Empire Steel Corporation,' *Acadiensis* 7, no. 1 (Autumn 1977), and Don Macgillivray,

'Henry Melville Whitney Comes to Cape Breton: The Saga of a Gilded Age Entrepreneur,' *Acadiensis* 9, no. 1 (Autumn 1979). On Algoma, see Duncan McDowall, *Steel at the Sault: Francis H. Clergue, Sir James Dunn, and the Algoma Steel Corporation, 1901–1956* (Toronto 1984).

30 See Vincent P. Carosso, *The Morgans: Private International Bankers, 1854–1913* (Cambridge, Mass., 1987), 466–74, 487–90, for details on the organization and financing of U.S. Steel in 1900–1.

31 These rumours had been circulating for some time. In 1907, for example, it was reported that U.S. Steel had given up options on properties at Thorold, Sarnia, and Owen Sound. Instead, it was to build a plant on 1,000 acres (404.7 hectares) employing four blast furnaces and 5,000 men at Sandwich, opposite Detroit (*MT*, 10 Aug. 1907, 216).

32 At the beginning of March 1910, the federal government announced that iron and steel bounties, which had been in force for fourteen years, would expire at the end of the fiscal year (*MT*, 5 Mar. 1910, 1034).

33 *MT*, 13 Feb. 1909, 1407.

34 *MT*, 18 May 1907, 1810.

35 HBK, A/170, Aitken to Fred R. Taylor, 18 Nov. 1909; G/3/9, Aitken to Cahan, 26 Nov. 1909; A/173, Aitken to the financial editor of the Montreal *Witness*; A/154, Fred W. Field to A.E. Jennings, 15 Nov. 1909; and A/134, A.J. Brown to Aitken, 24 Dec. 1909. The terms of the merger are set out in the *AFR* 10 (Apr. 1910), 178–9.

36 *AFR* 10 (Apr. 1910), 168. J.H. Plummer was a financier from Toronto who became president of DISCO in October 1903, succeeding James Ross, who had been named president temporarily on Henry M. Whitney's resignation in 1902; see Public Archives of Nova Scotia (PANS) microfilm, MG1/2155, manuscript biography of Graham Fraser by Joseph Dix Fraser, 135–6. See also entry for Frank Percy Jones in *Canadian Men and Women of the Time*, 2nd ed. (Toronto 1912; hereater *CMW*2), 591. Lafarge Canada archives, Narsted manuscript (LCA, Narsted), 110, reports that Jones, born in Brockville in 1869, worked in the shop and sales department of the Canadian General Electric Company until 1894, when he joined Scotia. Five years later he joined DISCO as a sales agent and then became general manager on Graham Fraser's retirement at the end of 1905.

37 Aitken tried to hire F.G.B. Allan, Canadian Portland Cement's experienced general manager, as interim manager of Canada Cement, but he refused 'unless it carries more permanent engagement' (HBK, A/139, Allan and Aitken correspondence, 14, 15, and 22 Sept. 1909).

38 Cahan was sent to Sydney to represent Aitken in the steel-coal merger negotiations in early November. At that time, Cahan was the acting president of

Canada Cement and spoke with F.P. Jones concerning both the coal-steel merger and the cement proposal. Aitken then spent an entire week in early November with Jones convincing him to leave DISCO for Canada Cement (HBK, A/139, Aitken's Nov. correspondence with F.P. Jones, and A/170, and Aitken to Tweedie, 11 Nov. 1909).

39 LCA, Canada Cement minutes, 18 Nov. 1909, with memorandum of agreement between Canada Cement and F.P. Jones dated 11 Nov. 1909. Kilbourn's statement (in *The Elements Combined*, 61) that Aitken 'snatched' Jones from DISCO 'at the unprecedented figure of $50,000' (twice the Prime Minister's salary), is incorrect. A.J.P. Taylor repeats this erroneous figure in *Beaverbrook* (New York 1972), 36.

40 LCA, Narsted, 111. The estimate of 600 shares is based on Jones's holding as registered on 1 Feb. 1911 (GLSE, 18000/153B/335, application to LSE for ordinary share quotation, dated 24 May 1911).

41 HBK, G/3/9, press release by James Ross (signed by Cahan!), dated 16 Nov. 1909.

42 PANS, R.E. Harris Papers, MG1/398/4, various newspaper clippings.

43 In December 1908 Harris and Cantley compiled a list of the number of preferred and common shares held outside the Maritimes, revealing the extent of their vulnerability; 76 per cent of Scotia's common shares were held in Quebec and Ontario, and brokers held 28 per cent of this total (PANS, Cantley letter-book, MG1/170, Cantley to Harris, 23 Dec. 1908).

44 The *MT* was also highly critical of the scheme (13 Mar. 1909, 1607, and 20 Mar. 1909, 1659).

45 HBK, A/151, Harris to Aitken, 9 Mar. 1909.

46 HBK, A/151, Aitken to Harris, 15 Mar. 1909.

47 HBK, A/164, Aitken to Peacock, 24 Mar. 1909.

48 HBK, A/133, Benn to Aitken, 25 Mar. 1909.

49 Inwood, 'Local Control,' 266–7. Inwood estimates that between 1901 and 1912, Scotia's cost of extracting ore increased by 250 per cent.

50 HBK, A/139, Jones to Aitken, 22 Nov. 1909. There were also quality problems; see Inwood, 'Local Control,' for a discussion of both low-grade coal and low-grade iron, and their impact on Scotia. The evidence in the Beaverbrook correspondence supports Inwood's hypothesis concerning Scotia's increasingly deficient resource base, bringing into question analyses that play down this factor; for example, L. Anders Sandberg, 'Dependent Development, Labour and the Trenton Steel Works, Nova Scotia, c. 1900–1943,' *Labour/Le Travail* 27, no. 1 (Spring 1991), 128.

51 *AFR* 9 (Apr. 1909), 188; *MT*, 27 Nov. 1909, 2221, and 4 Dec. 1909, 2321.

52 *MT*, 11 Dec. 1909, 2433.

53 PANS, R.E. Harris Papers, MG1/398/5; *Wall Street Journal*, 2 Dec. 1909.

54 *MT*, 15 Jan. 1910, 314. PANS, R.E. Harris papers, MG1/398/5.

55 PANS, Cantley letter-book, MG1/170, Cantley to W.F. Given, 22 Feb. 1910.

56 PANS, Cantley letter-book, MG1/170, Cantley to Harris, 12 Mar. 1910. One year later, McCurdy would get Sir Sandford Fleming to send his anti-Canada Cement circular so that he could share it with his Halifax cronies (NA, Fleming Papers, MG29/B1/30/214, McCurdy to Sandford Fleming, 13 May 1911).

57 This was revealed days after the Scotia meeting in the Halifax *Morning Chronicle*, 5 Apr. 1910, in an article entitled 'F.B. McCurdy Saved the Day for Scotia.'

58 Portions of the 'Scotia raid' story have already been told; see Inwood, 'Local Control,' 259–63; also Gregory P. Marchildon, 'International Corporate Law from a Maritime Base: The Halifax Firm of Harris, Henry, and Cahan,' in Carol Wilton, ed., *Beyond the Law: Lawyers and Business in Canada, 1830 to 1930* (Toronto 1990), 217–18. See Larry McCann and Jill Burnett, 'Social Mobility and the Ironmaster of Late Nineteenth Century New Glasgow,' in Larry McCann, ed., *People and Place: Studies of Small Town Life in the Maritimes* (Fredericton 1987), 75, which refers to the YMCA as 'the most popular of New Glasgow's clubs.'

59 Cantley, quoted in Halifax *Morning Chronicle*, 31 Mar. 1910. The meeting is recorded almost verbatim in this article. See also report in the *Eastern Chronicle*, 31 Mar. 1910.

60 Greenshields, quoted in Halifax *Morning Chronicle*, 31 Mar. 1910, in PANS, R.E. Harris papers, MG1/398/4, newspaper clippings on Scotia raid.

61 Although Forget and Greenshields had become the leaders of the central-Canadian group, Cantley still assumed that 'Aitken was the dangerous man in the affair.' He told one investor that he and Harris would eventually 'put a knot on his tail' (PANS, Cantley letter-book, MG1/170, letter to George Stout, 25 Apr. 1910).

62 Halifax *Morning Chronicle*, 6, 7, and 9 Apr. 1910, in PANS, R.E. Harris papers, MG1/398/4, Scotia raid. Although Harris did not sign the articles, the evidence points to his being the author, particularly his reference to the 'rumour' that Forget had sworn that 'only the men he feared among the directors were to be slain.' As Cantley had been left on Forget's proposed board, he would not likely have been the author of this sentence.

63 Halifax *Morning Chronicle*, 6 Apr. 1910, 1, in PANS, R.E. Harris papers, MG1/398/4, Scotia raid.

64 Forget ultimately sold his shares back to Harris and Cantley, who were terrified that they might get into Aitken's hands. Forget apparently told Harris and Cantley that Aitken was bidding for his shares, but no record of this can

be found in the Beaverbrook Papers and it is likely that Forget used this threat to get a higher price out of Harris and Cantley, who paid $80 a share at a time when share prices fluctuated between $78 and $80; see PANS, Cantley letter-book, MG1/170, Cantley to Harris, 30 June 1909, and *AFR* 12 (May 1912), 257, monthly prices quoted on MSE from 1902 to 1912.

65 Steel Company of Canada private archive (Stelco), 0256/06, McMaster to Wilcox, 9 Mar. 1910. According to Kilbourn (*The Elements Combined*, 61), Plummer eventually regretted his decision and so told William McMaster years later.

66 Kilbourn, *The Elements Combined*, 61–2; HBK, A/193, Aitken to Holt, 29 Apr. 1910; and *MT*, 11 June 1910, 2412. Of this amount, $3,700,000 was in cash, and $500,000 was in the assumption of long-term debt.

67 *MT*, 7 Nov. 1908, 759, and 21 Nov. 1908, 845. Aitken sold a part of his total interest, approximately 2,800 shares, at a price of $135. He advised his fellow shareholders to hold on to their shares as he believed that Montreal Trust would 'be much more successful owing to the strong connection of the [Royal] Bank' (HBK, A/130, Aitken to Charles Archer, July 1909).

68 Kilbourn, *The Elements Combined*, 61–2.

69 HBK, G/3/9, telegram, Aitken to Cahan, 9 Mar. 1910.

70 Stelco, 0256/06, McMaster to Birge, 31 Jan. 1910, and Price Waterhouse to McMaster with enclosures and copy to Aitken, 12 Mar. 1910.

71 Stelco, 0256/06 Whitten to Birge, 7 Mar. 1910, and Lloyd Harris to Wilcox, 8 Mar. 1910; 0256/07, printed memorandum of understanding between C.S. Wilcox, representing Hamilton Steel and Iron, William McMaster, representing the Montreal Rolling Mills, Cyrus A. Birge, representing Canada Screw, and Lloyd Harris, representing Canada Bolt and Nut, 28 Feb. 1910, with McMaster and Montreal Rolling Mills scored out of agreement.

72 Stelco, 0252/04, list of fourteen shareholders on record, 8 Feb. 1910. Farrell owned 2,672 shares out of 5,000. The next largest share holder was Molsons Bank, which held 717 shares.

73 HBK, A/193, Aitken to Holt, 12 Mar. 1910: Aitken said he was most interested in the 'alliance between the Dominion Wire Co. and the officials of the United States Steel Corporation, which possibly results in a certain amount of protection ... to the Canadian market in galvanized wire.'

74 Kilbourn, *The Elements Combined*, 70; Stelco, 0256/06, Farrell to Wilcox, 8 Oct. 1909.

75 HBK, A/193, Aitken to Holt, 12 Mar. 1910.

76 HBK, G/3/9, Aitken to Cahan, 9 Mar. 1910, and A/193, Aitken to Holt, 12 Mar. 1910. There is no indication of Aitken's thoughts on Algoma or why Algoma's president, Thomas Drummond, refused to enter the Canadian

Steel Corporation. According to McDowall (*Steel At the Sault*, chap. 3), Algoma performed well between 1908 and 1913 although its specialization in steel rail production masked some fundamental weaknesses in the company.

77 Kilbourn, *The Elements Combined*, 71.

78 Stelco, 0238/02, Canada Screw Company, list of preference and common shareholders, 31 Mar. 1910. Birge held 38 per cent of Canada Screw's shares, Whitton 6.1 per cent, and Wilcox 3.3 percent.

79 Stelco, 0282/12, Hamilton *Spectator*, 9 July 1910, 1.

80 Stelco, 0256/06, Birge to Whitton, 12 Feb. 1910.

81 HBK, G/3/9, Aitken to Cahan, 10 Mar. 1910, and A/193, Aitken to Holt, 12 Mar. 1910.

82 Stelco, 0282/17, RSC (Montreal) to Aitken (Waldorf Astoria, New York), 11 Apr. 1911, and V.M. Drury (RSC) to Aitken (Savoy Hotel, London). Montreal Rolling Mills' largest shareholders – McMaster, Clouston, Royal Trust Company, Sir Montague Allan, and Robert McKay – deposited their stock almost immediately.

83 In Kilbourn's *Elements Combined*, 71–7, the meeting at the Waldorf-Astoria in New York is said have been after Aitken's trip to England, sometime in late May or June. The documentation (Stelco, 0282/08, Waldorf-Astoria agreement dated 9 Apr. 1910, witnessed by F.P. Jones) however, indicates that the New York meeting preceded Aitken's trip to Europe in mid-April. The confusion is understandable given that the written agreement of 9 April was ultimately printed and dated 30 May 1910.

84 This description is drawn from Kilbourn's *Elements Combined*, 71–3, as corroborated by evidence in the Beaverbrook Papers, particularly the identity of those attending the Waldorf-Astoria meeting.

85 Beaverbrook Papers, University of New brunswick (UNBK), 72b/15, Aitken to Ross McMaster and reply, 9 and 12 Nov. 1957.

86 Holt was involved in the Montreal Rolling Mills purchase from the beginning (HBK, A/193, Aitken to Holt, 12 Mar. 1910).

87 In *The Elements Combined*, Kilbourn states that the Waldorf-Astoria negotiations took ten days, information that he received from Beaverbrook a few years before the latter's death. Although the documentation does not indicate the length of time, such complex negotiations could easily have taken so long.

88 Stelco, 0282/12, Stelco statement of assets broken into constituent companies, 1 July 1910.

89 The New York agreement of 9 Apr. 1910 was the same as that ultimately printed and dated 30 May 1910 (Stelco 0282/08, agreement dated 9 Apr. 1910). Agreement confirmed in Stelco (Canadian Steel Corporation) min-

utes of 14 June 1910, authorizing the purchase of the Montreal Rolling Mills 'upon a warranted net valuation of $4,000,000, of which at least $1,000,000 will be liquid assets.'

90 Stelco, 0256/06, Farrell to Aitken and reply, 15 June 1910, and Wilcox, Birge, Hobson, and Harris to Aitken, 14 June 1910.

91 Stelco, 0256/06, merger committee to Aitken, 9 Apr. 1910, and Aitken to Farrell and reply, 12 and 14 Apr. 1910.

92 HBK, A/193, Aitken to Holt, 29 Apr. 1910.

93 Anne Chisholm and Michael Davie, *Beaverbrook: A Life* (London 1992), 69.

94 HBK, A/193, Aitken to Holt, 29 Apr. 1910. The amount of RSC stock purchased by Lazard Bros. & Co. was not specified by Aitken in his letter to Holt, but it certainly was not a controlling interest as rumoured in the *MT*, 30 Apr. 1910, 1822.

95 Aitken did not borrow $5 million in Britain as suggested by Chisholm and Davie (*Beaverbrook*, 69); he borrowed only the $3.75 million cash needed for the Montreal Rolling Mills, since the steel syndicate itself had agreed to exercise Aitken's option on Dominion Wire (HBK, A/193, Aitken to Holt, 29 Apr. 1910).

96 Chisholm and Davie, *Beaverbrook*, 69–70.

97 Stelco, 0113/Montreal Rolling Mills minutes, 3 June 1910.

98 HBK, A/202, Plummer and Aitken correspondence, 28 May and 8 June 1910.

99 Stelco, 0252/05, articles in *Montreal Herald*, 2–4 June 1910.

100 *MT*, 11 June 1910, 2412.

101 GLSE, 18000/151B/31, documents filed with LSE application for quotation of Stelco bonds, 20 Oct. 1910: letters patent in name of 'Canadian Steel Corporation' dated 8 June 1910, and supplementary letters patent changing name to the 'Steel Corporation of Canada,' filed 22 June 1910.

102 Stelco, 0282/08, Stelco bond prospectus dated 1 July 1910.

103 Net fixed assets were assessed to be $343,469 more than previously, while net liquid assets were found to be $274,832 more; see Stelco, 0251/13, balance sheet for Montreal Rolling Mills to 30 June 1910, plus other accounting documentation, including draft setting out provisions of agreement of 12 July 1910 between the RSC and Stelco, and letter with enclosure, Price Waterhouse to H.H. Champ, Stelco treasurer, 17 Nov. 1910.

104 Stelco 0251/08, Montreal Rolling Mills minutes of special meeting of shareholders held at Montreal, 27 July 1910, Aitken and the RSC represented by V.M. Drury, since Aitken had already left for England by this time.

105 Kilbourn, *The Elements Combined*, 76–7.

106 Marchildon, 'International Corporate Law from a Maritime Base,' 218–25, discusses the dispute between Aitken and Cahan at greater length.

107 HBK, A/219, Bennett to Aitken, 19 Dec. 1909.

108 HBK, A/209, Aitken to Wilcox, 19 July 1910.

109 Aitken also wanted to supervise Benn; he told E.R. Wood that Benn and his English friends had been a little 'too hungry' in the Canadian Car flotation (HBK, A/209, Aitken to Wood, 1 Apr. 1910).

110 Chisholm and Davie, *Beaverbrook*, 73; Taylor, *Beaverbrook*, 43–4.

111 Aitken first signed the visitor book at Goudling's house in Wargrave, Berks, in late September (Chisholm and Davie, *Beaverbrook*, 73–4).

112 Sandra Gwyn, *Tapestry of War: A Private View of Canadians in the Great War* (Toronto 1992), 249.

113 Quoted in Taylor, *Beaverbrook*, 44.

114 Taylor, *Beaverbrook*, 43.

115 $488,000 Stelco bonds were earmarked for the Canadian public by the RSC at the same time as $4.5 million (£924,000) Stelco bonds were issued in London (*MT*, 16 July 1910; HBK, G/19/15, Stelco bond prospectus, London, 9 July 1910).

116 Gregory P. Marchildon, '"Hands across the Water": Canadian Industrial Financiers in the City of London,' *Business History* 34, no. 3 (July 1992), 86–7.

117 The issue was sold at a 13¢ discount on par and was offered simultaneously in London, Montreal, Toronto, Quebec City, Halifax, and Chicago by the RSC (*MT*, 5 Nov. 1910, 1916; *MT*, 12 Nov. 1910, 2028; and *MT*, 26 Nov. 1910, 2236). According to the *Canadian Journal of Commerce* (18 Nov. 1910, 741), demand was so strong that Aitken was able to sell the issue one point above the prospectus price.

118 *MT*, 12 Nov. 1910, 2021.

119 *MT*, 20 Nov. 1909, 2142; *MT*, 11 Dec. 1909, 2450; *MT*, 19 Mar. 1910, 1219; and *MT*, 18 June 1910, 2544. The Quebec office was established at the beginning of 1909 by Killam and was later managed by G.H. Doble (perhaps related to Arthur Doble) after Killam left for London, at which time R.M. White became the manager of the Toronto branch. Gladys Aitken's brother, Victor Drury, was the manager of the Montreal head office at this time.

120 HBK, A/219, Bennett to Aitken, 13 Nov. 1910: Bennett congratulates Aitken on being offered the North Cumberland constituency.

121 Chisholm and Davie, *Beaverbrook*, 75; Taylor, *Beaverbrook*, 44.

122 Letter of 14 Nov. 1910, quoted in Chisholm and Davie, *Beaverbrook*, 76–7.

123 Quoted in Chisholm and Davie, *Beaverbrook*, 79.

124 The meaning of the word 'speculate' is sufficiently vague that, objectively speaking, Aitken's activities could easily be classified as participating 'in any risky venture on the chance of making huge profits.' See *Webster's New World Dictionary*, 2nd College Edition (Toronto 1974), 1368.

125 HBK, A/209, Aitken to General Wilson, 28 June 1910.
126 HBK, G/18/13, Aitken to R.T.D. Aitken, 23 Apr. 1909.
127 Chisholm and Davie, *Beaverbrook*, 78–9.
128 Ibid., 81.
129 In fact his maiden speech, one year later, was on the subject he knew best – the Caribbean, and British-Canadian competition with the United States over economic influence in the region (Chisholm and Davie, *Beaverbrook*, 89).

10: Combines, Canada Cement, and the Reciprocity Election

1 Quotation from article entitled 'Trusts,' in *Grain Growers' Guide*, 19 Jan. 1910, 19.
2 *Debates of the House of Commons (DHC)*, 12 Apr. 1910, 6813.
3 The tariff reform campaign is well covered by Michael Balfour, *Britain and Joseph Chamberlain* (London 1985), and Aaron L. Friedberg, *The Weary Titan: Britain and the Experience of Relative Decline, 1895–1905* (Princeton 1988).
4 Beaverbrook Papers, House of Lords Record Office (HBK), A/28, Aitken to Dr Horatio Walker, 8 Nov. 1905.
5 HBK, A/36, Aitken to Rev. W.T.D. Moss, 18 May 1906.
6 Hugh Cudlipp, *The Prerogative of the Harlot: Press Barons and Power* (London 1980), 250.
7 Aitken finally sold the magazine in September 1911; see Anne Chisholm and Michael Davie, *Beaverbrook: A Life* (London 1992), 107.
8 Rev. Salem Bland, a Methodist minister and agrarian radical, regularly attacked what he called the 'rascalities of high finance' during the Laurier boom; quoted in Robert Craig Brown and Ramsay Cook, *Canada, 1896–1921: A Nation Transformed* (Toronto 1974), 146.
9 In *A Living Profit: Studies in the Social History of Canadian Business, 1883–1911* (Toronto 1974), Michael Bliss dissects the source of the attitude resulting in behaviour which he describes as the 'flight from competition.'
10 See the *Select Committee Report on Alleged Combinations in Manufactures, Trade and Insurance in Canada* (Ottawa 1888), submitted to the House of Commons on 16 May 1888. The report fuelled the demand for the removal of protectionist tariffs, which were popularly believed to be the 'cause' of price fixing. The Macdonald Conservatives, committed as they were to the National Policy of tariff protection, passed the anticombines legislation in order to cure the abuses of price fixing without affecting tariffs.
11 In particular, see Michael Bliss, 'Another Anti-Trust Tradition: Canadian Anti-Combines Policy, 1889–1910,' *Business History Review* 47, no. 2 (Summer 1973), and Tom Naylor, *The History of Canadian Business, 1867–1914*, vol. 2

(Toronto 1975), 162–94. For general information on the first anticombines legislation, see Paul K. Gorecki and William T. Stanbury, *The Objectives of Canadian Competition Policy, 1888–1983* (Montreal 1984), A. Ball, *Canadian Anti-Trust Legislation* (Baltimore 1934), Lloyd G. Reynolds, *The Control of Competition in Canada* (Cambridge, Mass., 1940), O.J. McDiarmid, *Commercial Policy in the Canadian Economy* (Cambridge, Mass., 1946), 189–207, and Maxwell Cohen, 'The Canadian Antitrust Laws: Doctrinal and Legislative Beginnings,' *Canadian Bar Review* 16, no. 3 (Sept. 1938).

12 *The Queen v. American Tobacco Company of Canada*; see *Revue de jurisprudence (Quebec)* 3 (1897), 453–64.

13 *DHC*, 12 Apr. 1910, 6843–5.

14 Bliss, *A Living Profit*.

15 In 1886, 44.3 per cent of Canada's total trade was with the United States compared to 43.7 per cent with Britain. In 1896 the percentage of trade with Britain had increased relative to the United States; but by 1901, 48.7 per cent of all Canadian trade was with the United States compared to 38.7 per cent with Britain. See F.H. Leacy, ed., *Historical Statistics of Canada* (Ottawa 1983), calculated from series G389–414.

16 L. Ethan Ellis, *Reciprocity 1911: A Study in Canadian-American Relations* (New Haven, Conn., 1939), 2–10, and McDiarmid, *Commercial Policy in Canada*, 203–29.

17 According to James J. Harpell, tariff protection and combines (cartels and mergers) were the two most important causes of high prices in Canada (*Canadian National Economy: The Cause of High Prices and Their Effect upon the Country* [Toronto 1911]).

18 Lyle Dick, 'Estimates of Farm-Making Costs in Saskatchewan, 1882–1914,' *Prairie Forum* 6, no. 2 (1981).

19 HBK, G/3/9, Aitken to Cahan, 15 Sept. 1909.

20 *Grain Growers' Guide*, 29 Sept. 1909, 14.

21 Entry for George H. Bradbury in *The Canadian Directory of Parliament, 1867–1967* (Ottawa 1968, hereafter *CDP*), 69; *DHC*, 16 Nov. 1909, 106–7. This exchange was duly reported on in the *Grain Growers' Guide*, 17 Nov. 1909, 17.

22 The *Grain Growers' Guide*, 28 Aug. 1909, 10, attacked the cement merger from the moment that the Canadian Consolidated Cement Company charter was taken out; the announcement of the charter, in the *Guide*'s view, was 'nothing more or less than the euphonious announcement that the people of Canada are to become *the victims of another vicious combine*' (emphasis in original).

23 *Monetary Times (MT)*, 18 Sept. 1909, 1209.

24 *MT*, 18 Sept. 1909, 1210, and interview, 17 Sept. 1909, 1213.

25 HBK, A/207, Aitken to the London *Times*, 10 Jan. 1910.

26 Aitken had, in fact, adopted a basing-point system of pricing in which delivered price was equal to the plant's base price plus the published freight rate
   from the plant to the market in question. On the basing-point system and its
   role in cement price collusion in the United States, see Samuel M. Loescher,
   Imperfect Collusion in the Cement Industry (Cambridge, Mass., 1959).

27 HBK, A/150, Aitken to William H. Dennis, proprietor of the Halifax *Herald*,
   12 Nov. 1909.

28 HBK, A/139, Aitken to Richards, 4 Sept. 1909, Aitken to Canadian Portland
   Cement, 6 Sept. 1909, Allan to Aitken, 9 Sept. 1909, and Thorn to Aitken with
   enclosures, 20 Dec. 1909.

29 Lafarge Canada private archive (LCA), Canada Cement compilation of retail
   price data from independent cement dealers in various Canadian cities, V.C.
   Hamilton's memorandum book. As retail prices are expressed in the form of
   annual statistics, I have relied on 1910 data as a proxy for post-merger prices,
   and on 1909 data as a proxy for premerger data.

30 National Archives of Canada (NA), Laurier Papers, MG26/G, reel C900,
   Miller to Laurier, 16 Dec. 1910.

31 HBK, A/207, Aitken to the London *Times*, 10 Jan. 1910.

32 HBK, A/157, Aitken to A.W. MacArthur of the Standard Ideal Company,
   30 Oct. 1909.

33 HBK, A/132, Aitken to H.C. Blair and reply, 22 and 24 Nov. 1909, and A/134,
   Thomson to Butler and reply, 26 and 27 Nov. 1909.

34 *DHC*, 18 Jan. 1910, 2057–60.

35 *Grain Growers' Guide*, 16 June 1910.

36 Glen Campbell in *DHC*, 12 Apr. 1910, 6914.

37 R. MacGregor Dawson, *William Lyon Mackenzie King: A Political Biography* (Toronto 1958), 198–205, and F.A. McGregor, *The Fall and Rise of Mackenzie King:
   1911–1919* (Toronto 1962), 40.

38 *DHC*, 18 Jan. 1910, 2057.

39 Bliss, 'Another Anti-Trust Tradition.'

40 *DHC*, 24 Jan. 1910, 2296–7.

41 *DHC*, 12 Apr. 1910, 6824.

42 *DHC*, 12 Apr. 1910, 6826–7.

43 J.A. Currie (North Simcoe, Ont.), in *DHC*, 12 Apr. 1910, 6880.

44 *CDP*, 147: Currie was managing director of the Imperial Steel Corporation
   and general manager of the Huronia Steel Company; *DHC*, 12 Apr. 1910,
   6884.

45 The most effective was Thomas S. Sproule, Conservative (Grey East, Ont.);
   see *DHC*, 12 Apr. 1910, 6874–91.

46 Nowhere in Aitken's correspondence is there an indication that Canada

Cement feared investigation after the passage of the law. Nor was Aitken ever again sent letters by his associates asking whether he had taken defensive measures to avoid an attack under the Combines Investigation Act. In a cartoon, Aitken's magazine, the *Canadian Century*, 19 Feb. 1910, did poke fun at Mackenzie King and his Combines Investigation Act.

47 Brown and Cook, *Canada, 1896–1921*, 159.

48 *Grain Growers' Guide*, 6 July 1910, 8.

49 *Grain Growers' Guide*, 13 July 1910, 26.

50 Various issues of the *Grain Growers' Guide*, July and August 1910.

51 *Industrial Canada* 11 (Sept. 1910), 119.

52 *Industrial Canada* 11 (Sept. 1910), 123–4; (Oct. 1910), 240–1, 247–8, 332; (Nov. 1910), 433–5, 440–6; and (Dec. 1910), 531.

53 Quoted in Brown and Cook, *Canada, 1896–1921*, 160.

54 Aitken had first conceived the idea shortly after his move to Montreal: HBK, A/44, R.T.D. Aitken to Aitken, 8 Nov. 1907), but it took him another two years to begin operations. A.J.P. Taylor (*Beaverbrook* [New York 1972], 35) suggests that Aitken's failed attempt to buy the Montreal *Gazette* prompted the *Canadian Century* venture. Chisholm and Davie (*Beaverbrook*, 98–9) suggest that he tried to buy the *Gazette* in February 1910, after having started the *Century*.

55 *Canadian Century*, 8 Jan. 1910, 3.

56 *Canadian Century*, 8 Jan. 1910, 7. Entry for Sir George Eulas Foster in *The Canadian Encyclopedia* (Edmonton 1985), 2:682, and *CDP*, 212. Only after his defeat in Saint John in 1900 did Foster leave New Brunswick to run for a House of Commons seat in Ontario. Foster's article provided Aitken with his introduction to Rudyard Kipling. On 14 Nov. 1910, Aitken sent Kipling a copy of a *Canadian Century* issue, pointing out Foster's piece. Kipling was impressed, and within a month he was meeting with Aitken on a regular basis. See Sandra Gwyn, *Tapestry of War: A Private View of Canadians in the Great War* (Toronto 1992), 248.

57 Watson Griffin, 'A Canadian Navy,' *Canadian Century*, 8 Jan. 1910, 9. Olivar Asselin, 'A Quebec View of Canadian Nationalism,' *Canadian Century*, 22 Jan. 1910, 7–8.

58 *Canadian Century*, 29 Jan. 1910, 20; 5 Feb. 1910, 20; and 19 Feb. 1910, 20.

59 *Canadian Annual Review* (*CAR*), 1910, 328–35.

60 This quotation is taken from G.F. Chipman's introduction to his edited record of the event: *The Siege of Ottawa* (Winnipeg 1911), 8.

61 As Chipman described it in the *Siege of Ottawa*, 'Canada sat up on Friday morning and rubbed its eyes to see that the farmers were at last coming to the front and were capable of doing business at Ottawa, as well as were the

manufacturers and other interests. Since morning newspapers throughout
the country had carried the story of the farmers' delegation, the House was,
for a change, full of both government and opposition members' (9).

62 Rob Macian, 'The Great Farmers' Delegation: Some Impressions,' *Canadian
Century*, 31 Dec. 1910, 14, 22.

63 Macian, 'Farmers' Delegation,' *Canadian Century*, 31 Dec. 1910, 22.

64 Chipman, *Siege of Ottawa*, 64.

65 NA, Laurier Papers, MG26/G, reel C900, Laurier to Miller, 17 Dec. 1910.

66 Henry Horton Miller (Grey S., Ont.) of Hanover, Ont., was elected to the
House of Commons in the general elections of 1904 and 1908, and subsequently became chairman of the Banking and Commerce Parliamentary
Committee. In the 1911 election, Miller lost to the Conservative candidate by
only forty-eight votes (*Parliamentary Guide 1910*, 149, and *Parliamentary Guide
1912*.)

67 NA, Laurier Papers, MG26/G, reel C897, Miller to Laurier, 16 Dec.
1910.

68 NA, Laurier Papers, MG26/G, reel C897, Laurier to Miller, 17 Dec. 1910. First
elected in 1904 and re-elected in 1908, Miller lost his Ontario seat of Grey
South in 1911, in part because of Laurier's decision to lower the tariff on
cement in the proposed reciprocity agreement (*CDP*, 366).

69 Confidential dispatch 61, from James Bryce to Governor General Earl Grey,
7 Apr. 1910, and 12 May 1910 with enclosed letter from P.C. Knox, U.S.
secretary of state, to Bryce, 12 May 1910, in *Documents on Canadian External
Relations*, vol. 1, *1909–1918* (Ottawa 1967), 776–7.

70 Letters between P.C. Knox, U.S. secretary of state, and W.S. Fielding,
minister of finance, 10, 12, 20, 24, and 28 Oct. 1910, in *Documents on
Canadian External Relations*, 1:779–83. As the governor general astutely
observed (confidential dispatch, governor general to colonial secretary, 30
Nov. 1910), although the objectives of both countries initially seemed at
variance – the United States wanted its manufactured products to have easy
entry into a rapidly industrializing Canada, while Canada wanted its natural
products to have a market in the densely populated cities of the United
States – recent increases in the price level had produced a demand for
reduction of duties on foreign food imports to the United States, as recent
congressional elections had illustrated.

71 *DHC*, 26 Jan. 1911, 2440–76; Ellis, *Reciprocity, 1911*, 11–70; Brown and Cook,
Canada, 1896–1921, 162–87. A majority of natural products were to be admitted free (schedule A) and the remainder were to be admitted at lower or
identical duties in both countries (schedule B). Agricultural implements
came under schedule B. A very few manufactured products from Canada

were to be allowed into the United States at a lower rate (schedule C), while duties on a few American manufactures, most notably cement, were to be significantly reduced (schedule D); see *CAR*, 1911, 28–30.

72 See Paul Stevens's introduction to his edited volume *The 1911 General Election: A Study in Canadian Politics* (Toronto 1970), 1–5, and Brown and Cook, *Canada, 1896–1921*, 161, 180.

73 *DHC*, 2 Feb. 1911, 2956. Borden simply wanted to embarrass the government. Not only was he a personal friend of Max Aitken and a business lawyer familiar with high-risk finance, but he was sympathetic to its methods.

74 *DHC*, 2 Feb. 1911, 2950–1.

75 Meighen, quoted in the *MT*, 4 Mar. 1911, 916.

76 *Grain Growers' Guide*, 26 Apr. 1911, 5.

77 *DHC*, 2 Feb. 1911, 2927–40. It was popularly believed that the inflation of the period was caused by the higher commodity prices imposed by mergers. This view was given scholarly cachet with the appearance of J.J. Harpell's *Canadian National Economy, the Causes of High Prices and Their Effect Upon the Country* (Toronto, 1911) – commented on in the *MT*, 25 Mar. 1911, 1232.

78 NA, Laurier Papers, MG26/G, reel C900, J.R. Dutton (Riverside Farms, Man.) to Laurier and reply, 8 and 14 Feb. 1911.

79 *MT*, 16 Sept. 1911, 1215.

80 HBK, A/155, Aitken to Killam, 20 Nov. 1909.

81 Quoted in Brown and Cook, *Canada, 1896–1921*, 92.

82 *Toronto Sun* article, reprinted in *Grain Growers' Guide*, 27 Apr. 1910.

83 A.A. Berle, 'Problems of Non-Par Stock,' *Columbia Law Review* 25 (1925). James C. Bonbright, 'The Danger of Shares without Par Value,' *Quarterly Journal of Economics* 38, no. 2 (May 1924). For a general review, see Louis Loss, *Securities Regulation* (Boston 1961).

84 On dissatisfaction within the Liberal government, see Robert D. Cuff, 'The Toronto Eighteen and the Election of 1911,' *Ontario History*, Dec. 1965; W.M. Baker, 'A Case Study of Anti-Americanism in English-Speaking Canada: The Election Campaign of 1911,' *Canadian Historical Review* 51, no. 4 (Dec. 1970); and Brown and Cook, *Canada, 1896–1921*, 181–4. Mackenzie King continued to support Laurier, despite his grave doubts about the political viability of the reciprocity agreement (NA, King Papers, MG26/J13, microfiche T24, diary entry, 18 Jan. 1911).

85 A Liberal, Harris had crossed the floor to the Conservatives to protest the reciprocity deal. Curry used his position in the CMA to fight reciprocity. See C.P. Stacey, *Canada and the Age of Conflict: A History of Canadian External Policies* (Toronto 1977), 148.

86 HBK, A/183, and various issues of the *Canadian Century*.

87 This story is recounted in Henry Borden, ed., *Robert Laird Borden: His Memoirs* (Toronto 1938), 320.

88 HBK, A/212, and quoted in Taylor, *Beaverbrook*, 59.

89 Robert Craig Brown, *Robert Laird Borden: A Biography* (Toronto 1975), 185.

90 HBK, G/19/Borden, Borden to Aitken, 5 Apr. 1911.

91 HBK, A/229, Aitken to Allan Davidson, quoted in Taylor, *Beaverbrook*, 59.

92 Beaverbrook Papers, National Archives of Canada (NABK), MG27/2/G1/ Borden, Borden (holograph, marked confidential) to Aitken, 1 May 1911.

93 HBK, H/80, Aitken to Doble, 20 June 1911.

94 HBK, C/50, Borden to Aitken, 9 May 1911.

95 Quoted in Chisholm and Davie, *Beaverbrook*, 90

96 He had previously sent the same printed pamphlet to every member of the Canada Cement board, prompting at least one extensive defence of the manner in which the merger was promoted, from J.M. Kilbourn (NA, Fleming Papers, MG29/B1/26/185, Kilbourn to Fleming, 24 Mar. 1911).

97 NA, Laurier Papers, MG26/G, reel C902, Sir Sandford Fleming to Laurier, 5 Apr. 1910.

98 NA, Laurier Papers, MG26/G, reel C902, Laurier to Fleming, 7 Apr. 1911.

99 NA, Fleming Papers, MG29/B1/30/214, Fleming to chairman, Private Bills Committee, 11 May 1911; HBK, G/19/Borden, clipping from the *Montreal Star*, 12 May 1911.

100 *CAR*, 1911, 360; *MT*, 6 May 1911, 1814.

101 HBK, H/81. Quotation is from a comment, on the Toronto *Globe*'s attack, in the *Montreal Star*, 26 May 1911.

102 HBK, G/19/Borden, clipping from *Montreal Star*, 12 May 1911.

103 *MT*, 3 June 1911, 2209–10.

104 *MT*, 24 June 1911, 2510; Chisholm and Davie, *Beaverbrook*, 91.

105 Gwyn, *Tapestry of War*, 251.

106 Taylor, *Beaverbrook*, 65.

107 Bennett Papers, University of New Brunswick (UNBEN), reel 470, Aitken to Bennett, 16 Aug. 1911.

108 Quoted in Chisholm and Davie, *Beaverbrook*, 90.

109 Quoted in Chisholm and Davie, *Beaverbrook*, 90.

110 HBK, H/80, Aitken to Doble, 20 June 1911.

111 HBK, H/80, telegram, Doble to Aitken, 18 May 1911.

112 NABK, MG27/2/G1. Borden to Aitken, 24 May 1911, and Bennett to Aitken, 11 Aug. 1911.

113 NABK, MG27/2/G1. Bennett to Aitken, 11 Aug. 1911. Bennett mentions Jones and his desire that Aitken should avoid the campaign.

114 HBK, G/19/21, Drury to Aitken, 13 July 1911.

115 Quoted in Chisholm and Davie, *Beaverbrook*, 537. Aitken wrote to Kipling that

he was spending an enormous sum of money on the Canadian antireciprocity campaign (*ibid.*, 96).

116 Quoted in Baker, 'Anti-Americanism in English-Speaking Canada,' 437.

117 Stacey, *Age of Conflict*, 148; Cahan's letter to the editor of the *Montreal Herald*, 2 Sept. 1911, reprinted in Stevens, *1911 General Election*, 143–4; entry for Forget, *CDP*, 209.

118 *CDP*, 148.

119 Quoted in Chisholm and Davie, *Beaverbrook*, 95.

120 Quoted in Gwyn, *Tapestry of War*, 251.

121 NA, Fleming Papers, MG29/B1/5/31, Sandford Fleming to Borden, 25 Oct. 1911.

122 NA, Fleming Papers, MG29/B1/126/65, printed circular.

123 NA, Fleming Papers, MG29/B1/5/31, Borden to Fleming, 15 Nov. 1911.

124 On Aitken's post-election visit, see Chisholm and Davie, *Beaverbrook*, 113.

125 This is what Aitken believed at any rate (Aitken to J.L. Stewart, 5 Dec. 1911, quoted in Chisholm and Davie, *Beaverbrook*, 538).

126 HBK, A/219. Bennett to Aitken, 18 Nov. 1911.

127 Ibid.

128 HBK, A/219. Bennett to Aitken, 9 Dec. 1911.

129 HBK, A/219. Bennett to Aitken (sometime in 1912).

130 George Smith Holmested and Thomas Langton, *The Judicature Act of Ontario and the Consolidated Rules of Practice and Procedure of the Supreme Court of the Judicature of Ontario* (Toronto 1905), chap. 7 (on examinations for discovery).

131 He bought a 40–acre site east of Spokane and hired the Fuller Engineering Company of Allentown, Pa, to begin erecting a cement plant that autumn costing $1 million. The 2,000 barrel-a-day-capacity plant was to be operational by the following summer (*MT*, 23 Sept. 1911, 1351).

132 HBK, G/3/6, 1st Irvin exam and Fleming exam.

133 McCord Museum (Montreal), Clouston Papers, obituary file.

134 NABK, Bennett to Aitken, 9 Dec. 1911. Ill for some time, Fleming was to die in Halifax on 22 July 1915 at eighty-eight years of age.

135 HBK, G/3/6, Meredith exam.

136 HBK, G/3/6, Fleming exam.

137 NA, Fleming Papers, MG29/B1/15/107, S.H. Fleming to Sandford Fleming, 9 Aug. 1911. Joe Irvin told Fleming (MG29/B1/23/170, letter, 16 Aug. 1911) that 'the Bank of Montreal and the Royal Trust Company were active parties in both Montreal and London in bringing about the deal for the Exshaw property which, as you know, resulted so disastrously for all concerned.'

138 HBK, G/3/6, 2nd Irvin exam, 30.

139 HBK, G/3/7, A.M. Stewart to Aitken, 31 Oct. 1913.

140 Chisholm and Davie, *Beaverbrook*, 542.
141 HBK, G/3/7, Doble to Aitken, 12 Nov. 1913.
142 UNBEN, reel 470, correspondence between Aitken and Bennett, 1910–13; *MT*, 7 Sept. 1912, 416.
143 *MT*, 8 Apr. 1911, 1419; *MT*, 6 Apr. 1912, 1424; and *MT*, 27 Apr. 1912, 1754.
144 NABK, reel A1776, Clarke to Aitken and reply, 15 and 30 Aug. 1911, and Clarke to Aitken, 19 Dec. 1911.
145 NABK, reel A1776, Clarke to Aitken and reply, 5 and 14 May 1913, and Clarke to Aitken, 22 Aug. 1914.
146 NABK, reel A1776, Aitken to Porto Rico Railways, 3 Nov. 1916.
147 NABK, reel A1776, Clarke to Lord Beaverbrook, 2 Mar. 1917.
148 NABK, reel A1776, Clarke to Aitken, 15 Aug. 1911, 6 Jan. 1912.
149 NABK, reel A1776, Clarke to Aitken, 27 July 1911 and 10 Apr. 1912.
150 HBK, G/3/6, Meredith exam, and Taylor, *Beaverbrook*, 79.
151 NABK, reel A1777, Aitken to Doble, 14 May 1914.
152 According to Douglas How (*Canada's Mystery Man of Finance* [Hantsport, NS 1986], 86), Aitken personally recruited Pitfield.
153 NABK, reel A1777, Doble to Aitken, 15 June 1914.
154 NABK, reel A1776, Giles to Aitken, 2 Jan. and 7 Apr. 1914, and reel A1777, Doble to Aitken, 1 May 1914.
155 On the Canadian public's perception of those individuals who profited in this way from the First World War, see Michael Bliss, *A Canadian Millionaire: The Life and Business Times of Sir Joseph Flavelle, Bart. 1858–1939* (Toronto 1978), chap. 14.
156 UNBEN, reel 470, Drury to Bennett, 20 Jan. 1915.
157 Killam purchased majority control in 1919 (Taylor, *Beaverbrook*, 79; Chisholm and Davie, *Beaverbrook*, 497; How, *Canada's Mystery Man*, 137–8; *MT*, 14 Jan. 1915, 7).
158 See Gwyn, *Tapestry of War*, for an account of Aitken's contribution to the Canadian war effort.

11: Conclusion: From Profits to Politics

1 Leacock, quoted in Ramsay Cook, 'Stephen Leacock and the Age of Plutocracy, 1903–1921,' in John S. Moir, ed., *Character and Circumstance: Essays in Honour of Donald Grant Creighton* (Toronto 1970), 169.
2 Beaverbrook Papers, University of New Brunswick, 80/1a, telegram, Aitken to Ross McMaster, 1 Oct. 1959.
3 Stephen Leacock, *Arcadian Adventures with the Idle Rich* (1914; reprint, Toronto 1959), chap. 2.

4 Quoted in Jesse Kornbluth, *Highly Confident: The Crime and Punishment of Michael Milken* (New York, 1992), 83–4.
5 In this, I agree with Michael Bliss's conclusions concerning the impact of the merger movement in his *Northern Enterprise: Five Centuries of Canadian Business* (Toronto 1987), 339.
6 Stanley Chapman, *The Rise of Merchant Banking* (London 1984), 98–103; P.L. Cottrell, *Industrial Finance, 1830–1914: The Finance and Organization of English Manufacturing Industry* (London 1980), 210–41; S.F. Van Oss, 'In Hooley Land,' *Journal of Finance* 5 (Jan. 1899).
7 See Jack Sexton, *Monenco: The First 75 Years* (np. 1982).
8 Douglas How, *Canada's Mystery Man of High Finance* (Hantsport, NS 1986), 50–3; Gregory P. Marchildon, 'The Montreal Engineering Company and International Power: Overcoming the Limitations of the Free-standing Utility' (unpublished manuscript, 1995).
9 A.J.P. Taylor, *Beaverbrook* (New York 1972), xiii.
10 National Archives of Canada, Fleming Papers, MG29/B1/5/32, J.A. Stevenson to Sandford Fleming, 14 Dec. 1911.
11 In the early 1920s, Frederick Guest, Winston Churchill's cousin, described Aitken as 'an adventurer with a closed past' who was 'subtle, ambitious, unscrupulous and unreliable,' words that were to follow Aitken to his grave; see Anne Chisholm and Michael Davie, *Beaverbrook: A Life* (London 1992), 194.

Appendix: The First Canadian Merger Wave in International Perspective

1 Richard Nelson, *Merger Movements in American Industry, 1895–1956* (Princeton 1959), 5.
2 Alfred D. Chandler, Jr, *The Visible Hand: The Managerial Revolution in American Business* (Cambridge, Mass., 1977), 331–9. For a comparison with Britain and Germany, see Chandler's *Scale and Scope: The Dynamics of Industrial Capitalism* (Cambridge, Mass., 1990).
3 This applies as much to Canada as to the United States. Over 80 per cent of all mergers between 1885 and 1918 were horizontal in nature.
4 Vincent P. Carosso, *The Morgans: Private International Bankers, 1854–1913* (Cambridge, Mass., 1987); H.O. O'Hagan, *Leaves from My Life*, 2 vols. (London 1929). Max Aitken foresaw the organizational difficulties posed by the eleven-firm Canada Cement merger and procured the most able 'outside' professional manager he could find for the company (Beaverbrook Papers, House of Lords Record Office [HBK], G/19/21, 1909 correspondence between Aitken and F.P. Jones).

5 Nelson, *Merger Movements*, 4. See also Shaw Livermore, 'The Success of Industrial Mergers,' *Quarterly Journal of Economics* 4, no. 4 (Nov. 1935).

6 Leslie Hannah, 'Mergers in British Manufacturing Industry, 1880–1918,' *Oxford Economic Papers* 26, no. 1 (Mar. 1974), 1.

7 Hannah, 'Mergers in British Manufacturing Industry.'

8 Leslie Hannah, 'Visible and Invisible Hands in Great Britain,' in Alfred D. Chandler, Jr, and H. Daems, eds., *Managerial Hierarchies: Comparative Perspectives on the Rise of the Modern Industrial Enterprise* (Cambridge, Mass., 1980), and *The Rise of the Corporate Economy*, 2nd ed. (London 1983), 22–40.

9 Leslie Hannah, 'The Political Economy of Mergers in British Manufacturing Industry between the Wars' (D Phil thesis, Oxford University, 1972), 143–5 and appendix D.

10 Richard Tilly, 'Mergers, External Growth, and Finance in the Development of Large-Scale Enterprise in Germany, 1880–1913,' *Journal of Economic History* 43, no. 3 (Sept. 1982).

11 On cartels in Canada, see Tom Naylor, *The History of Canadian Business, 1867–1914* (Toronto 1974), and Michael Bliss, *A Living Profit: Studies in the Social History of Canadian Business, 1883–1911* (Toronto 1974).

12 R.A. Brady, *The Rationalization Movement in German Industry* (Berkeley 1933); E. Maschke, 'Outline of the History of German Cartels from 1873 to 1914,' in Francois Crouzet et al., *Essays in European Economic History 1709–1914* (London 1969); F. Voigt, 'German Experience with Cartels and their Control during Pre-War and Post-War Periods,' in J.P. Miller, ed., *Competition, Cartels and their Regulation* (Amsterdam 1962); Jürgen Kocka, 'The Rise of the Modern Industrial Enterprise in Germany,' and Leslie Hannah, 'Mergers, Cartels and Concentration: Legal Factors in the U.S. and European Experience,' in N. Horn and Jürgen Kocka, eds., *Law and the Formation of the Big Enterprises in the 19th and Early 20th Centuries* (Göttingen 1979).

13 Hannah, *Rise of the Corporate Economy*, 21–6.

14 Jürgen Kocka, 'Family and Bureaucracy in German Industrial Management, 1850–1914: Siemens in Comparative Perspective,' *Business History Review* 45, no. 2 (Summer 1971).

15 Tilly, 'Mergers, External Growth, and Finance,' 642.

16 *Report of the Royal Commission on Price Spreads* (Ottawa 1935; hereafter, *Price Spreads Commission*). Some background to the Bennett government's decision to launch the price spreads inquiry of 1934 and to appoint the maverick Conservative, H.H. Stevens, as its chief investigator can be found in J.R.H. Wilbur, 'H.H. Stevens and R.B. Bennett, 1930–34,' *Canadian Historical Review* 43, no. 1 (Mar. 1962).

17 National Archives of Canada (NA), H.H. Stevens Papers, MG27/III/B9/94,

'Consolidations in Canadian Industry and Commerce, January 1, 1900 to December 31, 1933 (Confidential Report)' (hereafter referred to as Confidential Consolidations Report).

18 *Price Spreads Commission*, 28, 331.

19 There were a few inconsistencies such as the 1902 Nova Scotia Steel and Coal merger where bonded debt was not included. In addition, the figures were often slightly higher than my own figures, indicating that the compiler examined the level of issued capital a year or two after the merger while my procedure was to determine the amount of issued capital within the first six months of merger or less (Confidential Consolidations Report, 11–16).

20 Dominion Bureau of Statistics, *Standard Industrial Classification Manual* (Ottawa 1948; hereafter referred to as 1948 SIC).

21 See, for example, Statistic Canada's *Standard Industrial Classification 1980* (Ottawa, 1980).

22 In particular, the DBS series includes service sectors such as grain handling, amusements, and a third 'miscellaneous' catch-all trade category, which includes retail operations such as those of the United Cigar Stores Ltd of Canada (Confidential Consolidations Report).

23 J.C. Weldon, 'Consolidations in Canadian Industry, 1900–1948,' in L.A. Skeoch, ed., *Restrictive Trade Practices in Canada: Selected Readings* (Toronto 1966), 228–79.

24 Ibid,. 233.

25 H.G. Stapells, 'The Recent Consolidation Movement in Canadian Industry' (MA. thesis, University of Toronto, 1922), 16–34.

26 A. Ernest Epp, 'Cooperation among Capitalists: The Canadian Merger Movement 1909–13' (PhD diss., Johns Hopkins University, 1973), contains data on Canadian mergers from 1890 to 1913, but Epp's lack of industrial classification, narrowness of source, and sparseness of information severely limit the usefulness of his series. See also Gregory P. Marchildon, 'Promotion, Finance and Mergers in Canadian Manufacturing Industry, 1885–1918' (PhD diss., London School of Economics, 1990), 174.

27 I arrived at this judgment after a careful perusal of Paul Craven et al.'s relatively comprehensive 'Canadian Company Histories: A Checklist,' in *Communiqué* (Spring 1981), and after examining a number of company histories both on and off this checklist to determine their usefulness. The results were less than encouraging.

28 Although Canadian incorporated subsidiaries of American industrial enterprises are included in this definition, it is interesting to note that few of the numerous branch plants established in Canada during the Laurier boom engaged in merger activity. These subsidiaries relied largely on a strategy of

internal growth funded by profit retention and the occasional security flota-
tion, rather than on the strategies of external growth of their American parent
companies. See M. Wilkins, *The Emergence of Multinational Enterprise: American
Business Abroad from the Colonial Era to 1914* (Cambridge, Mass., 1970); H.G.J.
Aitken, *American Capital and Canadian Resources* (Cambridge, Mass., 1961); H.
Marshall et al., *Canadian-American Industry: A Study in International Investment*
(1936; rev. ed., Toronto 1976); and D.G. Paterson, *British Direct Investment in
Canada, 1890–1914* (Toronto 1976). See also *Monetary Times* (*MT*), 13 Nov.
1909, 2012–25, for a list of American branch plants in Canada. At this time,
Montreal had eighteen branch plants while Toronto, the magnet for such
activity in Canada, already had fifty-two branch companies.

29 Only three of these free-standing companies involved in merger activity were
included in the series: the British Columbia Canning Company merger of
1889, the Anglo-British Columbia Packing merger of 1890, and the North
American Pulp and Paper Companies Trust merger of 1915. For a discussion
of free-standing companies, see Mira Wilkins, 'The Free-Standing Company,
1870–1914: An Important Type of British Foreign Direct Investment,' *Economic History Review* 41, no. 2 (May 1988).

30 See introduction to Gregory P. Marchildon, ed., *Mergers and Acquisitions*
(Aldershot 1991), xi.

31 Although consolidation is not precisely defined by Nelson, his examples
imply the 'three-firm' definition (Nelson, *Merger Movements*, 21).

32 The British series for 1880–1918 is restricted to annual data.

33 Nelson, *Merger Movements*, 17.

34 Hannah admits that in constructing the British series 'it was sometimes difficult to distinguish ironstone mining from iron manufacture and gypsum
mines from the manufacture of plaster, so that some mining mergers may in
fact have been included in the series and classified to their related manufacturing industry' (Hannah, 'Mergers in British Manufacturing Industry,' 20).

35 For the detailed comparisons, see Marchildon, 'Promotion, Finance and
Mergers,' 195–205.

36 GNP estimates were based on Paul Bairoch's estimates for the United Kingdom in 1960 U.S. dollars ('Europe's Gross National Product: 1800–1975,'
Journal of European Economic History 5, no. 2 [Fall 1976]). Estimates for the per
capita level of industrialization (as measured by the volume of manufacturing production) for the United Kingdom and the United States as well as
Canada are found in Paul Bairoch, 'International Industrialization Levels
from 1750 to 1980,' *Journal of European Economic History* 11, no. 2 (Fall 1982).

37 Hannah, 'Mergers in British Manufacturing Industry,' 18; Nelson, *Merger
Movements*, 37.

38 See Marchildon, 'Promotion, Finance and Mergers', chap. 8.

Illustration Credits

Atlantic Advocate: Rev. William Aitken; John F. Stairs; Aitken wearing hat; Blake Burrill; Arthur J. Nesbitt; Walton Killam

Beaverbrook Papers, House of Lords Record Office: 'Maxie' Aitken at Harkins Academy; Aitken with Buckley, Bennett, and Walton Killam; Gladys Aitken; Lord Beaverbrook

National Archives: R.B. Bennett as young lawyer, PA117666; Sir Sandford Fleming, C51631; Rodolphe Forget, PA27236; Mackenzie King in ceremonial dress, PA27991; Wilfrid Laurier on 1910 western tour, C15568; Mackenzie King campaigning in 1911, C46311; Robert Borden, PA117660; Ward Pitfield, PA113116

Notman Photographic Archives, McCord Museum of Canadian History: Aitken in 1905, 156, 536-BII; Gerald Farrell, 175, 430-II; Edward Clouston, 149, 765-II; interior of Clouston's office, 81, 734-II; view of Montreal from Bank of Montreal, 3900; Richard Wilson-Smith, 119, 566-II; Arthur Doble, 1765, 581-BII; Nathaniel Curry, 178, 203-BII

Public Archives of Nova Scotia: Robert E. Harris; Charles H. Cahan; W.B. Ross and B.F. Pearson

Index